NINETEENTH-
CENTURY
ESSAYS

Classics of British Historical Literature

JOHN CLIVE, EDITOR

╔John Morley╗

—

Nineteenth-
Century
Essays

SELECTED AND WITH AN INTRODUCTION BY

PETER STANSKY

The University of Chicago Press

CHICAGO AND LONDON

ISBN: 0–226–53847–8 (clothbound); 0–226–53848–6 (paperbound)
Library of Congress Catalog Card Number: 73–116380
The University of Chicago Press, Chicago 60637
The University of Chicago Press, Ltd., London

Contents

83952

Series Editor's Preface

This series of reprints has one major purpose: to put into the hands of students and other interested readers outstanding—and sometimes neglected—works dealing with British history which have either gone out of print or are obtainable only at a forbiddingly high price.

The phrase Classics of British Historical Literature requires some explanation, in view of the fact that the two companion series published by the University of Chicago Press are entitled Classic European Historians and Classic American Historians. Why, then, introduce the word *literature* into the title of this series?

One reason is obvious. History, if it is to live beyond its own generation, must be memorably written. The greatest British historians—Clarendon, Gibbon, Hume, Carlyle, Macaulay—survive today, not merely because they contribute to the cumulative historical knowledge about their subjects, but because they were masters of style and literary artists as well. And even historians of the second rank, if they deserve to survive, are able to do so only because they can still be read with pleasure. To emphasize this truth at the present time, when much eminently solid and worthy academic history suffers from being almost totally unreadable, seems worth doing.

The other reason for including the word *literature* in the title of the series has to do with its scope. To read history is to learn about the past. But if, in trying to learn about the British past, one were to restrict oneself to the reading of formal works of history, one would miss a great deal. Often a historical novel, a sociological inquiry, or an account of events and institutions couched in semifictional form teaches us just as much about the past as does the "history" that calls itself by that name. And, frequently, these "informal" historical works turn out to be less well known than their merit deserves. By calling this series Classics of British Historical Literature it will be possible to include such books without doing violence to the usual nomenclature.

If John Morley can be categorized at all, it would have to be as that nowadays so elusive species, the man of letters. He was, of course, more than that; and most of us probably know him primarily either as a Liberal politician or as the voluminous biographer of Gladstone. But, like so many Victorians, he possessed and exercised a to us dazzlingly great variety of talents. And he appears in this volume in the guise of essayist, literary critic, and (perhaps above all) intellectual historian.

As Professor Stansky points out in introducing the very revealing and original selection of essays he has made for this volume, Morley liked to take as his subjects the ideas, works, and lives of the "culture heroes" of the English nineteenth century; and, in writing about them, demonstrated special interest in the intellectual climate within which they had their being and did their work. It was, of course, Morley's own climate—born one year after Victoria's accession, he outlived her reign by more than twenty years—and, fortunately for us, he happened to be particularly sensitive to changes of ideological wind, weather, and temperature.

Here they are, then, some of the giants of the age—Carlyle, Mill, Macaulay, George Eliot, Harriet Martineau, Arnold, Pater —sized up by a refined intelligence able to observe them within the intellectual context of their time. Labels, Morley wrote, were nothing more than devices for saving talkative persons the trouble of thinking. And readers of these essays need not expect the customary labels to be ritually attached to the great names. Instead, they can look forward to gaining fresh insights not only into some of the major currents and institutions of the nineteenth century in England—Liberalism, Radicalism, the decline of

Christian faith and the search for a substitute, changes in ethical and aesthetic values and standards, the function of periodical literature; but also into the mind and art of one of the most elegantly articulate observers and analysts of the contemporary scene, John Morley himself.

JOHN CLIVE

Editor's Introduction

John Morley holds an equivocal place among the late Victorians. In his own time he stood out equally as a man of letters, as a biographer, as an editor, and as a politician. Yet for all the variety of his activities and the considerable quality of his accomplishments, in none of them has he proved to be quite distinguished enough—the difference perhaps between being eminent and preeminent—to win an enduring place in the front rank. One has no wish to enter too large a claim for him, the kind of fashionable revisionist exercise in which a modest-sized figure is puffed up past recognition. Still, at the very least, it should be said that as a politician he is of genuine interest, and that much, but not all, of his immense literary production has fallen into undeserved neglect. One has the impression that nowadays Morley is little read; only a few of his books are still in print. The student in search of him must turn to the older libraries where his works fill a good-sized shelf. They range from collections of literary and historical pieces that had first appeared in magazines to ample, book-length biographies (of which the most famous, of course, is the life in three volumes of William Gladstone) to the shorter studies such as *On Compromise* (published in 1874 as a kind of successor to Mill's *On Liberty* but never to achieve a comparable classic status) to the *Memorandum on Resignation*, the swan song for Morley's sort of Liberalism, which was published in 1928, five years after his death, and describes his refusal to be part of the Liberal Cabinet that led Britain into the First World War.

If Morley has been neglected, he has not been ignored. Modern scholarship has paid him some attention as a man of letters and as a central figure in the serious journalism of the nineteenth century, especially in connection with the *Fortnightly Review,* which he edited from 1867 to 1882. A number of biographical studies have been written about him, among them two volumes by his disciple, F. W. Hirst, on his early life (1927), and most recently, D. A. Hamer's *John Morley: Liberal Intellectual in Politics* (1968). (A lack of papers and a certain cloudiness about Morley's personal life have made a full biography not feasible so far; and while his own two volumes of *Recollections* [1917] are pleasant and interesting reading, they are hardly a complete autobiography.) But it is chiefly as a politician that he has received attention from modern scholars, not only in studies of his role in the 1880s, when he was a central figure in the course of Gladstone's Irish policy, and in the 1890s, when he played an important if sometimes erratic part in the sad fortunes of the Liberal party at that time, but most particularly in his years as secretary of state for India, from 1905 to 1910, during the great Liberal governments of Sir Henry Campbell-Bannerman and Herbert Henry Asquith. In that office he surprised some by being much less permissive toward the Indians than had been expected from an advocate of Irish Home Rule, at the same time that he was the prime mover in the Morley-Minto Reforms which helped to start India on the road to self-government.

The foregoing will suggest a continued interest in Morley; even so, considering the wide range of his activities, he is still incompletely known. It is my hope that this volume will bring to contemporary attention one further and still too little recognized aspect of Morley's work: his writings as an intellectual historian, or commentator on the intellectual tendencies—literary, historical, philosophical, and political—of his own century. As an essayist he once held a position alongside Matthew Arnold and Leslie Stephen. Perhaps because he no longer appears as tough-minded as they, less concerned with concrete particulars and more given to generalizations, or because, simply, the political aspect of his life has taken a commanding place, his essays have never achieved a permanence comparable to theirs. His important essays—many of which are reprinted here—were written in the 1870s and 1880s, when he was writing regularly for the *Fortnightly*, and it was then, deservedly, that his literary reputation was at its height. Afterwards, entering upon his active period as a politician, he tended to treat the form as a variety of occasional discourse—cultivated after-dinner talk, one might say —and the later essays suffer from diffuseness and prolixity, vices that had threatened him from the first but that he had been able in his best work to curb.

Morley was born in 1838 in Blackburn in Lancashire, and he was never to lose a certain practicality and hardheadedness associated with the North country. These attitudes were reinforced by his religious background, as a Dissenter, a Non-Conformist, who looked upon the institutions of the rich and mighty with profound suspicion; and although he soon became a devout atheist, losing his faith while living in Wesley's rooms in Lincoln College, Oxford, he was always able to speak for the Non-Conformist conscience in his political attitudes.

A rise in the fortunes of the Morley family had been accompanied by a religious change. While his mother remained as she had been, a Methodist, his father became an Anglican convert. Morley senior, planning to pass on to his eldest son his lucrative practice as a surgeon, decided, in the characteristic fashion of families on the way up, that John, his second son, should take holy orders in the Church of England. His education was to reflect this aspect of a change in social status, for first he was sent to Hole's Academy, then to University College School, London, perhaps the very best school at the time open to a Non-Conformist, and then to Cheltenham College, a minor public school. Oxford was to be the appropriate crown to an educational career leading to the Anglican priesthood. But in 1859, that year of historical landmarks—among them the publication of Mill's *On Liberty*—Morley lost his faith, in part at least a result of having read *On Liberty*. He told his father so and refused to go on with the plans that had been made for him. The father responded to his son's announcement by cutting him off, and Morley, who had expected to stay at Oxford for four years, was forced to leave with a pass degree at the end of his third year. Thereupon, as so many young men have done before and since, he went to London to seek his fortune.

He tried some tutoring; he considered reading for the bar—but for that he would have needed greater financial resources than he had; and so he turned to free-lance journalism. He did not remain for long undiscovered. In 1860, at the age of 22, he was made editor of the *Literary Gazette;* a brief honor, for it was shortly to cease publication. Thereafter, from 1863 to 1867, he was a regular contributor to one of the most influential periodicals of the time, the *Saturday Review.* Here he received his training as a literary journalist, turning out two polished essays a week, but he was not allowed to write on political topics, for he was at the other end of the spectrum from the paper's official Tory policy. Early on he established the practice of republishing his essays in book form, bringing out *Modern Characteristics* in 1865 and *Studies in Conduct* in 1867, both anonymously, in keeping with the tradition of the *Saturday Review,* but contrary to his later principles. He came to regret these books, and he would not allow them to be reissued; *Studies in Conduct,* in fact, was never acknowledged. Morley was being needlessly severe, for the essays were perceptive in their insights, if slight in their substance. *Modern Characteristics* contained the essay "New Ideas," which caught the fancy of John Stuart Mill and, when he discovered the identity of its author, led to a close relationship between the two men that continued until Mill's death in 1873.

The first period of London journalism makes an impressive beginning. But Morley had yet to arrive at a clearly defined or firmly held point of view. Unlike so many Victorian intellectuals of a slightly older generation, he was not thrown into despair, or any form of distress, by the passing of the Reform Act of 1867. He considered himself a Radical, and certainly he became one on matters of education and Irish Home Rule, but he remained all his life profoundly disapproving of anything that might be termed socialism—this despite his friendship in his declining years with such younger men as Harold Laski and Ramsay MacDonald. In 1885 he wrote, "I am a cautious Whig by temperament, I am a sound Liberal by training, and I am a thorough Radical by observation and experience." Yet whatever his Radical position on certain issues, in general he was an elitist who believed in a democracy that should dedicate itself to ratifying the decisions of sage rulers from the middle and upper classes, rather than bothering to put forward leaders of its own from the multitude.

In 1867 he was appointed editor of the *Fortnightly Review,* when G. H. Lewes, who had founded the publication with Anthony Trollope in 1865 and had been editor since its inception, was forced to retire because of illness. The *Fortnightly*—despite its name it was published monthly—was opposed, except in rare instances, to anonymity for its authors, that prevailing custom in Victorian reviews, and many of its authors were spokesmen, or advocates, for Liberal and Radical causes. But the journal was not at all narrowly partisan, and it welcomed a wide range of contributors. Morley, though himself something of a Comtist, angrily rejected the contention that it was committed to Positivism. He edited the *Fortnightly* for fifteen years, and it was during those years that he established his claim as a Victorian man of letters.

In the columns of the *Fortnightly* Morley worked out an approach to the political and intellectual world that reflected four dominant interests that would continue in varying degrees throughout his life. A keen commentator on his own times, he wrote frequently on the political issues of the day—an aspect of his career that would be even more conspicuous during the three years, 1880 to 1883, when he was editor of a radical newspaper, the *Pall Mall Gazette,* and from 1883 to 1885, when he was editor of *Macmillan's Magazine* and wrote for it the "Review of the Month." In the *Fortnightly* his political commentary gained importance after he met Joseph Chamberlain and became for a time his collaborator and intellectual spokesman. A second of Morley's interests, the French eighteenth century through the early years of the Revolution, inspired a number of essays whose didactic purpose was to extract from the period the sort of hardheadedness he thought necessary for his own time—in effect a rejection of Rousseau and Robespierre in favor of Voltaire, Turgot, and Diderot. A third and related interest is represented by the lengthy studies, written for the *Fortnightly,* of Edmund Burke and Joseph de Maistre—somewhat odd heroes for a Radical, but he admired the cohesion and discipline of their thought, particularly Burke's. These, as well as many of his English studies, were part of a search for a coherent resolution to the intellectual problems that so troubled what he once called the "Age of Comfort." He came to feel ever more imperatively that he must possess a unifying idea and that politics itself should be reduced to one big idea, such as Home Rule, or Temperance, which would serve to unify the disparate strains of late nineteenth-century thought. The search was made even more difficult by his fear of any permanent total commitment—in his delicate and at times rather prissy way, Morley was a prosaic version of Tennyson's Ulysses. Throughout his writings one finds a kind of eclecticism linked to discrimination, for he was always selecting those aspects of various figures of past and present that could be combined in a logical, ideal synthesis. Yet in his life away from the page he tended to be less selective, and for a short time would commit himself wholeheartedly to one or another of his contemporaries whom he saw in heroic terms; then, in most cases— Gladstone being a notable exception—disillusionment would set in. In the period of the *Fortnightly* his heroes were Mill and Chamberlain. Ultimately he grew disillusioned with both—with Mill, however, only very slightly, after the posthumous publication of *Three Essays on Religion* which revealed, he felt, a lamentable soft-mindedness and acquiescence toward the possibility of the truth of Christian doctrine. With Chamberlain the disillusionment was complete, as the two men parted irrevocably in 1886 over the question of Home Rule for Ireland, Morley's great cause.

To my mind the most durable of the *Fortnightly* essays grow out of the fourth of his dominant interests: the ideas, works, and lives of certain of the great and near-great "culture heroes" of the English nineteenth century. His subjects extend from Byron to Matthew Arnold, and in his treatment of them it can be said that he is more concerned with their lives than their specific works, and more with their ideas than their lives. Reading his essay on George Eliot, for example, one would have only a vague notion of what her novels were; yet one would have a firm sense of the intellectual climate in which the novels were written.

The essay on Byron can be taken as representative of the collection as a whole, in its method and its excellence. In it Morley performed an admirable act of rehabilitation, writing at a time, 1870, when such an act was courageous and necessary—as he comments dryly, "Lord Byron is denied a place in Westminster Abbey and Lord Palmerston is not." The essay, though early, is a characteristic performance, for the tension in Morley's attitude toward his own time, his interest in both freedom and order, which made him both a Radical and an admirer of Burke, is evident in the contrasts in which it abounds. He pays tribute to Byron in a memorable sentence, "It was no small feat to rise to such a height that should command so much, and to exhibit with all the force of life a world that had broken loose from its mooring." And he writes approvingly of Byron as "the genuine exponent of that immense social movement which we sum up as the Revolution." If this is the radical speaking, it is the conservative who adds the counterweight: "That the whole movement in spite of its energy, was crude, unscientific, virtually abortive is most true. That it was presided over by a false conception of nature as a benign and purifying power, while she is in truth a stern force to be tamed and crushed, if society is to hold together, cannot be denied of the revolutionary movement then, any more than it can be denied of its sequels now."

Occasionally Morley's judgments, in the essay on Byron and elsewhere, have an unmistakable period flavor, as when he sighs over "Don Juan" with its "anti-social and licentious sentiment" and remarks "Here again, in the license of this literature, we see the finger of the Revolution, and of that egoism which makes the passions of the individual his own law." But such judgments have the virtue of reminding us that Morley was, after all, a man of his time, a contemporary of the queen and the laureate as well as of Matthew Arnold and Walter Pater. It is this that gives the essays gathered here so much value as contemporary evidence and makes them in themselves documents in intellectual history.

In these penetrating essays one sees Morley, the editor and public man of letters, sorting out, summing up, and by implication passing judgment on the intellectual tendencies of the Victorian epoch. At the same time they show the public man engaged in a private, ultimately unsuccessful attempt to fuse a coherent system out of the diversified elements he valued: humaneness on the one hand, and hardheadedness on the other. Somehow the two were to be conjoined, a reconciliation, one might say, between the pragmatic and the ideal—in this respect,

Morley's dilemma was emblematic of his age as well as peculiar to himself.

PETER STANSKY

A Note on the Text

When Morley reprinted his essays he subjected them to revision, which was most extensive in his earlier essays in the *Fortnightly Review*. In comparing texts I came to the conclusion that in the versions printed in the *Miscellanies,* particularly in the case of the essays printed here in part 1, the arguments were softened and overextended by revision. Hence I preferred to use the original versions of the essays as they appeared in periodical form. Later essays were hardly revised at all for publication in book form, since Morley had increasing demands made on his time, but I have used the text as found in the journals in all cases. Five of the essays included here have never, as far as I know, been reprinted.

Acknowledgments

I should like to express here my gratitude to Mrs. G. A. Morley for kindly granting permission to reprint these essays, and to A. F. Thompson, John W. Bicknell, and Stephen E. Koss, who shared their knowledge of John Morley with me.

Bibliographical Note

There is no life of John Morley. To date the most complete biographical studies, within the limits they have set themselves, are F. W. Hirst, *Early Life and Letters of John Morley,* 2 vols (London, 1927); and D. A. Hamer, *John Morley: Liberal Intellectual in Politics* (Oxford, 1968). Morley's period on the *Fortnightly Review* is partly covered in E. M. Everett, *The Party of Humanity: The Fortnightly Review and Its Contributors 1865–1874* (Chapel Hill, 1939) and on the *Pall Mall Gazette* in J. W. Robertson Scott, *The Life and Death of a Newspaper . . .* (London, 1952). His time as secretary of state for India is discussed in M. N. Das, *India Under Morley and Minto* (London, 1964); Stanley A. Wolpert, *Morley and India* (Los Angeles, 1967); and Stephen E. Koss, *John Morley at the India Office* (New Haven, 1969).

Essayistic book-length studies of some value are F. W. Knickerbocker, *Free Minds: John Morley and His Friends* (Cambridge, Mass., 1943); J. H. Morgan, *John, Viscount Morley* (London, 1924); and W. Staebler, *The Liberal Mind of John Morley* (Princeton, 1943). Perceptive essays are to be found by Basil Willey in *More Nineteenth Century Studies* (New York, 1956); by W. Menzies Whitelaw in Herman Ausubel et. al., eds., *Some Modern Historians of Britain* (New York, 1951); and by John Gross in *The Rise and Fall of the Man of Letters* (New York, 1969). John W. Bicknell is preparing the Morley section in the forthcoming *Victorian Prose Writers: A Guide to Research*. D. A. Hamer's study contains a very useful, if not complete, bibliography.

Part I

Byron

It is one of the singular facts in the history of literature that the most rootedly conservative country in Europe should have produced the poet of the Revolution. Nowhere is the antipathy to principles and ideas so profound, nor the addiction to moderate compromise so inveterate, nor the reluctance to advance away from the past so unconquerable, as in England; and nowhere in England is there so settled an indisposition to regard any thought or sentiment except in the light of an existing social order, nor so firmly passive a hostility to generous aspirations, as in the aristocracy. Yet it was precisely an English aristocrat who became the favourite poet of all the most highminded conspirators and socialists of continental Europe for half a century; one of the best of those, that is to say, who have borne the most unsparing testimony against the present ordering of society, and against the theological and moral conceptions which have guided and maintained it. The rank and file of the army has been equally inspired by the same fiery and rebellious strains against the order of God and the order of man. "The day will come," wrote Mazzini, thirty years ago, "when Democracy will remember all that it owes to Byron. England, too, will, I hope, one day remember the mission—so entirely English, yet hitherto overlooked by her—which Byron fulfilled on the Continent; the European rôle given by him to English literature,

This essay was first published in *Fortnightly Review,* n.s., 48 (December 1870): 650–73, and was reprinted in *Critical Miscellanies,* vol. 1 (London, 1877)—ed.

and the appreciation and sympathy for England which he awakened amongst us. Before he came, all that was known of English literature was the French translation of Shakespeare, and the anathema hurled by Voltaire against the 'intoxicated barbarian.' It is since Byron that we Continentalists have learned to study Shakespeare and other English writers. From him dates the sympathy of all the true-hearted amongst us for this land of liberty, whose true vocation he so worthily represented among the oppressed. He led the genius of Britain on a pilgrimage throughout all Europe."

The day of recollection has not yet come. It is only in his own country that Byron's influence has been a comparatively superficial one, and its scope and gist dimly and imperfectly caught, because it is only in England that the partisans of order hope to mitigate or avoid the facts of the Revolution by pretending not to see them, while the friends of progress suppose that all the fruits of change shall inevitably fall, if only they keep the forces and processes and extent of the change rigorously private and undeclared. That intense practicalness, which seems to have done so many great things for us and yet at the same moment mysteriously to have robbed us of all, forbids us even to cast a glance at what is no more than an aspiration. Englishmen like to be able to answer about the Revolution as those ancients answered about the symbol of another revolution, when they said that they knew not so much as whether there were a Holy Ghost or not. The same want of kindling power in the national intelligence which made of the English Reformation one of the most mean, tedious, and disgusting chapters in our history, has made the still mightier advance of the moderns from the social system and spiritual bases of the old state, in spite of our two national achievements of punishing a king with death and emancipating our slaves, just as unimpressive and semi-efficacious a performance in this country, as the more affrontingly hollow and halt-footed transactions of the sixteenth century. Lord Byron is denied a place in Westminster Abbey, and Lord Palmerston is not.

Just because it was wonderful that England should have produced Byron, it would have been wonderful if she had received any permanently deep impression from him, or preserved a lasting appreciation of his work, or cheerfully and intelligently

4

recognised his immense force. And accordingly we cannot help perceiving that generations are arising who know not Byron. This is not to say that he goes unread; but there is a vast gulf fixed between the author whom we read with pleasure and even delight, and that other to whom we turn at all moments for inspiration and encouragement, and whose words and ideas spring up incessantly and animatingly within us, unbidden, whether we turn to him or no.

For no Englishman now does Byron hold this highest place, and this is not unnatural in any way, if we remember in what a different shape the Revolution has now by change of circumstance and occasion come to present itself to those who are most ardent in the search after new paths. An estimate of Byron would be in some sort a measure of the distance that we have travelled within the last half century in our appreciation of the conditions of social change. The modern rebel is at least half acquiescence. He has developed a historic sense. The most hearty aversion to the prolonged reign of some of the old gods does not hinder him from seeing that what are now frigid and unlovely blocks were full of vitality and light in days before the era of their petrifaction. There is much less eagerness of praise or blame, and much less in knife and cautery, less confidence that new and right growth will naturally and necessarily follow upon demolition.

The Revolution has never had that long hold on the national imagination in England, either as an idol or a bugbear, which is essential to keep the poet who sings it in effective harmony with new generations of readers. More than this, the Byronic conception was as transitional and inadequate as the methods and ideas of the practical movers, who were to a man left stranded in every country in Europe during the period of his poetic activity. A transitional and unstable movement of society inevitably fails to supply a propulsion powerful enough to make its poetic expression eternal. There is no better proof of the enormous force of Byron's genius, than that it was able to produce so fine an expression of elements so intrinsically unfavourable to high poetry as doubt, denial, antagonism, and weariness. But this force was no guarantee for perpetuity of influence. Bare rebellion cannot endure, and no succession of generations can continue nourishing themselves on the poetry of complaint and the ideal-

isation of revolt. If, however, it is impossible that Byron should
be all to us that he was to a former generation, and if we find
no direct guidance in his muse, this is no reason why criticism
should pass him over, nor why there may not be something
peculiarly valuable in the noble freedom and genuine modernism
of his poetic spirit, to an age that is apparently only forsaking
the clerical idyll of one school, for the reactionary mediævalism
or paganism, intrinsically meaningless and issueless, of another.

Poetry, and not only poetry, but every other channel of emotional expression and æsthetic culture, confessedly moves with
the general march of the human mind, and art is only the transformation into ideal and imaginative shapes of a predominant
system and philosophy of life. Minor verse-writers may fairly be
consigned, without disrespect, to the region of the literature of
taste; and criticism of their work takes the shape of a discussion
of stray graces, of new turns, of little variations of shade and
colour, of their conformity to the accepted rules that constitute
the technics of poetry. The sublimer masters, though their technical power and originality, their beauty of form, strength of
flight, music and variousness of rhythm, are all full of interest
and instruction, yet, besides these precious gifts, come to us with
the size and quality of great historic forces, for they represent
the hope and energies, the dreams and the consummation, of the
human intelligence in its most enormous movements. To appreciate one of these, we need to survey it on every side. For these we
need synthetic criticism, which, after analysis has done its work,
and disclosed to us the peculiar qualities of form, conception, and
treatment, shall collect the products of this first process, construct
for us the poet's mental figure in its integrity and just coherence,
and then finally, as the sum of its work, shall trace the relations
of the poet's ideas, either direct or indirect, through the central
currents of thought, to the visible tendencies of an existing age.
The greatest poets reflect beside all else the broad-bosomed
haven of a rounded and positive faith, in which mankind has for
some space found shelter, unsuspicious of the new and distant
wayfarings that are ever in store. To this band of sacred bards few
are called, while perhaps not more than four high names would
fill the list of the chosen: Dante, the poet of Catholicism; Shak-

speare, of Feudalism; Milton, of Protestantism; and Goethe, of that new faith which is as yet without any universally recognised label, but whose heaven is an ever-closer harmony between the consciousness of man and all the natural forces of the universe; whose liturgy is culture, and whose deity is a certain composure of the human heart.

The far-shining pre-eminence of Shakspeare, apart from the incomparable fertility and depth of his natural gifts, arises secondarily from the larger extent to which he transcended the special forming influences, and refreshed his fancy and widened his range of sympathy by recourse to what was then the nearest possible approach to a historic or political method. To the poet, vision reveals a certain form of the truth, which the rest of men laboriously discover, and prove by the tardier methods of meditation and science. Shakspeare did not walk in imagination with the great warriors, monarchs, churchmen, and rulers of history, conceive their conduct, ideas, schemes, and throw himself into their words and actions, without strengthening that original taste which must have first drawn him to historical subjects, and without deepening both his feeling for the great progression of human affairs, and his sympathy for those relative modes of surveying and dealing with them, which are not more positive, scientific, and political, than they may be made truly poetic.

Again, while in Dante the inspiring force was spiritual, and in Goethe it was intellectual, we may say that both in Shakspeare and Milton it was political or social; in other words, with these two, the drama of the one, and the epic of the other, were each of them connected with ideas of government and the other external movements of men in society, and with the play of the sentiments which spring from them. We assuredly do not mean that in either of them, least of all in Shakspeare, there is an absence of the spiritual element. This would be at once to thrust them down into a lower place; for the spiritual is of the very essence of poetry. But with the spiritual there mixes in our Englishmen a most abundant leaven of recognition of the impressions and impulses of the outer forms of life, as well as of active sympathy with the every-day debate of the world. They are neither of them inferior to the highest in sense of the wide and unutterable things of the spirit; yet with both of them, more than with other poets

7

of the same rank, the man with whose soul and circumstance they have to deal is the πολιτικόν ζῷον, * no high abstraction of the race, but the creature with concrete relations and a full objective life. In Shakspeare the dramatic form helps partly to make this more prominent, though the poet's spirit shines forth thus, independently of the mould which it imposes on itself. Of Milton we may say, too, that, in spite of the supernatural machinery of his greatest poem, it bears strongly impressed on it the political mark, and that in those minor pieces, where he is avowedly in the political sphere, he still rises to the full height of his majestic harmony and noblest dignity.

Byron was touched by the same fire. The contemporary and friend of the most truly spiritual of all English poets, Shelley, he was himself among the most essentially political. Or perhaps one will be better understood, describing his quality as a quality of poetical worldliness, in its enlarged and generous sense of energetic interest in real transactions, and a capacity of being moved and raised by them into those lofty moods of emotion, which in more spiritual natures are only kindled by contemplation of the vast infinitudes that compass the human soul round about. That Shelley was immeasurably superior to Byron in all the rarer qualities of the specially poetic mind appears to us so unmistakably assured a fact, that difference of opinion upon it can only spring from a more fundamental difference of opinion as to what it is that constitutes this specially poetic quality. If more than anything else it consists in the power of transfiguring action, character, and thought, in the serene radiance of the purest imaginative intelligence, and the gift of expressing these transformed products in the finest articulate vibrations of emotional speech, then must we not confess that Byron has composed no piece which from this point may compare with *Prometheus* or the *Cenci,* any more than Rubens may take his place with Titian? We feel that Shelley transports the spirit to the highest bound and limit of the intelligible; and that with him thought passes through one superadded and more rarefying process than the other poet is master of. If it be true, as has been written, that "Poetry is the breath and finer spirit of all knowledge," we may say that Shelley teaches us

* "political animal"—ed.

8

to apprehend that further something, the breath and finer spirit of poetry itself. Contrasting, for example, Shelley's "Ode to the West Wind" with the famous and truly noble stanzas on the eternal sea which close the fourth canto of *Childe Harold*, who does not feel that there is in the first a volatile and unseizable element that is quite distinct from the imagination and force and high impressiveness or from any indefinable product of all of these united, which form the glory and power of the second? We may ask in the same way whether *Manfred*, where the spiritual element is as predominant as it ever is in Byron, is worth half a page of *Prometheus*.

To perceive and admit this is not to disparage Byron's achievements. To be most deeply penetrated with the differentiating quality of the poet, is not, after all, to contain the whole of that admixture of varying and moderating elements which goes to the composition of the broadest and most effective work. Of these elements, Shelley, with all his rare gifts of spiritual imagination and winged melodiousness of verse, was markedly wanting in a keen and omnipresent feeling for the course of human events. All nature stirred him, except the consummating crown of natural growth.

We do not mean anything so untrue as that Shelley was wanting either in deep humanity or in active benevolence, or that social injustice was a thing indifferent to him. Many a furious stanza remains to show how deeply and bitterly the spectacle of this injustice burnt into his soul. But these pieces are accidents. They do not belong to the immortal part of his work. An American original, unconsciously bringing the revolutionary mind to the climax of all utterances possible to it, has said that "men are degraded when considered as the members of a political organisation."[1] Shelley's position was on a yet more remote pinnacle than this. Of mankind he was barely conscious in his loftiest and divinest flights. His muse seeks the vague translucent spaces, where the care of man melts away in vision of the eternal forces, of which man may be but the fortuitous manifestation of an hour.

Byron, on the other hand, is never moved by the strength of his passion or the depth of his contemplation quite away from the

1. Thoreau.

round earth, and the civil animal who dwells upon it. Even his misanthropy is only an inverted form of social solicitude. His practical zeal for good and noble causes might teach us this. He never grudged either money or time or personal peril for the cause of Italian freedom, and his life was the measure and the cost of his interest in the liberty of Greece. Then again he was full not merely of wit, which is sometimes only an affair of the tongue, but of humour also, which goes much deeper, and it is of the essence of the humoristic nature, that whether sunny or saturnine, it binds the thought of him who possesses it to the wide medley of expressly human things. Byron did not misknow himself, nor misapprehend the most marked turn of his own character, when he wrote the lines:—

> I love not Man the less, but Nature more,
> From these our interviews, in which I steal
> From all I may be, or have been before,
> To mingle with the universe and feel
> What I can ne'er express, yet cannot all conceal.

It was this which made Byron a social force, a far greater force that Shelley either has been or can be. Men read in each page that he was one of like passions with themselves; that he had their own feet of clay, if he had other members of brass and gold and fine silver which they had none of; and that vehement sensibility, tenacious energy of imagination, a bounding swell of poetic fancy, had not obliterated, but had rather quickened, the sense of the highest kind of man of the world, which did not decay but waxed stronger in him with years. His openness to beauty and care for it were always inferior in keenness and in hold upon him to his sense of human interest, and the superiority in some respects of *Marino Faliero,* for example, where he handles a social theme in a worthy spirit, over *Manfred,* where he seeks a something tumultuously beautiful, is due to that subordination in his mind of purely æsthetic to social intention, which is one of the most strongly distinctive marks of the truly modern spirit. The admirable wit both of his letters, and of pieces like the *Vision of Judgment* and *Don Juan,* where wit reaches as high as any English writer has ever carried it, shows in another way the same vividness and reality of attraction which every side of human affairs possessed for this glowing and incessantly animated spirit.

In spite of a good many surface affectations, which may have cheated the lighter heads, but which may now be easily seen through, and counted off for as much as they are worth, Byron possessed a bottom of plain sincerity and rational sobriety which kept him substantially straight, real, and human, and made him the genuine exponent of that immense social movement which we sum up as the Revolution. If Keats's whole soul was absorbed by sensuous impressions of the outer world, and his art was the splendid and exquisite reproduction of these; if Shelley on the other hand distilled from the fine impressions of the senses by process of inmost mediation some thrice ethereal essence, "the viewless spirit of a lovely sound"; we may say of Byron that even in the moods when the mightiness and wonder of nature had most effectually possessed themselves of his imagination, his mind never moved for very long on these remote heights apart from the busy world of men, but returned again like the fabled dove from the desolate void of waters to the ark of mortal stress and human passion. Nature in her most dazzling aspects or stupendous parts is but the background and theatre of the tragedy of man.

We may find a secondary proof of this in the fewness of those fine descriptive strokes and subtle indirect touches of colour or sound which arise with incessant spontaneity where a mastering passion for nature steeps the mind in vigilant, yet half-unconscious observation. It is amazing through how long a catalogue of natural objects Byron sometimes takes us, without affixing to one of them any but the most conventional term, or a single epithet which might show that in passing through his mind it had yielded to him a beauty or a savour that had been kept a secret from the common troop. Byron is certainly not wanting in commanding image, as when Manfred likens the lines of foaming light flung along from the Alpine cataract to "the pale courser's tail, the Giant steed, to be bestrode by death." But imaginative power of this kind is not the same thing as that susceptibility to the minutest properties and unseen qualities of natural objects, which reveals itself in chance epithet of telling felicity, or phrase that opens to us hidden lights. Our generation is more likely to think too much than too little of this; for its favourite poet, however narrow in subject and feeble in moral treatment, is without any peer in the exquisitely original, varied, and imaginative art of his landscape touches.

This treatment of nature was in exact harmony with the method of revolutionary thought, which, from the time of Rousseau downwards, had appealed in its profound weariness of an existing social state to the solitude and seeming freedom of mountain and forest and ocean, as though the only cure for the woes of civilisation lay in annihilating it. This was an appeal less to nature than from man, just as we have said that Byron's was, and hence it was distinct from the single-eyed appreciation and love of nature for her own sake, for her beauty and terror and unnumbered moods, which has made of her the mistress and consoler of many men in these times. In the days of old faith, while the catholic gods sat yet firm upon their thrones, the loveliness of the universe shone to blind eyes. Saint Bernard in the twelfth century could ride for a whole day along the shore of the Lake of Geneva, and yet when in the evening his comrades spoke some word about the lake, he inquired, "What lake?" It was not mere difference of temperament that made the preacher of one age pass by in this marvellous unconsciousness, and the singer of another burst forth into that tender invocation of "clear, placid Leman," whose "contrasted lake with the wild world he dwelt in" moved him to the very depths. To Saint Bernard the world was as wild and confused as it was to Byron; but then he had gods many and saints many, and a holy church in this world, and a kingdom of heaven awaiting resplendent in the world to come. All this filled his soul with a settled certitude, too absorbing to leave any space for other than religious emotion. The seven centuries that flowed between the spiritual mind of Europe when Saint Bernard was its spokesman, and the spiritual mind of which Byron was the interpreter, had gradually dissolved these certitudes, and the faint lines of new belief and a more durable order were still invisible. The assurance of science was not yet rooted, nor had men as yet learned to turn back to the history of their own kind, to the long chronicle of its manifold experiences, for an adequate system of life and an inspiring social faith. So they fled, in spirit or in flesh, into unfamiliar scenes, and vanished from society, because society was not sufficiently social. The feeling was abnormal, and the method was fundamentally artificial. A sentimentalism arose, which is to art what the metaphysical method is to philosophy. Yet a literature was born of it, whose freshness, its force, elevation, and, above all, a self-assertion and peculiar aspiring freedom that have never been surpassed, still exert an irresistible attraction, even over minds that are furthest removed from the moral storm and disorder and the confused intellectual convictions of that extraordinary group. Perhaps the fact that their active force is spent, and that men find in them now only a charm and no longer a gospel, explains the difference between the admiration which some of us permit ourselves to feel for them, and the impatient dislike which they stirred in our fathers. Then they were a danger, because they were a force, misleading amiable and highminded people into blind paths. Now this is at an end, and, apart from their historic interest, the permanent elements of beauty draw us to them with a delight that does not diminish, as we recede further and further from the impotence of the aspirations which thus married themselves to lofty and stirring words. To say nothing of Rousseau, the father and founder of the nature-worship, which is the nearest approach to a positive side that the Revolution has ever possessed, how much fine colour and freshness of feeling there is in *Réné,* what a sense of air and space in *Paul et Virginie,* and what must they have been to a generation that had just emerged from the close parlours of Richardson, the best of the sentimentalists of the præ-revolutionary type? May we not say, too, in parenthesis, that the man is the votary, not of wisdom, but of a bald and shapeless asceticism, who is so excessively penetrated with the reality, the duties, the claims, and the constant hazards of civilisation, as to find in himself no chord responsive to that sombre pensiveness into which Obermann's unfathomable melancholy and impotence of will deepened, as he meditated on the mean shadows which men are content to chase for happiness, and on all the pigmy progeny of giant effort? "C'est peu de chose," says Obermann, "de n'être point comme le vulgaire des hommes; mais c'est avoir fait un pas vers las sagesse, que de n'être plus comme le vulgaire des sages." This penetrating remark hits the difference between

De Sénancourt himself and most of the school. He is absolutely free from the vulgarity of wisdom, and breathes the air of higher peaks, taking us through mysterious and fragrant pine-woods, where more than he may find meditative repose amid the heat and stress of that practical day, of which he and his school could never bear the burden.

In that *vulgaire des sages* of which De Sénancourt had none, Byron abounded. His work is in much the glorification of revolutionary commonplace. Melodramatic individualism reaches its climax in that long series of Laras, Conrads, Manfreds, Harolds, who present that fatal trilogy, in which crime is middle term between debauch and satiety, that forms the natural development of an anti-social doctrine in a full-blooded temperament. It was this temperament which, blending with his gifts of intellect, gave Byron the amazing copiousness and force that makes him the dazzling master of revolutionary emotion, because it fills his work with such variety of figures, such free change of incident, such diversity of passion, such a constant movement and agitation. It was this never-ceasing stir, coupled with a striking concreteness and an unfailing directness, which rather than any markedly correct or wide intellectual apprehension of things, made him so much more effective an interpreter of the moral tumult of the epoch than any one else. If we look for psychological delicacy, for subtle moral traits, for opening glimpses into unobserved depths of character, behold, none of these things are there. These were no gifts of his, any more than the divine gift of music was his. There are some writers whose words but half express the indefinable thoughts that inspired them, and to whom we have to surrender our whole minds with a peculiar loyalty and fulness, independent of the letter and printed phrase, if we would liquefy the frozen speech and recover for ourselves some portion of the imprisoned essence. This is very seldom a necessity with Byron. His words tell us all that he means to say, and do not merely hint nor suggest. The matter with which he deals is gigantic, and he paints with violent colours and a sweeping pencil. Yet he is free from that declamation with which some of the French poets of the same age, and representing a portion of the same movement, blow out their cheeks. An angel of reasonableness seems to watch over him, even when he comes most dangerously near to an extravagance. He is equally free from a strained antithesis, which would have been inconsistent not only with the breadth of effect required by Byron's art, but also with the peculiarly direct and forcible quality of his genius. In the preface to *Marino Faliero,* a composition that abounds in noble passages and rests on a fine and original conception of character, he mentions his "desire of preserving a nearer approach to unity than the irregularity which is the reproach of the English theatre." And this sound view of the importance of form, and of the barbarism to which our English genius is prone, from "Goody Blake and Harry Gill" up to the clownish savagery which occasionally defaces even plays attributed to Shakspeare, is collateral proof of the sanity and balance which marked the foundations of his character, and which at no point of his work ever entirely failed him. Byron's admiration for Pope was no mere eccentricity.

We may value this self-control the more, by remembering the nature of his subjects. We look out upon a wild revolutionary welter, of vehement activity without a purpose, boundless discontent without a hope, futile interrogation of nature in questions for which nature can have no answer, unbridled passion, despairing satiety, impotence. It is too easy, as the history of English opinion about Byron's poetic merit abundantly proves, to underrate the genius which mastered so tremendous a conflict, and rendered that amazing scene with the flow and energy and mingled tempest and forlorn calm which belonged to the original reality. The essential futility of the many moods, which went to make up all this, ought not to blind us to the enormous power that was needed for the reproduction of a turbulent and not quite aimless chaos of the soul, in which man seemed to be divorced alike from his brother men in the present, and from all the long succession and endeavour of men in the past. It was no small feat to rise to a height that should command so much, and to exhibit with all the force of life a world that had broken loose from its moorings.

It is idle to vituperate this anarchy, either from the point of view of a sour and precise Puritanism, or the more elevated point of a rational and large faith in progress. Wise men are like Burke, who did not know how to draw an indictment against a whole nation. They do not know how to think nothing but ill of a whole generation, that lifted up its voice in heartfelt complaint and wailing against the conceptions, forms, and rulers, human and divine, of a society that the inward faith had abandoned, but which clung to every outward ordinance; which only remembered that man had property, and forgot that he had a spirit. This is the complaint that rings through Byron's verse. It was this complaint that lay deep at the bottom of the Revolution, and took form in every possible kind of protest, from a dishevelled neckcloth up to a profession of atheism. Byron elaborated the common emotion, as the earliest modern poets elaborated the common speech. He gave it inflections, and distinguished its moods, and threw over it an air of system and coherency, and a certain goodly and far-reaching sonorousness. This is the usual function of the spiritual leader, who leaves no more in bulk in the minds of those whom he attracts than he found, but he leaves it articulate with many sounds, and vivid with the consciousness of a multitude of defined impressions.

That the whole movement, in spite of its energy, was crude, unscientific, virtually abortive, is most true. That it was presided over by a false conception of nature as a benign and purifying power, while she is in truth a stern force to be tamed and crushed, if society is to hold together, cannot be denied of the revolutionary movement then, any more than it can be denied of its sequels now. Nor need we overlook its fundamental error of tracing half the misfortunes and woes of the race to that social union, to which we are really indebted for all the happiness we know, including even this dignifying sensibility of the woes of the race; and the other half to a fictitious entity styled destiny, placed among the nethermost gods, which would be more rightly regarded as the infinitely modifiable influence exercised by one generation of ourselves upon those that follow.

Every one of these faults of thought is justly chargeable to Byron. They were deeply inherent in the Revolution. They coloured thoughts about government, about laws, about morals; they effected a transformation of religion, but resting on no basis of philosophical acceptance of history, this transformation was only temporary. They spread a fantastic passion, of which Byron was himself an example and a victim, for extraordinary outbreaks of a peculiar kind of material activity, that met the exigencies of an imperious will, while it had not the irksomeness of the self-control which would have exercised the will to more permanent profit. They destroyed faith in order, natural or social, actual or potential, and substituted for it an enthusiastic assertion of the claims of the individual to make his passions, aspirations, and convictions, a final and decisive law.

Such was the moral state which Byron had to render and interpret. His relation to it was a relation of exact sympathy. He felt the force of each of the many currents that united in one destructive stream, wildly overflowing the fixed banks, and then when it had overflowed, often, it must be confessed, stagnating in lazy, brackish pools, while new tributaries began to flow in together from far other quarters. The list of his poems is the catalogue of the elements of the revolutionary spirit. For of what manner is this spirit? It is not a masterful and impatient yearning after many good things, unsubdued and uninformed either by a just knowledge of the time and the means which are needed to bring men the fruits of their hope, or by a fit appreciation of orderly and tranquil activity for the common service, as the normal type of the individual life? And this is precisely the temper and the spirit of Byron. Nowhere else do we see drawn in such traits that colossal figure which has haunted Europe these four-score years and more, with its new-born passion, its half-controlled will, its constant cry for a multitude of unknown blessings under the single name of freedom, the one known and unadulterated word of blessing. If only truth, which alone of words is essentially divine and sacrosanct, had been the chief talisman of the Revolution, the movement would have been very different from that which we know. But to claim this or that in the name of truth, would have been to borrow the language which priests and presbyters, Dominic and Calvin, had made hateful. Freedom, after all, was the next best thing, for it is an indispensable condition of the best of all, but it could not lead men until the spirit of truth, which means science in the intellectual order, and justice in the social order, had joined company with it.

So there was violent action in politics, and violent and excessive stimulation in literature, the positive effects of the force moved in each sphere being deplorably small in proportion to the intense moral energy which gave the impulse. In literature the straining for mental liberty was the more futile of the two, because it expressed the ardent and hopeless longing of the individual for a life which we may perhaps best call life unconditioned. And this unconditioned life, which the Byronic hero vainly seeks, and not finding he fills the world with stormy complaint, is least of all likely to offer itself in any approximative form to men penetrated with gross and egotistical passions to their inmost core. The Byronic hero went to clasp repose in a frenzy. All crimson and aflame with passion, he groaned for evening stillness. He insisted on being free, in the corroding fetters of resentment and scorn for men. Conrad sought balm for disappointment of spirit in vehement activity of body. Manfred represents the confusion common to the type, between thirst for the highest knowledge, and proud violence of unbridled will. Harold is held in a middle way of poetic melancholy, equally far from a speechless despair and from gay and reckless license, by contemplation of the loveliness of external nature and the great exploits and perishing monuments of man in the past; but he equally with the others embodies the paradoxical hope that angry isolation and fretful estrangement from mankind is equivalent to emancipation from their pettiness, instead of being its very climax and demonstration. As if freedom of soul could exist without orderly relations of intelligence and partial acceptance between a man and the sum of surrounding circumstances. That universal protest which rings through Byron's work with a plangent resonance very different from the whimperings of punier men, is a proof that so far from being free, one's whole being is invaded and laid waste. It is no ignoble mood, and it was a most inevitable product of the mental and social conditions of western Europe at the close of the eighteenth century. Everlasting protest impetuous energy of will, melancholy and despondent reaction;—this is the revolutionary course. Cain and Conrad; then Manfred and Lara and Harold.

In studying that portion of the European movement which burst forth into flame in France between the fall of the Bastille and those fatal days of Vendémiaire, Fructidor, Floréal, Brumaire, in which the explosion came convulsively to its end, we seem to see a microcosm of the Byronic epos. The succession of moods is identical. Overthrow, rage, intense material energy, crime, profound melancholy, half-cynical dejection. The Revolution was the battle of Will against the social forces of a dozen centuries. Men thought that they had only to will the freedom and happiness of a world, and all nature and society would be plastic before their daring, as clay in the hands of the potter. They could only conceive of failure as another expression for inadequate will. Is not this one of the notes of Byron's Ode on the fall of Bonaparte? "L'audace, l'audace, et toujours l'audace." If Danton could have read Byron, he would have felt as one in front of a magician's glass. Every passion and fit, from the bloody days of September down to the gloomy walks by the banks of the Aube, and the prison-cry that "it were better to be a poor fisherman than to meddle with the governing of men," would have found itself there. It is true that in Byron we miss the firmness of noble and generous hope. This makes him a more veritable embodiment of the Revolution than such a precursor as Rousseau, in whom were all the unclouded anticipations of a dawn that opened to an obscured noon and a tempestuous night. Yet one knows not, in truth, how much of that violence of will and restless activity and resolute force was due less to confidence than to the urgent necessity which every one of us has felt, at some season and under some influence, of filling up spiritual vacuity by energetic material activity. Was this the secret of the mysterious charm that scenes of violent strife and bloodshed always had for Byron's imagination, as it was perhaps the secret of the black transformation of the social faith of '89 into the worship of the Conqueror of '99? Nowhere does Byron's genius show so much as its own incomparable fire and energy, nor move with such sympathetic firmness and amplitude of pinion, as in Lara, the Corsair, Harold, and other poems, where "Red Battle stamps his foot," and where

> The Giant on the mountain stands,
> His blood-red tresses deep'ning in the sun,
> With death-shot glowing in his fiery hands,
> And eye that scorcheth all it glows upon.

Yet other and intrinsically nobler passages, where this splendid imaginative energy of the sensations is replaced by the calmer glow of social meditation, prove that Byron was penetrated with the distinctively modern scorn and aversion for the military spirit, and the distinctively modern conviction of its being the most deadly of anachronisms. Such indirect satisfaction to the physical energies was to him, as their direct satisfaction was to the disillusioned France of '99, the relief demanded by a powerful nature for the impotence of hope and vision.

However this may have been, it may be confessed that Byron presents less of the flame of his revolutionary prototypes, and too much of the ashes. He came at the end of the experiment. But it is only a question of proportion. The ashes belong as much and as necessarily to the methods of the Revolution, in that phase, as do the blaze that first told men of possible light and warmth, and the fire which yet smoulders with abundant life underneath the grey cinders. And we have to remember that Byron came in the midst of a reaction; a reaction of triumph for the partisans of darkness and obstruction, who were assured that the exploded fragments of the old order would speedily grow together again, and a reaction of despondency for those who had filled themselves with illimitable and preemptory hopes. Silly Byronical votaries, who only half understood their idol and loved him for a gloom that in their own case was nothing but a graceful veil for selfishness and mental indolence, saw and felt only the melancholy conclusion, and had not travelled a yard in the burning path that led to it. They hugged Conrad's haughty gloom, but they would have trembled at the thought of Conrad's perilous expedition. They were proud despondent Laras after their manner, "lords of themselves, that heritage of woe," but the heritage would have been still more unbearable if it had involved Lara's bodily danger.

This shallowness has no part in Byron himself. His weariness was genuine outcome of the influence of the time upon a character consumed by passion. His lot was cast among spent forces, and while it is no hyperbole to say that he was himself the most enormous force of his time, he was only half conscious of this, if indeed he did not always inwardly shrink from crediting his own power and strength, as so many strong men habitually do, in spite of noisy and perpetual self-assertion. Conceit and presumption have not been any more fatal to the world, than the waste which comes of great men failing in their hearts to recognise how great they are. Many a man whose affectations and assumptions are a proverb, has lost the magnificent virtue of simplicity, for no other reason than that he needed courage to take his own measure, and so finally confirm to himself the reality of his pretensions. With Byron, as with some of his prototypes among the men of action in France and elsewhere, theatrical ostentation, excessive self-consciousness, extravagant claims, cannot hide from us that their power was secretly drained by an ever-present distrust of their own aims, their own methods, even of the very results they seemed to have achieved.

This diffidence was an inseparable consequence of the vast predominance of exalted passion over reflection, which is one of the revolutionary marks. Byron was fundamentally and substantially, as has been already said, one of the most rational of men. Hence when the passionate fit grew cold, as it always does in temperaments so mixed, he wanted for perfect strength a justification in thought. There are men whose being is so universally possessed by phantasies, that they never feel this necessity of reconciling the visions of excited emotion with the ideas of ordered reason. Byron was more vigorously constituted, and his susceptibility to the necessity of this reconciliation combined with his inability to achieve it to produce that cynicism which the simple charity of vulgar opinion attributes to the possession of him by unclean devils. It was his refuge, as it sometimes is with smaller men, from the disquieting confusion which was caused by the disproportion between his visions and aspirations, and his intellectual means for satisfying himself seriously as to their true relations and substantive value. Only the man arrives at practical strength who is convinced, whether rightly or wrongly, that he knows all about his own ideas that needs to be known. Byron never did thus know himself, either morally or intellectually. The higher part of him was consciously dragged down by the degrading reminiscence of the brutishness of his youth and its connections and associations, which hung like miasma over his spirit. He could not rise to that sublimest height of moral fervour, when a man intrepidly chases from his memory past evil done; suppresses the recollection of old corruptions, declares that he no longer belongs to them nor they to him, and is not frightened by the past from a firm and lofty respect for present dignity and worth. It is a good thing thus to overthrow the tyranny of the memory, and to cast out the body of our dead selves. That Byron never attained this good, though he was not unlikely to have done so, if he had lived longer, does not prove that he was too gross to feel its need, but it explains a moral weakness, which has left a strange and touching mark on some of his later works.

So in the intellectual order, he knew too much in one sense, and in another too little. The strong man is not conscious of gaps and cataclysms in the structure of his belief, or else he would in so far instantly cease to be strong. One living as Byron emphatically did in the truly modern atmosphere, was bound by all the conditions of the atmosphere to have mastered what we may style the natural history of his own ideas and convictions; to know something of their position towards fact and outer circumstance and possibility; above all to have some trusted standard for testing their value and assuring himself that they do really cover the field which he takes them to cover. People with a faith and people living in frenzy are equally under this law; but they take the completeness and coherency of their doctrine for granted. Byron was not the prey of habitual frenzy, and he was without a faith. That is to say he had no firm basis for his conceptions, and he was aware that he had none. The same unrest which drove men of that epoch to Nature, haunted them to the end, because they had no systematic conception of her working and of human relations with her. In a word there was no science. Byron was a warm admirer of the genius and art of Goethe, yet he never found out the central secret of Goethe's greatness, his luminous and coherent positivity. This is the crowning glory of the modern spirit, and it was the lack of this which went so far to neutralise Byron's hold of the other chief characteristics of that spirit, its freedom and spaciousness, its humaneness and wide sociality, its versatility and manysidedness, and passionate feeling for the great natural forces.

This positivity is the cardinal condition of strength, for times when theology lies in decay, and the abstractions which gradually replaced the older gods have in their turn ceased to satisfy the intelligence and mould the will. All competent persons agree that it is the first condition of the attainment of scientific truth. Nobody denies that men of action find in it the first law of successful achievement in the material order. Its varied but always superlative power in the region of æsthetics is only an object of recent recognition, though great work enough has been done in past ages by men whose recognition was informal and unexpressed. It is plain that in the different classes of æsthetic manifestation, there will be differences in objective shape and colour, corresponding to the varied limits and conditions of the matter with which the special art has to deal; but the critic may expect to find in all a profound unity of subjective impression, and that, the impression of a self-sustaining order and a self-sufficing harmony among all those faculties and parts and energies of universal life which come within the idealising range of art. In other words, the characteristically modern inspiration is the inspiration of law. The regulated play of forces shows itself as fit to stir those profound emotional impulses which wake the artistic soul, as ever did the gracious or terrible gods of antique or middle times. There are glories in Turner's idealisation of the energies of matter, which are at least as nobly imaginative and elevated, in spite of the conspicuous absence of the human element in them, as the highest products of the artists who believed that their work was for the service and honour of a deity.

It is as mistaken to suppose that this conviction of the supremacy of a cold and self-contained order in the universe is fatal to emotional expansion, as it would be to suppose it fatal to intellectual curiosity. Experience has shown in the scientific sphere, that the gradual withdrawal of natural operations from the grasp of the imaginary volitions of imaginary beings has not tamed, but greatly stimulated and fertilised, scientific curiosity as to the conditions of these operations. Why should it be otherwise in the æsthetic sphere? Why should all that part of our mental composition which responds to the beautiful and imaginative expression of real truths, be at once inflamed and satisfied by the thought that our whole lives and all the movements of the universe are the objects of the inexplicable caprice of Makers who are also Destroyers, and yet grow cold, apathetic, and unproductive, in the shadow of the belief that we can only know ourselves as part of a stupendous and inexorable succession of phenomenal conditions, moving according to laws that may be formulated positively but not interpreted morally, to new des-

tinies that are eternally unfathomable? Why should this conception of a coherent order, free from the arbitrary and presumptuous stamp of certain final causes, be less favourable either to the
ethical or the æsthetic side of human nature, than the older conception of the regulation of the course of the great series by a
multitude of intrinsically meaningless and purposeless volitions?
The alertness of our sensations for all sources of outer beauty
remains unimpaired. The old and lovely attitude of devout service
does not pass away to leave vacancy, but is transformed into a
yet more devout obligation and service towards creatures that
have only their own fellowship and mutual ministry to lean upon;
and if we miss something of the ancient solace of special and
personal protection, the loss is not unworthily made good by the
growth of an imperial sense of participation in the common
movement and equal destination of eternal forces.

To have a mind penetrated with this spiritual persuasion, is to
be in full possession of the highest strength that man can attain.
It springs from a scientific and rounded interpretation of the
facts of life, and is in a harmony which freshly found truths only
make more ample and elaborate, with all the conclusions of the
intellect in every order. The active energies are not paralysed by
the possibilities of enfeebling doubt, nor the reason drawn down
and stultified by apprehension lest its methods should discredit a
document, or its inferences clash with a dogma, or its light flash
unseasonably on a mystery. There is none of the baleful distortion
of hate, because evil and wrongdoing and darkness are acknowledged to be effects of causes, sums of conditions, terms in a series;
they are to be brought to their end or weakened and narrowed by
right action and endeavour, and this endeavour does not stagnate
in an antipathy, but concentrates itself in transfixing a cause. In
no other condition of the spirit than this in which firm acquiescence mingles with valorous effort, can a man be so sure of raising
a calm gaze and an enduring brow to the cruelty of circumstance.
The last appalling stroke of annihilation itself is measured with
purest fortitude by one whose religious contemplation dwells
most habitually upon the sovereignty of obdurate laws in the
vast revolving circle of physical forces, on the one hand, and, on
the other, upon that moral order which the vision and pity of
good men for their fellows, guiding the spontaneous energy of all

men in strife with circumstance, have raised into a structure sublimer and more amazing than all the majesty of outer nature.

In Byron's time the pretensions of the two possible answers to the great and eternally open questions of God, immortality, and the like, were independent of that powerful host of inferences and analogies, which the advance of physical discovery and the establishment of a historical order have since then brought into men's minds. The direct aggressions of old are for the most part abandoned, because it is felt that no fiercest polemical cannonading can drive away the impalpable darkness of error, but only the slow and silent presence of the dawning truth. *Cain* remains, a stern and lofty statement of the case against that theological tradition which so outrages, where it has not already too deeply depraved, the conscience of civilised man. Yet every one who is competent to judge, must feel how infinitely more free the mind of the poet would have been, if besides this just and holy rage, most laudable in its kind, his intellectual equipment had been ample enough and precise enough to have taught him that all the conceptions that races of men have ever held either about themselves or their deities have had a source in the permanently useful instincts of human nature, are capable of explanation, and of a historical justification, that is to say of the kind of justification which is in itself and of its own force the most instant destruction to what has grown to be an anachronism.

Byron's curiously marked predilection for dramatic composition, not merely for dramatic poems, as *Manfred* or *Cain,* but for genuine plays, as *Marino Faliero, Werner,* the *Two Foscari,* was the only sign of his approach to the historic or positive spirit. Dramatic art in its purest modern conception is genuinely positive; that is, it is the presentation of action, character, and motive, in a self-sufficing and self-evolving order. There are no final causes, and the first moving elements are taken for granted to begin with. The dramatist creates, but it is the climax of his work to appear to stand absolutely apart and unseen, while the play unfolds itself to the spectator, just as the greater drama of physical phenomenon unfolds itself to the scientific observer, or as the order of recorded history extends in natural process under the eye of the political philosopher. Partly, no doubt, the attraction which dramatic form had for Byron is to be explained by that revolutionary thirst for action, of which we have already spoken; but partly also it may well have been due to Byron's rudimentary and unsuspected affinity with the more scientific and constructive side of the modern spirit.

His idea of Nature, of which something has been already said, pointed in the same direction; for, although he made an abstraction and a goddess of her, and was in so far out of the right modern way of thinking about these outer forces, it is to be remembered that while this dominant conception of Nature as introduced by Rousseau and others into politics was most mischievous and destructive, its place and worth in poetry are very different; because here in the region of the imagination it had the effect, without any pernicious practical consequences, of giving shape and proportion to that great idea of Ensemble throughout the visible universe, which may be called the beginning and fountain of right knowledge. The conception of the relationship of the different parts and members of the vast cosmos was not accessible to Byron as it is to a later generation, but his constant appeal in season and out of season to all the life and movement that surrounds man, implied and promoted the widest extension of our consciousness of the wholeness and community of natural processes.

There was one very manifest evil consequence of the hold which this idea in its cruder shape gained over Byron and his admirers. The vastness of the material universe as they conceived and half adored it, entirely overshadowed the principle of moral duty, and social obligation. The domestic sentiment, for example, almost disappears in those works which made Byron most popular, or else only appears, to be banished with reproach. This is quite in accordance with the revolutionary spirit, which was in one of its most fundamental aspects a revolt on behalf of unconditioned individual rights, and against the family. If we accept what seems to be the fatal law of progress that excess on one side is only moderated by a nearly corresponding excess of an opposite kind, the Byronic dissolution of domestic feeling was not entirely without justification. There is probably no uglier growth of time than that form of gross, mean, spiritless domesticity which has always been very apt to fascinate the English imagination ever since the last great effort of the Rebellion, and which rose to the climax of its popularity when the mad and malignant George III. won all hearts by living like a farmer. Instead of the fierce light beating about a throne, it played lambently upon a sty. And the nation who admired, imitated. When the Regent came, and with him that coarse profligacy which has alternated with deadly dulness in the annals of the line, the honest part of the world was driven even further into domestic sentimentality of a greasy kind out of antipathy to the son, than it had gone from affection for the sire. Byron helped to clear the air of this. His fire, his lofty spaciousness of outlook, his spirited interest in great national causes, his romance, and the passion both of his animosity and his sympathy, acted for a while like an electric current, and every one within his influence became ashamed to barter the large heritage of manhood, with its many realms and illimitable interests, for the sordid ease of the hearth and the good word of the unworthy. He fills men with thoughts that shake down the unlively temple of comfort. This was good, to force whoever was not already too far sunk into the mire, high up to the larger atmosphere, whence they could see how minute an atom is man, how infinite and blind and pitiless the might that encompasses his little life. Many feeble spirits run back homewards from the horrid solitudes and abysses of *Manfred* and the moral terrors of *Cain* and even the despair of *Harold,* and burying themselves in warm domestic places, were comforted by the familiar restoratives and appliances. Firmer souls were not only exhilarated, but intoxicated by the potent and unaccustomed air. They went too far. They made war on the family, and the idea of it. Everything human was mischievously dwarfed, and the difference between right and wrong, between gratification of appetite and its control for virtue's sake, between the acceptance and the evasion of clear obligation, this became invisible or of no account in the new light. That constancy and permanence of which the family is the type, and which is the first condition alike of the stability and progress of society, were obliterated from thought. As if the wonders that have been wrought by this regulated constancy of the feeling of man for man in transforming human life, were not far more transcendently exalting than the contemplation of those glories of brute nature, which are barbaric in comparison.

It would be unjust not to admit that there are abundant passages in his poems, of too manifest depth and sincerity of feeling, for us to suppose that Byron himself was dead to the beauty of domestic sentiment. The united tenderness and dignity of Faliero's words to Angiolina before he goes to the meeting of the conspirators would, if there were nothing else, be enough to show how rightly in his better moods the poet appreciated the conditions of the family. Unfortunately, the better moods were not fixed, and we had *Don Juan,* where the wit and colour and power served to make an antisocial and licentious sentiment attractive to puny creatures, who were thankful to have their lasciviousness so gaily adorned. As for Great Britain, she deserved *Don Juan.* A nation, whose disrespect for all ideas and aspirations, that cannot be supported by a text, nor circulated by a religious tract society, was systematic, and where consequently the understanding is least protected against sensual sophisms, received no more than a just chastisement in "the literature of Satan." Here again, in the licence of this literature, we see the finger of the Revolution, and of that egoism which makes the passions of the individual his own law. Let us condemn and pass on, homily undelivered. If Byron injured the domestic idea on this side, let us not fail to observe how vastly he elevated it on others, and how, above all, he pointed to the idea above and beyond it, in whose light only can that be worthy, the idea of the country and a public cause. A man may be sure that the comfort of the hearth has usurped too high a place, when he can read without response the lines declaring that domestic ties must yield in "those who are called to the high destinies, Which purify corrupted commonwealths."

> We must forget all feelings save the one,—
> We must resign all passions save our purpose,—
> We must behold no object save our country,—
> And only look on death as beautiful,
> So that the sacrifice ascend to heaven
> And draw down freedom on her evermore.
>   *Calendaro.* But if we fail—
>   *I. Bertuccio.*   They never fail who die
> In a great cause: the block may soak their gore;
> Their heads may sodden in the sun; their limbs

Be strung to city gates and castle walls—
But still their spirit walks abroad. Though years
Elapse, and others share as dark a doom,
They but augment the deep and sweeping thoughts
Which overpower all others, and conduct
The world at last to freedom. What were we
If Brutus had not lived? He died in giving
Rome liberty, but left a deathless lesson—
A name which is a virtue, and a soul
Which multiplies itself throughout all time,
When wicked men wax mighty, and a state
Turns servile.

And the man who wrote this, was worthy to play an even nobler part than the one he had thus nobly described; for it was not many years after that Byron left all and laid down his life for the emancipation of a strange land, and "Greece and Italy wept for his death, as it had been that of the noblest of their own sons." Detractors have done their best to pare away the merit of this act of self-renunciation by attributing it to despair. That contemporaries of their own humour had done their best to make his life a load to him is true, yet to this talk of despair we may reply in the poet's own words,

When we know
All that can come, and how to meet it, our
Resolves, if firm, may merit a more noble
Word that this, to give it utterance.

There was an estimate of the value and purpose of a human life, which our Age of Comfort may fruitfully ponder.

It was the same impetuous and indomitable spirit of effort which moved Byron to his last heroic exploit, that made the poetry inspired by it so powerful in Europe from the deadly days of the Holy Alliance onwards. Cynical and misanthropical as he has been called, as though that were his sum and substance, he yet never ceased to glorify human freedom in tones that stirred the hearts of men and quickened their hope and upheld their daring as with the voice of some heavenly trumpet. You may, if you choose, find the splendour of the stanzas in the Fourth Canto on the Bourbon restoration, on Cromwell and Washington, a theatrical splendour. But for all that, they touched the noblest parts of men. They are alive with an exalted and magnanimous generosity, the one high virtue which can never fail to touch a multitude. Subtlety may miss them, graces may miss them, and reason may fly over their heads, but the words of a generous humanity on the lips of poet or chief have never failed to kindle divine music in their breasts. The critic may censure, and culture may wave a disdainful hand. As has been said, all such words "are open to criticism, and they are all above it." The magic still works. It is as though some mysterious and potent word from the gods had gone abroad over the face of the earth.

This larger influence was not impaired by Byron's ethical poverty. The latter was an inevitable consequence of his defective discipline. The triteness of his moral climax is occasionally startling. When Sardanapalus, for instance, sees Zarina torn from him, and is stricken with profound anguish at the pain with which he has filled her life, he winds up with such a platitude as this:—

> To what gulfs
> A single deviation from the track
> Of human duties leaves even those who claim
> The homage of mankind as their born due!

A hymn-writer might work up enough of passion for such a consummation as this. Once more, Byron was insufficiently furnished with positive intellectual ideas, and for want of these his most exalted words were constantly left sterile of definite and pointed outcome.

More than this, Byron's passionate feeling for mankind was narrowed, by his failure to include in his conception the long succession of generations, that stretch back into the past and lie far on in the misty distances of the future. This was a defect that his conception shares in common with the religion which, while sublimely bidding man to love his neighbour as himself, yet leaves him in the profundity of a concentrated regard for his own soul, to forget sacred reverence for the unseen benefactors of old time, and direct endeavour to be more to the future than even the benefactions of the past have been to him. No good man is without both these sentiments in germ. But to be fully effective, they need to be fused together into a single thought, completing that idea of humanity, which when imperfectly held so constantly misleads men into shortsighted action, effective only for the hour, and at the hour's end turning to something worse than ineffective. Only he stands aright, who from his little point of present possession ever meditates on the far-reaching lines which pass through his point from one interminable starlight distance to another. Neither the stoic pagan, nor the disciple of the creed which has some of the peculiar weakness of stoicism and not all its peculiar strength, could find Manfred's latest word untrue to himself:—

> The mind which is immortal makes itself
> Requital for its good or evil thoughts—
> Is its own origin of ill and end—
> And its own place and time—its innate sense,
> When stripped of this mortality, derives
> No colour from the fleeting things without:
> But is absorbed in sufferance or joy,
> Born from the knowledge of its own desert.

It is only when a man subordinates this absorption in individual sufferance and joy to the thought that his life is a trust for humanity, that he is sure of making it anything other than "rain fallen on the sand." In his own career Byron was loftier than the individualism of his creed, and for this reason, though he may have no place in our own Minster, he belongs to the band of far-shining men of whom Pericles declared the whole world to be the tomb.

Carlyle

The new edition of Mr. Carlyle's works of which some eighteen volumes are now in the hands of the public, may be taken for the final presentation of all that the author has to say to his contemporaries, and to possess the settled form in which he wishes his words to go to those of posterity who may prove to have ears for them. The edition will be complete in the course of another twelvemonth, and the whole of the golden Gospel of Silence will then be effectively compressed in thirty fine volumes. After all has been said about self-indulgent mannerisms, moral perversities, phraseological outrages, and the rest, these volumes will remain the noble monument of the industry, originality, conscientiousness, and genius of a noble character, and of an intellectual career that has exercised the profoundest sort of influence upon English feeling. Men who have long since moved far away from these spiritual latitudes, like those who still find an adequate shelter in them, can hardly help feeling as they turn over the pages of the now disused pieces which they once used to ponder daily, that whatever later teachers may have done in definitely shaping opinion, in giving specific form to sentiment, and in subjecting impulse to rational discipline, here was the friendly fire-bearer who first conveyed the Promethean spark, here the prophet who first smote the rock. That with this sense of obligation to the master, there mixes a less satisfactory reminiscence of

This essay was first published in *Fortnightly Review,* n.s., 43 (July 1870): 1–22, and was reprinted in *Critical Miscellanies,* vol. 1 (London, 1877)—ed.

youthful excess in imitative phrases, in unseasonably apostolic readiness towards exhortation and rebuke, in interest about the soul, a portion of which might more profitably have been converted into care for the head, is true in most cases. A hostile observer of bands of Carlylites at Oxford and elsewhere might have been justified in describing the imperative duty of work as the theme of many an hour of strenuous idleness, and the superiority of golden silence over silver speech as the text of endless bursts of jerky rapture, while a too constant invective against cant had its usual effect of developing cant with a difference. To the incorrigibly sentimental all this was sheer poison which continues tenaciously in the system. Others of robuster character no sooner came into contact with the world and its fortifying exigencies, than they at once began to assimilate the wholesome part of what they had taken in, while the rest falls gradually and silently out. When criticism has done its just work on the odious affectations of many of Mr. Carlyle's disciples, and about the nature of Mr. Carlyle's opinions and their worth as specific contributions, very few people will be found to deny that his influence in stimulating moral energy, in kindling enthusiasm for virtues worthy of enthusiasm, and in stirring a sense of the reality on the one hand and the unreality on the other of all that men can do or suffer, has not been surpassed by any teacher now living.

The degree of durability which this influence is likely to possess with the next and other generations is another and rather sterile question, which we are not now concerned to discuss. The unrestrained eccentricities which Mr. Carlyle's strong individuality has precipitated in his written style may, in spite of the poetic fineness of his imagination, which no historian or prose humourist has excelled, still be expected to deprive his work of that permanence which is only secured by classic form. The incorporation of so many phrases, allusions, nicknames, that belong only to the hour, inevitably makes the vitality of the composition conditional on the vitality of these transient and accidental elements which are so deeply imbedded in it. Another consideration is that no philosophic writer, however ardently his words may have been treasured and followed by the people of his own time, can well be cherished by succeeding generations, unless his name is associated through some specific and positive contribution with the central march of European thought and feeling. In other words, there is a difference between living in the history of literature or belief, and living in literature itself and in the minds of believers. Mr. Carlyle has been a most powerful solvent, but solvents are apt to become merely historic. The historian of the intellectual and moral movements of Great Britain during the present century, will fail ludicrously in his task if he omits to give a large and conspicuous space to the author of *Sartor Resartus*. But it is one thing to study historically the ideas which have influenced our predecessors, and another thing to seek in them an influence fruitful for ourselves. It is to be hoped that one may doubt the permanent soundness of Mr. Carlyle's peculiar speculations, without either doubting or failing to share that warm affection and tender reverence which his personality has worthily inspired in many thousands of his readers. He has himself taught us to separate these two sides of a man, and we have learnt from him to love Samuel Johnson without reading much or a word that the old sage wrote.

It is none the less, for what has just been said, a weightier and a rarer privilege for a man to give a stirring impulse to the moral activity of a generation than to write in classic style, and to have impressed the spirit of his own personality deeply upon the minds of multitudes of men, than to have composed most of those works which the world is said not willing to let die. Nor, again, is to say that this higher renown belongs to Mr. Carlyle, to underrate the less resounding, but most substantial, services of a definite kind which he has rendered both to literature and history. This work may be in time superseded with the advance of knowledge, but the value of the first service will remain unimpaired. It was he, as has been said, "who first taught England to appreciate Goethe"; and not only to appreciate Goethe, but to recognise and seek yet further knowledge of the genius and industry of Goethe's countrymen. His splendid drama of the French Revolution has done, and may be expected long to continue to do, more to bring before our slow-moving and unimaginative public the portentous meaning of that tremendous cataclysm, than all the other writings on the subject in the English language put together. His presentation of Puritanism and the Commonwealth and Oliver Cromwell first made the most elevating period of the national history in any way really intelligible. The Life of Frederick the Second, whatever judgment we may pass upon its morality, or even upon its place as a work of historic art, is a model of laborious and painstaking narrative of facts not before accessible to the reader of history. For all this, and for much other work eminently useful and meritorious even from the mechanical point of view, Mr. Carlyle deserves the warmest recognition. His genius gave him a right to mock at the ineffectiveness of Dryasdust, but his genius was also too true to prevent him from adding the always needful supplement of a painstaking industry that rivals Dryasdust's own most strenuous toil. Take out of the mind of the English reader of ordinary cultivation and the average journalist, usually a degree or two lower than this, their conceptions of the French Revolution and the English Rebellion, and their knowledge of German literature and history, as well as most of their acquaintance with the prominent men of the eighteenth century, and we shall see how much work Mr. Carlyle has done simply as schoolmaster. This, however, is emphatically a secondary aspect of his character and of the function which he has fulfilled in relation to the more active tendencies of modern opinion and feeling. We must go on to other ground, if we would find the field in which he has laboured most ardently and with most acceptance. History and literature have been with him, what they will always be with wise and understanding minds of creative and even of the higher critical faculty, only embodiments, illustrations, experiments, for ideas about religion, conduct, society, history, government, and all the other great heads and departments of a complete social doctrine. From this point of view, the time has perhaps come when we may fairly attempt to discern some of the tendencies which Mr. Carlyle has initiated, or accelerated and deepened, though assuredly many years must elapse before any adequate measure can be taken of their force and final direction.

It would be a comparatively simple process to affix the regulation labels of philosophy: to say that Mr. Carlyle is a Pantheist in religion (or a Pottheist, to use the alternative whose flippancy gave such offence to Sterling on one occasion), a Transcendentalist or Intuitionist in ethics, an Absolutist in politics, and so forth, with the addition of a cloud of privative or negative epithets at discretion. But classifications of this sort are the worst enemies of true knowledge. Such names are by the vast majority even of persons who think themselves educated, imperfectly apprehended, ignorantly interpreted, and crudely and recklessly applied. It is not too much to say that nine out of ten people who think they have delivered themselves of a criticism when they call Mr. Carlyle a Pantheist, could neither explain with any precision what Pantheism is, nor have ever thought of determining the parts of his writings where this particular monster is believed to lurk. Labels are devices for saving talkative persons the trouble of thinking. As we once said elsewhere, "the readiness to use general names in speaking of the greater subjects, and the fitness which qualifies a man to use them, commonly exist in inverse proportions. If we reflect on the conditions out of which ordinary opinion is generated, we may well be startled at the profuse liberality with which names of the widest and most complex and variable significance are bestowed on all hands. The majority of the ideas which constitute most men's intellectual stock-in-trade have accrued by processes quite distinct from fair reasoning and consequent conviction. This is so notorious that it is amazing how so many people can go on freely and rapidly labelling thinkers or writers with names which they themselves are not competent to bestow, and which their hearers are not competent either to understand generally or to test in the specific instance."

These labels are rather more worthless than usual in the present case, because Mr. Carlyle is ostentatiously illogical and defiantly inconsistent; and, therefore, the term which might correctly describe one side of his teaching or belief would be tolerably sure to give a wholly false impression of some of its other sides. The qualifications necessary to make any one of the regular epithets fairly applicable would have to be so many, that the glosses would virtually overlay the text. We shall be more likely to reach an instructive appreciation by discarding such substitutes for examination, and considering, not what pantheistic, absolutist, transcendental, or any other doctrine means, or what it is worth, but what it is that Mr. Carlyle means about men, their character, their relations to one another, and what that is worth.

With most men and women the master element in their opinions is obviously neither their own reason nor their own imagination, independently exercised, but only mere use and wont, chequered by fortuitous sensations, and modified in the better cases by the influence of a favourite teacher; while, in the worse, the teacher is the favourite who happens to chime in most harmoniously with prepossessions, or most effectually to nurse and exaggerate them. Among the superior minds the balance between reason and imagination is scarcely ever held exactly true, nor is either firmly kept within the precise bounds that are proper to it. It is a question of temperament which of the two mental attitudes becomes fixed and habitual, as it is a question of temperament how violently either of them straitens and distorts the normal faculties of vision. The man who prides himself on a hard head, which would usually be better described as a thin head, may and constantly does fall into a confirmed manner of judging character and circumstance, so narrow, one-sided, and elaborately superficial, as to make common sense shudder at the crimes that are committed in the divine name of reason. Excess, on the other side, leads people into emotional transports, in which the pre-eminent respect that is due to truth, the difficulty of discovering truth, the narrowness of the way that leads thereto, the merits of intellectual precision and definiteness, and even the merits of moral precision and definiteness, are all effectually veiled by purple or fiery clouds of anger, sympathy, and sentimentalism, which imagination has hung over the intelligence.

The familiar distinction between the poetic and the scientific temper is another way of stating the same difference. The one fuses or crystallises external objects and circumstances in the medium of human feeling and passion; the other is concerned with the relations of objects and circumstances among themselves, including in them all the facts of human consciousness, and with the discovery and classification of these relations. There is, too, a corresponding distinction between the aspects which conduct, character, social movement, and the objects of nature, are able to present, according as we scrutinise them with a view to exactitude of knowledge, or are stirred by some appeal which they make to our various faculties and forms of sensibility, our tenderness, sympathy, awe, terror, love of beauty, and all the other emotions in that momentous catalogue. The starry heavens have one side for the astronomer, as astronomer, and another for the poet, as poet. The nightingale, the skylark, the cuckoo, move one sort of interest in an ornithologist, and a very different sort in a Shelley or a Wordsworth. The hoary and stupendous formations of the inorganic world, the thousand tribes of insects, the great universe of plants, from those whose size and form and hue make us afraid as if they were deadly monsters, down to "the meanest flower that blows," all these are clothed with one set of attributes by scientific intelligence; and with another by sentiment, fancy, and imaginative association.

The contentiousness of rival schools of philosophy has obscured the application of the same distinction to the various orders of fact more nearly and immediately relating to man and the social union. One school has maintained the virtually unmeaning doctrine that the will is free, and therefore its followers never gave any quarter to the idea that man was as proper an object of scientific scrutiny morally and historically as they could not deny him to be anatomically and physiologically. Their enemies have been more concerned to dislodge them from this position than to fortify, organise, and cultivate their own. The consequences have not been without their danger. Poetic persons have rushed in where scientific persons ought not to have feared to tread. That human character and the order of events have their poetic aspect, and that their poetic treatment demands the rarest and most valuable qualities of mind, is a truth which none but narrow and superficial men of the world are rash enough to deny. But that there is a scientific aspect of these things, an order among them that can only be understood and criticised and effectually modified scientifically, by using all the caution and precision and infinite patience of the truly scientific spirit, is a truth that is constantly ignored even by men and women of the loftiest and most humane nature. In such cases misdirected and uncontrolled sensibility ends in mournful waste of their own energy, in the certain disappointment of their own aims, and where such sensibility is backed by genius, eloquence, and a peculiar set of public conditions, in prolonged and fatal disturbance of society. Rousseau was the great type of this triumphant and dangerous sophistry of the emotions. The Rousseau of these times for English-speaking nations is Thomas Carlyle. An apology is perhaps needed for mentioning one of such simple, veracious, disinterested, and wholly high-minded life, in the same breath with one of the least sane men that ever lived. Community of method, like misery, makes men acquainted with strange bedfellows. Two men of very different degrees of moral worth may notoriously both preach the same faith and both pursue the same method, and the method of Rousseau is the method of Mr. Carlyle. With each of them thought is an aspiration, and justice a sentiment, and society a retrogression. In other words, the writer who in these days has done more than anybody elese to fire men's hearts with a feeling for right and an eager desire for social activity, has with deliberate contempt thrust away from him the only instruments by which we can make sure what right is, and that our social action is wise and effective. A born poet, only wanting perhaps a clearer feeling for form and a firmer spiritual self-possession, to have added another name to the noble gallery of English singers, he has been driven by the impetuosity of his sympathies to attack the scientific side of social questions in an imaginative and highly emotional manner. Depth of benevolent feeling is unhappily no proof of fitness for handling complex problems, and a fine sense of the picturesque no more a qualification for dealing effectively with the difficulties of an old society, than the composition of Wordsworth's famous sonnet on Westminster Bridge was any reason for supposing that the author would have made a competent Commissioner of Works.

The deep unrest of unsatisfied souls meets its earliest solace in the effective and sympathetic expression of the same unrest from the lips of another. To look it in the face is the first approach to a sedative. To find our discontent with the actual, our yearning for an undefined ideal, our aspiration after impossible heights of being, shared and amplified in the emotional speech of a man of genius, is the beginning of consolation. Some of the most generous spirits a hundred years ago found this in the eloquence of Rousseau, and some of the most generous spirits of this time and place have found it in the writer of the *Sartor*. In ages not of faith, there will always be multitudinous troops of people crying for the moon. If such sorrowful pastime be ever permissible to men, it has been natural and lawful this long while in præ-revolutionary England, as it was natural and lawful a century since in præ-revolutionary France. A man born into a community where political forms, from the monarchy down to the popular chamber, are mainly hollow shams disguising the coarse supremacy of wealth, where religion is mainly official and political, and is ever too ready to dissever itself alike from the spirit of justice, the spirit of charity, and the spirit of truth, and where literature does not as a rule permit itself to discuss serious subjects frankly—a community, in short, where the great aim of all the classes and orders with power is by dint of rigorous silence, fast shutting of the eyes, and stern stopping of the ears, somehow to keep the social pyramid on its apex, and to preserve for England its glorious fame as a paradise for the well-to-do, a purgatory for the able, and a hell for the poor—why, a man born into all this with a heart something softer than a flint, and with intellectual vision something more acute than that of a Troglodyte, may well be allowed to turn aside and cry for moons for a season.

Impotent unrest, however, is followed in Mr. Carlyle by what is socially an impotent solution, just as it was with Rousseau. To bid a man do his duty in one page, and then in the next to warn him sternly away from Utilitarianism, from Political Economy, from any "theory of the Moral Sense," and from any other definite means of ascertaining what duty may chance to be, is but a bald and naked counsel. Spiritual nullity and material confusion in a society are not to be repaired by a transformation of egotism, querulous, brooding, marvelling, into egotism, active, practical, objective, not uncomplacent. The moral movements to which the instinctive impulses of humanity fallen on evil times uniformly give birth—early Christianity, for instance, or the socialism of Rousseau, may destroy a society, but they cannot save it unless in conjunction with organising Policy. A thorough appreciation of fiscal and economic truths was at least as indispensable for the life of the Roman Empire as the acceptance of a Messiah; and it was only in the hands of a great statesman like Gregory VII. that Christianity became at last an instrument powerful enough to save civilisation. What the moral renovation of Rousseau did for France, we all know. Now Rousseau's was far more profoundly social than the doctrine of Mr. Carlyle, which, while in name a renunciation of self, has all its foundations in the purest individualism. If we look among our own countrymen, we find that the apostle of self-renunciation is nowhere so beloved as by the best of those whom steady self-reliance and thrifty self-securing and a firm eye to the main chance have got successfully on in the world. This circumstance is honourable both to them and to him, as far as it goes, but it furnishes some reason for suspecting that our most vigorous moral reformer, so far from starting us in new grooves, has in truth only given new firmness and coherency to tendencies that were strongly marked enough in the national character before. He has increased the fervour of the country, but without materially changing its objects; there is all the less disguise among us as a result of his teaching, but no radical modification of the sentiments which people are sincere in. The most stirring general appeal to the benevolent emotions to be effective for more than negative purposes, must lead up to definite maxims and specific precepts. As a negative renovation Mr. Carlyle's doctrine was perfect. It effectually put an end to the mood of Byronism. May we say that with the neutralisation of Byron, his most decisive and special work came to an end? May we not say, further, that the true renovation of England, if such a process be ever feasible, will lie in a quite other method than this of emotion? It will lie not in mere moral earnestness, but in a more open intelligence; not in a more dogged resolution to work and be silent, but in a ready willingness to use the understanding. The poison of our sins, says Mr. Carlyle in his latest utterance, "is not intellectual dimness chiefly, but torpid unveracity of heart." Yes, but all unveracity, torpid or fervid, breeds intellectual dimness, and it is this last which prevents us from seeing a way out of the present ignoble situation. We need light more than heat; intellectual alertness, faith in the reasoning faculty, accessibility to new ideas. To refuse to use the intellect patiently and with system, to decline to seek scientific truth, to prefer effusive indulgence of emotion to the laborious and disciplined and candid exploration of new ideas, is not this, too, a torpid unveracity? And has not Mr. Carlyle, by the impatience of his method, done somewhat to deepen it?

It is very well to invite us to moral reform, to bring ourselves to be of heroic mind, as the surest way to "the blessed Aristocracy of the Wisest." But how shall we know the Wisest when we see them, and how shall a nation know, if not by keen respect and watchfulness for intellectual truth and the teachers of it? Much as we may admire Mr. Carlyle's many gifts, and highly as we may revere his character, it is yet very doubtful to us whether anybody has as yet learnt from him the precious lesson of scrupulosity and conscientiousness in actively and constantly using the intelligence. This would have been the solid foundation of the true hero-worship.

Let thus much have been said on the head of temperament. The historic position also of every writer is an indispensable key to many things in his teaching.[1] We have to remember in Mr. Carlyle's case, that he was born in the memorable year when the French Revolution, in its narrower sense, was closed by the Whiff of Grapeshot, and when the great century of emancipation and illumination was ending darkly in battles and confusion. During his youth the reaction was in full flow, and the lamp had been handed to runners who not only reversed the ideas and methods, but even turned aside from the goal of their precursors. Hopefulness and enthusiastic confidence in humanity when freed from the fetters of spiritual superstition and secular tyranny, marked all the most characteristic and influential speculations of the two generations before '89. The frightful failure which attended the splendid attempt to realise these hopes in a renewed and perfected social structure, had no more than its natural effect in turning men's minds back, not to the past of Rousseau's imagination, but to the past of recorded history. The single epoch in the annals of Europe since the rise of Christianity, for which no good word could be found, was the epoch of Voltaire. The hideousness of the Christian Church in the ninth and tenth centuries was passed lightly over by men who had only eyes for the moral obliquity of the Church of the Encyclopædia. The brilliant, but profoundly inadequate essays on Voltaire and Diderot were the outcome in Mr. Carlyle of the same reactionary spirit. Nobody now, we may suppose, who is competent to judge, thinks that that

1. The dates of Mr. Carlyle's principal compositions are these:—*Life of Schiller*, 1825; *Sartor Resartus*, 1831; *French Revolution*, 1837; *Chartism*, 1839; *Hero-Worship*, 1840; *Past and Present*, 1843; *Cromwell*, 1845; *Friedrich the Second*, 1858 (and following years); *Shooting Niagara*, 1867.

estimate of "the net product of tumultuous Atheism" of Diderot and his fellow workers, is a satisfactory account of the influence and significance of the Encyclopædia; nor that to sum up Voltaire, with his burning passion for justice, his indefatigable humanity, his splendid energy in intellectual production, his righteous hatred of superstition, as a supreme master of *persiflage,* can be at all a process partaking of finality. The fact that to the eighteenth century belong the subjects of more than half of these thirty volumes, is a proof of the fascination of the period for an author who has never ceased to vilipend it. The saying is perhaps as true in these matters as of private relations, that hatred is not so far removed from love as indifference is. Be that as it may, the Carlylean view of the eighteenth century as a time of mere scepticism and unbelief, is now clearly untenable to men who remember the fervour of Jean Jacques, and the more rational, but hardly less fervid faith of the disciples of Perfectibility. But this was not so clear fifty years since, when the crash and dust of demolition had not subsided enough to let men see how much had risen up behind. The fire of the new school had been taken from the very conflagration which they execrated, but they were not held back from denouncing the eighteenth century by the reflection that, at any rate, its thought and action had made ready the way for the nineteenth.

Mr. Carlyle himself has told us about Coleridge, and the movement of which Coleridge was the leader. That movement has led men in widely different ways. In one direction it has stagnated in the sunless swamps of a theosophy, from which a cloud of sedulous ephemera still suck a little spiritual moisture. In another it led to the sacramental and sacerdotal developments of Anglicanism. In a third, among men with strongly practical energy, to the benevolent bluster of a sort of Christianity which is called muscular because it is not intellectual. It would be an error to suppose that these and the other streams that have sprung from the same source did not in the days of their fulness fertilise and gladden many lands. The wordy pietism of one school, the mimetic rites of another, the romping heroics of the third, are degenerate forms. How long they are likely to endure, it would be rash to predict among a nation whose established teachers and official preachers are prevented by an inveterate timidity from trusting themselves to that disciplined intelligence, in which the superior minds of the last century had such courageous faith.

Mr. Carlyle drank in some sort at the same fountain. Coleridgean ideas were in the air. It was there, probably, that he acquired that sympathy with the past, that feeling of the unity of history, and that conviction of the necessity of binding our theory of history fast with our theory of other things, in all of which he so strikingly resembles the great Anglican leaders of a generation ago, and in gaining some of which so strenuous an effort must have been needed to modify the prepossessions of a Scotch Puritan education. No one has contributed more powerfully to that movement which, drawing force from many and various sides, has brought out the difference between the historian and the gazetteer or antiquary. One half of *Past and Present* might have been written by one of the Oxford chiefs in the days of the Tracts. Vehement native force was too strong for such a man to remain in the luminous haze which made the Coleridgean atmosphere. A well-known chapter in the *Life of Sterling,* which some, indeed, have found too ungracious, shows how little hold he felt Coleridge's ideas to be capable of retaining, and how little permanent satisfaction resided in them. Coleridge, in fact, was not only a poet but a thinker as well; he had science as well as imagination, but it was not science for headlong and impatient souls. Mr. Carlyle has probably never been able to endure a subdivision all his life, and the infinite ramifications of the central division between object and subject might well be with him an unprofitable weariness to the flesh.

In England, the greatest literary organ of the Revolution was unquestionably Byron, whose genius, daring, and melodramatic lawlessness exercised what now seems such an amazing fascination over the least revolutionary of European nations. Unfitted for scientific work and full of ardour, Mr. Carlyle found his mission in rushing with all his might to the annihilation of this terrible poet, who, like some gorgon, hydra, or chimera dire planted at the gate, carried off a yearly tale of youths and virgins from the city. In literature, only a revolutionist can thoroughly overmaster a revolutionist. Mr. Carlyle had fully as much daring

44

as Byron; his writing at its best, if without the many-eyed minuteness and sustained pulsing force of Byron, has still the full swell and tide and energy of genius; he is as lawless in his disrespect for some things established. He had the unspeakable advantage of being that which, though not in this sense, only his own favourite word of contempt describes, respectable; and, for another thing, of being ruggedly sincere. Carlylism is the male of Byronism. It is Byronism with thew and sinew, bass pipe and shaggy bosom. There is the same grievous complaint against the time and its men and its spirit, something even of the same despair, the same sense of the puniness of man in the centre of a cruel and frowning universe: but there is in Carlylism a deliverance from it all; indeed, the only deliverance possible. Against Byronism the ordinary moralist and preacher could really do nothing, because Byronism was an appeal that lay in regions of the mind only accessible by one with an eye and a large poetic feeling for the infinite whole of things. It was not the rebellion only in *Manfred,* nor the wit in *Don Juan,* nor the graceful melancholy of *Childe Harold,* which made their author an idol, and still makes him one to multitudes of Frenchmen and Italians, as well as of ourselves. The secret of it is the air and spaciousness, the freedom and elemental grandeur of Byron. Who has not felt this to be one of the glories of Mr. Carlyle's work, that it, too, is large and spacious, rich with the fulness of a sense of things unknown and wonderful, and ever in the tiniest part showing us the stupendous and overwhelming whole? Remember further, that while in Byron the outcome of this was rebellion, in Carlyle its outcome is reverence, a noble mood, which is one of the highest predispositions of the English character. Again, at the bottom of the veriest *frondeur* with English blood in his veins, in his most defiant moment there lies a conviction that after all something known as common sense is the measure of life, and that to work hard is a prime precept of common sense. Carlylism exactly hits this and brings it forward. We cannot wonder that Byronism was routed from the field.

It may have been in the transcendently firm and clear-eyed intelligence of Goethe that Mr. Carlyle first found a responsive encouragement to the profoundly positive impulses of his own spirit.[2] There is, indeed, a whole heaven betwixt the serenity, balance, and bright composure of the one, and the vehemence, passion, masterful wrath, of the other; and the vast, incessant, exact inquisitiveness of Goethe, finds nothing corresponding to it in Mr. Carlyle's multitudinous contempt and indifference, sometimes express and sometimes only very significantly implied, for forms of intellectual activity that do not happen to be personally congenial. But each is a god, though the one sits ever on Olympus, while the other is as one from Tartarus. There is in each, besides all else, a certain remarkable directness of glance, an intrepid and penetrating quality of vision, which defies analysis. Occasional turgidity of phrase and unidiomatic handling of language do not conceal the simplicity of the process by which Mr. Carlyle pierces through obstruction down to the abstrusest depths. And the important fact is that this abstruseness is not verbal, any more than it is the abstruseness of fog and cloud. His epithet, or image, or trope, shoots like a sunbeam on to the matter, throwing a transfigurating light, even where it fails to pierce to its central core.

Eager for a firm foothold, yet wholly revolted by the too narrow and unelevated positivity of the eighteenth century; eager also for some recognition of the wide realm of the unknowable, yet wholly unsatisfied by the transcendentalism of the English and Scotch philosophic reactions; he found in Goethe that truly free and adequate positivity which accepts all things as parts of a natural or historic order, and while insisting on the recognition of the actual conditions of this order as indispensable, and condemning attempted evasions of such recognition as futile and childish, yet opens an ample bosom for all forms of beauty in art and for all nobleness in moral aspiration. That Mr. Carlyle has reached this high ground we do not say. Temperament has kept him down from it. But it is after this that he has striven. The vacuum of pure transcendentalism he has always abhorred. Some

2. *Positive.* No English lexicon as yet seems to justify the use of this word in one of the senses of the French *positif,* as when M. Lanfrey, for instance, speaks of the *esprit positif* of Napoleon. We have no word, I believe, that exactly corresponds, so perhaps *positive* with this significance will become acclimatised. A distinct and separate idea of this particular characteristic is indispensable.

of Mr. Carlyle's favourite phrases have disguised from his readers the intensely practical turn of his whole mind. His constant presentation of the Eternities, the Immensities, and the like, has veiled his almost narrow adherence to plain record without moral comment, and his often cynical respect for the dangerous yet, when rightly qualified and guided, the solid formula that What is, is. The Eternities and Immensities are only a kind of awful background. The highest souls are held to be deeply conscious of these vast unspeakable presences, yet even with them they are only inspiring accessories; the true interest lies in the practical attitude of such men towards the actual and palpable circumstances that surround them. This spirituality, whose place in Mr. Carlyle's teaching has been so extremely mis-stated, sinks wholly out of sight in connection with such heroes as the coarse and materialist Bonaparte, of whom, however, the hero-worshipper, in earlier pieces, speaks with some laudable misgiving, and the not less coarse and materialist Frederick, about whom no misgiving is permitted to the loyal disciple. The admiration for military methods, on condition that they are successful—for Mr. Carlyle, like Providence, is always on the side of big and victorious battalions—is the last outcome of a devotion to vigorous action and practical effect, which no verbal garniture of a transcendental kind can hinder us from perceiving to be more purely materialist and unfeignedly brutal than anything which sprung from the reviled thought of the eighteenth century.

It is instructive to remark that another of the most illustrious enemies of that century and all its works, Joseph de Maistre, had the same admiration for the effectiveness of war, and the same extreme interest and concern in the men and things of war. He, too, declares that "the loftiest and most generous sentiments are probably to be found in the soldier"; and that war, if terrible, is divine and splendid and fascinating, the manifestation of a sublime law of the universe. We must, however, do De Maistre the justice to point out, first, that he gave a measure of his strange interest in Surgery and Judgment, as Mr. Carlyle calls it, to the public executioner, a division of the honours of social surgery which is no more than fair; while, in the second place, he redeems the brutality of the military surgical idea after a fashion, by an extraordinary mysticism, which led him to see in war a divine, inscrutable force, determining success in a manner absolutely defying all the speculations of human reason.[3] The biographer of Frederick apparently finds no inscrutable force at all, but only will, tenacity, and powder kept dry. There is a vast difference between this and the absolutism of the mystic.

Mr. Carlyle's influence, however, was at its height before this idolatry of the soldier became a paramount article in his creed; and it is devoutly to be hoped that not many of those whom he first taught to seize before all things fact and reality, will follow him into this torrid air, where only forces and never principles are facts, and where nothing is reality but the violent triumph of arbitrarily imposed will. There was once a better side to it all, when the injunction to seek and cling to fact was a valuable warning not to waste energy and hope in seeking lights which it is not given to man ever to find, with a solemn assurance added that in frank and untrembling recognition of circumstance the spirit of man may find a priceless, ever-fruitful contentment. The prolonged and thousand-times repeated glorification of Unconsciousness, Silence, Renunciation, all comes to this: We are to leave the region of things unknowable, and hold fast to the duty that lies nearest. Here, and nowhere else, is the Everlasting Yea. In action only can we have certainty.

Not even Comte himself has harder words for metaphysics than Mr. Carlyle. "The disease of Metaphysics" is perennial. Questions of Death and Immortality, Origin of Evil, Freedom and Necessity, are ever appearing and attempting to shape something of the universe. "And ever unsuccessfully: for what theorem of the Infinite can the Finite render complete? . . . . Metaphysical Speculation as it begins in No or Nothingness, so it must needs end in Nothingness; circulates and must circulate in endless vortices; creating, swallowing—itself."[4] Again, on the other side, he sets his face just as firmly against the excessive pretensions and unwarranted certitudes of the physicist. "The course of Nature's phases on this our little fraction of a Planet is partially known to us: but who knows what deeper courses these depend on; what infinitely larger Cycle (of causes) our little Epicycle revolves on? To the Minnow every cranny and pebble, and quality

3. *Soirées de Saint Pétersbourg.* 7ième Entretien.
4. *Characteristics,* Misc. Ess., iii. pp. 356–58.

and accident may have become familiar: but does the Minnow understand the Ocean tides and periodic Currents, the Trade-winds, and Monsoons, and Moon's Eclipses, by all which the condition of its little Creek is regulated, and may, from time to time (*un*miraculously enough), be quite overset and reversed? Such a minnow is Man; his Creek this Planet Earth; his Ocean the immeasurable All; his Monsoons and periodic Currents the mysterious course of Providence through Æons of Æons."[5] The inalterable relativity of human knowledge has never been more forcibly illustrated; and the two passages together fix the limits of the knowledge with a sagacity truly philosophic. Between the vagaries of mystics and the vagaries of physicists lies the narrow land of rational certainty, relative, conditional, experimental, from which we view the vast realm that stretches out unknown before us, and perhaps for ever unknowable; inspiring men with an elevated awe, and environing the interests and duties of their little lives with a strange sublimity. "We emerge from the Inane; haste stormfully across the astonished Earth; then plunge again into the Inane . . . . But whence? O Heaven, whither? Sense knows not; Faith knows not; only that it is through Mystery to Mystery."[6]

Natural Supernaturalism, the title of one of the cardinal chapters in Mr. Carlyle's cardinal book, is perhaps as good a name as another for this two-faced yet integral philosophy, which teaches us to behold with cheerful serenity the great gulf which is fixed round our faculty and existence on every side, while it fills us with that supreme sense of countless unseen possibilities and of the hidden, undefined movements of shadow and light over the spirit, without which the soul of man falls into hard and desolate sterility. In youth, perhaps, it is the latter aspect of Mr. Carlyle's teaching which first touches people, because youth is the time of indefinite aspiration; and it is easier, besides, to surrender ourselves passively to these vague emotional impressions, than to apply actively and contentedly to the duty that lies nearest, and to the securing of "that infinitesimallest product" on which the teacher is ever insisting. It is the Supernaturalism which stirs men first, until larger fulness of years and wider experience of life

5. *Sartor Resartus.* Bk. iii. ch. 8, p. 249.
6. *Ibid.,* p. 257.

draw them to a wise and not inglorious acquiescence in Naturalism. This last is the mood which Mr. Carlyle never wearies of extolling and enjoining under the name of Belief; and the absence of it, the inability to enter into it, is that Unbelief which he so bitterly vituperates, or, in another phrase, that Discontent which he charges with holding the soul in such desperate and paralysing bondage.

Novalis complained in bitter words, as we know, of the mechanical, prosaic, utilitarian, cold-hearted character of *Wilhelm Meister,* constituting it an embodiment of "artistic Atheism," while English critics as loudly found fault with its author for being a mystic. Exactly the same discrepancy is possible in respect of Mr. Carlyle's own writings. In one sense he may be called mystic and transcendental, in another baldly mechanical and even cold-hearted, just as Novalis found Goethe to be in *Meister.* The latter impression is inevitable in all who, like Goethe and like Mr. Carlyle, make a lofty acquiescence in the positive course of circumstance a prime condition at once of wise endeavour and of genuine happiness. The splendid fire and unmeasured vehemence of Mr. Carlyle's manner partially veil the depth of this acquiescence, which is really not so far removed from fatalism. The torrent of his eloquence, bright and rushing as it is, flows between rigid banks and over hard rocks. Devotion to the heroic does not prevent the assumption of a tone towards the great mass of the unheroic, which implies that they are no more than two-legged mill horses, ever treading a fixed, unalterable round. He practically denies other consolation to mortals than such as they may be able to get from the final and conclusive *Kismet* of the oriental. It is fate. Man is the creature of his destiny. As for our supposed claims on the heavenly powers, What right, he asks, hadst thou even to be. Fatalism of this stamp is the natural and unavoidable issue of a born positivity of spirit, uninformed by scientific meditation. It exists in its coarsest and most childish kind in adventurous freebooters of the type of Napoleon, and in a noble and not egotistic kind in Oliver Cromwell's pious interpretation of the order of events by the good will and providence of God.

Two conspicuous qualities of Carlylean doctrine flow from this fatalism, or poetised utilitarianism, or illumined positivity. One of them is a tolerably constant contempt for excessive nicety in moral distinctions, and an aversion to the monotonous attitude of praise and blame. In a country overrun and corroded to the heart, as Great Britain is, with cant and a foul mechanical hypocrisy, this temper ought to have had its uses in giving a much-needed robustness to public judgment. One might suppose from the tone of opinion among us, not only that the difference between right and wrong marks the most important aspect of conduct, which would be true, but that it marks the only aspect of it that exists, or that is worth considering, which is most profoundly false. Nowhere has Puritanism done us more harm than in thus leading us to take all breadth, and colour, and diversity, and fine discrimination, out of our judgments of men, reducing them to thin, narrow, and superficial pronouncements upon the letter of their morality, or the precise conformity of their opinions to accepted standards of truth, religious or other. Among other evils which it has inflicted, this inability to conceive of conduct except as either right or wrong, and, correspondingly in the intellectual order, of teaching except as either true or false, is at the bottom of that fatal spirit of *parti-pris* which has led to the rooting of so much injustice, disorder, immobility, and darkness in English intelligence. No excess of morality, we may be sure, has followed this excessive adoption of the exclusively moral standard; for no people, as the homely saying goes, are so thoroughly nasty as the over-nice. We have simply got for our pains a most unlovely leanness of judgment, and ever since the days when this temper set in until now, when a wholesome rebellion is afoot, it has steadily and powerfully tended to straiten character, make action mechanical, and impoverish art. As if there were nothing admirable in a man save unbroken obedience to the letter of the moral law, and that letter read in our own casual and local interpretation; and as if we had no faculties of sympathy, no sense for the beauty of character, no feeling for broad force and full-pulsing vitality.

To study manners and conduct and men's moral nature in such a way is as direct an error as it would be to overlook in the study of his body everything except its vertebral column and the bony framework. The body is more than "a mere anatomy." A character is much else besides being virtuous or vicious. In many of the characters in which some of the finest and most singular qualities of humanity would seem to have reached their furthest height, their morality was the side least worth discussing. The same may be said of the specific rightness or wrongness of opinion in the intellectual order. Let us condemn error or immorality, when the scope of our criticism calls for this particular function, but why rush to praise or blame, to eulogy or reprobation, when we should do better simply to explore and enjoy? Moral imperfection is ever a grievous curtailment of life, but many exquisite flowers of character, many gracious and potent things, may still thrive in the most disordered scene.

The vast waste which this limitation of prospect entails is the most grievous rejection of moral treasure, if it be true that nothing enriches the nature like wide sympathy and many-coloured appreciativeness. To a man like Macaulay for example, criticism was only a tribunal before which men were brought to be decisively tried by one or two inflexible tests, and then sent to join the sheep on the one hand or the goats on the other. His pages are the record of sentences passed, not the presentation of human characters in all their fulness and colour, and the consequence is that even now and so soon, in spite of all their rhetorical brilliance, their hold on men has grown slack. Contrast the dim depths into which his essay on Johnson is receding, with the vitality as of a fine dramatic creation which exists in Mr. Carlyle's essay on the same man. Mr. Carlyle knows as well as Macaulay how blind and stupid a creed was English Toryism a century ago, but he seizes and reproduces the character of his man, and this was much more than a matter of a creed. So with Burns. He was drunken and unchaste and thriftless, and Mr. Carlyle holds all these vices as deeply in reprobation as if he had written ten thousand sermons against them, but he leaves the fulmination to the hack moralist of the pulpit or the press, with whom words are cheap, easily gotten, and readily thrown forth. To him it seems better worth while, having made sure of some sterling sincerity and rare genuineness of vision and singular human quality, to dwell on, and do justice to that, than to accumulate commonplaces as to the viciousness of vice. Here we may perhaps find the explanation of the remarkable fact that though Mr. Carlyle has written about a large number of men of all varieties of opinion and temperament, and written with emphasis and point and strong feeling, yet there is not one of these judgments, however much we may dissent from it, which we could fairly put a finger upon as *saugrenu,* indecently absurd and unreasonable. Of how many writers of thirty volumes can we say the same?

That this broad and poetic temper of criticism has special dangers and needs to have special safeguards, is but too true. Even, however, if we find that it has its excesses, we may forgive much to the merits of a reaction against a system which has raised monstrous floods of sour cant round about us, and hardened the hearts and parched the sympathies of men by blasts from theological deserts. There is a point of view so lofty and so peculiar that from it we are able to discern in men and women something more than and apart from creed, and profession, and formulated principle; which indeed directs and colours this creed and principle as decisively as it is in its turn acted on by them, and this is their character or humanity. The least important thing about Johnson is that he was a Tory; and about Burns, that he drank too much and was incontinent; and if we see in modern literature an increasing tendency to mount to this higher point of view, this humaner prospect, there is no living writer to whom we owe more for it than Mr. Carlyle. The same principle which revealed the valour and godliness of Puritanism, has proved its most efficacious solvent, for it places character on the pedestal where Puritanism places dogma.

The second of the qualities which seem to flow from Mr. Carlyle's fatalism, and one much less useful among a people already far too deeply imbued with contempt for the fallen and the subject, is a deficiency of sympathy with masses of men. It would be easy enough to select passages where he talks of the dumb millions in terms of fine and sincere humanity, but detached passages cannot counterbalance the effect of a whole compact body of teaching. The multitude stands between Destiny on the one side, and the Hero on the other; a sport to the first, and as potter's clay to the second. *"Dogs, would ye then live for ever,"* Frederick cried to a troop who hesitated to attack a battery vomiting forth death and destruction. This is a measure of Mr. Carlyle's own valuation of the store we ought to set on the lives of the most. We know in what coarse outcome such an estimate of the dignity of other life than the life heroic has practically issued; in what barbarous vindication of barbarous law-breaking in Jamaica, in what inhuman softness for slavery, in what contemptuous and angry words for "Beales and his 50,000 Roughs," contrasted with gentle words for our adorable aristocracy, with "the politest and gracefullest kind of woman" to wife. Here is the end of the Eternal Verities, when one lets them bulk so big in his eyes as to shut out that perishable speck, the human race.

There is no passage which Mr. Carlyle so often quotes as the sublime—

> We are such stuff
> As dreams are made on; and our little life
> Is rounded with a sleep.

If the ever present impression of this awful, most moving, yet most soothing thought, be a law of spiritual breadth and height, there is yet a peril in it. Such an impression may inform the soul with a devout mingled sense of grandeur and nothingness, or it may blacken into cynicism and antinomian living for self and the day. It may be a solemn and holy refrain, sounding far off, but clear, in the dusty course of work and duty; or it may be the comforting chorus of a diabolic drama of selfishness and violence. As a reaction against religious theories, which make humanity over-abound in self-consequence, and fill individuals with the strutting importance of creatures with private souls to save or lose, even such cynicism as Byron's was wholesome and nearly forgivable. Nevertheless, the most important question that we can ask of any great teacher, as of the walk and conversation of any commonest person, remains this, how far has he strengthened and raised the conscious and harmonious dignity of humanity; how stirred in men and women, many or few, deeper and more active sense of the worth, and obligation, and innumerable possibilities, not of their own little lives, one or another, but of life collectively; how heightened the self-respect of the race? There is no need to plant oneself in a fool's paradise, with no eye for the weakness of men, the futility of their hopes, the irony of their fate, the dominion of the satyr and the tiger in their hearts. Laughter has a fore-place in life. All this we may see and show that we see, and yet so throw it behind the weightier facts of nobleness and sacrifice, of the boundless gifts which fraternal union has given, and has the power of giving, as to kindle in every breast, not callous to exalted impressions, the glow of sympathetic endeavour, and of serene exultation in the bond that makes "precious the soul of man to man."

This renewal of moral energy by spiritual contact with the mass of men, and by meditation on the dignity of mankind, is the very reverse of Mr. Carlyle's method. With him, it is good to leave the mass and fall down before the individual and be saved by him. The victorious hero is the true Paraclete. "Nothing so lifts a man from all his mean imprisonment, were it but for moments, as true admiration." And this is really the kernel of the Carlylean doctrine. The whole human race toils and moils, straining and energising, doing and suffering things multitudinous and unspeakable, in order that like the aloe tree it may once in a hundred years produce a flower. It is this hero that age offers to age, and the wisest worship him. Time and nature once and again distil from out of the lees and froth of common humanity some wondrous character of a potent and reviving property not much short of miraculous. This is the man who knows his own good cherishes in his inmost soul a sacred thing, an elixir of moral life. The Great Man is "the light which enlightens, which has enlightened the darkness of the world; a flowing light fountain, in whose radiance all souls feel that it is well with them." This is only another form of the anthropomorphic conceptions of deity. The divinity of the ordinary hierophant is clothed in the minds of the worshippers with the highest human qualities they happen to be capable of conceiving, and this is the self-acting machinery by which worship refreshes and recruits what is best in man. Mr. Carlyle has another way. He carries the process a step further, giving back to the great man what had been taken for beings greater than any man, and summoning us to trim the lamp of endeavour at the shrine of heroic chiefs of mankind. In that house there are many mansions, the resounding sanctuary of a vagabond polytheism. But each altar is individual and apart, and the reaction of this isolation upon the egoistic instincts of the worshipper has been only too evident. It is good for us to build temples to great names which recall special transfigurations of humanity; but it is better still, it gives a firmer nerve to purpose and adds a finer holiness to the ethical sense, to carry ever with us the unmarked, yet living tradition of the voiceless, unconscious effort of unnumbered millions of souls, flitting lightly away like showers of thin leaves, yet ever augmenting the elements of perfectness in man, and exalting the eternal contest. Mr. Carlyle has indeed written that generation stands indissolubly woven with generation; "how we inherit, not Life only, but all the garniture and form of Life, and work and speak, and even think and feel, as our fathers and primeval grandfathers from the beginning have given it to us"; how "mankind is a living, indivisible whole."[7] Even this, however, with the "literal communion of saints," which follows in connection with it, is only a detached suggestion, not incorporated with the body of the writer's doctrine. It does not neutralise the general lack of faith in the spontaneous virtue of masses of men, nor the universal tone of humouristic cynicism with which all but a little band, the supposed salt of the earth, are treated. Man is for Mr. Carlyle, as for the Calvinistic theologian, a fallen and depraved being, without much hope, except for a few of the elect. The best thing that can happen to the poor creature is, that he should be thoroughly well drilled. In other words, society does not really progress in its bulk; and the methods which were conditions of the original formation and growth of the social union, remain indispensable until the sound of the last trump. Was there not a profound and far-reaching truth wrapped up in Goethe's simple yet really inexhaustible monition, that if we would improve a man, it were well to let him believe that we already think him that which we would have him to be. The law that *noblesse oblige* has unwritten bearings in dealing with all men; all masses of men are susceptible of an appeal from that point. For this Mr. Carlyle seems to make no allowance.

Every modification of society is one of the slow growths of time, and to hurry impatiently after them by swift ways of military discipline and peremptory law-making, is only to clasp the near good, and one so superficial as hardly to be a good at all. It is easy to make a solitude and call it peace, to plant an iron heel and call it order. But read Mr. Carlyle's essay on Dr. Francia, and

---

7. *Organic Filaments* in the *Sartor*, Bk. iii. c. 7.

then ponder the history of Paraguay for these later years, and the accounts of its condition in the newspapers of to-day. "Nay, it may be," we learn from that remarkable piece, "that the benefit of him is not even yet exhausted, even yet entirely become visible. Who knows but, in unborn centuries, Paragueno men will look back to their lean iron Francia, as men do in such cases to the one veracious person, and institute considerations?"[8] Who knows, indeed, if only it prove that their lean iron Francia, in his passion for order and authority, did not stamp out the very life of the nation? Where organic growths are concerned, patience is the sovereign law; and where the organism is a society of men, the vital principle is a sense in one shape or another of the dignity of humanity. The recognition of this tests the distinction between the truly heroic ruler of the stamp of Cromwell, and the mere arbitrary enthusiast for external order, like Frederick.

One of Mr. Carlyle's chief and just glories is, that for more than thirty years he has clearly seen and kept constantly and conspicuously in his own sight and that of his readers the profoundly important crisis in the midst of which we are living. The moral and social dissolution in progress about us, and the enormous peril of sailing blindfold and haphazard, without rudder or compass or chart, have always been fully visible to him, and it is no fault of his if they have not become equally plain to his contemporaries. The policy of drifting has had no countenance from him. That a society should be likely to last with hollow and scanty faith, with no government, with a number of institutions hardly one of them real, with a steadily increasing mass of poverty-stricken and hopeless subjects; that, if it should last, it could be regarded as other than an abomination of desolation, he has boldly and often declared to be things incredible. We are not promoting the objects which the social union subsists to fulfil, nor applying with energetic spirit to the task of preparing a sounder state for our successors. The relations between master and servant, between capitalist and labourer, between landlord and tenant, between governing race and subject race, between the feelings and intelligence of the legislature and the feelings

8. *Misc. Ess.,* vi. 124.

and intelligence of the nation, between the spiritual power, literary and ecclesiastical, and those who are under it,—the anarchy
that prevails in all these, and the extreme danger of it, have been
with Mr. Carlyle a never-ending theme. What seems to many of
us the extreme inefficiency or worse of his solutions, still allows
us to feel grateful for the vigour and perspicacity with which he
has pressed on the world the urgency of the problem, and this is
one of the most distinguished of Mr. Carlyle's manifold titles
to pre-eminent honour.

The Man of Letters as Hero

We are not about to embark upon the stormy question whether Mr. Froude has rightly understood the function of the biographer, or has wisely played the part of one faithful to the memory of a departed friend. A hundred essays might be written on the casuistical points that an ingenious man might raise, and at the end of the hundredth the judgment of men would differ as widely as at the first. The work is done; if not the truth, at least the materials for truth, are out. The biographer states his case with that lucidity in which his pen seldom fails:—

> Carlyle exerted for many years an almost unbounded influence on the mind of educated England. His writings are now spread over the whole English-speaking world. They are studied with eagerness and confidence by millions who have looked and looked to him not for amusement, but for moral guidance, and those millions have a right to know what manner of man he really was. It may be, and I for one think it will be, that when time has levelled accidental distinctions, when the perspective has altered, and the foremost figures of this century are seen in their true proportions, Carlyle will tower far above all his contemporaries, and will then be the one person of them about whom the coming generations will care most to be informed. But whether I estimate his importance rightly or wrongly, he has played a part which entitles every one to demand a complete account of his character. He has come forward as a teacher of

This essay was first published in *Macmillan's Magazine*, 51 (November 1884): 62–70—ed.

mankind. He has claimed "to speak with authority, and not as the Scribes." He has denounced as empty illusion the most favourite convictions of the age. No concealment is permissible about a man who could thus take on himself the character of a prophet and speak to it in so imperious a tone.

It is not easy to see the answer to this. When a statesman dies, the world is not concerned to know the details of his private history, unless they affect his public probity. The coarse talk of Walpole, the debts of Pitt, the gambling of Fox, the bettings, the drinkings, the gallantries of other politicians whose day is over, do not and ought not to affect our judgment of them from the only point of view which the public has any right to take. The statesman is judged by his policy, by the wisdom of his aims, the success with which he attained them, and the lawfulness of the means that he allowed himself to use. One might say the same of a great painter, actor, dramatist, and even of the author, provided the author has not posed as prophet and teacher. If he have played that part, he cannot complain if he be judged by the standard which he has himself set up, and which he has acquired fame, glory, and the reverence of nations by holding before their gaze. The *Principia* would have been just as great a gift to mortals if Sir Isaac Newton had been a bad man instead of being a good one. The morality of the author of the *Novum Organum* has, indeed, exercised the lively interest and the curiosity of the world, partly because it turns upon points of history, and partly because it is one of that fixed class of recognised riddles at which successive generations of lettered men are never weary of trying their hands. But in Bacon's case, the question is one of public, rather than of private morals. Better, again, said Voltaire or some one else, better Racine, bad father, bad husband, bad friend, and good poet, than Racine, good father, good husband, good friend, and bad poet. Is this the true view, or are we to decline to enjoy *Hamlet* until we have satisfied ourselves about Shakespeare's moral character? Does it much matter to us whether Byron was a wicked profligate or not? Or are we to feel the beauty of *Childe Harold* and the sublimity of *Manfred* or *Cain* without asking ourselves whether the poet practised the sublime and beautiful in his daily walk and conversation? People will try to find out personal traits, so long as the world goes round, for curiosity about the personal history of famous figures springs eternal in the human breast and is inextinguishable, with or without material. But the value of Byron's poetry remains just what it was, be it great or little, whether the lenient or the merciful view of his character be the right one. Does the value of a Prophet remain what it was, if we find that he was a fierce railer, selfish and self-centred, harsh, presumptuous, alternately whining and cursing like a sturdy beggar, intolerant, inconsiderate? In a military commander or the ruler of an empire, these shortcomings touch us not an atom. Napoleon Bonaparte may have been as great a ruffian as any one pleases, may have behaved ill to Josephine, may have been the meanest tyrant that ever bullied a court; it is by weightier matters that he must be judged. The man with a gospel stands on another footing. Here we have a right to know, if we can, how the gospel worked. Such a man is a character as well as a doctrine, and the one may be, and ought to be, just as edifying as the other. What he was and did may teach us no less, may inspire and stimulate and guide us no less, than what he wrote down in books.

The difficulty is in being quite sure that even the most candid biographer can tell us what his hero was; can lay bare all the unspoken thoughts and silent motives; can effectually and truly reveal the inward history, which is, after all, the real tissue of the man's being. This is what Carlyle has himself most truly set forth in a passage cited by Mr. Froude from his Journal. "The chief elements of my little destiny," he said, "have all along lain deep below view or surmise, and never will or can be known to any son of Adam. I would say to any biographer, if any fool undertook such a task, 'Forbear, poor fool! Let no life of me be written; let me and my bewildered wrestlings lie buried here and be forgotten swiftly of all the world. If these write, it will be mere delusion and hallucination. The confused world never understood, nor will understand, me and my poor affairs. Not even the persons nearest to me could guess at them.' " This is true enough. In so extraordinary a genius as Carlyle, as sometimes in creatures of far commoner clay, the qualities that make the real man are deep below view or surmise. We easily know all about the outer act, but the spirit and inmost prompting of it, and all its relations to other parts of the doer's conduct are not to be so simply discerned.

Even the actual eyewitness, and it may be the sufferer from it, may wholly mistake and miscalculate the significance of something done or spoken. The half of us is misunderstanding, even between those who are most close to one another, and whom the action most concerns. How much more impossible, then, it is for those outside and at a distance to be confident that they know all and judge aright. The judgments of the world cannot be otherwise than rough, superficial, and somewhat haphazard; sound enough for practical purposes of human dealing, but not delicate enough, subtle, comprehensive, well-informed enough, to render it fit for the part of an Eternal Judge with no right of appeal.

Yet there is much in conduct as to which there can be no mistake, and if a man persists in acts that are inconsiderate and unkind, and in words that are harsh, ungenerous, biting, and wilfully ignorant, his fellows will judge him, prophet or no prophet. "Thou are inexcusable, O man," said the Apostle, "whosoever thou art that judgest: for wherein thou judgest another, thou condemnest thyself; for thou that judgest doest the same things." There is no function from which he who knows himself will more sedulously abstain than that of the moral judge of the character of another. Human nature is so subtle, intermixed, self-deceiving, that hesitation and leniency are the rules that come spontaneously to all save the Pharisee and the Cynic. Carlyle was himself, on the surface at all events, a Cynic of the Cynics; and as he chose to vent his spleen on most of the best of his contemporaries, he will have to take his chance. His friends can hardly claim for his benefit a tenderness that he so seldom extended to the rest of the world.

Of his relations to his wife, of which most is said, perhaps it is well to say least. Of all relations they are those of which even the nearest outside friend must know least. Their success or failure, the rights and wrongs of them, are constantly determined—outside the ordinary cases of coarse rupture—by elements too delicate to be capable of being either fully divulged or fairly seized. We can never be perfectly sure that we know all the relevant circumstances of the case. Perhaps we do not know them all here, in spite of Mr. Froude's ample exposure of many facts. Carlyle laughed his horse-laughter over the household troubles of Diderot, his quarrels with his wife, his gross indigestions, and all the

other *misères* of the unlucky philosopher,—not without an in-
uendo that he had fallen into them all as a result of his materialist
metaphysics, and that they only served him right. Yet no "black-
guard *philosophe*" of the band was more essentially reprobate in
all domestic duty than the transcendental Coleridge, and there is
many a scene in Cheyne Row that exactly recalls Diderot's interior
in the Rue Taranne. The greater is the pity. There are not in the
history of the Calamities of Authors more painful entries than
many here:—"Work ruined for this day. Imprudently expressed
complaints in the morning filled all the sky with clouds—por-
tending grave issues? Or only inane ones?" That is to say, we
take it, would his wife leave him altogether, as seems to have
been often threatened, and was once for a time actually attempted,
or would they go on in their "mutual misery"? The mutual misery
hardly abated. "A thick black cloud overshadowed his life for
many weary years." The fourteenth chapter—partially redeemed
from utter squalor by two letters to Mr. Carlyle from the noble-
minded Mazzini—is a dolorous piece of reading to all, and one
hopes they are not few, who would have given much to know that
the man of high thoughts, stern purpose, noble imagination,
fared through the world, if not with serenity, at least without
squalid perversities, wranglings, indignity.

Mr. Froude states the case generally in several places. It comes
to this, that when Carlyle was uncomfortable, he could not keep
it to himself, and made more of it than the reality justified. "His
wife suffered perhaps more than he from colds, and pains, and
sleeplessness; when her husband was dilating upon his own
sorrows, he often forgot hers, or made them worse by worry."
She on the other hand had a hot temper, and a tongue as biting
and as rasping as his own. She even described to Mr. Froude and
others, in Carlyle's presence, how he set out on an expedition,
drawing him "in her finest style of mockery—his cloak, his
knapsack, his broad-brimmed hat, his preparation of pipes, &c.
He laughed as loud as any of us; but it struck me even then that
the wit, however brilliant, was rather untender." The lady "had a
terrible habit of speaking out the exact truth, cut as clear as with
a graving tool, on occasions, too, when without harm it might
have been left unspoken." Even she and her mother were "seldom
together without a collision." In their most intimate talk Carlyle

had no gift of tender expansion. His letters are full of it, but in conversation he shrank from expressions of affection. "On the other hand he was keenly sensitive to what he thought unreasonable or silly. He was easily provoked; and his irritation would burst out in spurts of angry metaphor, not to be forgotten from their very point and force. Thus his letters failed in producing their full effect from their contrast with remembered expressions which had meant nothing." That Carlyle was imperious and exacting in his household is as certain as that Milton was, or that James Mill was. That he was self-centred, inconsiderate and even downright selfish can hardly be denied. Friends were amused by his peculiarities, but "for his wife, on whom the firesparks fell first always, and who could not escape from them, the trial was hard." His affection was undoubted, but it did not prevent outbursts under which for a fortnight at a time she felt as "if she were the keeper of a madhouse." Yet, says Mr. Froude, though both he and she were noble and generous, "his was the soft heart and hers the stern one." On the whole, it looks as if this were the truth, and here let us close the distressing page, only taking care not to forget that the head and the will ought to have a share in conduct as well as a soft heart. Carlyle was at bottom a sentimentalist, not a reasoner, and the sentimentalist's catastrophe overtook him. It will sound revolting to his disciples, but in truth Carlyle was in many important respects not unlike the favourite Prophet and Teacher of an earlier generation, the remarkable Jean Jacques (and there is even a letter of Rousseau's, by the way, to his Thérèse that is wonderfully like some in these volumes). Carlyle was a Rousseau who chanced to be, as Mr. Froude puts it, in everything Norse to the heart. To them both their times were utterly out of joint. In contempt for their literary contemporaries, they were singularly alike.

Carlyle has few good words to bestow. In all camps it is the same. Cardinal Newman "had not the intellect of a moderate-sized rabbit." The author of the *Christian Year* is "some little ape called Keble." George Sand is a mere French improper female, from every point of view objectionable and intolerable, though he admits in one place that he is made by what he calls her sentimentalisms so impatient of her (as also of Mazzini) "as often to be unjust to what of truth and genuine propriety of him is in them." But these great moral leaders ought not to allow themselves to be impatient and unjust. To be in everything Norse to the heart is not the only quality required for wise and equitable judgment. To be Norse in the heart, if you are not careful, is to be both brutal and silly. The brutality and silliness of some of Carlyle's utterances are more Norse than can be permitted.

Nothing is more striking than the fascination for Carlyle of the outer seeming of the people in whom he either was really interested, or knew that he was expected to be. His letters and journals are among other things the most extraordinary gallery of the portraits of contemporary notables. In the power of physiognomic description he is little short of a magician. The worst of it is that the one thing for which this eloquent talker about Work seems to have had least eye or thought, was the quality of the work that was being done by anybody with whom he is brought into contact. He can tell you that Sydney Smith was "a mass of fat and muscularity, with massive Roman nose, piercing hazel eyes, huge cheeks, shrewdness and fun, not humour or even wit, seemingly without soul altogether." Yet Sydney Smith had fought hard for all sorts of merciful improvements, and had helped to get them done; he had not contented himself with the random vehemence of such things as the *Latter-day Pamphlets,* in spite of the "soul" in them. Carlyle can tell us of Mr. Bright's nose and his pugnacious eye, and his coat-collar; but that Mr. Bright had achieved anything or set a mark for good or for ill on national affairs, seems to have been of no more interest to him than it would be to an artist with a commission for a portrait. In "Radical Grote"—one of the gentlest and most courteous of all the sons of men—he finds no more than "a man with strait upper lip, large chin, and open mouth (spout mouth); for the rest a tall man with dull thoughtful brows, and lank dishevelled hair, greatly the look of a prosperous Dissenting minister." No wonder that intercourse with his fellow creatures was so stale, flat, and unprofitable to one who could bring no more away from even the strongest heads of his time than mere external memorabilia of this description.

He goes down to stay with Mill at Mickleham in 1836, about a month after the death of James Mill. "They were as hospitable as they could be," says Carlyle, and he gives a pleasant picture of "the little drawing-room door of glass looking out into a rose

lawn, into green plains, and half a mile off to a most respectable
wooded and open broad-shouldered green hill." Then the inevitable grumble. "There was little sorrow visible in their house,
or rather none, nor any human feeling at all; but the strangest
unheimlich kind of composure and acquiescence, as if all human
spontaneity had taken refuge in invisible corners." As if there
could be no human feeling unless it shows itself in the hullabaloo
of an Irish wake, or the ceaseless sombre dronings and woful
ejaculations of the Old Prophet himself. As if Mill's feeling for
his father were not as deep as Carlyle's for his, simply because it
found a calmer and more rational expression; and as if Mill's
lament for the wife whom he had idolised, were not as passionate
as the dreary inarticulate moanings of Carlyle over the wife
whom he only idolised in memory after she had been taken away
from him. Even the illness which Mill had brought upon himself by his consuming ardour for knowledge and truth, excited
only disgust or contempt in his heroic friend. "His eyes go
twinkling and jerking with wild lights and twitches; his head is
bald, his face brown and dry," and so forth. As if this, or the like
of this, were the thing best worth saying and reporting. Mill, he
admits, "talked much and not stupidly—far from that." Surely a
sentence or two of this not stupid talk would have been better
worth putting down than these miserable items of his personal
appearance. Carlyle's tone in speaking of a man who was so much
superior to him in so many ways as Mill, is simply painful. Than
the *Autobiography,* Carlyle has never read "a more uninteresting
book, nor, I should say, a sillier. . . . It is wholly the life of a
logic-chopping engine, little more of human in it than if it had
been done by a thing of mechanised iron." Such talk inclines one
to think that to be calm, grave, dignified, serene, rational, was the
most sure means of provoking an explosion of contempt. Even
of Emerson, who had once been so radiant to him, Carlyle latterly
seems to have thought but poorly. What, then, are we to say for
a scheme of thinking, feeling, living, which at the end of many
years so extinguishes the sympathy and the hope of a man? "Do
not conjugate *ennuyer,* dear Jack," he wrote to his brother, "if
you can help it; conjugate *espérer* rather. Depend upon it, working, trying, is the only remover of doubt. It is an immense truth
that." Immense truth it is indeed, yet hardly in a page or a line of

the teacher's life do we see that it was of any practical use to him in that not unimportant part of the day when he is out of the workshop, and has to deal with the claims of others.

It is the same with most of the incidents of his time. All is bad. For the Great Exhibition, says his biographer, "he could have no feeling but contempt," because, forsooth, it was "a contrivance to bring in a new era, and do for mankind what Christianity had tried and failed to do." When the Duke of Wellington was buried, and the nation did its best in the ordinary way of such things to give outward evidence of its inward appreciation, Carlyle could see nothing but "a big bag of wind and nothingness." The crowd who go to see the lying-in-state were "all the empty fools of creation." The whole performance is "a painful, miserable kind of thing to me and others of a serious turn of mind." The serious turn of mind is just what is not there. Think how Goethe would have talked about such things, would have brushed the cant and insincerity and bad upholstery aside, and found some positive, genial, instructive, human word to say about exhibitions and crowds and pageants. He would have said something to Eckermann or to the Chancellor von Müller that would have been interesting, perhaps even useful, and in any case serious. What has an everlasting torrent of inhuman scolding to do with "a serious turn of mind?" It is the worst levity.

At Cologne, instead of yielding himself for a while to the sublime impressions of the great church, he "got no good of it, but rather mischief; the sight of those impious Christians doing their so-called worship there (a true devil-worship if ever there was one) [etcetera, etcetera] far transcended any little pleasure I could have got from the supreme of earthly masonry." If any one would measure this outbreak of inconsiderate spleen with the composure of a great spirit, let him turn to Goethe's few words about Saint Peter's at Rome. The church is not more empty, more hypocritical, more desperate than everything else. "Bunsen had once tried to enlist Carlyle's sympathies in the completion of Cologne Cathedral, showing him the plans, &c. Carlyle said nothing till obliged to speak. Then at last, being pressed to speak, he said, 'It is a very fine pagoda, if ye could get any sort of a God to put in it.' " Some will be inclined to ask themselves whether as grave a thing might not be said of the gorgeous structure that

Carlyle himself has raised in our literature. His imagination is resplendent, his humour incomparable, the spaciousness is imposing and awful, but where is the piety, the reverence, except in words? Is not the upshot of it all that the Devil and his angels have somehow got hold of our poor planet, and are its masters, driving our generation headlong like swine down steep places? It would be no great paradox to say that in many respects no atheism has ever been preached in this world of blacker dye than Carlyle's. The men of the eighteenth century, of whom he made so light, had at least the fire of humane hope burning with a bright and a steadfast flame within them, illusory enough in many cases, but still giving warmth and light while it lasted. They attacked what they held wrong and mischievous, but they had in them the spirit of practical direction. It was not all anathema. Without disparaging some sides of Carlyle as a spiritual force, we see in him as a directing practical force only distraction in his own efforts, and too often ignorant and presumptuous detraction of the efforts of others. Mr. Froude tells us boldly, taking the bull by the horns, that Carlyle "lived to see most of the unpalatable doctrines which the Pamphlets contained, verified by painful experience and practically acted on." Of this we would fain hear further and better particulars. If it were said of Bentham, or the early Edinburgh Reviewers, or of some others on whom Carlyle poured his boisterous scorn, such a statement would be unintelligible and reasonably true. But in turning over once more the familiar pages of the Latter-day Pamphlets, we feel that they are as little capable of being "practically acted on" as the wailings of the Prophet Jeremiah, or the shoutings of Philoctetes on his island.

His Edinburgh address in 1866, according to Mr. Froude, brought a low-priced edition of his works "into a strange temporary popularity with the reading multitude. *Sartor,* 'poor beast,' had struggled into life with difficulty, and its readers since had been few, if select. Twenty thousand copies of the shilling edition of it were now sold instantly on its publication. It was now admitted universally that Carlyle was 'a great man.' *Yet he saw no inclination, not the slightest, to attend to his teaching."* That very plain truth, which becomes still plainer as the years roll over us, was due to the fact that his teaching was all heat and no light; it emancipated men from the spirit of convention, but did not furnish them with a new leading; was a glorious appeal to the individual to look into his own soul, but gave him no practical key by which he might read what he found there. For that we have all had to look elsewhere, and some have found it in one source and others in another. "Carlyle," says Mr. Froude, "taught me a creed which I could then accept as really true; which I have held ever since, with increasing confidence as the interpretation of my existence, and the guide of my conduct, so far as I have been able to act up to it." Nobody living is Mr. Froude's superior in the art of clear exposition when he has something to expound, but we look through his account of Carlyle in vain for anything worthy of the name of a creed. Sublime and moving aspirations, poetic and devout ejaculations, yes: but a creed, no.

How imperfectly Carlyle's creed was a guide to conduct, or even to opinion, for its inventor and first owner, we learn here. Carlyle, said Mazzini, "loves calm and silence *platonically*." So too was his love too nearly platonic for Resignation (Entsagen), Acquiescence, Faith, and all the other cardinal articles of his spiritual programme. We know of no biography in the world more impregnated with mutiny, and (in Carlyle's sense) with Impiety. This is not the fault of the biographer. He has only painted the scenes and the character as they were.

The resplendent poetic genius, of course, stands where it did, the penetrating humour, the vivid glance, the noble imagination and solemnity. There is no need for pity, whatever else there may be, for one who could so feed the mind and heart through the eye as to have such communings with nature as here:—

> My days pass along here, where a multiplicity of small things still detains but does not occupy me, in a most silent, almost Sabbath-like manner. I avoid all company whatever—except the few poor greedy-minded, very stupid rustics who have some affairs with me, which I struggle always to despatch and cut short. I see nobody; I do not even read much. The old hill and rivers , the old earth with her star firmaments and burial-vaults, carry on a mysterious, unfathomable dialogue with me. It is eight years since I have seen a spring, and in such a mood I never saw one. It seems all new and original to me—beautiful, almost solemn. Whose great laboratory is that? The hills stand snow-

69

powdered, pale, bright. The black hailstorm awakens in them, rushes down like a black swift ocean tide, valley answering valley; and again the sun blinks out, and the poor sower is casting his grain into the furrow, hopeful he that the Zodiacs and far Heavenly Horologes have not faltered; that there will be yet another summer added for us and another harvest. Our whole heart asks with Napoleon: "Messieurs, who made all that? *Be silent,* foolish Messieurs!"

Yet this is not the only or the uniform impression; the beholder reflected as many moods as he found. At Newby the scene has changed. There he watches "the going and coming of the great Atlantic brine, which rushes up and down every twelve hours since the creation of the world, never forgetting its work; a most huge unfortunate looking thing, doomed to a career of transcendent monotony, the very image as of a grey objectless monotony."

Here is another scene:—

Avoiding crowds and highways, I went along Battersea Bridge, and then by a wondrous path across cow fields, mud ditches, river embankments, over a waste expanse of what attempted to pass for country, wondrous enough in darkening dusk, especially as I had never been there before, and the very road was uncertain. I had left my watch and my purse. I had a good stick in my hand. Boat people sat drinking about the Red House; steamers snorting about the river, each with a lantern at its nose. Old women sat in strange cottages, trimming their evening fire. Bewildered-looking, mysterious coke furnaces (with a very bad smell) glowed at one place; I know not why. Windmills stood silent. Blackguards, improper females, and miscellanies sauntered, harmless all. Chelsea lights burnt many-hued, bright over the water in the distance —under the great sky of silver, under the great still twilight. So I wandered full of thoughts, or of things I could not think.

With one more, we may close:—

Yesterday I set out in the rough wind, while the weather was dry, for a long walk. I went by Penpont, up Scaur Water, round the foot of Tynron Doon. I had all along been remembering a poor little joiner's cottage which I saw once when poor Auntie and you and I went up on ponies. This ride, this cottage, which was the centre of it in my memory, I would again recall, by looking at the places—the places which still abide while all else vanishes so soon. It was a day of tempestuous wind; but the sun occasionally shone; the country was green, bright; the hills of an almost spiritual clearness, and broad swift storms of hail came dashing down from them on this hand and that. It was a kind of *preternatural* walk, full of sadness, full of purity.

The Scaur Water, the clearest I ever saw except one, came brawling down, the voice of it like a lamentation among the winds, answering me as the voice of a brother wanderer and lamenter, wanderers like me through a certain portion of eternity and infinite space. Poor brook! yet it was nothing but drops of water. My thought alone gave it an individuality. It was *I* that was the wanderer, far older and stronger and greater than the Scaur, or any river or mountain, or earth, planet, or thing.

Whether Mr. Froude is right in thinking that Carlyle is the one person among his contemporaries about whom the coming generations will care most to be informed, it is impossible to be sure. Most critics, however, will be inclined to assent to the estimate of Lord Beaconsfield in that singular and truly admirable letter, here published, in which he offered to Carlyle an honourable mark of national recognition. Tennyson and Carlyle are likely to be the two conspicuous names in the literature of the middle of our century. In Carlyle's permanence as a spiritual force we have little belief. His teaching is not sane, it is vague, it is not true. There is, however, no occasion for an examination of it here. The question which these volumes will make men ask themselves is, as we have said, how the Gospel worked. One part of the answer is plain. Carlyle's life and character cannot and will not take their place in the temple of those whose mere name is an incitement to the love of virtue and the love of truth, like Socrates, Plato, Marcus Aurelius. Mr. Froude concludes his task with the immortal words from the Funeral Oration of Pericles, about the unwritten memory of illustrious men abiding in the hearts and minds of all mankind, and there standing for an everlasting monument. But who will close the story of Carlyle's life in the devout and elevated mood in which Tacitus finishes his noble picture of Agricola? As a great poet, as an artist of the highest power, Carlyle's fame can hardly grow pale. But who will take him as an example of conduct, of self-discipline, of wise and

virtuous government of life in the world in which we find ourselves? A sublime sense of the solemnity of life is not enough:
above all things we need measure. The Beautiful, as he has many
a time said, is the Good. For the beautiful in character, in de-
meanour, in human relation, men will still turn to other types
than Carlyle. When they seek to quicken the love of what is good
in youthful souls by pictures of wise and magnanimous living,
they will hardly send the ingenuous learner the story of Cheyne
Row. Grace, affection, charity, divine equity, sober charm of life
—not for these things or any of them will the name of Carlyle
be dear to human history.

If we seek a standard, Carlyle himself has given it. "Here,"
he said of a great figure of our age, "here is a mind of the most
subtle and tumultuous elements; but it is governed in peaceful
diligence, and its impetuous and ethereal faculties work softly
together for good and noble ends. He may be called a philosopher; for he loves and has practised as a man the wisdom which
as a poet he inculcates. Composure and cheerful seriousness seem
to breathe over all his character. There is no whining over human
woes; it is understood that we must simply all strive to alleviate
or remove them. There is no noisy battling for opinions; but a
persevering effort to make Truth lovely. . . . An air of majestic
repose and serene humanity is visible throughout his works. In
no line of them does he speak with asperity of any man; scarcely
ever even of a thing. He knows the good and loves it; he knows
the bad and hateful, and rejects it, but in neither case with violence; his love is calm and active; his rejection is implied rather
than pronounced." It is not given to all to reach to this high
serenity. But teachers less Olympian than Goethe have come near
to the ideal even in our own "bankrupt age." The life of Emerson
at Concord, and of Mill at Blackheath and Avignon, tends more
to edification than the life of Carlyle, with all its tumultuous
emotions, and all its strange celestial imaginings.

Macaulay

It is told of Strafford that before reading any book for the first time, he would call for a sheet of paper, and then proceed to write down upon it some sketch of the ideas that he already had upon the subject of the book, and of the questions that he expected to find answered. No one who has been at the pains to try the experiment, will doubt the usefulness of Strafford's practice: it gives to our acquisitions from books clearness and reality, a right place and an independent shape. At this moment we are all looking for the biography of an illustrious man of letters, written by a near kinsman, who is himself naturally endowed with keen literary interests, and who has invigorated his academic cultivation by practical engagement in considerable affairs of public business. Before taking up Mr. Trevelyan's two volumes, it is perhaps worth while, on Strafford's plan, to ask ourselves shortly what kind of significance or value belongs to Lord Macaulay's achievements, and to what place he has a claim among the forces of English literature. It is seventeen years since he died, and those of us who never knew him nor ever saw him may now think about his work with that perfect detachment which is impossible in the case of actual contemporaries.

That Macaulay comes in the very front rank in the mind of the ordinary bookbuyer of our day is quite certain. It is an amusement

This essay was first published in *Fortnightly Review*, n.s., 112 (April 1876): 494–513, and was reprinted in *Critical Miscellanies*, vol. 1 (London, 1877) —ed.

with some people to put an imaginary case of banishment to a desert island, with the privilege of choosing the works of one author, and no more, to furnish literary companionship and refreshment for the rest of a lifetime. Whom would one select for this momentous post? Clearly the author must be voluminous, for days on desert islands are many and long; he must be varied in his moods, his topics, and his interests; he must have a great deal to say, and must have a power of saying it that shall arrest a depressed and dolorous spirit. Englishmen, of course, would with mechanical unanimity call for Shakespeare; Germans could hardly hesitate about Goethe; and a sensible Frenchman would pack up the ninety volumes of Voltaire. It would be at least as interesting to know the object of a second choice, supposing the tyrant were in his clemency to give us two authors. In the case of Englishmen there is some evidence as to a popular preference. A recent traveller in Australia informs us that the three books which he found on every squatter's shelf, and which at last he knew before he crossed the threshold that he should be sure to find, were Shakespeare, the Bible, and Macaulay's Essays. This is only an illustration of a feeling about Macaulay that has been almost universal among the English-speaking peoples.

We may safely say that no man obtains and keeps for a great many years such a position as this, unless he is possessed of some very extraordinary qualities, or else of common qualities in a very uncommon and extraordinary degree. The world, says Goethe, is more willing to endure the Incongruous than to be patient under the Insignificant. Even those who set least value on what Macaulay does for his readers, may still feel bound to distinguish the elements that have given him his vast popularity. The inquiry is not a piece of merely literary criticism, for it is impossible that the work of so imposing a writer should have passed through the hands of every man and woman of his time who has even the humblest pretensions to cultivation, without leaving a very decided mark on their habits both of thought and expression. As a plain matter of observation, it is impossible to take up a newspaper or a review, for instance, without perceiving Macaulay's influence both in the style and the temper of modern journalism, and journalism in its turn acts upon the style and temper of its enormous uncounted public. The man who now succeeds in catching the ear of the writers of leading articles, is in the position that used to be held by the head of some great theological school, whence disciples swarmed forth to reproduce in ten thousand pulpits the arguments, the opinions, the images, the tricks, the gestures, and the mannerisms of a single master.

Two men of very different kinds have thoroughly impressed the journalists of our time, Macaulay and Mr. Mill. Mr. Carlyle we do not add to them; he is, as the Germans call Jean Paul, *der Einzige.* And he is a poet, while the other two are in their degrees serious and argumentative writers, dealing in different ways with the great topics that constitute the matter and business of daily discussion. They are both of them practical enough to interest men handling real affairs, and yet they are general or theoretical enough to supply such men with the large and ready common- places which are so useful to a profession that has to produce literary graces and philosophical decorations at an hour's notice. It might perhaps be said of these two distinguished men that our public writers owe most of their virtues to the one, and most of their vices to the other. If Mill taught some of them to reason, Macaulay tempted more of them to declaim: if Mill set an example of patience, tolerance, and fair examination of hostile opinions, Macaulay did much to encourage oracular arrogance, and a rather too thrasonical complacency; if Mill sowed ideas of the great economic, political, and moral bearings of the forces of society, Macaulay trained a taste for superficial particularities, trivial circumstantialities of local colour, and all the parapher- nalia of the pseudo-picturesque.

Of course nothing so obviously untrue is meant as that this is an account of Macaulay's own quality. What is empty pretension in the leading article was often a warranted self-assertion in Macaulay; what is little more than testiness in it, is in him often a generous indignation. What became and still remain in those who have made him their model, substantive and organic vices, the foundation of literary character and intellectual temper, were in him the incidental defects of a vigorous genius. And we have to take a man of his power and vigour with all his drawbacks, for the one are wrapped up in the other. Charles Fox used to apply to Burke a passage that Quintilian wrote about Ovid. "Si animi sui affectibus temperare quam indulgere maluisset," quoted Fox, "quid vir iste praestare non potuerit!"* But this is really not at all certain either of Ovid, or Burke, or anyone else. It suits moralists to tell us that excellence lies in the happy mean and nice balance of our faculties and impulses, and perhaps in so far as our own contentment and an easy passage through life are involved, what they tell us is true. But for making a mark in the world, for rising to supremacy in art or thought or affairs—whatever those aims may be worth—a man possibly does better to indulge rather than to chide or grudge his genius, and to pay the penalties for his weaknesses rather than run any risk of multilating those strong faculties of which they happen to be an inseparable accident. Versatility is not a universal gift among the able men of the world; not many of them have so many gifts of the spirit as to be free to choose by what pass they will climb "the steep where Fame's proud temple shines afar." If Macaulay had applied himself to the cultivation of a balanced judgment, of tempered phrases, and of relative propositions, he would probably have sunk into an impotent tameness. A great pugilist has sometimes been converted from the error of his ways, and been led zealously to cherish gospel graces, but the hero's discourses have seldom been edifying. Macaulay, divested of all the exorbitancies of his spirit and his style, would have been a Samson shorn of the locks of his strength.

Although, however, a writer of marked quality may do well to let his genius develope its spontaneous forces without too assiduous or vigilant repression, trusting to other writers of equal strength in other directions, and to the general fitness of things and operation of time, to redress the balance, still it is the task of criticism in counting up the contributions of one of these strong men to examine the mischiefs no less than the benefits incident to their work. There is no puny carping or cavilling in the process. It is because such men are strong that they are able to do harm, and they may injure the taste and judgment of a whole generation, just because they are never mediocre. That is implied in strength. Macaulay is not to be measured now merely as if he were the author of a new book. His influence has been a distinct literary force, and in an age of reading, this is to be a distinct

* "If he had preferred to control rather than indulge his emotions, what that man could not have accomplished!"—ed.

force in deciding the temper, the process, the breadth, of men's opinions, no less than the manner of expressing them. It is no new observation that the influence of an author becomes in time something apart from his books, and that a certain generalised or abstract personality impresses itself on our minds, long after we have forgotten the details of his opinions, the arguments by which he enforced them, and even, what are usually the last to escape us, the images by which he illustrated them. Phrases and sentences are a mask: but we detect the features of the man behind the mask. This personality of a favourite author is a real and powerful agency. Unconsciously we are infected with his humours; we apply his methods; we find ourselves copying the rhythm and measure of his periods; we wonder how he would have acted, or thought, or spoken in our circumstances. Usually a strong writer leaves a special mark in some particular region of mental activity: the final product of him is to fix some persistent religious mood, or some decisive intellectual bias, or else some trick of the tongue. Now Macaulay has contributed no philosophic ideas to the speculative stock, nor has he developed any one great historic or social truth. His work is always full of a high spirit of manliness, probity, and honour; but he is not of that small band to whom we may apply Mackintosh's thrice and four times enviable panegyric on the eloquence of Dugald Stewart, that its peculiar glory consisted in having "breathed the love of virtue into whole generations of pupils." He has painted many striking pictures, and imparted a certain reality to our conception of many great scenes of the past. He did good service in banishing once for all those sentimental Jacobite leanings and prejudices which had been kept alive by the sophistry of the most popular of historians, and the imagination of the most popular of romance-writers. But where he set his stamp has been upon style; style in its widest sense, not merely on the grammar and mechanism of writing, but on what De Quincey described as its *organology;* style, that is to say, in its relation to ideas and feelings, its commerce with thought, and its reaction on what one may call the temper or conscience of the intellect.

Let no man suppose that it matters little whether the most universally popular of the serious authors of a generation—and Macaulay was nothing less than this—effects *style coupé* or *style soutenu.* The critic of style is not the dancing-master, declaiming on the deep ineffable things that lie in a minuet. He is not the virtuoso of supines and gerundives. The morality of style goes deeper "than dull fools suppose." When Comte took pains to prevent any sentence exceeding two lines of his manuscript or five of print; to restrict every paragraph to seven sentences; to exclude every hiatus between two sentences or even between two paragraphs; and never to reproduce any word, except the auxiliary monosyllables, in two consecutive sentences; he justified his literary solicitude by insisting on the wholesomeness alike to heart and intelligence of submission to artificial institutions. He felt, after he had once mastered the habit of the new yoke, that it became the source of continual and unforeseeable improvements even in thought, and he perceived that the reason why verse is a higher kind of literary perfection than prose, is that verse imposes a greater number of rigorous forms. We may add that verse itself is perfected, in the hands of men of poetic genius, in proportion to the severity of this mechanical regulation. Where Pope or Racine had one rule of metre, Victor Hugo has twenty, and he observes them as rigorously as an algebraist or an astronomer observes the rules of calculation or demonstration. One, then, who touches the style of a generation acquires no trifling authority over its thought and temper, as well as over the length of its sentences.

The first and most obvious secret of Macaulay's place on popular bookshelves is that he has a true genius for narration, and narration will always in the eyes not only of our squatters in the Australian bush, but of the many all over the world, stand first among literary gifts. The common run of plain men, as has been noticed since the beginning of the world, are as eager as children for a story, and like children they will embrace the man who will tell them a story, with abundance of details and plenty of colour, and a realistic assurance that it is no mere make-believe. Macaulay never stops to brood over an incident or a character, with an inner eye intent on penetrating to the lowest depth of motive and cause, to the furthest complexity of impulse, calculation, and subtle incentive. The spirit of analysis is not in him, and the divine spirit of meditation is not in him. His whole mind runs in action and movement; it busies itself with eager interest in all objective particulars. He is seized by the external and the superficial, and revels in every detail that appeals to the five senses. "The brilliant Macaulay," said Emerson, with slight exaggeration, "who expresses the tone of the English governing classes of the day, explicitly teaches that *good* means good to eat, good to wear, material commodity." So ready a faculty of exultation in the exceeding great glories of taste and touch, of loud sound and glittering spectacle, is a gift of the utmost service to the narrator who craves immense audiences. Let it be said that if Macaulay exults in the details that go to our five senses, his sensuousness is always clean, manly, and fit for honest daylight and the summer sun. There is none of that curious odour of autumnal decay that clings to the passion of a more modern school for colour and flavour and the enumerated treasures of subtle indulgence.

Mere picturesqueness, however, is a minor qualification compared with another quality which everybody assumes himself to have, but which is in reality extremely uncommon; the quality, I mean, of telling a tale directly and in straightforward order. In speaking of Hallam, Macaulay complained that Gibbon had brought into fashion an unpleasant trick of telling a story by implication and allusion. This provoking obliquity has certainly increased rather than declined since Hallam's day, and it has reached its height and climax in the latest addition of all to our works of popular history, Mr. Green's clever book upon the English People. Mr. Froude, it is true, whatever may be his shortcomings on the side of sound moral and political judgment, has admirable gifts in the way of straightforward narration, and Mr. Freeman, when he does not press too hotly after emphasis and abstains from overloading his account with superabundance of detail, is usually excellent in the way of direct description. Still, it is not merely because these two writers are alive and Macaulay is not, that most people would say of him that he is unequalled in our time in his mastery of the art of letting us know in an express and unmistakable way exactly what it was that happened, though it is quite true that in many portions of his too elaborated History of William the Third he describes a large number of events about which, I think, no sensible man can in the least care either how they happened, or whether indeed they happened at all or not.

Another reason why people have sought Macaulay is that he has in one way or another something to tell them about many of the most striking personages and interesting events in the history of mankind. And he does really tell them something. If any one will be at the trouble to count up the number of those names that belong to the world and time, about which Macaulay has found not merely something, but something definite and pointed to say, he will be astonished to see how large a portion of the wide historic realm is traversed in that ample flight of reference, allusion, and illustration, and what unsparing copiousness of knowledge gives substance, meaning, and attraction to that blaze and glare of rhetoric.

Macaulay came upon the world of letters, just as the middle classes were expanding into enormous prosperity, were vastly increasing in numbers, and were becoming more alive than they had ever been before to literary interests. His essays are as good as a library; they make an incomparable manual and vade-mecum for a busy uneducated man who has curiosity and enlightenment enough to wish to know a little about the great lives and great thoughts, the shining words and many-coloured complexities of action, that have marked the journey of man through the ages. Macaulay had an intimate acquaintance both with the imaginative literature and the history of Greece and Rome, with the literature and the history of modern Italy, of France, and of England. Whatever his special subject, he contrives to pour into it with singular dexterity a stream of rich, graphic, and telling illustrations from all these widely diversified sources. Figures from history, ancient and modern, sacred and secular; characters from plays and novels from Plautus down to Walter Scott and Jane Austen; images and similes from poets of every age and every nation, "pastoral, pastoral-comical, historical-pastoral, tragical-historical"; shrewd thrusts from satirists, wise saws from sages, pleasantries caustic or pathetic from humorists; all throng Macaulay's pages with the bustle and variety and animation of some glittering masque and cosmoramic revel of great books and heroical men. Hence, though Macaulay was in mental constitution one of the very least Shakespearean writers that ever lived, yet he has the Shakespearean quality of taking his reader through an immense gallery of interesting characters and striking situations. No writer can now expect to attain the widest popularity as a man of letters unless he gives to the world *multa* as well as *multum*. Sainte-Beuve, the most eminent man of letters in France in our generation, wrote no less than twenty-seven volumes of his incomparable *Causeries*. Mr. Carlyle, the most eminent man of letters in England in our generation, has taught us that silence is golden in thirty volumes. Macaulay was not so exuberantly copious as these two illustrious writers, but he had the art of being as various without being so voluminous.

There has been a great deal of deliberate and systematic imitation of Macaulay's style, often by clever men who might well have trusted to their own resources. Its most conspicuous vices are very easy to imitate, but it is impossible for any one who is less familiar with literature than Macaulay was, to reproduce his style effectively, for the reason that it is before all else the style of great literary knowledge. Nor is that all. Macaulay's knowledge was not only very wide; it was both thoroughly accurate and instantly ready. For this stream of apt illustrations he was indebted to his extraordinary memory, and his rapid eye for contrasts and analogies. They come to the end of his pen as he writes; they are not laboriously hunted out in indexes, and then added by way of afterthought and extraneous interpolation. Hence quotations and references that in a writer even of equal knowledge, but with his wits less promptly about him, would seem mechanical and awkward, find their place in a page of Macaulay as if by a delightful process of complete assimilation and spontaneous fusion.

We may be sure that no author could have achieved Macaulay's boundless popularity among his contemporaries, unless his work had abounded in what is substantially Commonplace. Addison puts fine writing in sentiments that are natural without being obvious, and this is a true account of the "law" of the exquisite literature of the Queen Anne men. We may perhaps add to Addison's definition, that the great secret of the best kind of popularity is always the noble or imaginative handling of Commonplace. Shakespeare may at first seem an example to the contrary; and indeed is it not a standing marvel that the greatest writer of a nation that is distinguished among all nations for the pharisaism, puritanism, and unimaginative narrowness of its judgments on conduct and type of character, should be paramount over all writers for the breadth, maturity, fulness, subtlety, and infinite variousness of his conception of human life and nature? One possible answer to the perplexity is that the puritanism does not go below the surface in us, and that Englishmen are not really limited in their view by the too strait formulas that are supposed to contain their explanations of the moral universe. On this theory the popular appreciation of Shakespeare is the irrepressible response of the hearty inner man to a voice in which he recognises the full note of human nature, and those wonders of the world which are not dreamt of in his professed philosophy. A more obvious answer than this is that Shakespeare's popularity with the many is not due to those finer glimpses that are the very essence of all poetic delight to the few, but to his thousand other magnificent attractions, and above all, after his skill as a pure dramatist and master of scenic interest and situation, to the lofty or pathetic setting with which he vivifies, not the subtleties or refinements, but the commonest and most elementary traits of the commonest and most elementary human moods. The few with minds touched by nature or right cultivation to the finer issues, admire the supreme genius which takes some poor Italian tale, with its coarse plot and gross personages, and shooting it through with threads of variegated meditation, produces a masterpiece of penetrative reflection and high pensive suggestion as to the deepest things and most secret parts of the life of men. But to the general these finer threads are undiscernible. What touches them, and most rightly touches them and us all, in the Shakespearean poetry, are topics eternally old, yet of eternal freshness, the perennial truisms of the grave and the bride-chamber, of shifting fortune, the surprises of destiny, the emptiness of the answered vow. This is the region in which the poet wins his widest if not his hardest triumph, the region of the noble Commonplace.

A writer dealing with such matters as principally occupied Macaulay has not the privilege of resort to these great poetic inspirations. Yet history, too, has its generous commonplace, its plausibilities of emotion, and no one has ever delighted more than Macaulay did to appeal to the fine truisms that cluster round love of freedom and love of native land. The high rhetorical topics of liberty and patriotism are his readiest instruments for kindling a glowing reflection of these magnanimous passions in the breasts of his readers. That Englishman is hardly to be envied who can read without a glow such passages as that in the History about Turenne being startled by the shout of stern exultation with which his English allies advanced to the combat, and expressing the delight of a true soldier when he learned that it was ever the fashion of Cromwell's pikemen to rejoice greatly when they beheld the enemy; while even the banished cavaliers felt an emotion of national pride when they saw a brigade of their countrymen, outnumbered by foes and abandoned by friends, drive before it in headlong route the finest infantry of Spain, and force a passage into a counterscarp which had just been pronounced impregnable by the ablest of the marshals of France. Such prose as this is not less thrilling to a man who loves his country, than the spirited verse of the Lays of Ancient Rome. And the commonplaces of patriotism and freedom would never have been so powerful in Macaulay's hands if they had not been inspired by a sincere and hearty faith in them in the soul of the writer. His unanalytical turn of mind kept him free of any temptation to think of love of country as a prejudice, or a passion for freedom as an illusion. The cosmopolitan or international idea which such teachers as Cobden have tried to impress on our stubborn islanders, would have found in Macaulay not lukewarm or sceptical adherence, but pointblank opposition and denial. He believed as stoutly in the supremacy of Great Britain in the history of the good causes of Europe, as M. Thiers believes in the supremacy of France, or Mazzini believed in that of Italy. The thought of the prodigious industry, the inventiveness, the stout enterprise, the free government, the wise and equal laws, the noble literature, of this fortunate island and its majestic empire beyond the seas, and the discretion, valour, and tenacity by which all these great material and still greater intangible possessions had been first won and then kept against every hostile comer whether domestic or foreign, sent through Macaulay a thrill, like that which the thought of Paris and its heroisms moves in the great poet of France, or sight of the dear city of the Violet Crown moved in an Athenian of old. Thus habitually, with all sincerity of heart, to offer to one of the greater popular prepossessions the incense due to any other idol of superstition, sacred and of indisputable authority, and to let this adoration be seen shining in every page, is one of the keys that every man must find who would make a quick and sure way into the temple of contemporary fame.

It is one of the first things to be said about Macaulay, that he was in exact accord with the common average sentiment of his day on every subject on which he spoke. His superiority was not of that highest kind which leads a man to march in thought on the outside margin of the crowd, watching them, sympathising with them, hoping for them, but apart. Macaulay was one of the middle-class crowd in his heart, and only rose above it by extraordinary gifts of expression. He had none of that ambition which inflames some hardy men, to make new beliefs and new passions enter the minds of their neighbours; his ascendancy is due to literary pomp, not to fecundity of spirit. No one has ever surpassed him in the art of combining resolute and ostentatious common sense of a slightly coarse sort in choosing his point of view, with so considerable an appearance of dignity and elevation in setting it forth and impressing it upon others. The elaborateness of his style is very likely to mislead people into imagining for him a corresponding elaborateness of thought and sentiment. On the contrary, Macaulay's mind was really very simple, strait, and with as few notes in its register, to borrow a phrase from the language of vocal compass, as there are few notes, though they are very loud, in the register of his written prose. When we look more closely into it, what at first wore the air of dignity and elevation, in truth rather disagreeably resembles the narrow assurance of a man who knows that he has with him the great battalions of public opinion. We are always quite sure that if Macaulay had been an Athenian citizen towards the ninety-fifth Olympiad, he would have taken sides with Anytus and Meletus in the impeachment of Socrates. A popular author must take the accepted maxims for granted in a thoroughgoing way. He must suppress any whimsical fancy for applying the Socratic elenchus, or any other engine of criticism, scepticism, or verification, to those sentiments or current precepts of morals, which may in fact be very two-sided and may be much neglected in practice, but which the public opinion of his time requires to be treated in theory and in literature as if they had been cherished and held sacred *semper, ubique, et ab omnibus*.

This is just what Macaulay does, and it is commonly supposed to be no heavy fault in him or any other writer for the common public. Man cannot live by analysis alone, nor nourish himself on the secret delights of irony. And if Macaulay had only reflected the more generous of the prejudices of mankind, it would have been well enough. Burke, for instance, was a writer who revered the prejudices of a modern society as deeply as Macaulay did; he believed society to be founded on prejudices and held compact by them. Yet what size there is in Burke, what fine perspective, what momentum, what edification! It may be pleaded that there is the literature of edification, and there is the literature of knowledge, and that the qualities proper to the one cannot lawfully be expected from the other, and would only be very much out of place if they should happen to be found there. But there are two answers to this. First, Macaulay in the course of his varied writings discusses all sorts of ethical and other matters, and is not simply a chronicler of party and intrigue, of dynasties and campaigns. Second, and more than this, even if he had never travelled beyond the composition of historical record, he could still have sown his pages, as does every truly great writer, no matter what his subject may be, with those significant images or far-reaching suggestions, which suddenly light up a whole range of distant thoughts and sympathies within us; which in an instant affect the sensibilities of men with a something new and unforeseen; and which awaken, if only for a passing moment, the faculty and response of the diviner mind. Tacitus does all this, and Burke does it, and that is why men who care nothing for Roman despots or for Jacobin despots, will still perpetually turn to those writers almost as if they were on the level of great poets or very excellent spiritual teachers.

One secret is that they, and all such men as they were, had that of which Macaulay can hardly have had the rudimentary germ, the faculty of deep abstract meditation and surrender to the fruitful "leisures of the spirit." We can picture Macaulay talking, or making a speech in the House of Commons, or buried in a book, or scouring his library for references, or covering his blue foolscap with dashing periods, or accentuating his sentences and barbing his phrases; but can anybody think of him as meditating, as modestly pondering and wondering, as possessed for so much as ten minutes by that spirit of inwardness which has never been wholly wanting in any of those kings and princes of literature, with whom it is good for men to sit in counsel? He seeks Truth, not as she should be sought, devoutly, tentatively, and with the air of one touching the hem of a sacred garment, but clutching her by the hair of the head and dragging her after him in a kind of boisterous triumph, a prisoner of war and not a goddess.

All this finds itself reflected, as the inner temper of a man always is reflected, in his style of written prose. The merits of his prose are obvious enough. It naturally reproduces the good qualities of his understanding, its strength, manliness, and directness. That exultation in material goods and glories of which we have already spoken makes his pages rich in colour, and gives them the effect of a sumptuous gala-suit. Certainly the brocade is too brand-new, and has none of the delicate charm that comes to such finery when it is a little faded. Again, nobody can have any excuse for not knowing exactly what it is that Macaulay means. We may assuredly say of his prose what Boileau says of his own poetry—"Et mon vers, bien ou mal, dit toujours quelque chose." This is a prodigious merit, when we reflect with what fatal alacrity human language lends itself in the hands of so many performers upon the pliant instrument, to all sorts of obscurity, ambiguity, disguise and pretentious mystification. Scaliger is supposed to have remarked of the Basques and their desperate tongue: " 'Tis said the Basques understand one another; for my part, I will never believe it." The same pungent doubt might apply to loftier members of the hierarchy of speech than that forlorn dialect, but never to English as handled by Macaulay. He never wrote an obscure sentence in his life, and this may seem a small merit, until we remember of how few writers we could say the same.

Macaulay is one of those who think prose as susceptible of polished and definite form as verse, and he was, we should suppose, of those also who hold the type and mould of all written language to be spoken language. There are more reasons for demurring to the soundness of the latter doctrine than can conveniently be made to fill a digression here. For one thing, spoken language necessarily implies one or more listeners, whereas written language may often have to express meditative moods and trains of inward reflection that move through the mind without trace of external reference, and that would lose their special traits by the introduction of any suspicion that they were to be overheard. Again, even granting that all composition must be supposed to be meant by the fact of its existence to be addressed to a body of readers, it still remains to be shown that indirect address to the inner ear should follow the same method and rhythm as address directly through impressions on the outer organ. The attitude of the recipient mind is different, and there is the symbolism of a new medium between it and the speaker. The writer, being cut off from all those effects which are producible by the physical intonations of the voice, has to find substitutes for them by other means, by subtler cadences, by a more varied modulation, by firmer notes, by more complex circuits, than suffice for the utmost perfection of spoken language, which has all the potent and manifold aids of personality. In writing, whether it be prose or verse, you are free to produce effects whose peculiarity one can only define vaguely by saying that the senses have one part less in them than in any other of the forms and effects of art, and the imaginary voice one part more. But the question need not be laboured here, because there can be no dispute as to the quality of Macaulay's prose. Its measures are emphatically the measures of spoken deliverance. Those who have made the experiment, pronounce him to be one of the authors whose works are most admirably fitted for reading aloud. His firmness and directness of statement, his spiritedness, his art of selecting salient and highly coloured detail, and all his other merits as a narrator keep the listener's attention, and make him the easiest of writers to follow.

Although, however, clearness, directness, and positiveness are master qualities and the indispensable foundations of all good style, yet does the matter plainly by no means end with them. And it is even possible to have these virtues so unhappily proportioned and inauspiciously mixed with other turns and casts of mind, as to end in work with little grace or harmony or fine tracery about it, but only overweening purpose and vehement will. And it is overweeningness and self-confident will that are the chief notes of Macaulay's style. It is no benignity. Energy is doubtless a delightful quality, but then Macaulay's energy is energy without momentum, and he impresses us more by a strong volubility than by volume. It is the energy of interests and intuitions, which though they are profoundly sincere if ever they were sincere in any man, are yet in the relations which they comprehend, essentially superficial.

Still, trenchancy whether in speaker or writer is a most effective tone for a large public. It gives them confidence in their man, and prevents tediousness—except to those who reflect how delicate is the poise of truth, what steeps and pits encompass the dealer in unqualified propositions. To such persons, a writer who is trenchant in every sentence of every page, who never lapses for a line into the contingent, who marches through the intricacies of things in a blaze of certainty, is not only a writer to be distrusted, but the owner of a doubtful and displeasing style. It is a great test of style to watch how an author disposes of the qualifications, limitations, and exceptions that clog the wings of his main proposition. The grave and conscientious men of the seventeenth century insisted on packing them all honestly along with the main proposition itself within the bounds of a single period. Burke arranges them in tolerably close order in the paragraph. Dr. Newman, that winning writer, disperses them lightly over his page. Of Macaulay it is hardly unfair to say that he dispatches all qualifications into outer space before he begins to write, or if he magnanimously admits one or two here and there, it is only to bring them the more imposingly to the same murderous end.

We have spoken of Macaulay's interests and intuitions wearing a certain air of superficiality; there is a feeling of the same kind about his attempts to be genial. It is not truly festive. There is no abandonment in it. It has no deep root in moral humour, and is merely a literary form, resembling nothing so much as the hard geniality of some clever college tutor of stiff manners entertaining undergraduates at an official breakfast-party. This is not because his tone is bookish; on the contrary, his tone and level are distinctly those of the man of the world. But one always seems to find that neither a wide range of cultivation nor familiar access to the best Whig circles had quite removed the stiffness and self-conscious precision of the Clapham Sect. We would give much for a little more flexibility, and would welcome even a slight consciousness of infirmity. As has been said, the only people whom men cannot pardon are the perfect. Macaulay is like the military king who never suffered himself to be seen, even by the attendants in his bedchamber, until he had time to put on his uniform and jack-boots. His severity of eye is very wholesome; it makes his writing firm, and firmness is certainly one of the first qualities that good writing must have. But there is such a thing as soft and considerate precision, as well as hard and scolding precision. Those most interesting English critics of the generation slightly anterior to Macaulay,—Hazlitt, Lamb, De Quincey, Leigh Hunt, —were fully his equals in precision, and yet they knew how to be clear, acute, and definite, without that edginess and inelasticity which is so conspicuous in Macaulay's criticisms, alike in their matter and their form.

To borrow the figure of an old writer, Macaulay's prose is not like a flowing vestment to his thought, but like a suit of armour. It is often splendid and glittering, and the movement of the opening pages of his History is superb in its dignity. But that movement is exceptional. As a rule there is the hardness, if there is also often the sheen, of highly-wrought metal. Or, to change our figure, his pages are composed as a handsome edifice is reared, not as a fine statue or a frieze "with bossy sculptures graven" grows up in the imaginative mind of the statuary. There is no liquid continuity, such as indicates a writer possessed by his subject and not merely possessing it. The periods are marshalled in due order of procession, bright and high-stepping; they never escape under an impulse of emotion into the full current of a brimming stream. What is curious is that though Macaulay seems ever to be brandishing a two-edged gleaming sword, and though he steeps us in an atmosphere of belligerency, yet we are never conscious of inward agitation in him, and perhaps this alone would debar him from a place among the greatest writers. For they, under that reserve, suppression, or management, which is an indispensable condition of the finest rhetorical art, even when aiming at the most passionate effects, still succeed in conveying to their readers a thrilling sense of the strong fires that are glowing underneath. Now when Macaulay advances with his hectoring sentences and his rough pistolling ways, we feel all the time that his pulse is as steady as that of the most practised duelist who ever ate fire. He is too cool to be betrayed into a single phrase of happy improvisation. His pictures glare, but are seldom warm. Those strokes of minute circumstantiality which he loved so dearly, show that even in moments when his imagination might seem to be moving both spontaneously and ardently, it was really only a literary instrument, a fashioning tool and not a melting flame. Let us take a single example. He is describing the trial of Warren Hastings. "Every step in the proceedings," he says, "carried the mind either backward through many troubled centuries to the days when the foundations of our constitution were laid; or faraway over boundless seas and deserts, to dusky nations living under strange stars, worshipping strange gods, and writing strange characters from right to left." The odd trivality of the last detail, its unworthiness of the sentiment of the passage, leaves the reader checked; what sets out as a fine stroke of imagination dwindles down to a sort of literary conceit. And so in other places, even where the writer is most deservedly admired for gorgeous picturesque effect, we feel that it is only the literary picturesque, a kind of infinitely glorified newspaper-reporting. Compare, for instance, the most imaginative piece to be found in any part of Macaulay's writings with that sudden and lovely apostrophe in Carlyle, after describing the bloody horrors that followed the fall of the Bastille in 1789:—"O evening sun of July, how, at this hour, thy beams fall slant on reapers amid peaceful woody fields; on old women spinning in cottages; on ships far out in the silent main; on balls at the Orangerie of Versailles, where high-rouged dames of the Palace are even now dancing with double-jacketed Hussar-officers;—and also on this roaring Hell-porch of a Hôtel de Ville!" Who does not feel in this the breath of poetic inspiration, and how different it is from the mere composite of the rhetorician's imagination, assiduously working to order?

This remark is no disparagement of Macaulay's genius, but a classification of it. We are interrogating our own impressions, and asking ourselves among what kind of writers he ought to be placed. Rhetoric is a good and worthy art, and rhetorical authors are often more useful, more instructive, more really respectable than poetical authors. But it is to be said that Macaulay as a rhetorician will hardly be placed in the first rank by those who have studied both him and the great masters. Once more, no amount of embellishment or emphasis or brilliant figure suffices to produce this intense effect of agitation rigorously restrained; nor can any beauty of decoration be in the least a substitute for that touching and penetrative music which is made in prose by the repressed trouble of grave and high souls. There is a certain music, we do not deny, in Macaulay, but it is the music of a man everlastingly playing for us rapid solos on a silver trumpet, never the swelling diapasons of the organ, and never the deep ecstasies of the four magic strings. That so sensible a man as Macaulay should keep clear of the modern abomination of dithyrambic prose, that rank and sprawling weed of speech, was natural enough; but then the effects which we miss in him, and which, considering how strong the literary faculty in him really was, we are almost astonished to miss, are not produced by dithyramb but by repression. Of course the answer has been already given; Macaulay, powerful and vigorous as he was, had no agitation, no wonder, no tumult of spirit, to repress. The world was spread out clear before him; he read it as painly and as certainly as he read his books; life was all an affair of direct categoricals.

This was at least one secret of those hard modulations and shallow cadences. How poor is the rhythm of Macaulay's prose, we only realise by going with his periods fresh in our ear to some true master of harmony. It is not worth while to quote passages from an author who is in everybody's library, and Macaulay is always so much like himself that almost any one page will serve for an illustration exactly as well as any other. Let anyone turn to his character of Somers, for whom he had much admiration, and then turn to Clarendon's character of Falkland;—"a person of such prodigious parts of learning and knowledge, of that inimitable sweetness and delight in conversation, of so flowing and obliging a humanity and goodness to mankind, and of that primitive simplicity and integrity of life, that if there were no other brand upon this odious and accursed civil war than that single loss, it must be most infamous and execrable to all posterity." Now Clarendon is not a great writer, not even a good writer, for he is prolix and involved, yet we see that even Clarendon, when he comes to a matter in which his heart is engaged, becames sweet and harmonious in his rhythm. If we turn to a prose-writer of the very first place, we are instantly conscious of a still greater difference. How flashy and shallow Macaulay's periods seem as we listen to the fine ground-base that rolls in the melody of the following passage of Burke's, and it is taken from one of the least ornate of all his pieces:—

> You will not, we trust, believe, that, born in a civilized country, formed to gentle manners, trained in a merciful religion, and living in enlightened and polished times, where even foreign hostility is softened from its original sternness, we could have thought of letting loose upon you, our late beloved brethren, these fierce tribes of savages and cannibals, in whom the traces of human nature are effaced by ignorance and barbarity. We rather wished to have joined with you in bringing gradually that unhappy part of mankind into civility, order, piety, and virtuous discipline, than to have confirmed their evil habits and increased their natural ferocity by fleshing them in the slaughter of you, whom our wiser and better ancestors had sent into the wilderness with the express view of introducing, along with our holy religion, its humane and charitable manners. We do not hold that all things are lawful in war. We should think every barbarity, in fire, in wasting, in murders, in tortures, and other cruelties, too horrible and too full of turpitude for Christian mouths to utter or ears to hear, if done at our instigation, by those who we know will make war thus if they make it at all, to be, to all intents and purposes, as if done by ourselves. We clear ourselves to you our brethren, to the present age, and to future generations, to our king and our country, and to Europe, which, as a spectator, beholds this tragic scene, of every part or share in adding this last and worst of evils to the inevitable mischiefs of a civil war.
>
> We do not call you rebels and traitors. We do not call for the vengeance of the crown against you. We do not know how to qualify millions of our countrymen, contending with one heart for an admission to privileges which we have ever thought our own happiness and honor, by odious and unworthy names. On the contrary, we highly revere the principles on which you act, though we lament some of their effects. Armed as you are, we embrace you, as our friends and as our brethren by the best and dearest ties of relation.

It may be said that there is a patient injustice in comparing the prose of a historian criticising or describing great events at second hand, with the prose of a statesman taking active part in great events, fired by the passion of a present conflict, and stimulated by the vivid interest of undetermined issues. If this be a well grounded plea, and it may be so, then of course it excludes a contrast not only with Burke, but also with Bolingbroke, whose fine manners and polished gaiety give us a keen sense of the grievous garishness of Macaulay. If we may not imitate a comparison between Macaulay and great actors on the stage of affairs, at least there can be no objection to the introduction of Southey as a standard of comparison. Southey was a man of letters pure and simple, and it is worth remarking that Macaulay himself admitted that he found so great a charm in Southey's style, as nearly always to read it with pleasure, even when Southey was talking nonsense. Now, take any page of the Life of Nelson or the Life of Wesley; consider how easy, smooth, natural, and winning is the diction and the rise and fall of the sentence, and yet how varied the rhythm and how nervous the phrases; and then turn to a page of Macaulay, and wince under its stamping emphasis, its over-coloured tropes, its exaggerated expressions, its unlovely staccato. Southey's history of the Peninsular War is now dead, but if any of my readers has a copy on his highest shelves, I would venture to ask him to take down the third volume, and read the concluding pages, of which Coleridge used to say that they were the finest specimen of historic eulogy he had ever read in English, adding with forgivable hyperbole, that they were more to the Duke's fame and glory than a campaign. "Foresight and enterprise with our commander went hand in hand; he never advanced but so as to be sure of his retreat; and never retreated but in such an attitude as to impose upon a superior enemy," and so on through the sum of Wellington's achievements. "There was something more precious than these, more to be desired than the high and enduring fame which he had secured by his military achievements, the satisfaction of thinking to what end those achievements had been directed; that they were for the deliverance of two most injured and grievously oppressed nations; for the safety, honour, and welfare of his own country; and for the general interests of Europe and of the civilized world. His campaigns were sanctified by the cause; they were sullied by no cruelties, no crimes; the chariot-wheels of his triumphs have been followed by no curses;

his laurels are entwined with the amaranths of righteousness, and upon his death-bed he might remember his victories among his good works."

With this exquisite modulation still delighting the ear, we open Macaulay's Essays and stumble on such sentences as this: "That Tickell should have been guilty of a villany seems to us highly improbable. That Addison should have been guilty of a villany seems to us highly improbable. But that these two men should have conspired together to commit a villany seems to us improbable in a tenfold degree." Ὦ μιαρὸν, καὶ παμμιαρὸν, καὶ μιαρώτατον! *
Surely this is the very burlesque and travesty of a style. Yet it is a characteristic passage. It would be easy to find a thousand examples of the same vicious workmanship, and it would be difficult to find a page in which these cut and disjointed sentences are not the type and mode of the prevailing rhythm.

What is worse than want of depth and fineness of intonation in a period is all gross excess of colour, because excess of colour is connected with graver faults in the region of the intellectual conscience. Macaulay is a constant sinner in this respect. The wine of truth is in his cup a brandied draught, a hundred degrees above proof, and he too often replenishes the lamp of knowledge with naphtha instead of fine oil. It is not that he has a spontaneous passion for exuberant decoration, which he would have shared with more than one of the greatest names in literature. On the contrary, we feel that the exaggerated words and dashing sentences are the fruit of deliberate travail, and the petulance or the irony of his speech is mostly due to a driving predilection for strong effects. His memory, his directness, his aptitude for forcing things into firm outline, and giving them a sharply defined edge,—these and other singular talents of his all lent themselves to this intrepid and indefatigable pursuit of effect. And the most disagreeable feature is that Macaulay was so often content with an effect of an essentially vulgar kind, offensive to taste, discordant to the fastidious ear, and worst of all, at enmity with the whole spirit of truth. By vulgar we certainly do not mean homely, which marks a wholly different quality. No writer can be more homely than Mr. Carlyle,

* "Oh abominable, oh completely abominable, oh most abominable!"—ed.

alike in his choice of particulars to dwell upon, and in the terms
or images in which he describes or illustrates them, but there is
also no writer further removed from vulgarity. Nor do we mean
that Macaulay too copiously enriches the tongue with infusion
from any Doric dialect. For such raciness he had little taste. What
we find in him is that quality which the French call brutal. The
description, for instance, in the essay on Hallam, of the license of
the Restoration, seems to us a coarse and vulgar picture, whose
painter took the most garish colours he could find on his palette
and laid them on in untempered crudity. And who is not sensible
of the vulgarity and coarseness of the account of Boswell? "If he
had not been a great fool, he would not have been a great writer.
. . . he was a dunce, a parasite, and a coxcomb," and so forth, in
which the shallowness of the analysis of Boswell's character
matches the puerile rudeness of the terms. Here, again, is a sentence about Montesquieu. "The English at that time," Macaulay
says of the middle of the eighteenth century, "considered a
Frenchman who talked about constitutional checks and fundamental laws as a prodigy not less astonishing than the learned pig
or musical infant." And he then goes on to describe the author of
one of the most important books that ever were written as "specious but shallow, studious of effect, indifferent to truth—the
lively President," and so forth, stirring in any reader who happens
to know Montesquieu's influence, a singular amazement. We are
not concerned with the judgment upon Montesquieu, nor with the
truth as to contemporary English opinion about him, but a writer
who devises an antithesis to such as man as Montesquieu in
learned pigs and musical infants, deliberately condescends not
merely to triviality or levity but to flat vulgarity of thought, to
something of mean and ignoble association. Though one of the
most common, this is not Macaulay's only sin in the same unfortunate direction. He too frequently resorts to vulgar gaudiness.
For example, there is in one place a certain description of an
alleged practice of Addison's. Swift had said of Esther Johnson
that "whether from her easiness in general, or from her indifference to persons, or from her despair of mending them, or from
the same practice which she most liked in Mr. Addison, I cannot
determine; but when she saw any of the company very warm in a

wrong opinion, she was more inclined to confirm them in it than to oppose them. It prevented noise, she said, and saved time."[1] Let us behold what a picture Macaulay draws on the strength of this passage. "If his first attempts to set a presuming dunce right were ill-received," Macaulay says of Addison, "he changed his tone, 'assented with civil leer,' and lured the flattered coxcomb deeper and deeper into absurdity." To compare this transformation of the simplicity of the original into the grotesque heat and overcharged violence of the copy, is to see the homely maiden of a country village transformed into the painted flaunter of the city.

One more instance. We should be sorry to violate any sentiment of τὸ σεμνόν * about a man of Macaulay's genius, but what is a decorous term for a description of the doctrine of Lucretius's great poem, thrown in parenthetically, as the "silliest and meanest system of natural and moral philosophy"? Even disagreeable artifices of composition may be forgiven when they serve to vivify truth, to quicken or to widen the moral judgment, but Macaulay's hardy and habitual recourse to strenuous superlatives is fundamentally unscientific and untrue. There is no more instructive example in our literature than he, of the saying that the adjective is the enemy of the substantive.

In 1837 Jeffrey saw a letter written by Macaulay to a common friend, and stating the reasons for preferring a literary to a political life. Jeffrey thought that his illustrious ally was wrong in the conclusion to which he came. "As to the tranquillity of an author's life," he said, "I have no sort of faith in it. And as to fame, if an author's is now and then more lasting, it is generally longer withheld, and except in a few rare cases it is of a less pervading or elevating description. A great poet or a great *original* writer is above all other glory. But who would give much for such a glory as Gibbon's? Besides, I believe it is in the inward glow and pride of consciously influencing the destinies of mankind, much more than in the sense of personal reputation, that the delight of either poet or statesman chiefly consists." And Gibbon had at least the advantage of throwing himself into a controversy destined to endure for centuries. He, moreover, was specifically a

1. Forster's "Swift," i. 265.
* "reverence"—ed.

historian, while Macaulay has been prized less as a historian proper, than as a master of literary art. Now a man of letters, in an age of battle and transition like our own, fades into an ever-deepening distance, unless he has while he writes that touching and impressive quality,—the presentiment of the eve; a feeling of the difficulties and interests that will engage and distract mankind on the morrow. Nor can it be enough for enduring fame in any age merely to throw a golden halo round the secularity of the hour, or to make glorious the narrowest limitations of the passing day. If we think what a changed sense is already given to criticism, what a different conception now presides over history, how many problems on which he was silent are now the familiar puzzles of even superficial readers, we cannot help feeling that the eminent man whose life we are all about to read, is the hero of a past which is already remote, and that he did little to make men better fitted to face a present of which, close as it was to him, he seems hardly to have dreamed.

Part II

The Death of Mr. Mill

The tragic commonplaces of the grave sound a fuller note as we mourn for one of the greatest among the servants of humanity. A strong and pure light is gone out, the radiance of a clear vision and a beneficent purpose. One of those high and most worthy spirits to arise from time to time to stir their generation with new mental impulses in the deeper things, has perished from among us. The death of one who did so much to impress on his contemporaries that physical law works independently of moral law, marks with profounder emphasis the ever ancient and ever fresh decree that there is one end to the just and the unjust, and that the same strait tomb awaits alike the poor dead whom nature or circumstance imprisoned in mean horizons, and those who saw far and felt passionately and put their reason to noble uses. Yet the fulness of our grief is softened by a certain greatness and solemnity in the event. The teachers of men are so few, the gift of intellectual fatherhood is so rare, it is surrounded by such singular gloriousness. The loss of a powerful and generous states-man, or of a great master in letters or art, touches us with many a vivid regret. The Teacher, the man who has talents and has virtues, and yet has a further something which is neither talent nor virtue, and which gives him the mysterious secret of drawing men after him, leaves a deeper sense of emptiness than this; but lamentation is at once soothed and elevated by a sense of sacred-

This essay was first published in *Fortnightly Review,* n.s., 78 (June 1873): 669–76, and was reprinted in *Critical Miscellanies,* vol. 3 (London, 1886)—ed.

ness in the occasion. Even those whom Mr. Mill honoured with his friendship, and who must always bear to his memory the affectionate veneration of sons, may yet feel their pain at the thought that they will see him no more, raised into a higher mood as they mediate on the loftiness of his task and the steadfastness and success with which he achieved it. If it is grievous to think that such richness of culture, such full maturity of wisdom, such passion for truth and justice, are now by a single stroke extinguished, at least we may find some not unworthy solace in the thought of the splendid purpose they have served in keeping alive, and surrounding with new attractions, the difficult tradition of patient and accurate thinking in union with unselfish and magnanimous living.

Much will one day have to be said as to the precise value of Mr. Mill's philosophical principles, the more or less of his triumphs as a dialectician, his skill as a critic and an explorer, and his originality as a discoverer. However this trial may go, we shall at any rate be sure that with his reputation will stand or fall the intellectual repute of a whole generation of his countrymen. The most eminent of those who are now so fast becoming the front line, as death mows down the veterans, all bear traces of his influence, whether they are avowed disciples or avowed opponents. If they did not accept his method of thinking, at least he determined the questions which they should think about. For twenty years no one at all open to serious intellectual impressions has left Oxford without having undergone the influence of Mr. Mill's teaching, though it would be too much to say that in that grey temple where they are ever burnishing new idols, his throne is still unshaken. The professional chairs there and elsewhere are more and more being filled with men whose minds have been trained in his principles. The universities only typify his influence on the less learned part of the world. The better sort of journalists educated themselves on his books, and even the baser sort acquired a habit of quoting from them. He is the only writer in the world whose treatises on highly abstract subjects have been printed during his lifetime in editions for the people, and sold at the price of railway novels. Foreigners from all countries read his books as attentively as his most eager English disciples, and

sought his opinion as to their own questions with as much reverence as if he had been a native oracle. An eminent American who
came over on an official mission which brought him into contact
with most of the leading statesmen throughout Europe, said to
the present writer:—"The man who impressed me most of them
all was Stuart Mill; you placed before him the facts on which you
sought his opinion. He took them, gave you the different ways in
which they might fairly be looked at, balanced the opposing considerations, and then handed you a final judgment in which
nothing was left out. His mind worked like a splendid piece of
machinery; you supply it with raw material, and it turns you out
a perfectly finished product." Of such a man England has good
reason to be very proud.

He was stamped in many respects with specially English quality. He is the latest chief of a distinctively English school of
philosophy, in which, as has been said, the names of Locke,
Hume, Adam Smith, and Bentham, (and Mr. Mill would have
added—James Mill) mark the line of succession—the school
whose method subordinates imagination to observation, and
whose doctrine lays the foundations of knowledge in experience,
and the tests of conduct in utility. Yet, for all this, one of his most
remarkable characteristics was less English than French; his constant admission of an ideal and imaginative element in social
speculation, and a glowing persuasion that the effort and wisdom
and ingenuity of men are capable, if free opportunity is given by
social arrangements, of raising human destiny to a pitch that is at
present beyond our powers of conception. Perhaps the sum of
all his distinction lies in this union of stern science with infinite
aspiration, of rigorous sense of what is real and practicable with
bright and luminous hope. He told one who was speaking of
Condorcet's *Life of Turgot,* that in his younger days whenever
he was inclined to be discouraged, he was in the habit of turning
to this book, and that he never did so without recovering possession of himself. To the same friend, who had printed something
in this *Review* comparing Mr. Mill's repulse at Westminster with
the dismissal of the great minister of Lewis XVI., he wrote:—"I
never received so gratifying a compliment as the comparison of
me to Turgot; it is indeed an honour to me that such an assimilation should have occurred to you." Those who have studied the

character of one whom even the rigid Austin thought worthy to be called "the god-like Turgot," know both the nobleness and the rarity of this type.

Its force lies not in single elements but in that combination of an ardent interest in human improvement with a reasoned attention to the law of its conditions, which alone deserves to be honoured with the high name of wisdom. This completeness was one of the secrets of Mr. Mill's peculiar attraction for young men, and for the comparatively few women whose intellectual interest was strong enough to draw them to his books. He satisfied the ingenuous moral ardour which is instinctive in the best natures, until the dust of daily life dulls or extinguishes it, and at the same time he satisfied the rationalistic qualities, which are not less marked in the youthful temperament of those who by-and-by do the work of the world. This mixture of intellectual gravity with a passionate love of improvement in all the aims and instruments of life, made many intelligences alive, who would otherwise have slumbered, or sunk either into a dry pedantry on the one hand, or a windy, mischievous philanthrophy on the other. He showed himself so wholly free from the vulgarity of the sage. He could hope for the future, without taking his eye from the realities of the present. He recognised the social destination of knowledge, and kept the elevation of the great art of social existence ever before him, as the ultimate end of all speculative activity.

Another side of this rare combination was his union of courage with patience, of firm non-conformity with silent conformity. Compliance is always a question of degree, depending on time, circumstance, and subject. Mr. Mill hit the exact mean, equally distant from timorous caution and self-indulgent violence. He was unrivalled in the difficult art of conciliating as much support as was possible and alienating as little sympathy as possible, for novel and extremely unpopular opinions. He was not one of those who strive to spread new faiths by brilliant swordplay with buttoned foils, and he was not one of those who run amuck among the idols of the tribe and the marketplace and the theatre. He knew how to kindle the energy of all who were likely to be persuaded by his reasoning, without stimulating in a corresponding degree the energy of persons whose convictions he attacked. Thus he husbanded the strength of truth, and avoided wasteful friction. Probably no English writer that ever lived has done so much as Mr. Mill to cut at the very root of the theological spirit, yet there is only one passage in the whole of his writings—I mean a well-known passage in the book on Liberty—which could possibly give any offence to the most devout person. His conformity, one need hardly say, never went beyond the negative degree, nor ever passed beyond the conformity of silence. That guilty and grievously common pusillanimity which leads men to make or act hyprocritical professions, always moved his deepest abhorrence. And he did not fear publicly to testify his interest in the return of an atheist to parliament.

His courage was not of the spurious kind arising from anger, or ignorance of the peril, or levity, or a reckless confidence. These are all very easy. His distinction was that he knew all the danger to himself, was anxious to save pain to others, was buoyed up by no rash hope that the world was to be permanently bettered at a stroke, and yet for all this he knew how to present an undaunted front to a majority. The only fear he ever knew was fear lest a premature or excessive utterance should harm a good cause. He had measured the prejudices of men, and his desire to arouse this obstructive force in the least degree compatible with effective advocacy of any improvement, set the single limit to his intrepidity. Prejudices were to him like physical predispositions, with which you have to make your account. He knew, too, that they are often bound up with the most valuable elements in character and life, and hence he feared that violent surgery which in eradicating a false opinion fatally bruises at the same time a true and wholesome feeling which may cling to it. The patience which with some men is an instinct, and with others a fair name for indifference, was with him an acquisition of reason and conscience.

The value of this wise and virtuous mixture of boldness with tolerance, of courageous speech with courageous reserve, has been enormous. Along with his direct pleas for freedom of thought and freedom of speech, it has been the chief source of that liberty of expressing unpopular opinions in this country without social persecution, which is now so nearly complete, that he himself was at least astonished by it. The manner of his dialectic, firm and vigorous as the dialectic was in matter, has gradually introduced mitigating elements into the atmosphere of opinion. Partly, no doubt, the singular tolerance of free discussion which now prevails in England—I do not mean that it is at all perfect—arise from the prevalent scepticism, from indifference, and from the influence of some of the more highminded of the clergy. But Mr. Mill's steadfast abstinence from drawing wholesale indictments against persons or classes whose opinions he controverted, his generous candour, his scupulous respect for any germ of good in whatever company it was found, and his large allowances, contributed positive elements to what might otherwise have been the negative tolerance that comes of moral stagnation. Tolerance of distasteful notions in others became associated in his person at once with the widest enlightenment, and the strongest conviction of the truth of our own notions.

His career, besides all else, was a protest of the simplest and loftiest kind against some of the most degrading features of our society. No one is more alive than he was to the worth of all that adds grace and dignity to human life; but the sincerity of this feeling filled him with aversion for the make-believe dignity of a luxurious and artificial community. Without either arrogance or bitterness, he stood aloof from that conventional intercourse which is misnamed social duty. Without either discourtesy or cynicism, he refused to play a part in that dance of mimes which passes for life among the upper classes. In him, to extraordinary intellectual attainments was added the gift of a firm and steadfast self-respect, which unfortunately does not always go with them. He felt the reality of things, and it was easier for a workman than for a princess to obtain access to him. It is not always the men who talk most affectingly about our being all of one flesh and blood, who are proof against those mysterious charms of superior rank, which do so much to foster unworthy conceptions of life in English society; and there are many people capable of accepting Mr. Mill's social principles and the theoretical corollaries they contain, who yet would condemn his manly plainness and austere consistency in acting on them. The too common tendency in us all to moral slovenliness, and a lazy contentment with a little flaccid protest against evil, finds a constant rebuke in his career. The indomitable passion for justice which made him strive so long and so tenaciously to bring to judgment a public official, whom he conceived to be a great criminal, was worthy of one of the stoutest patriots in our seventeenth-century history. The same moral thoroughness stirred the same indignation in him on a more recent occasion, when he declared it "a permanent disgrace to the Government that the iniquitous sentence on the gas-stokers was not remitted as soon as passed."

Much of his most striking quality was owing to the exceptional degree in which he was alive to the constant tendency of society to lose some excellence of aim, to relapse at some point from the standard of truth and right which had been reached by long previous effort, to fall back in height of moral ideal. He was keenly sensible that it is only by persistent striving after improvement in our conceptions of duty, and improvement in the external means for realising them, that even the acquisitions of past generations are retained. He knew the intense difficulty of making life better by ever so little. Hence at once the exaltation of his own ideas of truth and right, and his eagerness to conciliate anything like virtuous social feeling, in whatever intellectual or political association he found it. Hence also the vehemence of his passion for the unfettered and unchecked development of new ideas on all subjects, of originality in moral and and social points of view; because repression, whether by public opinion or in any other way, may be the means of untold waste of gifts that might have conferred on mankind unspeakable benefits. The discipline and vigour of his understanding made him the least indulgent of judges to anything like charlatanry, and effectually prevented his willingness to let the smallest good element be lost, from degenerating into that weak kind of universalism which nullifies some otherwise good men.

Some great men seize upon us by the force of an imposing and majestic authority; their thoughts impress the imagination, their words are winged, they are as prophets bearing high testimony that cannot be gainsaid. Bossuet, for instance, or Pascal. Others, and of these Mr. Mill was one, acquire disciples not by a commanding authority, but by a moderate and impersonal kind of persuasion. He appeals not to our sense of greatness and power in a teacher, which is noble, but to our love of finding and embracing truth for ourselves, which is still nobler. People who like their teacher to be as a king publishing decrees with herald and trumpet, perhaps find Mr. Mill colourless. Yet this habitual effacement of his own personality marked a delicate and very rare shade in his reverence for the sacred purity of truth.

Meditation on the influence of one who has been the foremost instructor of his time in wisdom and goodness quickly breaks off, in this hour when his loss is fresh upon us, and changes into affectionate reminiscences for which silence is most fitting. In such an hour thought turns rather to the person, than the work, of the master whom we mourn. We recall his purity, simplicity, gentleness, heroic self-abnegation; his generosity in encouraging, his eager readiness in helping; the warm kindliness of his accost, the friendly brightening of the eye. The last time I saw him was a few days before he left England. He came to spend a day with me in the country, of which the following rough notes happened to be written at the time in a letter to a friend:—

> He came down by morning train to G. station, where I was waiting for him. He was in his most even and mellow humour. We walked in a leisurely way and through roundabout tracks for some four hours along the ancient green road which you know, over the high grassy downs, into old chalk pits picturesque with juniper and yew, across heaths and commons, and so up to our windy promontory, where the majestic prospect stirred him with lively delight. You know he is a fervent botanist, and every ten minutes he stooped to look at this or that on the path. Unluckily
>
> I am ignorant of the very rudiments of the matter, so his parenthetic enthusiasms were lost upon me.
>
> Of course he talked, and talked well. He admitted that Goethe had added new points of view to life, but has a deep dislike of his moral character; wondered how a man who could draw the sorrows of a deserted woman like Aurelia, in *Wilhelm Meister,* should yet have behaved so systematically ill to women. Goethe tried as hard as he could to be a Greek, yet his failure to produce any thing perfect in form except a few lyrics proves the irresistible expansion of the modern spirit, and the inadequateness of the Greek type to modern needs of activity and expression. Greatly

prefers Schiller in all respects; turning to him from Goethe is like going into the fresh air from a hot-house.

Spoke of style; thinks Goldsmith unsurpassed; then Addison comes. Greatly dislikes the style of Junius and of Gibbon; indeed thinks meanly of the latter in all respects, except for his research, which alone of the work of that century stands the test of nineteenth-century criticism. Did not agree with me that George Sand's is the high-water mark of prose, but yet could not name anybody higher, and admitted that her prose stirs you like music.

Seemed disposed to think that the most feasible solution of the Irish University question is a Catholic University, the restrictive and obscurantist tendencies of which you may expect to have checked by the active competition of life with men trained in more enlightened systems. Spoke of Home Rule.

Made remarks on the difference in the feeling of modern refusers of Christianity as compared with that of men like his father, impassioned deniers, who believed that if only you broke up the power of the priest and checked superstition, all would go well—a dream from which they were partially awakened by seeing that the French revolution, which overthrew the Church, still did not bring the millennium. His radical friends used to be very angry with him for loving Wordsworth. 'Wordsworth, I used to say, is against you, no doubt, in the battle which you are now waging, but after you have won, the world will need more than ever those qualities which Wordsworth is keeping alive and nourishing.' In his youth mere negation of religion was a firm bond of union, social and otherwise, between men who agreed in nothing else.

Spoke of the modern tendency to pure theism, and met the objection that it retards improvement by turning the minds of some of the best men from social affairs, by the counter-proposition that it is useful to society, apart from the question of its truth,—useful as a provisional belief, because people will identify serviceable ministry to men with service of God. Thinks we cannot with any sort of precision define the coming modification of religion, but anticipates that it will undoubtedly rest upon the solidarity of mankind, as Comte said, and as you and I believe. Perceives two things, at any rate, which are likely to lead men to invest this with the moral authority of a religion; first, they will become more and more impressed by the awful fact that a piece of conduct to-day may prove a curse to men and women scores and even hundreds of years after the author of it is dead; and second, they will more and more feel that they can only satisfy their sentiment of gratitude to seen or unseen benefactors, can only repay the untold benefits they have inherited, by diligently maintaining the traditions of service.

And so forth, full of interest and suggestiveness all through. When he got here, he chatted to R. over lunch with something of the simple amiableness of a child about the wild flowers, the ways of insects, and notes of birds. He was impatient for the song of the nightingale. Then I drove him to our roadside station, and one of the most delightful days of my life came to its end, like all other days, delightful and sorrowful.

Alas, the sorrowful day which ever dogs our delight, followed very quickly. The nightingale that he longed for fills the darkness with music, but not for the ear of the dead master; he rests in the deeper darkness where is unbroken silence. We may console ourselves with the reflection offered by the dying Socrates to his sorrowful companions; he who has arrayed the soul in her own proper jewels of moderation, and justice and courage, and nobleness and truth, is ever ready for the journey when his time comes. We have lost a great teacher and example of knowledge and virtue, but men will long feel the presence of his character, making them ashamed of what is indolent or selfish, and encouraging them to all disinterested labour, both in trying to do good, and in trying to find out what the good is,—which is harder.

Mr. Mill's
Doctrine of Liberty

Mr. Mill's memorable plea for social liberty was little more than an enlargement, though a very important enlargement, of the principles of the still more famous Speech for Liberty of Unlicensed Printing with which Milton ennobled English literature two centuries before. Milton contended for free publication of opinion mainly on these grounds: First, that the opposite system implied the "grace of infallibility and incorruptibleness" in the licensers. Second, that the prohibition of bold books led to mental indolence and stagnant formalism both in teachers and congregations, producing the "laziness of a licensing church." Third, that it "hinders and retards the importation of our richest merchandise, truth," for the commission of the licenser enjoins him to let nothing pass which is not vulgarly received already, and "if it come to prohibiting, there is not aught more likely to be prohibited than truth itself, whose first appearance to our eyes, bleared and dimmed with prejudice and custom, is more unsightly and unplausible than many errors, even as the person is of many a great man slight and contemptible to see to." Fourth, that freedom is in itself an ingredient of true virtue, and "they are not skilful considerers of human things who imagine to remove sin by removing the matter of sin; that virtue therefore, which is but a youngling in the contemplation of evil, and knows not the utmost that vice promises to her followers, and rejects it, is but a blank

This essay was first published in *Fortnightly Review,* n.s., 80 (August 1873): 234–56—ed.

virtue, not a pure; her virtue is but an excremental virtue, which was the reason why our sage and and serious poet Spenser, whom I dare be known to think a better teacher than Scotus or Aquinas, describing true temperance under the form of Guion, brings him in with his palmer through the cave of Mammon and the tower of earthly bliss, that he might see and know and yet abstain."

The four grounds on which Mr. Mill contends for the necessity of freedom in the expression of opinion to the mental well-being of mankind are virtually contained in these. His four grounds are, (1) that the silenced opinion may be true; (2) it may contain a portion of truth, essential to supplement the prevailing opinion; (3) vigorous contesting of opinions that are even wholly true is the only way of preventing them from sinking to the level of uncomprehended prejudices; (4) without such contesting, the doctrine will lose its vital effect on character and conduct.

But Milton drew the line of liberty at what he calls "neighbour-ing differences, or rather indifferences." The Arminian contro-versy had loosened the bonds with which the newly liberated churches of the Reformation had made haste to bind them-selves again, and weakened that authority of confession, which had replaced the older but not more intolerant authority of the universal church. Other controversies which raged during the first half of the seventeenth century,—those between Catholics and Protestants, between prelatists and presbyterians, between Socinians and Trinitarians, between latitudinarians, puritans, and sacramentalists,—all tended to weaken theological exclusiveness. This slackening, however, was no more than partial. Roger Wil-liams, indeed, the Welsh founder of Rhode Island, preached, as early as 1631, the principles of an unlimited toleration, extend-ing to Catholics, Jews, and even infidels. Milton stopped a long way short of this. He did not mean "tolerated popery and open superstition, which, as it extirpates all religious and civil supremacies, so itself should be extirpate, provided first that all charitable and compassionate means be used to win and regain the weak and the misled: that also which is impious or evil absolutely either against faith or manners no law can possibly permit that intends not to unlaw itself."

Locke, writing five and forty years later, somewhat widened these limitations. His question was not merely whether there should be free expression of opinion, but whether there should furthermore be freedom of worship and of religious union. He answered both questions affirmatively,—not on the semi-sceptical grounds of Jeremy Taylor, which is also one of the grounds taken by Mr. Mill, that we cannot be sure that our own opinion is the true one,—but on the strength of his definition of the province of the civil magistrate. Locke held that the magistrate's whole juris-diction reached only to civil concernments, and that "all civil power, right, and dominion, is bounded to that only care of promoting these things; and that it neither can nor ought in any manner to be extended to the saving of souls. This chiefly because the power of the civil magistrate consists only in outward force, while true and saving religion consists in the inward persuasion of the mind, without which nothing can be acceptable to God, and such is the nature of the understanding that it cannot be compelled to the belief of anything by outward force. . . . It is only light and evidence that can work a change in men's opinions; and that light can in no manner proceed from corporal sufferings, or any other outward penalties." "I may grow rich by an art that I take not delight in; I may be cured of some disease by remedies that I have not faith in; but I cannot be saved by a religion that I distrust and a ritual that I abhor." (*First Letter concerning Toleration.*) And much more in the same excellent vein. But Locke fixed limits to toleration. 1. No opinions contrary to human society, or to those moral rules which are necessary to the pres-ervation of civil society, are to be tolerated by the magistrate. Thus, to take examples from our own day, a conservative minister would think himself right on this principle in suppressing the Land and Labour League, a Catholic minister in dissolving the Education League, and any minister in making mere membership of the Mormon sect a penal offence. 2. No tolerance ought to be extended to "those who attribute unto the faithful, religious, and orthodox, that is in plain terms unto themselves, any peculiar privilege or power above other mortals, in civil concernments; or who upon pretence of religion do challenge any manner of authority over such as are not associated with them in their ecclesiastical communion." As I have seldom heard of any sect, except the Friends, who did not challenge as much authority as it could possibly get over persons not associated with it, this would amount to a universal proscription of religion; but Locke's principle might at any rate be invoked against Ultramontanism in some circumstances. 3. Those are not at all to be tolerated who deny the being of God. The taking away of God, *though but even in thought,* dissolves all society; and promises, covenents, and oaths, which are the bonds of human society, have no hold on such. Thus the police ought to close Mr. Bradlaugh's Hall of Science, and perhaps on some occasions the Positivist School.

Locke's principles depended on a distinction between civil concernment, which he tries to define, and all other concernments. Warburton's arguments on the alliance between church and state turned on the same point, as did the once famous Bangorian controversy. This distinction would fit into Mr. Mill's cardinal position, which consists in a distinction between the things that only affect the doer or thinker of them, and the things that affect other persons as well. Locke's attempt to divide civil affairs from affairs of salvation was satisfactory enough for the comparatively narrow object with which he opened his discussion. Mr. Mill's account of civil affairs is both wider and more definite; naturally so, as he had to maintain the cause of tolerance in a much more complex set of social conditions, and amid a far greater diversity of speculative energy, than any one dreamed of in Locke's time. Mr. Mill limits the province of the civil magistrate to the repression of acts that directly and immediately injure others than the doer of them. So long as acts, including the expression of opinions, are purely self-regarding, it seems to him expedient in the long run that they should not be interfered with by the magistrate. He goes much further than this. Self-regarding acts should not be interfered with by the magistrate; not only self-regarding acts, but all opinions whatever, should, moreover, be as little interfered with as possible by public opinion, except in the way of vigorous argumentation and earnest persuasion in a contrary direction; the silent but most impressive solicitation of virtuous example; the wise and careful upbringing of the young, so that when they enter life they may be most nobly fitted to choose the right opinions and obey the right motives.

The considerations by which he supports this rigorous confinement of external interference on the part of government, or the unorganized members of the community whose opinion is called public opinion, to cases of self-protection, are these, some of which have been already stated:—

1. By interfering to suppress opinions or experiments in living, you may resist truths and improvements in a greater or less degree.

2. Constant discussion is the only certain means of preserving the freshness of truth in men's minds, and the vitality of its influence upon their conduct and motives.

3. Individuality is one of the most valuable elements of well-being, and you can only be sure of making the most of individuality if you have an atmosphere of freedom, encouraging free development and expansion.

4. Habitual resort to repressive means of influencing conduct tends more than anything else to discredit and frustrate the better means, such as education, good example, and the like.

The principle which he deduces from these considerations is— "that the sole end for which mankind are warranted, individually or collectively, in interfering with the liberty of action of any of their number is self-protection; the only purpose for which power can be rightfully exercised over any member of a civilised community, is to prevent harm to others. His own good, either physical or moral, is not a sufficient warrant. He cannot be rightfully compelled to do or forbear because it will make him happier, because in the opinion of others to do so would be wise, or even right. These are good reasons for remonstrating with him, or reasoning with him, or persuading him, or entreating him, but not for compelling him, or visiting him with any evil in case he do otherwise. To justify that, the conduct from which it is desired to deter him must be calculated to produce evil to others."

Two disputable points in the above doctrine are likely at once to reveal themselves to the least critical eye. First, that doctrine would seem to check the free expression of disapproval; one of the most wholesome and indispensable duties which anybody with interest in serious questions has to perform, and the non-performance of which would remove the most proper and natural penalty from frivolous or perverse opinions and obnoxious conduct. Mr. Mill deals with this difficulty as follows:—"We have a right in various ways to act upon our unfavourable opinion of any one, not to the oppression of his individuality, but in the exercise of ours. We are not bound, for example, to seek his society; we have a right to avoid it (though not to parade the avoidance), for we have a right to choose the society most accept-able to us. We have a right, and it may be our duty, to caution others against him, if we think his example or conversation likely to have a pernicious effect on those with whom he associates. We may give others a preference over him in optional good offices, except those which tend to his improvement. In these various modes a person may suffer very severe penalties at the hands of others for faults which directly concern only himself; but he suffers these penalties only in so far as they are the natural, and as it were the spontaneous, consequences of the faults themselves, not because they are purposely inflicted on him for the sake of punishment." This appears to be a satisfactory way of meeting the objection. For though the penalties of disapproval may be just the same, whether deliberately inflicted, or naturally and spontaneously falling on the object of such disapproval, yet there is a very intelligible difference between the two processes in their effect on the two parties concerned. A person imbued with Mr. Mill's principle would feel the responsibility of censorship much more seriously; would reflect more carefully and candidly about the conduct or opinion of which he thought ill; would be more on his guard against pharisaic censoriousness and that desire to be ever judging one another, which Milton well called the strong-hold of our hypocrisy. The disapproval of such a person would have an austere colour, a gravity, a self-respecting reserve, which could never belong to an equal degree of disapproval in a person who had started from the officious principle, that if we are sure we are right, it is straightway our business to make the person whom we think wrong smart for his error. And in the same way such disapproval would be much more impressive to the person whom it affected. If it was justified, he would be like a froward child who is always less effectively reformed—if reformable at all—by angry chidings and passionate punishments, than by the sight of a cool and austere displeasure which lets him persist in his forwardness if he chooses.

The second weak point in the doctrine lies in the extreme vagueness of the terms, protective and self-regarding. The practical difficulty begins with the definition of these terms. Can any opinion or any serious part of conduct be looked upon as truly and exclusively self-regarding? This central ingredient in the discussion seems insufficiently laboured in the essay on Liberty. Yet it is here more than anywhere else that controversy is needed to clear up what is in just as much need of elucidation, whatever view we may take of the inherent virtue of freedom—whether we look on freedom as a mere negation, or as one of the most powerful positive conditions of attaining the highest kind of human excellence.

We may best estimate the worth and the significance of the doctrine of liberty by considering the line of thought and observation which led to it. To begin with, it is in Mr. Mill's hands something quite different from the same doctrine as preached by the French revolutionary school; indeed one might even call it reactionary in respect of the French theory of a hundred years back. It reposes on no principle of abstract right, but like all the rest of its author's opinions, on principles of utility and experience. Dr. Arnold used to divide reformers into two classes, popular and liberal; the first he defined as seekers of liberty, the second as seekers of improvement; the first were the goats, and the second were the sheep. Mr. Mill's doctrine denied the mutual exclusiveness of the two parts of this classification, for it made improvement the end and the test, but it proclaimed liberty to be the means. Every thinker now perceives that the strongest and most durable influences in every western society lead in the direction of democracy, and tend with more or less rapidity to throw the control of social organization into the hands of numerical majorities. There are many people who believe that if you only make the ruling body big enough, it is sure to be either very wise itself, or very eager to choose wise leaders. Mr. Mill, as any one who is familiar with his writings is well aware, did not hold this opinion. He had no more partiality for mob rule than De Maistre or Goethe or Mr. Carlyle. He saw its evils more clearly than any of these eminent men, because he had a more scientific eye, and because he had had the invaluable training of a political administrator on a large scale and in a most responsible post. But he did not content himself with seeing these evils, and he wasted no energy in passionate denunciation of them, which he knew must prove futile. Guizot said of De Tocqueville that he was an aristocrat who accepted his defeat. Mr. Mill was too penetrated by popular sympathies to be an aristocrat in De Tocqueville's sense, but he, likewise, was full of ideas and hopes which the unchecked or undirected course of democracy would defeat without chance of reparation. This fact he accepted, and from this he started. Mr. Carlyle, and one or two rhetorical imitators, poured malediction on the many-headed populace, and with a rather pitiful impatience insisted that the only hope for men lay in their finding and obeying a strong man, a king, a hero, a dictator. How he was to be found, neither the master nor his still angrier and more impatient mimics could ever tell us. The scream of this whole school is a mockery.

Now Mr. Mill's doctrine laid down the main condition of finding your hero; namely, that all ways should be left open to him, because no man, nor majority of men, could possibly tell by which of these ways their deliverers were from time to time destined to present themselves. Wits have caricatured all this by asking us whether by encouraging the tares to grow you give the wheat a better chance. This is as misleading as such metaphors usually are. The doctrine of liberty rests on a faith drawn from the observation of human progress, that though we know wheat to be serviceable and tares to be worthless, yet there are in the great seed-plot of human nature a thousand rudimentary germs, not wheat and not tares, of whose properties we have not had a fair opportunity of assuring ourselves. If you are too eager to pluck up the tares, you are very likely to pluck up with them these untried possibilities of human excellence, and you are, moreover, very likely to injure the growing wheat as well. The demonstration of this lies in the recorded experience of mankind.

Nor is this all. Mr. Mill's doctrine does not lend the least countenance to the cardinal opinion of some writers in the last century, that the only need of human character and of social institutions is to be let alone. He never said that we were to leave the ground uncultivated to bring up whatever might chance to grow. On the contrary, the ground was to be cultivated with the utmost care and knowledge, and with a view to prevent the growth of tares—but cultivated in a certain manner. You may take the method of the Inquisition, of the more cruel of the

Puritans, of De Maistre, of Mr. Carlyle; or you may take Mr. Mill's method of cultivation. According to the doctrine of Liberty, we are to devote ourselves to prevention, as the surest and most wholesome mode of extirpation. Persuade, argue, cherish virtuous example; bring up the young in habits of right opinion and right motive; shape your social arrangements so as to stimulate the best parts of character. By these means you will gain all the advantages that could possibly have come of heroes and legislative dragooning, as well as a great many more which neither heroes nor legislative dragooning could ever have secured.

It is well with men, Mr. Mill said moreover, in proportion as they respect truth. Now they at once prove and strengthen their respect for truth by having an open mind to all its possibilities, while at the same time they hold firmly to their own proved convictions, until they hear better evidence to the contrary. There is no anarchy, nor uncertainty, nor paralysing air of provisionalness in such a frame of mind. So far it is from being fatal to loyalty or reverence, that it is an indispensable part of the groundwork of the only loyalty that a wise ruler or teacher would care to inspire—the loyalty springing from a rational conviction that in a field open to all comers he is the best man they can find. Only on condition of liberty without limit is the ablest and most helpful of "heroes" sure to be found; and only on condition of liberty without limit are his followers sure to be worthy of him. You must have authority, and yet must have obedience. The noblest and deepest and most beneficient kind of authority is that which rests on an obedience that is rational, deliberate, and spontaneous.

The same futile impatience which animates the political utterances of Mr. Carlyle and his more weak-voiced imitators, takes another form in men of a different training or temperament. They insist that if the majority has the means of preventing vice by law, it is folly and weakness not to resort to those means. The superficial attractiveness of such a doctrine is obvious. Criminal lawyers and passionate philanthropists treat it as self-evident. The doctrine of liberty implies a broader and a more patient view. It says:—"Even if you could be sure that what you take for vice is so—and the history of persecution shows how careful you should be in this preliminary point—even then it is an undoubted and, indeed, a necessary tendency of this facile repressive legislation to make those who resort to it, neglect the more effective, humane, and durable kinds of preventive legislation. You pass a law (if you can) putting down drunkenness; there is a neatness in such a method very attractive to fervid and impatient natures. Would you not have done better to leave that law unpassed, and apply yourselves sedulously instead to the improvement of the dwellings of the more drunken class, to the provision of amusements that might compete with the ale-house, to the extension and elevation of instruction, and so on? You may say that this should be done, and yet the other should not be left undone; but, as matter of fact and history, the doing of the one has always gone with the neglect of the other, and ascetic law-making in the interests of virtue, has never been accompanied either by law-making or any other kinds of activity for making virtue easier or more attractive. It is the recognition how little punishment can do, that leaves men free to see how much social prevention can do." I believe, then, that what seems to the criminal lawyers and passionate philanthropists self-evident, is in truth an illusion, springing from a very shallow kind of impatience, heated in some of them by the addition of a cynical contempt for human nature and the worth of human existence.

If people believe that the book of social or moral knowledge is now completed, that we have turned over the last page and heard the last word, much of the foundation of Mr. Mill's doctrine would disappear. But those who hold this can hardly have much to congratulate themselves upon. If it were so, and if governments were to accept the principle that the only limits to the enforcement of the moral standard of the majority are the narrow expediencies of each special case, without reference to any deep and comprehensive principle covering all the largest social considerations, why then the society to which we ought to look with most admiration and envy is the Eastern Empire during the ninth and tenth centuries, when the Byzantine system of a thorough subordination of the spiritual power had fully consolidated itself.

Mr. Stephen's recent examination of Mr. Mill's doctrine does not seem to contribute much to its rectification. Many passages in that examination read as if the author had not by any means grasped the principle which he repudiates in so operose a manner. The dialectic has an imposing air of strictness and cogency, yet it continually lands you in the fallacy of Irrelevancy. Mr. Stephen labours certain propositions which Mr. Mill never denied, such as that society ought to have a moral standard and ought to act upon it. He proves the contradictory of assertions which his adversary never made, as when he cites judicial instances which imply the recognition of morality by the law. He wishes to prove that social coercion would in many cases tend to make men virtuous. He does so by proving that the absence of coercion does not tend in such cases to make men virtuous. Of course the latter proposition is no more equivalent to the former, than the demonstration of the inefficacy of one way of treating disease is equal to a demonstration of the efficacy of some other way. A short glance at some of Mr. Stephen's propositions will be a convenient mode of setting Mr. Mill's doctrine in a clearer light.

1. "Before he affirmed that in Western Europe and America the compulsion of adults for their own good is unjustifiable, Mr. Mill ought to have proved that there are among us no considerable differences in point of wisdom, or that if there are, the wiser part of the community does not wish for the welfare of the less wise." Why so? Mr. Mill's very proposition is that though there is a wiser part, and though the wiser part may wish well to the less wise, *yet* even then the disadvantages of having a wise course forced upon the members of civilised societies exceed the disadvantages of following an unwise course freely. Mr. Stephen's allegation of the points which Mr. Mill should have proved, rests on the assumption of the very matter at issue—namely, whether freedom is not in itself so valuable an element in social life (in civilised communities), that for the sake of it we should be content to let the unwiser part have their own way in what concerns themselves only.

2. "Look at our own time and country, and mention any single great change which has been effected by mere discussion. Can a single case be mentioned in which the passions of men were interested where the change was not carried by fear—that is to say ultimately by the fear of revolution?" It may be said, parenthetically, first, that it was free discussion which converted the force, and brought it over to the side of the change; say Free

Trade, or the Reform of Parliament, or the Irish Land Act. And secondly, that there is all the difference between the fear of a revolution and a revolution actual, and this is a powerful argument in favour of the unlimited discussion which Mr. Mill vindicates, and of the social system that favours it. But, apart from this, have these great changes been made by force in the sphere which Mr. Mill set apart from the operation of force? Was the imposition of the corn-duties a purely self-regarding act? Did the duties hurt nobody but the imposers? Was the exclusion of householders under ten pounds rental from the electoral body a self-regarding act? If not, Mr. Stephen is only beating the air by this talk about force being the *ultima ratio*. It is an organic part of Mr. Mill's doctrine that the whole social force may be exerted in matters which concern others than the doers. Then, Mr. Stephen retorts, "the principle cannot be applied to the very cases in which it is most needed—cases where men happen to be living under a political or social system with the principles or with the working of which they are not satisfied, and in which they may fight out their differences, the conqueror determining the matter in dispute according to his own will." Is this in the least degree true? Take the most memorable of these cases, the first French Revolution. Will Mr. Stephen seriously contend that the principle of leaving self-regarding acts alone could not have been applied to any parts of that transaction? Hardly so, if he reflects that the most monstrous acts of the Revolution were exactly due to the neglect of this very truth, that there is a province of thought and action—the self-regarding, namely—which ought to be free from social or legislative interference. It was precisely because the Jacobins, headed by Robespierre and Saint Just, borrowed the principles of Hobbes and Rousseau, as Mr. Stephen does; it was precisely because they rode roughshod over such a principle as Mr. Mill's, interfered alike with self-regarding conviction and self-regarding act, and adopted Mr. Stephen's formula of the *à priori* expediency of identifying the law-maker and the moralist, that the worst exploits and most fantastic aspirations which are associated with the French Revolution stained and perverted the movement. To say therefore that Mr. Mill's principle is incapable of application in the cases where it is most needed, or that "it assumes the existence of an ideal state of things in which every one has precisely the position which he ought to hold," is either to forget the most tremendous event in modern history, or else to show that you have never fully considered what Mr. Mill's principle is.

3. "If the object aimed at is good, if the compulsion employed such as to attain it, and *if the good obtained overbalances the inconvenience of the compulsion, I do not understand how upon utilitarian principles the compulsion can be bad.* I may add that this way of stating the case shows that Mr. Mill's simple principle is really a paradox. It can be justified only by showing as a fact that, self-protection apart, no good object can be attained by any compulsion which is not in itself a greater evil than the absence of the object which the compulsion obtains." The words in italics are introduced in a way, and have a significance, which show that, strange as it may appear, Mr. Stephen failed from beginning to end of his criticism to see that the very aim and object of Mr. Mill's essay is to show on utilitarian principles that compulsion in a definite class of cases, the self-regarding parts of conduct namely, and in societies of a certain degree of development, is always bad. Mr. Stephen's third proviso in the above quotation could never be complied with in self-regarding acts, according to his adversary's doctrine, and that it could never be complied with, was the central object of Mr. Mill's reasoning. He did show, or thought he had shown, that "as a fact," the good obtained in self-regarding acts could not overbalance the general inconvenience of the compulsion. I do not see that Mr. Stephen has anywhere directly confronted this position in the only manner proper to confute it, namely, by an enumeration, first, of the advantages of compulsion in self-regarding acts, second, of its disadvantages, followed by an attempt to strike the balance between the sum of the advantages and the sum of the disadvantages. The last three lines of the above quotation involve a similar misunderstanding. What Mr. Mill had to show was, not that any good object attained by compulsion was "in itself" a greater evil than the absence of the object procured by the compulsion, but something quite different, namely this; that though compulsion may procure objects which are good, yet the general consequences of the compulsion more than counterbalance the special good. Thus, to take a well-known illustration; sobriety might perhaps

be procured by some form of coercive legislation, but the evil inherent in such legislation, its enervating effect on character, its replacement of self-control, self-respect, and the rest, by a protective paternal will from without, would more than counterbalance the advantages of sobriety so gained. This may be a mistake. Mr. Mill may or may not prove his case. But where is the sense of calling such a position a paradox?

Hence Mr. Stephen's third and favourite test of the utility of coercion,—that it should not be employed at too great an expense —is a mere *ignoratio elenchi** as against Mr. Mill, who held that in all self-regarding matters it was necessarily employed at too great an expense. This position Mr. Mill defended on strictly utilitarian principles, which have been already stated. Mr. Stephen has missed one of the cardinal points in the whole contention, that "it is of importance not only what men do, but also what manner of men they are that do it." It is its robust and bracing influence on character which makes wise men prize freedom, and strive for the enlargement of its province. "They are not skilful considerers of human things," wrote Milton, "who imagine to remove sin by removing the matter of sin. Though ye take from a covetous man his treasure, he has yet one jewel left, ye cannot bereave him of his covetousness. Banish all objects of lust, shut up all youth into the severest discipline that can be exercised in any hermitage, ye cannot make them chaste that came not thither so. Suppose we could expel sin by this means; look how much we thus expel of sin, so much we expel of virtue. And were I the chooser, a dram of well-doing should be preferred before many times as much the forcible hindrance of evil-doing. For God sure esteems the growth and completing of one virtuous person more than the restraint of ten vicious."

The same omission to recognise that the positive quality of liberty is the essence of the doctrine which Mr. Stephen has hastily taken upon himself to disprove, is seen in such statements as that "Discussions about liberty are in truth discussions about a negation. Attempts to solve the problems of government and society by such discussions are like attempts to discover the nature of light and heat by inquiries into darkness and cold." This, by

* "ignorance of truth"—ed.

the way, is not so felicitous as Mr. Stephen's illustrations sometimes are, for assuredly he would be a very wretched kind of
investigator who thought he could discover the laws of heat
without reference to the conditions of cold, or the laws of light
without reference to the conditions of darkness. But is it true that
liberty is a negation? You may certainly say, if you choose, that
freedom from import duties is a negation, but even then I am
not aware that the comparative advantages of free trade and
protection are incapable of being profitably discussed. Mr. Mill,
however, held that liberty was much more than a negation; and
that there is plenty of evidence in the various departments of the
history of civilisation that freedom exerts a number of positively
progressive influences. It was Mr. Stephen's business to refute
this, if he could. That he has failed to do so, further than by a
number of blunt assertions and reassertions to the contrary, is a
proof either that he was not able to refute the most essential part
of Mr. Mill's doctrine, or else that he did not perceive in what
its essential part consisted. Metaphors about wasps in a garden,
and imaginary dialogues with the waters of a stagnant marsh,
and the like, really do not help us. Mr. Stephen had to prove two
things. First he had to show that freedom from interference in
the expression of opinion and in purely self-regarding acts, is not
a good thing in its general consequences. Most people, he says,
cannot be improved by free discussion. "I confine myself to saying
that the utmost conceivable liberty would not in the least degree
tend to improve them." But he should not have confined himself
to saying this. He should have tried to demonstrate it, which I
cannot see that he does. Second, Mr. Stephen had to show that
though liberty cannot improve people, compulsion or restraint
can. Instead of this, he takes for granted that because liberty
would not improve people, therefore compulsion must. An assumption that begs the whole question at issue.

Mr. Carlyle, more tersely than Mr. Stephen, has boldly said, in
one of the Latter Day Pamphlets, that most people are fools. Mr.
Mill himself in the book which has occasioned the present controversy has said something of the same sort. The essay on Liberty
is in fact one of the most aristocratic books ever written (I do not
mean British aristocratic, "with the politest and gracefullest kind
of woman to wife"). It is not Mr. Carlyle, but Mr. Mill, who

speaks of "that miscellaneous collection of a few wise and many foolish individuals, called the public." "No government by a democracy or a numerous aristocracy ever did or could rise above mediocrity, except in so far as the sovereign Many have let themselves be guided by the counsel and influence of a more highly gifted and instructed One or Few. The initiation of all wise or noble things comes and must come from individuals; generally at first from some one individual." "On any matter not self-evident, there are ninety-nine persons totally incapable of judging of it, for one who is capable." In the face of passages like these it is rather absurd to say that "the great defect of Mr. Mill's later writings is that he has formed too favourable an estimate of human nature"; and it is particularly absurd in a writer who, two hundred pages further on in the very same book, assures us that it would be easy to show from Mr. Mill's later works, "what a low opinion he has of mankind at large." Which of the two contradictory assertions that he has made does Mr. Stephen elect to stand by?

But now mark the use which Mr. Mill makes of his proposition that ninety-nine men are incapable of judging a matter not self-evident, and only one man capable. For this reason, he argues, leave the utmost possible freedom of thought, expression, discussion, to the whole hundred, because on no other terms can you be quite sure that the judgment of the hundredth man, the one judgment you want, will be forthcoming or will have a chance of making itself effectively heard over the incapable judgments? Mr. Stephen says otherwise. He declares it to be an idle dream "to say that one man in a thousand really exercises much individual choice as to his religious or moral principles, and I doubt whether it is not an exaggeration to say that one man in a million is capable of making any very material addition to what is already known or plausibly conjectured on these matters." *Argal,* beware of accepting any nonsensical principle of liberty which shall leave this millionth man the best possible opening for making his material addition; by the whole spirit of your legislation, public opinion, and social sentiment, habitually discourage, freeze, browbeat, all that eccentricity which would be sure to strike all the rest of the million in the one man and his material addition. If Mr. Stephen's book does not mean this, it means nothing, and his contention with Mr. Mill's doctrine of liberty is only a joust of very cumbrous logomachy.

We can thus understand how Mr. Stephen comes to accuse Mr. Mill of worshipping mere variety and "confounding the proposition that variety is good with the proposition that goodness is various." Mr. Mill deliberately held that variety is good on the ground that it is the essential condition of the appearance and growth of those new ideas, new practices, new sentiments, some of which must contain the germs of all future improvements in the arts of existence. It shows an incapacity to understand the essence of the doctrine, to deal with it by such statements as that it involves "a worship of mere variety." It plainly does no such thing. Mr. Mill prizes variety, not at all as mere variety, but because it furnishes most chances of new forms of good presenting themselves and acquiring a permanent place. He prized that eccentricity which Mr. Stephen so heartly dislikes, because he perceived that all new truth and new ways of living, must from the nature of things always appear eccentric to persons accustomed to old opinions and old ways of living; because he saw that most of the personages to whom mankind owes its chief steps in moral and spiritual advance were looked upon by contemporaries as eccentrics, and very often cruelly ill treated by them (on Mr. Stephen's principles) for eccentricity, which was in truth the very deliverance of humanity from error or imperfection. Not all novelties are improvements, but all improvements are novel, and you can only, therefore, be sure of improvements by giving eccentricity a fair hearing, and free room for as much active manifestation as does no near, positive, recognisable, harm to other people.

Mr. Stephen, however, has a very qualified faith in improvement. He seems to think that the only change in the world is the constant multiplication of the total number of its inhabitants. One of the most extraordinary pieces in his book is a very strained passage after the manner of Mr. Carlyle—only not every one can bend the bow of the great Ulysses—to the effect that the world is like a sort of Stilton cheese, filled with so many millions of indomitable cheese-mites. Apart from the lofty poetic quality and delicate picturesqueness of the trope, it carries its author too far. If men are cheese-mites, I no not see why, for example, able lawyers should strain every nerve, writing articles, reading papers, urging politicians, stimulating ministers, merely in order that a puny group of these cheese-mites, say as many as you could press up on a thumb-nail—to sustain the nobility of the image—may have their laws done up into a code. Mr. Carlyle was much more consistent. He told men they were shadows, and he pursued with loud bursts of not always musical laughter, Political Economy, and Bentham, and parliamentary Reform, and everything else that has made the England of to-day a better place for men or mites to live in than it was half a century ago. Mr. Stephen, to do him justice, gives us very little of this kind of talk. It would be the stultification of his own special ability if he did so. For law, equally with freedom, is only interesting and only worth a serious man's attention in the way of reform, in so far as the progress and the improvement which Mr. Stephen burlesques in the above passage are substantive realities. But his conception of the possibilities of improvement is a narrow one. He draws hard and fast lines in respect of each of the greater interests of men, and anything beyond them he brands as eccentric and chimerical. Mr. Stephen some years ago hurt the feelings of old-fashioned metaphysicians by delineating the case of an imaginary world in which two straight lines should be universally supposed to include a space. It is a matter of regret that he has not an equally courageous and powerful imagination in the region of morals. If he had, he would have less trouble in sympathizing with the idea that the limits of human improvement, though they exist in every direction, have as yet not only not been reached, but are not even visible. And if he had appreciated this idea he would have seen deeper into Mr. Mill's principle than to detect, in one of the conditions attending it, nothing beyond a worship of mere variety.

And after all, even if it were so, is he warranted in taking for granted that worship of variety is less creditable or in any way more singular than worship of unity? Whatever the value of progress may be, says Mr. Stephen, "unity in religious belief would further it." But we really cannot be expected to take Mr. Stephen's authority for this. Such a proposition is one part of the great question at issue. I am not aware that the Byzantine empire, where there eventually existed a more complete unity of belief

than has ever existed in any other part of Christendom, was the
scene of any remarkable furtherance of progress in consequence.
Or take the great theocracies, ancient Egypt, Islam under the
Caliphs, India under Buddhists or Brahmins. What element of
progress did this unity give? Is not unity of religious belief the
very note of stationary societies? It is no doubt true that unity
in religious belief as in other things will slowly draw nearer, as
the result of the gradual acceptance by an increasing number of
men of common methods of observing and interpreting experience. As Mr. Mill says—"As mankind improved, the number of
doctrines which are no longer disputed or doubted will be constantly on the increase; and the well-being of mankind may almost be measured by the number and gravity of the truths which
have reached the point of not being contested." But all the consequences of this quasi-unity may not prove to be beneficial, or
favourable to progress, nor is it at all clear, as Mr. Stephen takes
for granted, that unity of religious belief would further progress,
unless you replaced the discussions to which such unity had put
an end, by some other equally dividing subject of equal interest
to an equal number of people. In Mr. Stephen's opinion it would
be impossible ever to find any other such subject, for he lays down
the proposition which, I confess, strikes me as truly extravagant
that "If we were all of one mind, and that upon reasonable
grounds, about the nature of men, and their relation to the world
or worlds in which they live, [this is equivalent to previous expressions about "the attainment of religious truth"], we should
be able *at once and with but little difficulty* to solve all the great
moral and political questions which at present distract and divide
the world."

4. A good deal of rather bustling ponderosity is devoted to
proving that the actual laws in many points do assume the existence of a standard of moral good and evil, and that this proceeding is diametrically opposed to Mr. Mill's fundamental
principles. To this one would say, first, that the actual existence
of laws of any given kind is wholly irrelevant to Mr. Mill's contention, which is, that it would be better if laws of such a kind
did not exist. Second, Mr. Mill never says, nor is it at all essential
to his doctrine to hold, that a government ought not to have "a
standard of moral good and evil, which the public at large have

an interest in maintaining and in many cases enforcing." He only set apart a certain class of cases to which the right or duty of enforcement of the current standard does not extend—the self-regarding cases. Mr. Stephen would not have been any wider of the mark if he had devoted an equal number of pages to demonstrating against Mr. Mill that not only society, but an individual, ought to have a standard of good and evil, which he is to maintain through good report and ill report. Mr. Mill no more denied this of a government than he denied it of an individual. All he said was—"It is a mistake to enforce your standard on me, if my non-recognition of it does no harm to any one but myself. Clearly there is a number of matters—lying, unchastity, and so forth—in which there is no attempt to enforce the recognised standard of good and evil. I extend this class of neglected breaches of the current laws of morals, so as to include all self-regarding matters whatever." Consequently, the statement that the assumption of a standard of moral good and evil which the public at large have an interest in many cases in enforcing, is diametrically opposed to Mr. Mill's fundamental principle, involves a misunderstanding of that principle; and such a statement ignores the plain fact that this principle does emphatically recognize the right of the state to enforce that part of its moral code which touches such acts as are not self-regarding.

A similar neglect to master the real position taken by Mr. Mill is shown in Mr. Stephen's remarks about Pilate, and his parallel of the case of a British officer confronted by a revolutionary teacher in India. "If it is said that Pilate ought to have respected the principle of religious liberty as propounded by Mr. Mill, the answer is that if he had done so, he would have run the risk of setting the whole province in a blaze." Then in such a case Mr. Mill expressly lays down the limitation proper to the matter, in a passage to which Mr. Stephen appears not to have paid attention. "No one pretends," says Mr. Mill, "that actions should be as free as opinions. On the contrary, even opinions lose their immunity when the circumstances in which they are expressed are such as to constitute a positive instigation to some mischievous act. An opinion that corn-dealers are starvers of the poor, or that private property is robbery, ought to be unmolested when simply circulated through the press, but may justly incur punishment when delivered orally to an excited mob assembled before the house of a corn-dealer, or when handed about among the same mob in the form of a placard. Acts of whatever kind, which, without justifiable cause, do harm to others, may be, and in the more important cases absolutely require to be, controlled by the unfavourable sentiment, and when needful, by the active interference of mankind."

5. Let us take a concrete case with which Mr. Stephen furnishes us.

> A set of young noblemen of great fortune and hereditary influence, the representatives of ancient names, the natural leaders of the society of large districts, pass their whole time and employ all their means in gross debauchery. Such people are far more injurious to society than common pickpockets, but Mr. Mill says that if any one having the opportunity of making them ashamed of themselves uses it in order to coerce them into decency, he sins against liberty, unless their example does assignable harm to specific people. It might be right to say, "You the Duke of A. by extravagantly keeping four mistresses, set an example which induced your friend F. to elope with Mrs. G. and you are a great blackguard for your pains, and all the more because you are a duke." I could never be right to say, "You, the Duke of A. are scandalously immoral and ought to be made to smart for it, though the law cannot touch you."

But these two forms of remonstrance by no means exhaust the matter. An advocate of Mr. Mill's principle might say to the debauched duke one of three things: (*a*) "Your grace ought to be made to smart, only it is not worth while for the sake of making a poor creature like you smart, to invoke a principle which would endanger really fruitful experiments in living." (*b*) "We are much indebted to you for destroying your influence and character. Society will be more than compensated for the loss of your social services by the admirable deterrent effect which so hideous a spectacle as your grace, so conspicuous as your high station makes you, will exert over other dukes and men, in spite of your friend F., who imitates you. You are the Helot among dukes." (*c*) "My duke, codifiers and others would like to make you smart by law. We less peremptory heads perceive that you do smart. You smart by being the poor gross creature you are." Any of these rebukes would lie in the mouths of those who accepted Mr. Mill's principle, while the single rebuke which Mr. Stephen has imputed to such persons is the least adequate of the four, and is certainly not the rebuke to be found in the Essay on Liberty.

Take another case put by Mr. Stephen:—

> A number of persons form themselves into an association for the purpose of countenancing each other in the practice of seducing women, and giving the widest possible extension to the theory that adultery is a good thing. They carry out their objects by organizing a system for the publication and circulation of lascivious novels and pamphlets calculated to inflame the passions of the young and inexperienced. The law of England would treat this as a crime. It would call such books obscene libels, and a combination for such a purpose a conspiracy. Mr. Mill would not only regard this as wrong, but he would regard it as an act of persecution if the newspapers were to excite public indignation against the parties concerned by language going one step beyond the calmest discussion of such an experiment in living.

I venture to propound two questions to Mr. Stephen. Is the practice of seducing women a self-regarding practice? And is the *circulation* of pamphlets calculated to inflame the passions of the young an act that hurts nobody but the circulator? The answer to these questions shows the illustration to be utterly pointless. It shows the assertion that on Mr. Mill's principles police interference would be wrong and public anger would be of the nature of persecution, to be a prodigious piece of misrepresentation. There was in the last century a famous case exactly in point, that of Wilkes and the Franciscans of Medmenham Abbey. These dabauchees were as gross and scandalous a set of profligates as ever banded together. But they conformed to the conditions laid down in the doctrine of liberty, and no one thought of interfering with them. The law in this respect was conformable to Mr. Mill's principle. The exception to this non-interference shows the true side of this principle, and confirms the popular acceptance of it, under the circumstances described in Mr. Stephen's imaginary and, for the purposes of the discussion, quite inapposite case. Wilkes printed at his private press a few copies of the *Essay on Woman,* a ribald poem. The government contrived by corrupting a compositor to obtain a copy of it, it was ordered that Wilkes should be prosecuted for publishing a blasphemous libel, and he was convicted by the Court of King's Bench. This conviction has always been held a miscarriage of law, because there was no real publication. Mr. Mill's doctrine condemns the prosecution of Wilkes for the *Essay on Woman,* as all public opinion since has condemned it. A man has a right to keep poisons in his closet, it has been finely said, though he has no right publicly to distribute them for cordials—which is exactly Mr. Mill's position. Does Mr. Stephen hold that Wilkes was justifiably punished for this improperly imputed crime? If not, where is the force of his illustration?

6. At the bottom of all Mr. Stephen's argumentation lies a fundamental reluctance to admit that there are such things as self-regarding acts at all. This reluctance implies a perfectly tenable proposition, a proposition which has been maintained by nearly all religious bodies in the world's history in their non-latitudinarian stages. Comte denied the existence of such a division among acts, and made care of health, cleanliness, sobriety, and the rest, into social obligations.[1] Mr. Stephen does not exactly deny either the possibility or the expediency of recognising the distinction between acts that effect only the doer and acts that affect the rest of society. But if he does not deny this, neither does he admit it, nor treat admission of it as all important to the controversy. Yet that, I submit, ought to have been the field of his discussion on Mr. Mill's doctrine, for it is from that that the other differences really spring. In default of this larger principle, he is constanly obliged to fall back on illustrations of the consequences which might, and very probably would, happen to other people from conduct that seems fairly definable as self-regarding. There is one objection obviously to be made to these illustrations. The connection between the act and its influence on others is so remote, using the word in a legal sense, though quite certain, distinct, and traceable, that you can only take the act out of the self-regarding category, by a process which virtually denies the existence of any such category. You must set a limit to this "indirect and at a distance argument," as Locke called a similar plea, and the setting of this limit is the natural supplement to Mr.

1. In the matter of health Mr. Mill professed the same opinion. See his *Auguste Comte and Positivism,* p. 147.

Mill's "simple principle." Set it where you will, it must, to be a limit at all, come a long way short of Mr. Stephen's notion of self-protection.

In fact Mr. Stephen has failed to state in a definite and intelligible way his conception of the analysis of conduct on which the whole doctrine of Liberty rests. To some persons that analysis as performed by Mr. Mill seems metaphysical and arbitrary. To distinguish the self-regarding from the other parts of conduct strikes them not only as unscientific, but as morally and socially mischievous. They insist that there is a social as well as a personal element in every human act, though in very different proportions, while there is no gain, they contend, and there may be much harm, in trying to mark off actions in which the personal element decisively preponderates, from actions of another sort. Mr. Mill did so distinguish actions, nor was his distinction either metaphysical or arbitrary in its source. As a matter of observation, and for the practical purposes of morality, there are kinds of action whose consequences do not go beyond the doer of them. No doubt, you may say that by engaging in these kinds in any given moment, the doer is neglecting the actions in which the social element preponderates, and therefore even acts that seem purely self-regarding have indirect and negative consequences to the rest of the world. But to allow considerations of this sort to prevent us from using a common-sense classification of acts by the proportion of the personal element in them, is as unreasonable as if we allowed the doctrine of the conservation of physical force, or the evolution of one mode of force into another, to prevent us from classifying the affections of matter independently, as light, heat, motion, and the rest. The division between self-regarding acts and others, then, rests on observation of their actual consequences. And why was Mr. Mill so anxious to erect self-regarding acts into a distant and important class, so important as to be carefully and diligently secured by a special principle of liberty? Because observation of the recorded experience of mankind teaches us that the recognition of this independent provision is essential to the richest expansion of human faculty. To narrow or to repudiate such a province, and to insist exclusively on the social bearing of each part of conduct, is to limit the play of motives, and to thwart the doctrine—which Mr. Stephen at any rate is not likely to disown—that "mankind obtain a greater sum of happiness when each pursues his own, under the rules and conditions required by the rest, than when each makes the good of the rest his only object." To narrow or to repudiate such a province is to tighten the power of the majority over the minority, and to augment the authority of whatever sacerdotal or legislative body may represent the majority. Whether the lawmakers are laymen in parliament, or priests of humanity exercising the spiritual power, it matters not. Mr. Stephen and Comte rest their respective aspirations on a common principle—the assertion of the social element in every part of conduct. If Comte had lived to read the essay on Liberty he would have attacked it on the same side, by denying the possibility of saying of any part of conduct that it is self-regarding. Only he would have denied it boldly, while Mr. Stephen denies it in a timorous manner—not unnatural, perhaps, in one who holds that self is the centre of all things, and that we have no motives that are not self-regarding.

7. We may now notice one or two of Mr. Stephen's *obiter dicta*.

(*a*) "No rational man can doubt that Christianity, taken as a whole and speaking broadly, has been a blessing to men." Personally I am of Mr. Stephen's opinion that Christianity has been a blessing to men, but I should think twice before feeling myself entitled on the strength of this conviction to deny the title of "rational man" to such persons as the learned and laborious Gibbon, the shrewd, versatile, humane Voltaire, the scientific D'Alembert, the philosophic Condorcet. But would these eminent men have doubted what Mr. Stephen says no rational man can doubt, if they had seen the Revolution? Condorcet, at any rate, saw the Revolution, and it did not shake his conviction, and men like James Mill and Mr. Grote came after the Revolution, and both of them doubted, or went beyond doubting, the beneficence of Christianity. Mr. Stephen makes too much play with his rational man, and reasonable people. The phrase does not really come to much more than the majority of the males of a generation, engaged in the pleasing exercise of "that hide-bound humour which they call their judgment."

(*b*) "There are innumerable propositions on which a man may have a rational assurance that he is right, whether others are or are not at liberty to contradict him. Every proposition of which we are assured by our own senses falls under this head." Were not men assured by their own senses that the earth is a plane, and that the sun revolves round the earth? It may be said that before Copernicus they had a rational assurance that they were right in this. The belief was not correct, but it was a rational assurance. Precisely; and people would have lived to this day with their erroneous rational assurance uncorrected, unless Copernicus had been at liberty to contradict them.

(*c*) "The cry for liberty in short is a general condemnation of the past." Not condemnation at all, in any accurate or serious sense. In buying a new coat I do not condemn the old one; on the contrary, I look to it with gratitude for helpful service, though it is now worn out or has become too scanty for me. We do not believe that the principle of all things is water, or that number is the principle of matter; but the rejection of such notions is not equivalent to a condemnation of Thales and Pythagoras. On the contrary, we are thoroughly appreciative of the services rendered by them and their now worn-out speculations in first setting the human intelligence to work in a certain direction. The catholic church has contributed immensely to the progress of civilisation; to believe that it has now become retrogressive and obscurantist is not to condemn its past, but its present. Many of the forces of the past are now spent, but to hold this is a very different thing from saying that they never were forces, or that as forces they did no good, and a very different thing from condemning them —unless Mr. Stephen insists on using condemnation in the same arbitrary and unprecedented senses which he assigns to coercion. Mr. Stephen lacks historical perspective; he does not practise the historic method; we see no flexibility in his premises or his conclusions, nor any reference of them to specific social stages. He is one of those absolute thinkers who bring to the problems of society the methods of geometry. The cry for liberty, he says, "has shattered to pieces most of the old forms in which discipline was a recognised and admitted good,"—as if this were really the one cause, and is if the old forms had not been previously disorganized by internal decrepitude, the result of their association with one or two great groups of ideas which had been slowly robbed of their vitality by a large number of various forces.

(*d*) "If Mr. Mill's view of liberty had always been adopted and acted on to its full extent—if it had been the view of the first Christians or of the first Mahommedans—every one can see that there would have been no such thing as organized Christianity or Mahommedanism in the world." To this one might reply by asking how we know that there might not have been something far better in their stead. We know what we get by effective intolerance, but we cannot ever know what possible benefactions we lose by it.

(*e*) "Concede the first principle, that unfeigned belief in the Roman Catholic creed is indispensably necessary to salvation, or the first principle, that the whole Roman Catholic system is a pernicious falsehood and fraud, and it will be found impossible to stop short of the practical conclusions of the Inquisition and the Terror. Every real argument against their practical conclusions is an argument to show either that we cannot be sure as to the conditions of salvation, or that the Roman Catholic religion has redeeming points about it." Unless we agree to limit the meaning of "real" arguments to such as would convince the author of these assertions, such a statement is wholly inadequate. You may believe that the Roman Catholic religion is a pernicious falsehood and fraud, and that it has no redeeming point about it, and still stop short of the Terror, and not only of the Terror but of any coercive interference whatever, in consequence of this consideration, namely that falsehoods and frauds in religion are not to be extirpated by massacre or any penalties of that kind. Why is not that a real argument?

Nor is this the only possible restraining consideration. I may be convinced that I could stamp out the given form of pernicious belief by persecution, but yet may be of opinion that for various reasons—such as the effect of persecution on the character of the persecutor, the colour and bias given to my own true creed by associating it with cruelty to a false one, and so forth—for these reasons the evils incident to violent repression would counterbalance the evils incident to the tolerance of a faith without a single redeeming point. Why is not that also a real argument? Mr. Stephen asks any one who doubts his position to try to frame an argument which could have been addressed with any chance of success to Philip II. against the persecution of the Protestants, or to Robespierre against the persecution of Catholicism. Well, the two arguments I have just offered might well have been addressed alike to Philip II. and to Robespierre. The fact that they would have had no chance of success, which I admit, is just what explains the abhorrence with which the world regards their names. They are arguments resting on a balance of expediencies, as shown through the experience of mankind. But Robespierre was proof against such arguments. He believed with Rousseau and Mr. Stephen in the duty of putting down vice and error coercively. He shared Mr. Stephen's enthusiasm "for a powerful and energetic minority, sufficiently vigorous to impose their will on their neighbours, having made up their minds as to what is true," and so forth. Well, according to the doctrine of liberty, this energetic way of violently imposing your will on other people, by guillotine or act of parliament, is as futile as it is hateful, and not only a crime but a mistake. Like the boisterous pæans of literary men in honour of coercive energy, eagerness to resort to drastic remedies is the outcry of mere unscientific impatience.

Mr. Mill's Autobiography

Chercher en gémissant—search with many sighs—that was Pascal's notion of praiseworthy living and choosing the better part. Search, and search with much travail, strikes us as the chief intellectual ensign and device of that illustrious man whose record of his own mental nurture and growth we have all been reading. Everybody endowed with energetic intelligence has a measure of the spirit of search poured out upon him, and acts on the Socratic maxim that the life without inquiry is a life to be lived by no man. But it is the rare distinction of a very few to accept the maxim in its full significance, to insist on an open mind as the true secret of wisdom, to press the examination and testing of our convictions as the true way at once to stability and growth of character, and thus to make of life what it is so good for us that it should be, a continual building up, a ceaseless fortifying, and enlargement and multiplication of the treasures of the spirit. To make a point of "examining what was said in defence of all opinions, however new or however old, in the conviction that even if there were errors there might be a substratum of truth underneath them, and that in any case the discovery of what it was that made them plausible would be a benefit to truth," to thrust out the spirit of party, of sect, of creed, of the poorer sort of self-esteem, of futile contentiousness, and so to seek and again seek with undeviating singleness of mind the right interpretation of our

This essay was first published in *Fortnightly Review,* n.s., 85 (January 1874): 1–20, and was reprinted in *Critical Miscellanies,* vol. 3 (London, 1886)—ed.

experiences—here is the genuine seal of intellectual mastery and the true stamp of a perfect rationality.

The men to whom this is the ideal of the life of the reason, and who have done anything considerable towards spreading a desire after it, deserve to have their memories gratefully cherished even by those who do not agree with all their positive opinions. Reflect a little on the conditions of human existence; on the urgent demand which material necessities inevitably make on so immense a proportion of our time and thought; on the space which is naturally filled up by the activity of absorbing affections; on the fatal power of mere tradition and report over the indifferent, and the fatal power of inveterate prejudice over so many even of the best of those who are not indifferent. Then we shall know better how to value such a type of character and life as Mr. Mill has now told us the story of, in which intellectual impressionableness on the most important subjects of human thought was so cultivated as almost to acquire the strength and quick responsiveness of emotional sensibility. And this, without the too common drawback to great openness of mind, namely loose beliefs, taken up to-day and silently dropped to-morrow, vacillating opinions, constantly being exchanged for their contraries, feeble convictions, appearing, shifting, vanishing, in the quicksands of an unstable mind. Nobody will impute any of these disastrous weaknesses to Mr. Mill. His impressionableness was of the valuable positive kind, which adds and assimilates new elements from many quarters, without disturbing the organic structure of the whole. What he says of one stage in his growth remained generally true of him until the very end:—"I found the fabric of my old and taught opinions giving way in many fresh places, and I never allowed it to fall to pieces, but was incessantly occupied in weaving it anew. I never in the course of my transition was content to remain, for ever so short a time, confused and unsettled. When I had taken in any new ideas I could not rest till I had adjusted its relation to my old opinions, and ascertained exactly how far its effect ought to extend in modifying or superseding them." This careful and conscientious recognition of the duty of having ordered opinions, and of responsibility for these opinions being both as true and as consistent with one another as taking pains with his mind could make them, distinguished Mr.

Mill from the men who flit aimlessly from doctrine to doctrine as the flies of a summer day dart from point to point in the vacuous air. It distinguished him also from those sensitive spirits who fling themselves down from the heights of rationalism suddenly into the pit of an infallible church; and from those who, like La Mennais, move violently between faith and reason, between tradition and inquiry, between the fulness of deference to authority and the fulness of self-assertion.

All minds of the first quality move and grow; they have a susceptibility to many sorts of new impressions, a mobility, a feeling outwards, which makes it impossible for them to remain in the stern fixity of an early implanted set of dogmas, whether philosophic or religious. In stoical tenacity of character, as well as in intellectual originality and concentrated force of understanding, some of those who knew both tell us that Mr. Mill was inferior to his father. But who does not feel in the son the serious charm of a power of adaptation and pliableness which we can never associate with the hardy and more rigorous nature of the other? And it was just because he had this sensibility of the intellect, that the history of what it did for him is so edifying a performance for a people like ourselves, among whom that quality is so extremely uncommon. For it was the sensibility of strength and not of weakness, nor of mere over-refinement and subtlety. We may estimate the significance of such a difference, when we think how little, after all, the singular gifts of a Newman or a Maurice have done for their contemporaries, simply because these two eminent men allowed consciousness of their own weakness to "sickly over" the spontaneous impulses of their strength.

The wonder is that the reaction against such an education as that through which James Mill brought his son,—an education so intense, so purely analytical, doing so much for the reason and so little for the satisfaction of the affections,—was not of the most violent kind; that the crisis through which nearly every youth of good quality has to pass, and from which Mr. Mill, as he has told us, by no means escaped, did not land him in some of the extreme forms of transcendentalism. If it had done so, the reward of the journey would no doubt have been more abundant in melodramatic incidents, would have done more to tickle the fancy of "the present age of loud disputes but weak convictions," and been found more touching by the large numbers of talkers and writers who seem to think that a history of a careful man's opinions on grave and difficult subjects ought to have all the rapid movements and unexpected turns of a romance, and that a book without rapture and effusion and a great many capital letters must be joyless and disappointing. Those of us who dislike literary hysteria as much as we dislike the coarseness that mistakes itself for force, may well be glad to follow the mental history of a man who knew how to move and grow without any of these reactions and leaps on the one hand, or any of that overdone realism on the other, which may all make a more striking picture, but which do assuredly more often than not mark the ruin of a mind and the nullification of a career. If we are now and then conscious in the book of a certain want of spacing, of changing perspectives and long vistas; if we have perhaps a sense of being too narrowly enclosed; if we miss the relish of humour or the occasional relief of irony; we ought to remember that we are busy not with a work of imagination or art, but with the practical record of the formation of an eminent thinker's mental habits and the succession of his mental attitudes; and the formation of such mental habits is not a romance, but the most arduous of real concerns. If we are led up to none of the enkindled summits of the soul, and plunged into none of its abysses, that is no reason why we should fail to be struck by the pale flame of strenuous self-possession, or touched by the ingenuousness and simplicity of the speaker's accents. A generation continually excited by vehement sterile narratives of storm and stress and spiritual shipwreck, might do well, if it knew the things that pertained to its peace, to ponder the unvarnished history of a man who though not one of the picturesque victims of the wasteful torments of an uneasy spiritual self-consciousness, yet laboured so patiently after the gifts of intellectual strength, and did so much permanently to widen the judgments of the world.

If Mr. Mill's autobiography has no literary grandeur, nor artistic variety, it has the rarer merit of presenting for our contemplation a character that was infested by none of the small passions, and warped by none of the more unintelligent attitudes of the human mind; and we have to remember that it is exactly these, the smaller passions on the one hand, and slovenliness of intelligence on the other, which are even worse agencies in spoiling the worth of life and the advance of society than the more imposing vices either of thought or sentiment. Many have told the tale of a life of much external eventfulness. There is a rarer instructiveness in the quiet career of one whose life was an incessant education, a persistent strengthening of the mental habit of "never accepting half-solutions of difficulties as complete; never abandoning a puzzle, but again and again returning to it until it was cleared up; never allowing obscure corners of a subject to remain unexplored, because they did not appear important; never thinking that I perfectly understood any part of a subject until I understood the whole." It is true that this mental habit is not so singular in itself, for it is the common and indispensable merit of every truly scientific thinker. Mr. Mill's distinction lay in the deliberate intention and the systematic patience with which he brought it to the consideration of moral and religious and social subjects, were hitherto, for reasons that are not difficult to seek, the empire of prejudice and passion has been so much stronger, so much harder to resist, than in the field of physical science.

Here, where sect is so ready to succeed sect, and school comes after school, with constant replacement of one sort of orthodoxy by another sort, until even the principle of relativity becomes the base of a set of absolute and final dogmas, and the very doctrine of uncertainty itself becomes fixed in a kind of authoritative nihilism, it is a signal gain that we now have a new type, with the old wise device, μέμνησο 'απιστεῖν—*be sure you distrust*—distrust your own bias; distrust your supposed knowledge; constantly try, prove, fortify your firmest convictions. And all this, throughout the whole domain where the intelligence rules. It was characteristic of a man of this type that he should have been seized by that memorable passage in Condorcet's *Life of Turgot* to which Mr. Mill refers, and which every man with an active interest in serious affairs should bind about his neck and write on the tablet of his heart.

Turgot [says his wise biographer] always looked upon anything like a sect as mischievous. . . . From the moment that a sect comes into existence all the individuals composing it become answerable for the faults and errors of each one of them. The obligation to remain united leads them to suppress or dissemble all truths that might wound anybody whose adhesion is useful to the sect.They are forced to establish in some form a body of doctrine, and the opinions which make a part of it, being adopted without inquiry, become in due time pure prejudices. Friendship stops with the individuals; but the hatred and envy that any of them may arouse extends to the whole sect. If this sect be formed by the most enlightened men of the nation, if the defence of truths of the greatest importance to the common happiness be the object of its zeal, the mischief is still worse. Everything true or useful which they propose is rejected without examination. Abuses and errors of every kind always have for their defenders that herd of presumptuous and mediocre mortals who are the bitterest enemies of all celebrity and renown. Scarcely is a truth made clear, before those to whom it would be prejudicial crush it under the name of a sect that is sure to have already become odious, and are certain to keep it from obtaining so much as a hearing. Turgot, then, was persuaded that perhaps the greatest ill you can do to truth is to drive those who love it to form themselves into a sect, and that these in turn can commit no more fatal mistake than to have the vanity or the weakness to fall into the trap.

Yet we know that with Mr. Mill as with Turgot this deep distrust of sect was no hindrance to the most careful systematisation of opinion and conduct. He did not interpret manysidedness in the flaccid watery sense which flatters the indolence of so many of our contemporaries, who like to have their ears amused with a new doctrine each morning, to be held for a day, and dropped in the evening, and who have little more seriousness in their intellectual life than the busy ephemera of a midsummer noon. He says that he looked forward "to a future which shall unite the best qualities of the critical with the best qualities of the organic periods; unchecked liberty of thought, unbounded freedom of individual action in all modes not hurtful to others; but also convictions as to what is right and wrong, useful and pernicious, deeply engraven on the feelings by early education and general unanimity of sentiment, and so firmly grounded in reason and the true exigencies of life, that they shall not like all former and present creeds, religious, ethical, and political, require to be periodically thrown off and replaced by others." This was in some sort the type at which he aimed in the formation of his own character—a type that should combine organic with critical quality, the strength of an ordered set of convictions, with the pliability and the receptiveness in face of new truth are indispensable to these very convictions being held intelligently and in their best attainable form. We can understand the force of the eulogy on John Austin, that he manifested "an equal devotion to the two cardinal points of Liberty and Duty." These are the correlatives in the sphere of action to the two cardinal points of Criticism and Belief in the sphere of thought.

We can in the light of this double way of viewing the right balance of the mind the better understand the combination of earnestness with tolerance, which inconsiderate persons are apt to find so awkward a stumbling-block in the scheme of philosophic liberalism. Many people in our time have so ill understood the doctrine of liberty, that in some of the most active circles in society they now count you a bigot if you hold any proposition to be decidedly and unmistakably more true than any other, and pronounce you intemperate if you show anger and stern disappointment because men follow the wrong course instead of the right one. Mr. Mill's explanation of the vehemence and decision of his father's disapproval, when he did disapprove, and his refusal to allow honesty of purpose in the doer to soften his disapprobation of the deed, gives the reader a worthy and masculine notion of true tolerance. James Mill's "aversion to many intellectual errors, or what he regarded as such, partook in a certain sense of the character of a moral feeling. . . . None but those who do not care about opinions will confound this with intolerance. Those, who having opinions which they hold to be immensely important, and their contraries to be prodigiously hurtful, have any deep regard for the general good, will necessarily dislike as a class and in the abstract, those who think wrong what they think right, and right what they think wrong: though they need not be, nor was my father, insensible to good qualities in an opponent, nor governed in their estimation of individuals by one general presumption, instead of by the whole of their character. I grant that an earnest person, being no more infallible than other men, is liable to dislike people on account of opinions which do not merit dislike; but if he neither himself does them any ill office, nor connives at its being done by others, he is not intolerant: and the forebearance which flows from a conscientious sense of the importance to mankind of the equal freedom of all opinions is the only tolerance which is commendable, or to the highest moral order of minds, possible." This is another side of the co-ordination of Criticism and Belief, of Liberty and Duty, which attained in Mr. Mill himself a completeness that other men, less favoured in education and with less active power of self-control, are not likely to reach, but to reach it ought to be one of the prime objects of their mental discipline. The inculcation of this peculiar morality of the intelligence is one of the most urgently needed processes of our time, when the circumstance of our being in the very depths of a period of transition from one spiritual basis of though to another leads men to be content with holding a quantity of vague, confused, and contradictory opinions, and to invest with the honourable name of candour a weak reluctance to hold any one of them earnestly.

Mr. Mill experienced in the four or five last years of his life the disadvantage of trying to unite fairness towards the opinions from which he differed, with loyalty to the positive opinions which he accepted. "As I had shown in my political writings," he says, "that I was aware of the weak points in democratic opinions, some Conservatives, it seems, had not been without hopes of finding me an opponent of democracy: as I was able to see the Conservative side of the question, they presumed that like them I could not see any other side. Yet if they had really read my writings, they would have known that after giving full weight to all that appeared to me well grounded in the arguments against democracy, I unhesitatingly decided in its favour, while recommending that it should be accompanied by such institutions as were consistent with its principle and calculated to ward off its inconveniences." This was only one illustration of what constantly happened, until at length, it is hardly too much to say, a man who had hitherto enjoyed a singular measure of general reverence because he was supposed to see truth in every doctrine, became downright unpopular among many classes in the community, because he saw more truth in one doctrine than another, and brought the propositions for whose acceptance he was most in earnest eagerly before the public. A study of Mr. Mill's most characteristic mental habit was never more needed than by a generation which is so enamoured of Evolution as the key-word to universal development, as to believe that the true philosophy is to wait in the patience of a sublime contemplation until all abuses have evolved themselves out of the way, no matter how powerful the interests supporting them, and all prejudice and selfishness spontaneously transformed themselves into enlightenment and benevolence, no matter how little trouble is taken by those who happen to have most light and most public spirit.

In a similar way the Autobiography shows us the picture of a man uniting profound self-respect with a singular neutrality where his own claims are concerned, a singular self-mastery and justice of mind, in matters where with most men the sense of their own personality is wont to be so exacting and so easily irritated. The history of intellectual eminence is too often a history of immoderate egoism. It has perhaps hardly ever been given to any one who exerted such influence as Mr. Mill did over his contemporaries, to view his own share in it with such discriminativeness and equity as marks every page of his book, and as used to mark every word of his conversation. Knowing as we all do the last infirmity of even noble minds, and how deep the desire to erect himself Pope and Sir Oracle lies in the spirit of a man with strong convictions, we may value the more highly as well for its rarity as for its intrinsic worth Mr. Mill's quality of self-effacement, and his steadfast care to look anywhere rather than in his own personal merits for the source of any of those excellences which he was never led by false modesty to dissemble.

Many people seem to find the most interesting figure in the book that stoical father, whose austere, energetic, imperious, and relentless character showed the temperament of the Scotch Covenanter of the seventeenth century, inspired by the principles and philosophy of France in the eighteenth. No doubt, for those in search of strong dramatic effects, the lines of this strenuous indomitable nature are full of impressiveness.[1] But one ought to be able to appreciate the distinction and strength of the father, and yet also be able to see that the distinction of the son's strength was in truth more really impressive still. We encounter a modesty that almost speaks the language of fatalism. Pieces of good fortune that most people would assuredly have either explained as due to their own penetration, or to the recognition of their worth by others, or else would have refrained from dwelling upon, as being no more than events of secondary importance, are by Mr. Mill invariably recognised at their full worth or even above it, and invariably spoken of as fortunate accidents, happy turns in the lottery of life, or in some other quiet fatalistic phrase, expressive of his deep feeling how much we owe to influences over which we have no control and for which we have no right to take any credit. His saying that "it would be a blessing if the doctrine of necessity could be believed by all *quoad* the characters of others, and disbelieved in regard to their own," went even further than that, for he teaches us to accept the doctrine of necessity *quoad* the most marked felicities of life and character, and to lean lightly or not at all upon it in regard to our demerits. Humility is a rationalistic, no less than a Christian grace—not humility in face of error or arrogant pretensions or selfishness, nor a humility that paralyses energetic effort, but a steadfast consciousness of all the good gifts which our forerunners have made ready for us, and of the weight of our responsibility for transmitting

1. In an interesting volume just published (*The Minor Works of George Grote,* edited by Alexander Bain. London: Murray), we find Grote confirming Mr. Mill's estimate of his father's psychagogic quality. "His unpremeditated oral exposition," says Grote of James Mill, "was hardly less effective than his prepared work with his pen; his colloquial fertility in philosophical subjects, his power of discussing himself, and stimulating others to discuss, his ready responsive inspirations through all the shifts and windings of a sort of Platonic dialogue,—all these accomplishments were to those who knew him, even more impressive than what he composed for the press. Conversation with him was not merely instructive, but provocative to the observant intelligence. Of all persons whom we have known, Mr. James Mill was the one who stood least remote from the lofty Platonic ideal of Dialectic—τοῦ διδόναι καὶ δέχεσθαι λόγον (the giving and receiving of reasons)—competent alike to examine others or to be examined by them in philosophy. When to this we add a strenuous character, earnest convictions, and single-minded devotion to truth, with an utter disdain of mere paradox, it may be conceived that such a man exercised powerful intellectual ascendancy over youthful minds," etc.—*Minor Works of George Grote,* p. 284.

these helpful forces to a new generation not diminished but augmented.

In more than one remarkable place the Autobiography shows us distinctly what all careful students of Mr. Mill's books supposed, that with him the social aim, the repayment of the services of the past by devotion to the services of present and future, was predominant over any merely speculative curiosity or abstract interest. His preference for deeply reserved ways of expressing even his strongest feelings prevented him from making any expansive show of this governing sentiment. Though no man was ever more free from any taint of that bad habit of us English, of denying or palliating an abuse or a wrong, unless we are prepared with an instant remedy for it, yet he had a strong aversion to mere socialistic declamation. Perhaps, if one may say so without presumption, he was not indulgent enough in this respect. I remember once pressing him with the enthusiasm of my youth for Victor Hugo—an enthusiasm which I am glad to think that time does nothing to weaken. Mr. Mill, admitting, though not too lavishly, the superb imaginative power of this poetic master of our time, still counted it a fatal drawback to Hugo's worth and claim to recognition that "he has not brought forward one single practical proposal for the improvement of the society against which he is incessantly thundering." I venture to urge that it is unreasonable to ask a poet to draft acts of parliament, and that by bringing all the strength of his imagination and all the majestic fulness of his sympathy to bear on the social horrors and injustices which still lie so thick about us, he kindled an inextinguishable fire in the hearts of men of weaker initiative and less imperial gifts alike of imagination and sympathy, and so prepared the forces out of which practical proposals and specific improvements may be expected to issue. That so obvious a kind of reflection should not have previously interested Mr. Mill's judgment in favour of the writer of the *Outcasts,* the *Legend of the Ages,* the *Contemplations,* only shows how strong was his dislike to all that savoured of the grandiose, and how afraid he always was of every thing that seemed to dissociate emotion from rationally directed effort. That he was himself inspired by this emotion of pity for the common people, of divine rage against the injustice of the strong to the weak, in a degree not inferior to Hugo himself, his whole career most effectually demonstrates.

It is this devotion to the substantial good of the many, though practised without the noisy or ostentatious professions of more egoistic thinkers, which binds together all the parts of his work, from the *System of Logic* down to his last speech on the Land Question. One of the most striking pages in the Autobiography is that in which he gives his reasons for composing the refutation of Hamilton, and as some of these especially valuable passages in the book seem to be running the risk of neglect in favour of those which happen to furnish material for the idle, pitiful gossip of London society, it may be well to reproduce it.

The difference [he says] between these two schools of philosophy, that of Intuition, and that of Experience and Association, is not a mere matter of abstract speculation; it is full of practical consequences, and lies at the foundation of all the greatest differences of practical opinion in an age of progress. The practical reformer has continually to demand that changes be made in things which are supported by powerful and widely spread feelings, or to question the apparent necessity and indefeasibleness of established facts; and it is often an indispensable part of his argument to show how those powerful feelings had their origin, and how those facts came to seem necessary and indefeasible. There is therefore a natural hostility between him and a philosophy which discourages the explanation of feelings and moral facts by circumstances and association, and prefers to treat them as ultimate elements of human nature; a philosophy which is addicted to holding up favourite doctrines as intuitive truths, and deems intuition to be the voice of Nature and of God, speaking with an authority higher than that of our reason. In particular, I have long felt that the prevailing tendency to regard all the marked distinctions of human character as innate, and in the main indelible, and to ignore the irresistible proofs that by far the greater part of those differences whether between individuals, races, or sexes, are such as not only might but naturally would be produced by differences in circumstances, is one of the chief hindrances to the rational treatment of great social questions, and one of the greatest stumbling-blocks to human improvement. This tendency has its source in the intuitional metaphysics which characterized the reaction of the nineteenth century against the eighteenth, and it is a tendency so agreeable to human indolence, as well as to conservative interests generally, that unless attacked at the very root, it is sure to be carried to even a greater length than is really justified by the more moderate forms of the intuitional philosophy. . . . Considering then the writings and fame of Sir W. Hamilton as the great fortress of the intuitional philosophy in this country, a fortress the more formidable from the imposing character, and the in many respects great personal merits and mental endowments of the man, I thought it might be a real service to philosophy to attempt a thorough examination of all his most important doctrines, and an estimate of his general claims to eminence as a philosopher; and I was confirmed in this resolution by observing that in the writings of at least one, and him one of the ablest, of Sir W. Hamilton's followers, his peculiar doctrines were made the justification of a view of religion which I hold to be profoundly immoral—that it is our duty to bow down in worship before a Being whose moral attributes are affirmed to be unknowable by us, and to be perhaps extremely different from those which, when speaking of our fellow-creatures, we call by the same name.

Thus we see that even where the distance between the object of his inquiry and the practical well-being of mankind seemed farthest, still the latter was his starting point, and the doing "a real service to philosophy" only occurred to him in connection with a still greater and more real service to those social causes for which and which only philosophy is worth cultivating. In the *System of Logic* the inspiration had been the same.

The notion that truths extend to the mind, [he writes], may be known by intuition or consciousness, independently of observation and experience, is, I am persuaded, in these times, the great intellectual support of false doctrines and bad institutions. By the aid of this theory every inveterate belief and every intense feeling of which the origin is not remembered, is enabled to dispense with the obligation of justifying itself by reason, and is erected into its own all-sufficient voucher and justification. There never was an instrument better devised for consecrating all deep-seated prejudices. And the chief strength of this false philosophy in morals, politics, and religion, lies in the appeal which it is accustomed to make to the evidence of mathematics and of the cognate branches of physical science. To expel it from these is to drive it from its stronghold. . . . In attempting to clear up the real nature of the evidence of mathematical and physical truths, the *System of Logic* met the intuitive philosophers on grounds on which they had previously been deemed unassailable; and gave its own explanation from experience and association of that peculiar character of what are called necessary truths, which is adduced as proof that their evidence must come from a deeper source than experience. Whether this has been done effectually is still *sub judice;* and even then, to deprive a mode of thought so strongly rooted in human prejudices and partialities of its mere speculative support, goes but a very little way towards overcoming it; but though only a step, it is a quite indispensable one; for since, after all, prejudice can only be successfully combated by philosophy, no way can really be made against it permanently, until it has been shown not to have philosophy on its side.

This was to lay the basis of a true positivism by the only means through which it can be laid firmly, by establishing at the bottom of men's minds the habit of seeking explanations of all phenomena in experience, and building up from the beginning the great positive principle that we can only know phenomena and only know them experientially. We see, from such passages as the two that have been quoted, that with Mr. Mill, no less than Comte, the ultimate object was to bring people to extend positive modes of thinking to the master subjects of morals, politics, and religion. Mr. Mill, however, with a wisdom which Comte unfortunately did not share, refrained from any rash and premature attempt to decide what would be the results of this much-needed extension. He knew that we were as yet only just coming in sight of the stage where these most complex of all phenomena can be fruitfully studied on positive methods, and he was content with doing as much as he could to expel other methods from men's minds, and to engender the positive spirit and temper. Comte, on the other hand, presumed at once to draw up a minute plan of social reconstruction, which contains some ideas of great beauty and power, some of extreme absurdity, and some which would be very mischievous if there were the smallest chance of their ever being realised. "His book stands," Mr. Mill truly says of the *Système de Politique Positive,* "a monumental warning to thinkers on society and politics of what happens when once men lose sight in their speculations of the value of Liberty and Individuality."

It was his own sense of the value of Liberty which led to the production of the little tractate which Mr. Mill himself thought likely to survive longer than anything else that he had written, "with the possible exception of the *Logic*," as being "a kind of philosophic text-book of a single truth, which the changes progressively taking place in modern society tend to bring out into ever stronger relief; the importance to man and society, of a large variety in types of character, and of giving full freedom to human nature to expand itself in innumerable and conflicting directions." The present writer has so recently had occasion in these pages[2] to discuss the subject of this single truth, in connection with an elaborate attack upon it by the Goliah of the London evening press, against whom he ventured to go up and sling seven or more smooth stones from the brook, that it would be mere self-repetition to urge more in the matter. It seems to us, however, that Mr. Mill's plea for Liberty in the abstract, invaluable as it is, still is less important than the memorable application of this plea and of all the arguments supporting it to that half of the human race whose individuality has hitherto been blindly and most wastefully repressed. The little book on the Subjection of Women, though not a capital performance like the Logic, was the capital illustration of the modes of reasoning about human character set forth in his Logic applied to the case in which the old metaphysical notion of innate and indelible differences is still nearly as strong as ever it was, and in which its moral and social consequences are so inexpressibly disastrous, so superlatively powerful in keeping the ordinary level of the aims and achievements of life low and meagre. The accurate and unanswerable reasoning no less than the noble evaluation of this great argument; the sagacity of a hundred of its maxims on individual conduct and character no less than the combined rationality and beauty of its aspirations for the improvement of collective social life, make this piece probably the best illustration of all the best and richest qualities of its author's mind, and it is fortunate that a subject of such incomparable importance should have been first effectively presented for discussion in so worthy and pregnant a form.

It is interesting to know definitely from the Autobiography,

2. See an article on "Mr. Mill's Doctrine of Liberty," in the *Fortnightly Review* for July, 1873. [Reprinted in present collection.—ed.]

what is implied in the opening of the book itself, that a zealous belief in the advantages of abolishing the legal and social inequalities of women was not due to the accident of personal intimacy with one or more women of exceptional distinction of character. What has been ignorantly supposed in our own day to be a crotchet of Mr. Mill's was the common doctrine of the younger proselytes of the Benthamite school, and Bentham himself was wholly with them; as, of course, were other thinkers of an earlier date, Condorcet for instance. In this as in other subjects Mr. Mill did not go beyond his modest definition of his own originality—the application of old ideas in new forms and connections, or the originality "which every thoughtful mind gives to its own mode of conceiving and expressing truths which are common property." Or shall we say that he had an originality of a more genuine kind, which made him first diligently acquire what in a remarkable phrase he calls *plenary possession* of truths, and then transfuse them with sympathetic and contagious enthusiasm?

It is often complained that the book on Women has the radical imperfection of not speaking plainly on the question of the limitations proper to divorce. The present writer once ventured to ask Mr. Mill why he had left this important point undiscussed. Mr. Mill replied that it seemed to him impossible to settle the expediency of more liberal conditions of divorce, "first, without hearing much more fully than we could possibly do at present the ideas held by women in the matter; second, until the experiment of marriage with entire equality between man and wife had been properly tried." People who are in a hurry to get rid of their partners may find this very halting kind of work, and a man who wants to take a new wife before sunset may well be irritated by a philosopher who tells him that the question may possibly be capable of useful discussion towards the middle of the next century. But Mr. Mill's argument is full of force and praiseworthy patience.

The union of boundless patience with unshaken hope was one of Mr. Mill's most conspicuous distinctions. There are two crises in the history of grave and sensitive natures. One on the threshold of manhood, when the youth defines his purpose, his creed, his aspirations; the other towards the later part of middle life, when circumstance has strained his purpose, and tested his creed, and given to his aspirations a cold and practical measure. The second crisis, though less stirring, less vivid, less coloured to the imagination, is the weightier probation of the two, for it is final and decisive; it marks not the mere unresisted force of youthful impulse and implanted predispositions, as the earlier crisis does, but the resisting quality, the strength, the purity, the depth, of the native character, after the many princes of the power of the air have had time and chance of fighting their hardest against it. It is the turn which a man takes about the age of five-and-forty, that parts him off among the sheep on the right hand or the poor goats on the left. This is the time of the grand moral climacteric; when genial unvarnished selfishness, or coarse and ungenial cynicism, or querulous despondency, finally chokes out the generous resolve of a fancied strength which had not yet been tried in the furnace of circumstance.

Mr. Mill did not escape the second crisis, any more than he had escaped the first, though he dismisses it in a far more summary manner. The education, he tells us, which his father had given him with such fine solicitude, had taught him to look for the greatest and surest source of happiness in sympathy with the good of mankind on a large scale, and had fitted him to work for this good of mankind in various ways. By the time he was twenty, his sympathies and passive susceptibilities had been so little cultivated, his analytic quality had been developed with so little balance in the shape of developed feelings, that he suddenly found himself unable to take pleasure in those thoughts of virtue and benevolence which had hitherto only been associated with logical demonstration and not with sympathetic sentiment. This dejection was dispelled mainly by the influence of Wordsworth— a poet austere yet gracious, energetic yet sober, penetrated with feeling for nature yet penetrated with feeling for the homely lot of man. Here was the emotional synthesis, binding together the energies of the speculative and active mind by sympathetic interest in the common feelings and common destiny of human beings.

For some ten years more (1826–36) Mr. Mill hoped the greatest things for the good of society from reformed institutions. That was the period of parliamentary changes, and such hope was natural and universal. Then a shadow came over this confidence, and Mr. Mill advanced to the position that the choice of political institutions is subordinate to the question, "what great improvement in life and culture stands next in order for the people concerned, as the condition of their further progress." In this period he composed the *Logic* (published 1843) and the *Political Economy* (1848). Then he saw what all ardent lovers of improvement are condemned to see, that their hopes have outstripped the rate of progress; that fulfilment of social aspiration is tardy and very slow of foot; and that the leaders of human thought are never permitted to enter into the Promised Land whither they are conducting others. Changes for which he had worked and from which he had expected most, came to pass, but, after they had come to pass, they were "attended with much less benefit to human well-being than I should formerly have anticipated, because they had produced very little improvement in that which all real amelioration in the lot of mankind depends on, their intellectual and moral state. . . . . I had learnt from experience that many false opinions may be exchanged for true ones, without in the least altering the habit of mind of which false opinions are the result." This discovery appears to have brought on no recurrence of the dejection which had clouded a portion of his youth. It only set him to consider the root of so disappointing a conclusion, and led to the conviction that a great change in the fundamental constitution of men's modes of thought must precede any marked improvement in their lot. He perceived that society is now passing through a transitional period "of weak convictions, paralysed intellects, and growing laxity of principle," the consequence of the discredit in the more reflective minds of the old opinions on the cardinal subjects of religion, morals, and politics, which have now lost most of their efficacy for good, though still possessed of life enough to present formidable obstacles to the growth of better opinion on those subjects.

Thus the crisis of disappointment which breaks up the hope and effort of so many men who start well, or else throws them into poor and sterile courses, proved in this grave, fervent, and most reasonable spirit only the beginning of more serious endeavours in a new and more arduous vein. Hitherto he had been, as he says, "more willing to be content with seconding the superficial improvements which had begun to take place in the common opinions of society and the world." Henceforth he kept less and less in abeyance the more heretical part of his opinions, which he began more and more clearly to discern as "almost the only ones, the assertion of which tends in any way to regenerate society." The crisis of middle age developed a new fortitude, a more earnest intrepidity, a greater boldness of expression about the deeper things, an interest profounder than ever in the improvement of the human lot. The book on the *Subjection of Women,* the *Liberty,* and probably some pieces that have not yet been given to the world, are the notable result of this ripest, loftiest, and most inspiring part of his life.

This judgment does not appear to be shared by the majority of those who have published their opinions upon Mr. Mill's life and works. Perhaps it would have been odd if such a judgment had been common. People who think seriously of life and its conditions either are content with those conditions as they exist, or else they find them empty and deeply unsatisfying. Well, the former class, who naturally figure prominently in the public press, because the press is the more or less flattering mirror of the prevailing doctrines of the day, think that Mr. Mill's views of a better social future are chimerical, utopian, and sentimental. The latter class compensate themselves for the pinchedness of the real world about them by certain rapturous ideals, centring in God, a future life, and the long companionship of the blessed. The consequence of this absorption either in the immediate interests and aims of the hour, or in the interests and aims of an imaginary world which is supposed to await us after death, has been a hasty inclination to look on such a life and such purposes as are set forth in the Autobiography as essentially jejune and dreary. It is not in the least surprising that such a feeling should prevail. If it were otherwise, if the majority of thoughtful men and women were already in a condition to be penetrated by sympathy for the life of "search with many sighs," then we should have already gone far on our way towards the goal which a Turgot or a Mill set for human progress. If society had at once recognised the full attractiveness of a life arduously passed in consideration of the means by which the race may take its next step forward in the improvement of character and the amelioration of the common lot, and this not from love of God nor hope of recompense in a world to come, and still less from hope of recompense or even any very firm assurance of fulfilled aspiration in this world, then that fundamental renovation of conviction for which Mr. Mill sighed, and that evolution of a new faith to which he had looked forward in the far distance, would already have come to pass.

Mr. Mill has been ungenerously ridiculed for the eagerness and enthusiasm of his contemplation of a new and better state of human society. Yet we have always been taught to consider it the mark of the loftiest and most spiritual character, for one to be capable of rapturous contemplation of a new and better state in a future life. Why do you not recognise the loftiness and spirituality of those who make their heaven in the thought of the wider light and purer happiness that in the immensity of the ages may be brought to new generations of men by long force of vision and endeavour? What great element is wanting in a life guided by such a hope? Is it not disinterested, and magnanimous, and purifying, and elevating? The countless beauties of association which cluster round the older faith may make the new seem bleak and chilly, but when what is now the old faith was itself new, that too may well have struck, as we know that it did strike, the adherent of the mellowed pagan philosophy as crude, meagre, jejune, dreary.

Then Mr. Mill's life as disclosed to us in these pages has been called joyless by that sect of religious partisans whose peculiarity is to mistake boisterousness for unction. Was the life of Christ himself, then, so particularly joyful? Can the life of any man be joyful who sees and feels the tragic miseries and hardly less tragic follies of the earth? The old Preacher, when he considered all the oppressions that are done under the sun, and beheld the tears of such as were oppressed and had no comforter, therefore praised the dead which are already dead more than the living which are yet alive, and declared him better than both, which hath not yet been, who hath not seen the evil work that is done under the sun. Those who are willing to trick their understandings and play fast and loose with words may, if they please, console themselves with the fatuous commonplaces of a philosophic optimism; may with eyes tight shut cling to the notion that they live in the best of all possible worlds, or discerning all the anguish that may be compressed into threescore years and ten, still try to accept the Stoic's paradox that pain is not an evil. Or, most wonderful and most common of all, they may find this joy of which they talk, in meditating on the moral perfections of the omnipotent Being for whose diversion the dismal panorama of all the evil work done under the sun was bidden to unfold itself, and who sees that it is very good. Those who are capable of a continuity of joyous emotion on these terms may well complain of Mr. Mill's story as dreary; and so may the school of Solomon, who commended mirth because a man hath no better thing than to eat and to drink and to be merry. People, however, who are prohibited by their intellectual conditions from finding full satisfaction either in spiritual raptures or in pleasures of sense, may think the standard of happiness which Mr. Mill sought and reached, not unacceptable and not unworthy of being striven after.

Mr. Mill's conception of happiness in life is more intelligible if we contrast it with his father's. The Cynic element in James Mill, as his son now tells us, was that he had scarcely any belief in pleasures; he thought few of them worth the price which has to be paid for them, and he set down the greater number of the miscarriages in life as due to an excessive estimate of them. "He thought human life a poor thing at best, after the freshness of youth and of unsatisfied curiosity had gone by. . . . . He would sometimes say that if life were made what it might be, by good government and good education, it would be worth having; but he never spoke with anything like enthusiasm even of that possibility." We should shrink from calling even this theory dreary, associated as it is with the rigorous enforcement of the heroic virtues of temperance and moderation, and the strenuous and careful bracing up of every faculty to face the inevitable and make the best of it. At the bottom it is the theory of many of the bravest souls, who fare grimly through life in the mood of leaders of forlorn hopes, denying pleasures, yet very sensible of the stern delight of fortitude. We can have no difficulty in understanding that, when the elder Mill lay dying, "his interest in all things and persons that had interested him through life was undiminished, nor did the approach of death cause the smallest wavering (as in so strong and firm a mind it was impossible that

it should) in his convictions on the subject of religion. His principal satisfaction, after he knew that his end was near, seemed
to be the thought of what he had done to make the world better
than he found it; and his chief regret in not living longer, that
he had not had time to do more."

Mr. Mill, however, went beyond this conception. He had a
belief in pleasures, and thought human life by no means a poor
thing to those who knew how to make the best of it. It was essential both to the stability of his utilitarian philosophy, and to the
contentment of his own temperament, that the reality of happiness should be vindicated, and he did both vindicate and attain it.
A highly pleasurable excitement that should have no end, of
course he did not think possible; but he regarded the two constituents of a satisfied life, much tranquillity and some excitement,
as perfectly attainable by many men, and as ultimately attainable
by very many more. The ingredients of this satisfaction he set
forth as follows:—a willingness not to expect more from life
than life is capable of bestowing; an intelligent interest in the
objects of mental culture; genuine private affections; and a sincere interest in the public good. What, on the other hand, are the
hindrances which prevent these elements from being in the possession of every one born in a civilized country? Ignorance; bad
laws or customs, debarring a man or woman from the sources of
happiness within reach; and "the positive evils of life, the great
sources of physical and mental suffering—such as indigence,
disease, and the unkindness, worthlessness, or premature loss of
objects of affection." But every one of these calamitous impedi-
ments is susceptible of the weightiest modification, and some of
them of final removal. Mr. Mill had learnt from Turgot and
Condorcet—two of the wisest and noblest of men, as he justly
calls them—among many other lessons, this of the boundless improveableness of the human lot, and we may believe that he read
over many a time the pages in which Condorcet delineated the
Tenth Epoch in the history of human perfectibility, and traced
out in words of finely reserved enthusiasm the operation of the
forces which should consummate the progress of the race. "All
the grand sources of human suffering," Mr. Mill thought, "are in
a great degree, many of them almost entirely, conquerable by
human care and effort; and though their removal is grievously

slow—though a long succession of generations will perish in the breach before the conquest is completed, and this world becomes all that, if will and knowledge were not wanting, it might easily be made—yet every mind sufficiently intelligent and generous to bear a part, however small and unconspicuous, in the endeavour, will draw a noble enjoyment from the contest itself, which he would not for any bribe in the form of selfish indulgence consent to be without."

We thus see how far from dreary this wise and benign man actually found his own life; how full it was of cheerfulness, of animation, of persevering search, of a tranquillity lighted up at wholesome intervals by flashes of intellectual and moral excitement. That it was not seldom crossed by moods of despondency is likely enough, but we may at least be sure that these moods had nothing in common with the vulgar despondency of those whose hopes are centred in material prosperity in this world and spiritual prosperity in some other: they were the dejection of a magnanimous spirit, that could only be cast down by some new hindrance to the spread of reason and enlightenment among men, or some new weakening of their incentives to right doing.

Much has been said against Mr. Mill's strictures on society, and his withdrawal from it. If we realise the full force of all that he says of his own purpose in life, it is hard to see how either his opinion or his practice could have been different. He ceased to be content with "seconding the superficial improvements" in common ways of thinking, and saw the necessity of working at a fundamental re-constitution of accepted modes of thought. This in itself implies a condemnation of a social intercourse that rests on the base of conventional ways of looking at things. The better kind of society, it is true, appears to contain two classes; not only the class that will hear nothing said hostile to the greater social conventions, the popular theology among them, but also another class who will tolerate or even encourage attack on the greater social conventions, and a certain mild discussion of improvements in them—provided only neither attack nor discussion be conducted in too serious a vein. A new idea about God, or property, or the family, is handed round among the company, as ladies of quality in Queen Anne's time handed round a black page or a

China monster. In Bishop Butler's phrase, these people only want to know what is said, not what is true. To be in earnest, to show that you mean what you say, to think of drawing blood in the encounter, is thought, and perhaps very naturally thought, to be a piece of bad manners. Social intercourse can only exist either pleasantly or profitably among people who share a great deal of common ground in opinion and feeling. Mr. Mill, no doubt, was always anxious to find as much common ground as he honestly could, for this was one of the most characteristic maxims of his propagandism; but a man who had never been brought up in the popular religion, and who had been brought up in habits of the most scrupulous fair dealing with his own understanding; who had never closed his mind to new truths from likely sources, but whose character was formed, and whose mind was made up on the central points of opinion, was not in a position to derive much benefit from those who in all respects represent a less advanced stage of mental development, while all the benefit which they were in a position to derive from him could not be adequately secured by reading what he wrote. Perhaps there is nothing wiser among the wise things written in the Autobiography than the remarks on the fact that persons of any mental superiority who greatly frequent society are greatly deteriorated by it. "Not to mention loss of time, the tone of their feelings is lowered: they become less in earnest about those of their opinions respecting which they must remain silent in the society they frequent: they come to look on their most elevated objects as unpractical, or at least too remote from realisation to be more than a vision or a theory: and if, more fortunate than most, they retain their higher principles unimpaired, yet with respect to the person and affairs of their own day, they insensibly adopt the modes of feeling and judgment in which they can hope for sympathy from the company they keep." That a man loses something, nay, that he loses much, by being deprived of animating intercourse with other men, Mr. Mill would probably have been the first to admit. Where that intercourse can be had, nothing is more fit to make the judgment robust, nothing more fit to freshen and revive our interests, and clothe them with reality. Even second-rate companionship has some clear advantages. The question is whether these advantages outweigh the equally clear disadvantages. Mr. Mill was persuaded that they do not.

Those whom disgust at the aimlessness and insignificance of most of our social intercourse may dispose to withdrawal from it —and their number will probably increase as the reaction against intellectual flippancy goes on—will do well to remember that Mr. Mill's retirement and his vindication of it sprang from no moral valetudinarianism. He did not retire to gratify any self-indulgent whim, but only in order to work the more uninterruptedly and definitely. The Autobiography tells us what pains he took to keep himself informed of all that was going on in every part of the world, and those who knew him will perhaps agree that he was more widely and precisely informed of the transactions of the day in every department of activity all over the world, than any other person of their acquaintance. People should remember, further, that though Mr. Mill saw comparatively little of men after a certain time, yet he was for many years of his life in constant and active relations with men. It was to his experience in the India Office that he attributed some of his most serviceable qualities, especially this: "I learnt how to obtain the best I could, when I could not obtain everything; instead of being indignant or dispirited because I could not have entirely my own way, to be pleased and encouraged when I could have the smallest part of it; and when even that could not be, to bear with complete equanimity the being overruled altogether." In these words we seem almost to hear the modest and simple tones of the writer's own voice.

Mr. Mill's
Three
Essays on Religion

In the few well-considered words which are prefixed to this volume, we are told that Mr. Mill not only habitually declined to be hurried into premature decision on any point to which he did not think that he had given sufficient time and labour to have exhausted it to the utmost limit of his own thinking powers: "even after he had arrived at definite conclusions he refused to allow the curiosity of others to force him to the expression of them before he had bestowed all the elaboration in his power upon their adequate expression, and before, therefore, he had subjected to the test of time, not only the conclusions themselves, but also the form into which he had thrown them. The same reasons, therefore, which made him cautious in the spoken utterance of his opinion in proportion as it was necessary to be at once precise and comprehensive in order to be properly understood, which in his judgment was pre-eminently the case in religious speculation, were the reasons which made him abstain from publishing his Essay on Nature for upwards of fifteen years, and might have led him still to withhold the others which now appear in the same volume." This is an adequate explanation of the reserve on religious subjects which has long puzzled Mr. Mill's followers, and perhaps even scandalized some of the more

Nature: The Utility of Religion: Theism. By John Stuart Mill. London: Longmans. 1874. [These essays were first published in two parts in *Fortnightly Review,* n.s., 95 (November 1874):634–51, and n.s., 97 (January 1875):103–31—ed.]

ardent and on-pressing spirits. That fear of the odium attaching to the expression of his true opinions had anything to do with this prolonged reserve, is a supposition equally inconsistent with the strength and courage of his character as it was known to his private friends, and with some conspicuous acts of his public career.

On the whole, we are inclined to think that comparatively little odium will be excited by Mr. Mill's opinions, now that they have at length been given to us, along with a rigorously careful statement of the reasons which led him finally to adopt them, after an equally careful examination of the hostile and competing opinions. At first there may be, indeed there already has been, a certain shock at the outspokenness with which Mr. Mill repudiates some of the ideas that are most cherished by the less instructed or less thoughtful among believers. But it is the foundation of the superstructure about which the wiser heads are solicitous. And of the foundations, I am not sure that Mr. Mill does not leave them as much as they want. Theologians who know their trade, with the aid of no shiftier logic than they and their hearers are accustomed to, will certainly be able to construct a far more respectable kind of defence than they had any reason to hope, out of Mr. Mill's concluding admissions. His volume is, no doubt, thoroughly destructive of the doctrines which the more strict and literal adherents of the current supernatural creed count of the highest sacredness and importance. To the mystic articles of the faith which still remains the main organ of spiritual life in the West, his vigorous dialectic gives no quarter. On the common conception of the attributes of a Supreme Being he makes a most unsparing attack. Even the cardinal propositions that such a Being exists, and that this Being has endowed men with the quality of being immortal, he reduces from the august rank of certainties to the humbler place of holy possibilities. To the orthodox believer, however lax the form of orthodoxy may be, Mr. Mill's conclusions will seem objectionable enough. All this is true; yet considering both the intensity and the direction of the apprehensions of the theological world at present, how terrified men are at the prospect of being driven by science headlong into a forlorn wilderness of atheism and materialism, we may see reason for anticipating a certain sense of relief when it is found that, so far from shutting the door of hope on all the old religious doctrines, the chief English propagator of positive modes of thought in this generation closes his speculative work in the world with the following propositions:—

That such evidence as there is points to the creation of the present order of the universe by an Intelligent Mind, whose power over the materials was not absolute, whose benevolence was not his sole inducement, but yet who desired the good of his creatures (p. 243).

That to the conception of the rational sceptic it remains possible that "Christ was actually what he supposed himself to be—not God, for he never made the smallest pretension to that character and would probably have thought such a pretension as blasphemous as it seemed to the men who condemned him—but a man charged with a special, express, and unique commission from God to lead mankind to truth and virtue" (p. 255).

That, though there is no assurance whatever of a life after death, on grounds of natural religion, yet "to any one who feels it conducive either to his satisfaction or to his usefulness to hope for a future state as a possibility, there is no hindrance to his indulging that hope" (p. 210).

Finally with reference to revelation and its miracles, this—

> What can be said with truth on the side of Miracles amounts only to this: Considering that the order of nature affords some evidence of the reality of a Creator, and of his bearing good-will to his creatures though not of its being the sole prompter of his conduct towards them: considering, again, that all the evidence of his existence is evidence also that he is not all-powerful, and in our ignorance of the limits of his power we cannot positively decide that he was able to provide for us by the original plan of Creation all the good which it entered into his intentions to bestow upon us or even to bestow any part of it at any earlier period than that at which we actually received it,—considering these things, when we consider further that a gift, extremely precious, came to us which though facilitated was not apparently necessitated by what had gone before, but was due, as far as appearances go, to the peculiar mental and moral endowments of one man, and that man openly proclaimed that it did not come from himself but from God through him, then we are entitled to say that there is nothing so inherently impossible or absolutely

incredible in this supposition as to preclude any one from hoping
that it may perhaps be true. [Pp. 239–40.]

Undoubtedly to those who have dwelt with exultation in the
blazing sunlight of dogmatic convictions, these twilight hopes
and tepid possibilities will seem miserably desolate. Yet such
persons will nourish a certain private thankfulness for the
buckler with which Mr. Mill has furnished them against the fiery
darts of the dogmatic unbeliever. They will henceforth believe
themselves to have his authority for retorting on the denier, that
he, and not they, is the irrational person, the offender against the
laws of evidence; and that if they have been too apt to confound
a low degree of probability with certainty, the denier has been
just as apt to confound a low degree of probability with impossi-
bility. They will contrast the iron unfaith of James Mill, that
more than Roman figure of the *Autobiography,* with the eagerness of his son and most important disciple to restore the domain
of the supernatural, after it has been removed from the region of
Belief, into the region of Hope. So long as this domain of the
supernatural is left to them in one quarter or another, they will
feel that nothing is lost. Concede to them the region of hope, and
they will count pretty surely on making the old growths thrive in
it with the old vigour of the region of belief. Indeed at no time
in our generation has their thought been very much stronger, nor
has it had much more to say for itself, than its father, the wish.
Being told that they may now only wish for what they used to
think assured, most of them will hardly be sensible of any serious
difference in their frame of mind.

The general drift of Mr. Mill's new volume may be described
as setting in the following directions:—

(*a*) The displacement of the idea of a providential government by an all-powerful Being for the good of his creatures.

(*b*) The substitution in its stead of the idea of the possibility,
and, in a low degree, even the probability, of the government of
the universe by a Being with limited powers.

(*c*) The admission of certain supernatural potentialities as
proper objects of rational hope, though not capable of demonstration.

(*d*) The vindication of such a hope, as a legitimate aid and an effective support of "that real, though purely human religion, which sometimes calls itself the Religion of Humanity and sometimes that of Duty."

It will thus be seen that his latest work bears one of the well-known marks of all that has come from Mr. Mill's hand. While expelling with keen dialectic the ungrounded or self-contradictory ideas in which natural theology has been so fruitful, he shows the most subtle apprehension of all the valuable associations that were bound up in those ideas, nor is he content to part company with them until he has satisfied himself that they are susceptible of a certain transformation, which shall preserve what is precious and helpful to the imagination, while it throws off all that is unacceptable to the right reason. Some persons, indeed, as we shall presently see, may think that this anxiety not to go further in the negative direction than the evidence warrants, has caused Mr. Mill to grant positions which are not at all unlikely to be the springs of a new and mischievous reaction towards supernaturalism. That is the opinion of the present writer. A hundred years ago some of the seventeen atheists whom Hume met at D'Holbach's table, cried out about Voltaire—"Mais il est bigot; il est déiste!" It is not impossible that something may be said in the same spirit, of Mr. Mill's creed of low probabilities and faintly cheering potentialities. And few persons will be able to overcome a consciousness of incongruity in the author's final appeal to a mystic sentiment which in other parts of the book he had shown such good reason for counting superfluous. With all profound respect and unalterable affection for Mr. Mill's character and memory, I for one cannot help regarding the most remarkable part of the book as an aberration not less grave than the aberrations with which he rightly charged Comte.

One powerful element in the continuation of the present condition of religious anarchy is to be found in the vicious habit of substituting the history of a conception, or group of conceptions, for a scientific inquiry into its truth and its correspondence with reality or fitness. The only wisdom, according to this accomplished school, is to know what has been thought upon the great questions of human interest in different ages and under diversified intellectual conditions; not to press forward with all the apparatus of induction and ratiocination in search of true answers of our own, but to be content with collecting in an intelligent and systematic way the guesses which men have made from time to time in their attempts to solve the inscrutable riddles. The interesting thing about an opinion, they say, is not so much its more or less of truth, as its place and order in the classification of the mental experiences of the race. The literature of knowledge, rather than of direct discussion, is the true literature of emancipation. The effect of the adoption of this point of view to the exclusion of search after dogmatic truth is obviously to make even those who would be revolted by the more vulgar or direct forms of an universal scepticism, still willing to believe that all positive opinions alike are tolerably true. The late Mr. Maurice, for example, seems to have lived in this mood of the intellect; and the tendency of our present ideals of culture is to make such a mood stronger and more widely spread. Any one can see that its immediate influence must be to prolong the existing epoch of decay in religious opinions. It arrests the mind at the moment when it would otherwise deliberately pass forth from the declining beliefs and set out "voyaging on strange seas of thought" in search of beliefs more reconcilable with reason and knowledge. Now Mr. Mill was always fully alive to the value of studying opinions in their relations to institutions and customs, as well as to one another. He had plenty of that historic sense, which he noticed as deficient in Bentham. But his training, which was marked by the characteristic spirit of the eighteenth century, prevented him from putting the history of ideas before an inquiry into the ideas themselves, and in the present essays as elsewhere he treats as the most important relations which an opinion can have, its direct relations with the facts which constitute its object and matter. He confronts the current propositions of natural theology directly with the circumstances of nature, and thus takes the student out of the luminous haze with which the historic method, when not supplemented by the dogmatic method, envelopes the great religious issues. In examining moral and religious doctrines we are not merely assorting dried plants in classes for a herbarium, but testing their active qualities and specific properties. "Pray do not call it by any name," cried Dorothea in *Middlemarch,* speaking of the belief which she had found out to comfort her life, "you will say it is Persian or something else geographical. It is my life." One hopeful feature about the discussion which Mr. Mill's book must raise is that it will bring men face to face with opinions themselves as elements in human life, and not merely with their Persian or other geographical source. "The most important quality of an opinion," he says (p. 128), "on any momentous subject, is its truth or falsity, which to us resolves itself into the sufficiency of the evidence on which it rests. It is indispensable that the subject of religion should from time to time be reviewed as a strictly scientific question, and that its evidences should be tested by the same scientific methods, and on the same principles, as those of any of the speculative conclusions drawn by physical science." In other words enumeration and comparison of different ways of interpreting the facts of the universe are not to supersede the duty of definite judgment of this or that interpretation on the merits.

The first of the three essays is entitled *Nature,* and consists of an examination of the various ways in which the word Nature and its derivatives are employed to convey ideas of approval and even moral obligation. It has conveyed such ideas in all ages from the Stoics and Epicureans down to Rousseau, and from Rousseau down to the most recent and characteristic deliverances of the modern mind. "That any mode of thinking, feeling, or acting, is 'according to nature' is usually accepted as a strong argument for its goodness. If it can be said with any plausibility that 'nature enjoins' anything, the propriety of obeying the injunction is by most people considered to be made out: and conversely, the imputation of being contrary to nature is thought to bar the door against any pretension on the part of the thing so designated to be tolerated or excused; and the word unnatural has not ceased to be one of the most vituperative epithets in the language." The object of the essay is to inquire into the foundation of this practice of current speech; into the truth of the doctrines which make Nature a test of right and wrong, good and evil, and which attach any merit or approval to following, imitating, or obeying Nature.

The reader will soon understand, as he proceeds with Mr. Mill's argument, that the ultimate purpose and main undercurrent of it is a double one. The glorification of Nature has been, as Mr. Mill says, "one of the most copious sources of false taste, false philosophy, false morality, and even bad law." In all of these fields it has been mischievous, but the two most important regions in which it has misled men are those of theology and morals. In the one it has been connected with an idea, at once untenable and depraving, of certain of the attributes of a deity. In the other it has been associated with notions about human conduct and the test of right and wrong in it, which have retarded social progress by disparaging the improvement that man's own effort has made in his character and circumstances, and by substituting a fanciful conformity to Nature, instead of the promotion of happiness, as the standard of good and evil. This being the twofold tendency of the habit of exalting Nature, to assail that exaltation successfully is, in the first place, to undo some of the most serious work of the writers on natural theology; and, in the second place, to overthrow the most fundamental positions of the à priori school of moralists. Such an assault bears first on the attributes of a creator, and second on the proper pattern and standard of the conduct of men. It leads to the two propositions: that Nature is not at all creditable to the moral goodness of its creator, if we suppose such a being to be omnipotent; and not at all a desirable model for human beings, whose only safe guide must always be not Nature, but utility or the general good. To look at Nature really and as she is, is to perceive that the common religious explanation of the order of Nature is self-contradictory, and inconsistent with the facts for which it professes to account. It is at the same time to see that the scheme of Nature cannot have had for its sole or even principal object the good of human or other sentient beings, and therefore that all useful action consists in alteration and improvement of the spontaneous course of Nature, alike in external circumstance and in man's impulses and motives. Here, then, is the key to the significance of Mr. Mill's first essay, and its bearings on the other two essays by which it is accompanied.

A passage in the *Autobiography* is worth transcribing in this connection—a portion of that memorable account of the elder Mill, which will always remain one of the most striking pieces in the anthology of the characters of our British worthies.

I have heard my father say [Mr. Mill writes] that the turning-point of his mind on the subject—[Revelation and Natural Religion]—was reading Butler's "Analogy." That work, of which he always continued to speak with respect, kept him, as he said, for some considerable time a believer in the divine authority of Christianity; by proving to him that whatever are the difficulties in believing that the Old and New Testaments proceed from, or record the acts of, a perfectly wise and good being, the same and still greater difficulties stand in the way of the belief, that a being of such a character can have been the Maker of the universe. He considered Butler's argument as conclusive against the only opponents for whom it was intended. Those who admit an omnipotent as well as perfectly just and benevolent maker and ruler of such a world as this, can say little against Christianity but what can, with at least equal force, be retorted against themselves. . . . He found it impossible to believe that a world so evil was the work of an Author combining infinite power with perfect goodness and righteousness. . . . The Sabæan or Manichean theory of a Good and an Evil Principle, struggling against each other for the government of the universe, he would not equally have condemned. . . . He would have regarded it as a mere hypothesis; but he would have ascribed to it no depraving influence. As it was, his aversion to religion, in the sense usually attached to the term, was of the same kind with that of Lucretius: he regarded it with the feelings due not to a mere mental delusion, but to a great moral evil.

Thus early was the germ of the present essay planted.

The examination proceeds on a line which, with much abbreviation, we shall now endeavour to trace. In what sense is the word Nature employed, when associated with eulogistic ideas? It has two principal meanings. In the one, it denotes all the powers existing either within us or without us, and everything which takes place through those powers. In the other, it denotes only what happens without the voluntary and intentional agency of man. This distinction, which Mr. Mill arrives at after the manner of the Socrates of a Platonic dialogue, has to be borne carefully in mind throughout the essay, which might be described as an argumentative separation of the good and the righteousness in the world from the wrong and the degradation, and an ascription of all the former to the voluntary agency of man, and all the latter to the spontaneous course of nature undisturbed by man. As we shall see at the close of our remarks it is not only the à priori moralists nor the natural theòlogians whom such a line of reasoning effects. The school of evolution, while repudiating theological explanations, yet is slowly fashioning Nature and her processes into a divinity whose lineaments are acquiring a strong likeness to the central figure in the crumbling temple of natural theology.

Now in the first sense, where Nature means the entire system of things, with the aggregate of all their properties, it is superfluous and unmeaning to bid us follow Nature. We have no power to do anything else. "Every action is the exertion of some natural power, and its effects of all sorts are so many phenomena of nature, produced by the powers and properties of some of the objects of nature, in exact obedience to some law or laws of nature. When I voluntarily use my organs to take in food, the act and its consequences take place according to the laws of nature: if instead of food I swallow poison, the case is exactly the same" (p. 16). The continual talk about obeying the laws of nature is therefore absurd and useless. To tell us to follow Nature in this sense is to prescribe a rule of right conduct which agrees quite as well with wrong conduct. There is perhaps a rational notion at the bottom of this confused kind of injunction, namely, that we shall do well to study Nature and the actual properties of things, with a view to making such properties serve our purpose and check our conduct. But the promoters of the doctrine of following Nature undoubtedly intend much more by it than mere study of the properties of things, for the sake of adapting means to ends and giving effect to our wishes and intentions. They uphold conformity to Nature not merely as a prudential but as an ethical maxim. "Right action, must mean something more and other than merely intelligent action: yet no precept beyond this last can be connected with the word Nature in the wider and more philosophical of its acceptations. We must try it therefore in the other sense, that in which Nature stands distinguished from Art, and denotes, not the whole course of the phenomena which come under our observation, but only their spontaneous course."

Now it is obvious that the maxim of following Nature in this second sense, is not superfluous, as we have seen to be the case in the first meaning; but it is absurd. The whole process of civilisation, from digging and ploughing, up to the production of the most refined works of art, is plainly an interference with the spontaneous order of things. "All praise of Civilisation, or Art, or Contrivance is so much dispraise of Nature [in the second of the two principal meanings of the word]; an admission of imperfection which it is man's business, and merit, to be always endeavouring to correct or mitigate." And this brings the writer face to face with a central position of religious persons from the most primitive times down to our own day. In early times, there is a very distinct, active, and detrimental consciousness that human improvements are a censure on nature, which is the work of the gods. Inventions are at first either treated as impious, or else understood to be the voluntary communication of some god to a favoured mortal. With the extension of human experience and the enlarged intelligence of man's interpretation of this experience, such identification of acquiescence in things as they are with reverence for the Being who is believed to have made them what they are, grows weaker. "But the imputation of prying into the secrets of the Almighty long remained a powerful weapon of attack against unpopular inquirers into nature; and the charge of presumptuously attempting to defeat the designs of Providence, still retains enough of its original force to be thrown in as a make-weight along with other objections, when there is a desire to find fault with any new exertion of human forethought and contrivance."

No one, indeed, asserts it to be the intention of the Creator that the spontaneous order of the creation should not be altered, or even that it should not be altered in any new way. But there still exists a vague notion that though it is very proper to control this or the other natural phenomenon, the general scheme of nature is a model for us to imitate: that with more or less liberty in details, we should on the whole be guided by the spirit and general conception of nature's own ways: that they are God's work, and as such perfect; that man cannot rival their unapproachable excellence, and can best show his skill and piety by attempting, in however imperfect a way, to reproduce their likeness; and that if not the whole, yet some particular parts of the spontaneous order of nature, selected according to the speaker's predilections, are, in a peculiar sense, manifestations of the

Creator's will; a sort of finger-posts pointing out the direction which things in general, and therefore our voluntary actions, are intended to take. Feelings of this sort, though repressed on ordinary occasions by the contrary current of life, are ready to break out whenever custom is silent, and the native promptings of the mind have nothing opposed to them but reason. [Pp. 23–24.]

This consideration of the hindrance which the great à priori fallacy of the perfection of nature has interposed in the way of progress (and is not modern science in danger of breeding a corresponding à posteriori fallacy of the perfection of nature?), brings the writer to one of the chief destructive propositions of his book, which, he asserts in different places with a great variety of expression. Here it is put thus: "The order of nature, in so far as unmodified by man, is such as no being, whose attributes are justice and benevolence, would have made, with the intention that his rational creatures should follow it as an example." In other words, creation cannot be the entire work of a Being of unlimited power, and at the same time animated by the spirit of justice and benevolence. Hence the universe is not a proper object for that moral admiration which rhetorical theologians ecstatically lavish upon it. The greater natural phenomena strike us with astonishment rising into awe. Their enormous duration in time, their prodigious extension in space, the vastness of their forces, affect us with a profound sense of sublimity, but "this is more allied to terror than to any moral emotion." It is no admiration of excellence. "Those in whom awe produces admiration may be æsthetically developed, but they are morally uncultivated." We are all aware from familiar personal experience how readily disposed people are to translate awe and affright into some formula of pietistic reverence. And we are aware, too, how the same formulas serve also to express an overflowing emotion inspired by scenes of natural tranquillity and plenty and comfort. In neither case is the moral inference warranted, nor the moral imputation of praise to the power or powers who made the universe, justifiable. For we are bound to survey the forces of nature as a whole. The result of such a survey is described by Mr. Mill in a passage of singular energy that may recall Tennyson's famous stanzas on the man—

Who trusted God was love indeed,
And love Creation's final law—
Though Nature, red in tooth and claw,
With ravin, shriek'd against his creed.

In sober truth, nearly all the things which men are hanged or imprisoned for doing to one another, are Nature's every-day performances. Killing, the most criminal act recognised by human laws, Nature does once to every being that lives; and in a large proportion of cases, after protracted tortures such as only the greatest monsters whom we read of ever purposely inflicted on their living fellow-creatures. If, by an arbitrary reservation, we refuse to account anything murder but what abridges a certain term supposed to be allotted to human life, nature also does this to all but a small percentage of lives, and does it in all the modes, violent or insidious, in which the worst human beings take the lives of one another. Nature impales men, breaks them as if on the wheel, casts them to be devoured by wild beasts, burns them to death, crushes them with stones like the first Christian martyr, starves them with hunger, freezes them with cold, poisons them by the quick or slow venom of her exhalations, and has hundreds of other hideous deaths in reserve, such as the ingenious cruelty of a Nabis or a Domitian never surpassed. All this, Nature does with the most supercilious disregard both of mercy and of justice, emptying her shafts upon the best and noblest indifferently with the meanest and worst; upon those who are engaged in the highest and worthiest enterprises, and often as the direct consequence of the noblest acts; and it might almost be imagined as a punishment for them. She mows down those on whose existence hangs the well-being of a whole people, perhaps the prospects of the human race for generations to come, with as little compunction as those whose death is a relief to themselves, or a blessing to those under their noxious influence. Such are Nature's dealings with life. Even when she does not intend to kill, she inflicts the same tortures in apparent wantonness. In the clumsy provision which she has made for that perpetual renewal of animal life, rendered necessary by the prompt termination she puts to it in every individual instance, no human being ever comes into the world but another human being is literally stretched on the rack for hours or days, not unfrequently issuing in death. Next to taking life (equal to it according to a high authority) is taking the means by which we live; and Nature does this too on the largest scale and with the most callous indifference. A single hurricane destroys the hopes of a season; a flight of locust, or an

inundation, desolates a district; a trifling chemical change in an
edible root starves a million of people. The waves of the sea, like
banditti, seize and appropriate the wealth of the rich and the
little all of the poor with the same accompaniments of stripping,
wounding, and killing as their human antitypes. Everything, in
short, which the worst men commit either against life or property
is perpetrated on a larger scale by natural agents. Nature has
noyades more fatal than those of Carrier; her explosions of fire-
damp are as destructive as human artillery; her plague and
cholera far surpass the poison-cups of the Borgias. Even the love
of "order" which is thought to be a following of the ways of
Nature, is in fact a contradiction of them. All which people are
accustomed to deprecate as "disorder" and its consequences, is
precisely a counterpart of Nature's ways. Anarchy and the Reign
of Terror are overmatched in injustice, ruin, and death, by a
hurricane and a pestilence. [Pp. 28–31.]

It is of no avail, proceeds Mr. Mill, to urge that all these things
possess an occult quality of promoting good and wise ends. Even
if it were so, that would be no reason why it is religious or moral
in us to follow nature. The end is no moral warrant for the means.
Hidden good often comes out of human misdeeds and crimes, but
that does not prevent them from remaining misdeeds and crimes.
And in like manner if in the order of nature good comes out
of the mass of misery and injustice with which the world has
always teemed, that does not lessen the significance of the fact
that the method by which this supposed good is attained is a
method of misery and injustice. Then the writer once more
presses the conclusion from which there is no real escape, that
"if the maker of this world *can* all that he will, he wills misery."
And this brings him to one of the main propositions of the book:
—"The only admissible moral theory of Creation is that the
Principle of Good *cannot* at once and altogether subdue the
powers of evil either physical or moral; could not place mankind
free from the necessity of an incessant struggle with the malefi-
cent powers, or make them always victorious in that struggle, but
could and did make them capable of carrying on the fight with
vigour and with progressively increasing success. Of all the
religious explanations of the order of nature, this alone is neither
contradictory to itself, nor to the facts for which it attempts to
account" (p. 39).

Another line of theological argument is next considered.

Though it may be hard, the natural theologian contends, to maintain that Nature as a whole is a type of perfect wisdom and benevolence, yet we may discern the image of the moral qualities which we have been wont to ascribe to the Creator stamped on some portion of his work. The element in the construction of the world which seems particularly fitted to afford special indication of the Creator's wish, is to be found in the instincts of human beings. Mr. Mill accords to this exaltation of instinct more importance as a hostile argument than we should have thought it deserved at this time of day; but orthodox theologians, at any rate, ought not to complain of the zeal and thoroughness with which he deals blow after blow upon the natural and unregenerate man. No Calvinistic divine could be more hearty in denouncing the uncleanness and degradation of man without grace; though with the Calvinist grace means a mystic infusion from the divine spirit, while Mr. Mill sets all good down to the eminently artificial discipline by which man's own action has purged the old Adam. One by one, the author examines the claims of the natural man to what in a civilized state we counted elementary virtues. The natural man is pugnacious and irascible, but he has not true courage. He has a bestial lack of cleanliness. He is a liar. He is unjust. He is profoundly selfish, being at the best sympathetically selfish, an *égoïste à deux, à trois,* or *à quatre.* The effect of such a survey (pp. 46–54) is to prove "that the duty of man is the same in respect to his own nature, as in respect to the nature of all other things, namely not to follow but to amend it." And man, until the germs of good within him have been slowly and laboriously trained, and until the evil growths which were most luxuriant in him when he was nearest to the Creator's hand have been extirpated,—man is as little the image of a moral divinity as the forces of the cosmos outside of man are such an image.

But all natural wishes, it is said, must have been implanted for a purpose. God would not have endowed us with impulses unless he had designed them to have a certain sphere of legitimate action: therefore to contemn nature so far as to refuse to pay any deference to human instincts is to contemn the purposes of God. To which Mr. Mill replies as follows:—

> I conceive that there is a radical absurdity in all these attempts to discover, in detail, what are the designs of Providence, in order

when they are discovered to help Providence in bringing them
about. Those who argue, from particular indications, that
Providence intends this or that, either believe that the Creator can
do all that he will or that he cannot. If the first supposition is
adopted—if Providence is omnipotent, Providence intends
whatever happens, and the fact of its happening proves that
Providence intended it. If so, everything which a human being
can do, is predestined by Providence and is a fulfilment of its designs. But if, as is the more religious theory, Providence intends
not all which happens, but only what is good, then indeed man
has it in his power, by his voluntary actions, to aid the intentions
of Providence; but he can only learn those intentions by considering what tends to promote the general good, and not what man
has a natural inclination to; for, limited as, on this showing, the
divine power must be, by inscrutable but insurmountable obstacles, who knows that man could have been created without desires
which never are to be, and even which never ought to be, fulfilled? The inclinations with which man has been endowed, as
well as any of the other contrivances which we observe in Nature,
may be the expression not of the divine will, but of the fetters
which impede its free action; and to take hints from these for the
guidance of our own conduct may be falling into a trap laid by
the enemy. The assumption that everything which infinite goodness can desire, actually comes to pass in this universe, or at least
that we must never say or suppose that it does not, is worthy only
of those whose slavish fears make them offer the homage of lies
to a Being who, they profess to think, is incapable of being de-
ceived and holds all falsehood in abomination.

Again there are some propensities of which no good use can
possibly be made, and which are only fit for extirpation, that is
for starvation by disuse. Take, for instance, a propensity that is
common enough in the East and in Southern Europe, a delight in
cruelty for its own sake, "a particular kind of voluptuous excitement" at the sight of pain. Even, however, if it could be proved
that every elementary impulse in human nature has its good side,
and may by proper pains be made more useful than hurtful, this
would still do very little for those who wish to set up these impulses as guides to the wishes and purposes of Providence. Were
it not for discipline, in other words, a process not following
nature, but removing us more and more from nature, even the
impulses which are necessary to our preservation, the most ele-

mentary of them all, would make human "life an exaggerated likeness of the odious scene of violence and tyranny which is exhibited by the rest of the animal kingdom, except in so far as tamed and disciplined by man."

> There, indeed, those who flatter themselves with the notion of reading the purposes of the Creator in his works, ought in consistency to have seen grounds for inferences from which they have shrunk. If there are any marks at all of special design in creation, one of the things most evidently designed is that a large proportion of all animals should pass their existence in tormenting and devouring other animals. They have been lavishly fitted out with the instruments necessary for that purpose; their strongest instincts impel them to it, and many of them seem to have been constructed incapable of supporting themselves by any other food. If a tenth part of the pains which have been expended in finding benevolent adaptations in all nature, had been employed in collecting evidence to blacken the character of the Creator, what scope for comment would not have been found in the entire existence of the lower animals, divided, with scarcely an exception, into devourers and devoured, and a prey to a thousand ills from which they are denied the faculties necessary for protecting themselves! If we are not obliged to believe the animal creation to be the work of a demon, it is because we need not suppose it to have been made by a Being of infinite power. But if imitation of the Creator's will as revealed in nature, were applied as a rule of action in this case, the most atrocious enormities of the worst men would be more than justified by the apparent intention of Providence that throughout all animated nature the strong should prey upon the weak.

To conclude the main line of argument. The favourable prejudgment which follows the word Nature when it is employed as a distinctive term for certain parts of character as contrasted with other parts, is just as unwarranted as when Nature means the whole sum of human impulses. Language abounds with uses of the word natural, which set up a presumption in favour of the quality to which the epithet is applied. Mr. Mill "can perceive only one sense in which nature or naturalness in a human being, are really terms of praise, and then the praise is only negative; namely when used to denote the absence of affectation." Otherwise to say that a piece of conduct is unnatural is no argument for its being blamable, "since even the most criminal actions are to a being like man not more unnatural than most of the virtues." And, on the other side, the plea in extenuation of a culpable act, that it was natural, ought never to be admitted. In each case it is a slovenly and seriously misleading use of language.

The leading conclusions of the essay are finally summed up as follows:—

> The word Nature has two principal meanings: it either denotes the entire system of things, with the aggregate of all their properties, or it denotes things as they would be, apart from human intervention.
>
> In the first of these senses, the doctrine that man ought to follow nature is unmeaning; since man has no power to do anything else than follow nature; all his actions are done through, and in obedience to, some one or many of nature's physical or mental laws.
>
> In the other sense of the term, the doctrine that man ought to follow nature, or, in other words, ought to make the spontaneous course of things the model of his voluntary actions, is equally irrational and immoral.
>
> Irrational, because all human action whatever, consists in altering, and all useful action in improving, the spontaneous course of nature.
>
> Immoral, because the course of natural phenomena being replete with everything which when committed by human beings is most worthy of abhorrence, any one who endeavoured in his actions to imitate the natural course of things would be universally seen and acknowledged to be the wickedest of men.
>
> The scheme of Nature regarded in its whole extent, cannot have had, for its sole or even principal object, the good of human or other sentient beings. What good it brings to them, is mostly the result of their own exertions. Whatsoever, in nature, gives indication of beneficent design, proves this beneficence to be armed only with limited power; and the duty of man is to co-operate with the beneficent powers, not by imitating but by perpetually striving to amend the course of nature—and bringing that part of it over which we can exercise control, more nearly into conformity with a high standard of justice and goodness.

We proceed to suggest one or two criticisms upon this very vigorous piece of argumentation. On Mr. Mill's treatment of the old mystery of evil as the handiwork of a benevolent and all-powerful Being not much is left to be said. The enigma is as old as the Book of Job, and it never can be solved on any theistic hypothesis, unless men surrender either the Creator's omnipotence, as Mr. Mill does, or his benevolence and sense of justice, as, without meaning it, a man like De Maistre does. It may be worth while to glance for a moment at a rival theory, which will help us the better to place Mr. Mill's line of objection to all theories of that kind. We may as well take De Maistre as any one else, for he was one of the most acute and least dishonest of modern apologists for the ways of God to man. De Maistre started from the doctrine that *Deus est auctor mali quod est pœna, non autem mali quod est culpa.** Man's will is free. He falls into sin; the ruler of the world exacts a penalty, and these penalties constitute the pain and misery of the world. The objection to this was that the penalties are distributed in block, following no moral law, but falling alike on the just and the unjust, just as happiness or exemption from penalties falls on both alike. De Maistre evaded this objection—which had many years before been pressed upon the world with new force in Voltaire's splendid poem on the Earthquake of Lisbon—by the singular doctrine that a certain amount of transgression in the world called for a certain amount of vengeance, and that God chastises all men, as a pro-consul might chastise a whole province by fine and decimation, for the offences of some. This may or may not be true. It is as possible an explanation as that which Mr. Mill suggests. But it effectually reduces the Creator to the rank of a vindictive, pitiless, and blind judge. Whatever else it may be, then, such an explanation strips Nature, or the mechanism by which the Deity at once leads men into temptation and then punishes them indiscriminately for yielding to it, of all commendable moral attributes. Yet this theory is only the orthodox scheme of things with one or two ingenious variations in the reading. It involves not a whit more sophistication alike of the understanding and the moral sense, than is involved in every popular version of the western creed. Mr. Mill's rebellion against all such theories of the cosmic plan was first declared in the examination of Hamilton, and with a vehemence that startled many of his readers. That men

* "God is the author of evil which is punishment but not of that which is the guilt itself"—ed.

should pay the tribute of their worship and homage and ever-lasting praise to a Being capable of devising and carrying out a plan so heinously immoral, filled him with rational indignation. The present essay is, on one side of it, a further expression of the same feeling, and a fuller elaboration of the grounds for it.

The severance of all association between the standards of ethics and the course of nature—and this is the main object of the essay—is intended to go far beyond a mere correction of a fallacy of common speech. Mr. Mill inherited from Turgot and Condorcet the idea of perfectibility. Though he refrained from any such extravagant specification of the kinds and degrees of human perfection as the latter of these two eminent men ventured upon, yet no other element played so important a part in his moral and social thinking as a conviction of the immense and at present inconceivable pitch to which human happiness is capable of being raised by the exertion of reason and the strengthened practice of social devotion. This is the key alike to the *Liberty,* the *Utilitarianism,* and to some of the most original chapters in the *Political Economy.* To bring this conviction of the immense improveableness both of the arrangements of society and of the character of men, into a leading place among our habitual notions and most active inspirations, it is necessary to displace the metaphysical idea of Nature as a force presiding over the destinies of humanity, and benignly shaping them to higher and more prosperous ends. To encourage men to energetic endeavour in the path of improvement, no argument is so potent as the exhibition of the improvement which their endeavour has already achieved in the long process of the ages. And this exhibition must be, what Mr. Mill has made it, a demonstration of triumphs over Nature, if we use the word to describe all that takes place spontaneously without the voluntary intervention of man, including man's own primitive impulses.

Against the Nature of theologians and metaphysicians with a moral purpose, Mr. Mill's case is abundantly made out. But a different view has come into fashion, which does not make Nature a moral force, any more than Mr. Mill allows it to be one, but yet which presents it in a way that lays bare in Mr. Mill's essay a certain philosophical inadequateness. We are told in the Introductory Notice that the essay on Nature was written between 1850 and 1858, and that the author would certainly have referred to the writings of Mr. Darwin if that illustrious man's speculations had been fully before the world when the essay was composed. It can never, I think, be sufficiently deplored that the author did not find time to give us the result of his meditations as to the effect upon his own long-settled line of thought of the theory of Evolution and its moral and sociological applications. For the conception of experience has undergone a radical change since the time of Mr. Mill's most important productivity. The Experience philosophy has established itself to an extent and over a field which, when he published the *System of Logic*—the new starting-point of that philosophy in this generation—he could hardly have thought possible for a far longer time than the process has actually taken. But in this process the fundamental idea is being revolutionised. The Experience on which the dominant philosophy is based, and to which its professors appeal, is not that mere surface of experience which lies immediately under our personal observation. It is a prolonged ascending series of experiences; or as it has been well put, not a horizontal but a transverse section of natural phenomena. Experience is that of the species, not of the individual.

The Nature of Mr. Mill's essay is partly the result of the survey of a horizontal surface. This does not interfere with the substantial truth of the conclusions to which he comes, because they follow from the Methods of Nature, and these are the same from the moral point of view whether we examine them in the light of the experience of the individual or generation, or that of the whole hierarchy of being. But the rapidity with which the Nature of science is stepping to the throne of the older Nature of theology, makes one regret that Mr. Mill did not deal with the first as well as with the second.

For there are signs of danger that the conception of Nature which seems to flow from the evolutional theory may produce that very result upon human conduct, the result, namely, of disparaging the share of the voluntary agency of man in improving the conditions of his existence, against which it was Mr. Mill's object to place us on our guard in the present essay. There is an ancient story of a creature which had only one eye, and whose enemy was a sea-monster; it was careful then to feed with its single eye turned to the sea; and lo, there came up a monster from the land side unseen, and quickly devoured it. And while utilitarians have been doing battle against the Nature of theology and of metaphysics, there has sprung up the Nature of evolution, the great self-unfolding force of progressive development. Civilisation on the evolutional theory is no more artificial than nature is artificial. It is a part of nature, all of a piece, as has been said, with the development of the embryo or the unfolding of a flower. The modifications which our race has undergone and still undergoes are the consequences of a law that underlies the whole organic creation. What becomes of man's voluntary agency in face of this?

Again, "all good customs," Mr. Mill justly says, "presuppose that there must have been individuals better than the rest who set the customs going" (p. 48). But these individuals are, in early societies at any rate, no more nor less than spontaneously presented variations of character, as independent of the voluntary agency of man as the variation of organism which ended in the development of man himself. Those who lead the way in improvement, even if we adopt the theory that they do no more than seize, concentrate, and fix progressive forces that were already working to special ends, are born with new gifts, predispositions, aptitudes,—the result of common qualities in uncommon quantity and proportion—which are what enable their possessors to do what others, their predecessors and contemporaries, could not do, or failed to discern the advantages of doing. Mr. Mill, indeed, says in one place (p. 53) that it is only through the fostering of good germs "commenced early and not counteracted by unfavourable influences, that in *some happily circumstanced specimens* of the human race, the most elevated sentiments of which humanity is capable become a second nature, stronger than the first," etc. If under the denomination of happy "circumstances" we include the conditions of internal organization, this is consistent with the theory we are discussing. But circumstances ordinarily mean with Mr. Mill, as with other writers, the external conditions, the outside medium which surrounds us. He goes on to say:—"Even those gifted organizations which have attained the like excellence by self-culture, owe it essentially to the same cause; for what self-culture would be possible without aid from the general sentiments of mankind delivered through books, and from the contemplation of exalted characters real or ideal? This artificially created or at least artificially perfected nature of the best and noblest human beings is the only nature which it is ever commendable to follow" (p. 54). It is surely difficult to think that great intellectual reformers like Socrates or Descartes, or so marvellous an imagination as Shakespeare, or so keen and singular a spirit as Voltaire, or one with such an ear for the inner spiritual voices as the writer of the *Imitatio,* were in their most distinctive part artificially created; or they were in their distinctive part any less spontaneously presented variations of the human type than those successive changes which are the origin of new species in the organic kingdom. The fact that the qualities of these rarer souls were only qualities possessed by other men enlarged or intensified, makes no difference to the argument. If it be this exaggeration of ordinary faculties which produces the extraordinary results, then that is as momentous a fact of spontaneous variation as if the results had been produced by faculties hitherto unknown.

The reconciliation of the truths in Mr. Mill's doctrine would perhaps proceed in some such way as this. If it cannot be denied that no amount of taking thought, nor anything else short of natural intervention, will produce those variations in mental type that lead the race a distinct step forward, it still remains equally true that such variations would be thrown away and lost unless external circumstances were such as to allow of their preservation. In other words, the state of society into which these men of exceptional natural qualities are born, is as important an element in the ultimate result as the fact of such men having arisen. Again, apart from the great leaders in the march of human progress, it is the set of surrounding circumstance which determines character. The vast majority of mankind follow mechanically; they lack gifts of initiative. In proportion as they lack these, is the influence upon them of their social environment supreme. Now the modifiableness of these social conditions becomes greater as the society grows more complex. As civilisation advances, a community grows increasingly susceptible of modification, because the number of social interests is every day multiplied, and the relations of the social system within and without are more and more close and intricate. But is not this only another way of saying that the share of man in guiding his own destinies increases in proportion to the growth of civilisation? In other words, the secondary and derivative causes of social movement play an increasingly effective part. The field over which these causes operate grows wider and more varied. And the mere consciousness that this is so, that the part which he can play in assisting them, is in itself an active stimulant to intelligent and energetic exertions. Human effort is the channel through which the transforming forces are poured. Human forethought, contrivance, energy, sociability, are the indispensable conditions of the continuance of the long process of development. Even if these conditions are, as we know them to be, dependent on a long series of antecedents that were never within the control of us who are now alive, that fact of what is to us as a fatalistic origin of the impulses and circumstances does not commit us to anything like an acquiescence in fatalistic destination. The evolutionist would admit this as fully as Mr. Mill would claim it. And on the other hand, Mr. Mill's contention involves no denial of the truth that the limits of human effort are fixed at any given time by the antecedent social conditions. But all this needs to be carefully and elaborately worked out. It constitutes, as it seems to us, the most important philosophical problem of this particular time.

We now come to the two essays which naturally excite the most eager interest in a time of religious fermentation. To us both the conclusions at which Mr. Mill arrives, and, what is even more important, the spirit of the conclusions, are a rather keen surprise. But notwithstanding this, Mr. Mill's treatment of his subject certainly on the whole makes it more interesting, and not less so. We may think the reasoning at some points halt of foot; we may discern arguments unclinched; we may deplore the virtual elevation of naked and arbitrary possibilities into the place of reasonable probabilities. Still it would be mere petulance, even where the pages least carry conviction to those who were fed on the *System of Logic,* not to be sensible of a certain breath of pensive sincerity, a deep-eyed solicitude for tender consciences, an anxious allowance for diversity of mental operation and temperament.

There is a meditative simplicity of tone which affects us as if we had overheard the speeches in unconscious soliloquy. But it must always be a poor way of showing respect to one's best teacher, to veil or muffle our strong dissent. Mr. Mill had a greater aversion for nothing than for the spirit of sect, or the personal partisanship of a philosophic school. He would have counted it a great fault if the humblest disciple of Plato had feared to renounce the reactionary doctrine of the *Laws*. He would not have thought less ill of a follower of his own who should be deterred either by the deepest consciousness of intellectual and moral inferiority, or by the recollection of personal kindness, from stating such objections as might occur to him against any new deliverance, with all the freedom and directness at his command.

The essay on the Utility of Religion is an attempt to answer three questions. Is religion of direct service to temporal interests, a direct instrument of social good? Is it useful in improving and ennobling individual human nature? If its utility in either of these two ways be allowed, must the form of religion necessarily be supernatural, involving a journey beyond the boundaries of the world which we inhabit, and beyond anything which could be supplied by the idealisation of our earthly life?

The great importance of a discussion of these particular issues at the present moment is undeniable. As ordinary men find themselves losing the conviction of old beliefs, the more readily they lean on the notion that such beliefs are socially indispensable. That idea enables them to reconcile conformity and its numerous conveniences, with the gratification of their intellectual vanity by private disbelief. Most recent controversies are marked by obliqueness, evasiveness, a shiftiness of issue. These disagreeable features of discussion are due in the better sort of disputants to an uncertainty in their minds whether it may not be the case that in the sphere of religion, disclosure of the truth will inflict irreparable moral injury both on human nature and on organized society. The French Revolution first made this apprehension of the social perilousness of truth an important element in European thought. The insurrection of Paris in 1871 operated strongly in the same direction in our own day. It has inclined even freethinkers "of the baser sort" to regard truth as by no means coincident under all circumstances with social welfare, and superstition as by no means an inconsiderable element in preserving social stability. Apart from social utility, many persons, as Mr. Mill says—

> Having observed in others or experienced in themselves elevated feelings which they imagined incapable of emanating from any other source than religion, have an honest aversion to anything tending as they think to dry up the fountain of such feelings. They, therefore, either dislike and disparage all philosophy, or addict themselves with intolerant zeal to those forms of it in which intuition usurps the place of evidence, and internal feeling is made the test of objective truth. *The whole of the prevalent metaphysics of the present century is one tissue of suborned evidence in favour of religion;* often of Deism only, but in any case involving a misapplication of noble impulses and speculative capacities, among the most deplorable of those wretched wastes of human faculties which make us wonder that enough is left to keep mankind progressive, at however slow a pace. It is time to consider, more impartially and therefore more deliberately than is usually done, whether all this straining to prop up beliefs which require so great an expense of intellectual toil and ingenuity to keep them standing, yields any sufficient return in human well-being; and whether that end would not be better served by a frank recognition that certain subjects are inaccessible to our faculties, and by the application of the same mental powers to the strengthening and enlargement of those other sources of virtue and happiness which stand in no need of the support or sanction of supernatural beliefs and inducements. [P. 72.]

First, then, is religious belief an instrument of social good? As a supplement to human laws, as "an auxiliary to the thief-catcher and hangman," Mr. Mill thinks that its office could be dispensed with. The influence with which religion is commonly credited in this way, is really due to conditions that would make any moral system equally efficacious, even a system devoid of religious sanction or association. Such conditions are these:—(1) Religion is backed by the whole weight of social authority, and this social authority powerfully affects the *involuntary* leanings of men. (2) The whole energy of the impressions of early education goes to the side of religious beliefs. (3) The force of public opinion operates directly on the voluntary sentiments in favour of the religious belief which it countenances, whether men's involuntary sentiments are affected by it or not. Thus if we deduct from the social influence attributed to religion what it owes to motives not directly religious, but derived from social authority, from the effect of early education, and from the power of public opinion, we find that its intrinsic force as a moral deterrent becomes hardly worth taking into account. Where the power of public opinion has been on one side, and on the other only a religious obligation, it is the former which triumphs. Mr. Mill refers to Bentham's three illustrations of this; namely, customary oaths, duelling, and sexual irregularities. In each of these cases public opinion approved or pardoned what the religion of the society condemned, and the religious penalties were the less dreaded of the two. Perhaps Mr. Mill might have produced a broader historic instance still in the institution of slavery. "Neither the doctrines of Christianity," says Mr. Finlay, "nor the sentiments of humanity have ever yet succeeded in extinguishing slavery where the soil could be cultivated with profit by slave labour. No Christian community of slaveholders has yet voluntarily abolished slavery. In no country where it prevailed, has rural slavery ceased, until the price of productions raised by slave labour has fallen so low as to leave no profit to the slave-holder." That is to say, the religious motive was more than counterbalanced by the favour of a public opinion which was inspired by material interests.

It would have been enough for Mr. Mill's purpose to stop at the position that religion has been powerful in producing certain great effects on human conduct, "not by its intrinsic force, but because it has wielded the additional and more mighty power of public opinion." All that he has to show is that religious sanctions work only when aided by public opinion. But in one passage he seems to favour the questionable opinion that religious sanctions are not the operative part of the matter.

> Rewards and punishments postponed to that distance of time, and never seen by the eye, are not calculated, even when infinite and eternal, to have, on ordinary minds, a very powerful effect in opposition to strong temptation. Their remoteness alone is a prodigious deduction from their efficacy, on such minds as those which most require the restraint of punishment. A still greater

abatement is their uncertainty, which belongs to them from the very nature of the case: for rewards and punishments administered after death, must be awarded not definitely to particular actions, but on a general survey of the person's whole life, and he easily persuades himself that whatever may have been his peccadilloes, there will be a balance in his favour at the last. All positive religions aid this self-delusion. Bad religions teach that divine vengeance may be bought off, by offerings, or personal abasement; the better religions, not to drive sinners to despair, dwell so much on the divine mercy, that hardly any one is compelled to think himself irrevocably condemned. The sole quality in these punishments which might seem calculated to make them efficacious, their overpowering magnitude, is itself a reason why nobody (except a hypochondriac here and there) ever really believes that he is in any very serious danger of incurring them. Even the worst malefactor is hardly able to think that any crime he has had it in his power to commit, any evil he can have inflicted in this short space of existence, can have deserved torture extending through an eternity. Accordingly religious writers and preachers are never tired of complaining how little effect religious motives have on men's lives and conduct, notwithstanding the tremendous penalties denounced. [Pp. 89–90.]

There is much wholesome truth in this. Religious motives are undoubtedly immeasurably less effectual than it is the fashion for preachers to assert in their arguments with sceptics. But the above passage seems to allege more than is necessary. I think it would be very hard to show that religious motives, however derived and shaped, have in a general way little effect. Nor is that of the essence of the question. The question is whether motives dissociated from religion, and solely dependent for their force on social authority, early education, and public opinion, would suffice to prompt good conduct, as effectually—whether that be little or much—as motives not thus dissociated from religion. It perhaps gives an equivocal help towards an affirmative answer, to disparage the potency of religious motives; because experience shows this potency to be not inconsiderable, though we believe it to be derivative. In short, Mr. Mill's account of the existing state of feeling about the religious sanctions is not so obviously and unqualifiedly true, that an opponent may not be able to make its questionableness a means of evading the central issue. That issue is whether public opinion could not avail to enforce morality without supernatural sanctions. Do we not best answer this, not by asserting the nullity of such sanctions, which is very doubtful as matter of fact, but by showing that their efficaciousness costs in other ways more than it is worth?

Mr. Mill next considers this objection—that though human motives may be sufficient to make moral rules obeyed, yet were it not for the religious idea we should not have had the moral rules themselves. This is one of those arguments which the official apologists resort to, not out of the fulness of their own historical knowledge, or because they have any evidence that their allegation is at all true, but because they know how difficult it will be for their opponents to prove that it is false. In such cases it is enough to meet them by a direct traverse, throwing the burden of proof upon them. What moral rule do we possess which cannot be found to have had an existence independent of its association with religion? And this even if its power in the world be proved to be due to its having been adopted by some religion? Mr. Mill does not meet the objection in this way. He partially admits the fact, and then endeavours to turn it. The admission is of a very unstable and doubtful kind. "I grant that some of the precepts of Christ as exhibited in the Gospels—rising far above the Paulism which is the foundation of ordinary Christianity—carry some kinds of moral goodness to a greater height than had ever been attained before, though much even of what is supposed to be peculiar to them is equalled in the Meditations of Marcus Antoninus, which we have no ground for believing to have been in any way indebted to Christianity" (pp. 97–98).

After this not very firm treatment of the proposition that we owe to religion the moral rules which everybody agrees that it would be desirable to preserve, Mr. Mill proceeds to argue the consequence of the admission. Even if it be true that religion has given us the moral rules, he maintains that the highest moralities which we owe to Christ, for instance, "are surely in sufficient harmony with the intellect and feelings of every good man or woman, to be in no danger of being let go, after having been once acknowledged as the creed of the best and foremost portion of our species. There will be, as there have been, shortcomings enough for a long time to come in acting on them; but that they should be forgotten, or cease to be operative on the human conscience, while human beings remain cultivated or civilised, may be pronounced once for all impossible" (p. 99).

One could perhaps wish that the line of argument which is suggested here had been rather more laboured. For if anybody chooses to maintain that we are expecting the effect to follow after we have withdrawn the cause, this position is at first sight a plausible one enough. Mr. Fitzjames Stephen, for example, says of a sense of duty which is justified by a certain form of religion, that "if the belief should ever fail, the sense of duty which grows out of it would die by degrees," and he warns people who are inclined to think otherwise, that "though custom makes some duties so easy to some people that they are discharged as a matter of course, there are others which it is extremely difficult to discharge at all; and that obvious immediate self-interest, in its narrowest shape, is constantly eating away the edges of morality, and would destroy it if it had not something deeper for its support than an historical or physiological explanation."

The answer to this kind of view is that it overlooks the persistent tendency of moral truths to take a permanent place in character, which in time becomes quite independent of the conditions that first opened a way for them into men's minds. Such a tendency is explained by the accumulated strength of habit; by the fitness of these moral truths to the circumstances of life; and by their harmony, as Mr. Mill expresses it, with the intellect and feelings of every good man or woman. Kant talks of the process which exalts "a social consent that had been *pathologically* extorted from the mere necessities of situation into a *moral* union." An analogous process transforms the base of moral ideas. It exalts them from the superstitions of their origin into rational truths finally built into the higher types of human nature. It is untrue that self-interest is always eating away the edges of morality. On the contrary, the history of civilisation shows morality offering a surface that is continually growing more and more indurated against the tooth of self-interest. Civilisation has been brought to its present point by a gradually increasing preponderance of the moral over the purely egoistic impulses. This is plainly one of the most important sides of what we mean by social progress. We have no better ground for assuming a spontaneous tendency towards retrogression in a moral type that has once definitely established itself, than we have for assuming the corresponding tendency in the type of a physical species that has once acquired its definite marks. Nor would it be true, in presence of these considerations, to say that we who expect strongly altruistic morality to survive after being divorced from the religious system which first made a gospel of it, shall be expecting an effect after removing the cause. The religious system may have been the cause of the spread of altruistic habit, and its confirmation among human impulses. But that habit itself becomes in time a new cause; a new ground and antecedent for its own persistency. This shortly indicates the fuller answer that it is to be made to those who urge that by tampering with religion you are knocking away the only props of the morality that was first practised in association with it. And we may add, in fine, that whatever may have been the original debt of morality to religion, it can by no means exceed the subsequent debt of religion to morality. "One of the hardest burdens," as Mr. Mill says, "laid upon the other good influences of human nature has been that of improving religion itself" (p. 75). Or, as it has been expressed, "The history of the civilisation of the earth is the history of the civilisation of Olympus."

The second and third questions of the essay are both answered by Mr. Mill affirmatively. Religion is of value to the individual, improving and satisfying man's nature, apart from its influence on society as a whole. And, secondly, these benefits of religion may be attained without travelling beyond the boundaries of human existence. The general conclusion of the second essay is that the sense of unity with mankind and a deep feeling for the general good may be cultivated into a sentiment and a principle which would fulfil the functions of religion better than any form whatever of supernaturalism. "It is not only entitled to be called a religion; it is a better religion than any of those which are ordinarily called by that title" (p. 110). The reasons given for the latter proposition are, first, that such a sentiment would be disinterested, whereas supernatural religion is bound up with interested fears and hopes. Second, that it involves no torpidity nor twist in either intellectual or moral faculties, such as is in-

separable from the acceptance of any known form of supernatural religion.

A serious drawback to the value of this otherwise most weighty
essay is that we are unable to find in it a true or even a consistent
account of what Religion is. Mr. Mill considers religion to be the
expression of the same cravings as those which inspire Poetry:
the cravings for "ideal conceptions grander and more beautiful
than we see realised in the prose of human life." The distinction
between poetry and religion is that religion is the product of a
yearning to know "whether these imaginative conceptions have
realities answering to them in some other world than ours." Now
I find myself unable to derive from the pages in which these
remarks occur, taken in conjunction with the remainder of the
essay, a clear and firm idea of what the writer took to be the
essence of religion. Here, as we have seen, he apparently mentions
it as an essential and permanent element in religion as distinct
from poetry, that it is concerned with actual or supposed
realities *"in some other world than ours."* This qualification is
obviously of vital moment. Yet at p. 109 it disappears, and we are
only told that "the essence of religion is the strong and earnest
direction of the emotions and desires towards an ideal object,
recognised as of the highest excellence, and rightfully paramount
over all selfish objects of desire." But is this ideal object to be
looked for in other worlds than ours? It would seem not, because
the very gist of all this part of the essay is that "the idealisation of
our earthly life is capable of supplying a poetry, and, in the best
sense of the word, a religion, equally fitted to exalt the feelings
and still better calculated to ennoble the conduct, than any belief
respecting the unseen powers." To this we utter a fervent Amen;
but then what has become of that definition of religion which
marked its scope "in some other world than ours"? Another
striking passage in the same way places the region of the religious
imagination in the land of the unseen and unknowable:—

> Human existence is girt round with mystery: the narrow region
> of our experience is a small island in the midst of a boundless
> sea, which at once awes our feelings and stimulates our imagina-
> tion by its vastness and its obscurity. To add to the mystery, the
> domain of our earthly existence is not only an island in infinite
> space, but also in infinite time. The past and the future are alike

shrouded from us: we neither know the origin of anything which is, nor its final destination. If we feel deeply interested in knowing that there are myriads of worlds at an immeasurable, and to our faculties inconceivable, distance from us in space; if we are eager to discover what little we can about these worlds, and when we cannot know what they are, can never satiate ourselves with speculating on what they may be; it is not a matter of far deeper interest to us to learn, or even to conjecture, from whence came this nearer world which we inhabit; what cause or agency made it what it is, and on what powers depend its future fate? Who would not desire this more ardently than any other conceivable knowledge, so long as there appeared the slightest hope of attaining it? What would not one give for any credible tidings from that mysterious region, any glimpse into it which might enable us to see the smallest light through its darkness, especially any theory of it which we could believe, and which represented it as tenanted by a benignant and not a hostile influence? But since we are able to penetrate into that region with the imagination only, assisted by specious but inconclusive analogies derived from human agency and design, imagination is free to fill up the vacancy with the imagery most congenial to itself; sublime and elevating if it be a lofty imagination, low and mean if it be a grovelling one. [Pp. 102–3.]

In view of such a conception as this, whether right or not, the Religion of Duty lacks a vital mark of religion, and cannot be regarded as more than a highly poetised morality.

Whatever the explanation may be, it is surely in the worst degree inconvenient and confusing to pass from one sense of the word to another, and silently to relegate what was first declared to be of the essence, to the region of the separable accident. To speak a little more at large—is it clear that we can extract from the sentences of Mr. Mill such a comprehensive and penetrating notion of religion as shall at once take in these two states of mind —one of them yearning after knowledge of some other world than ours, the other satisfied with some ideal object, of which we only may ask that it shall be of the highest excellence and paramount over all selfish objects of desire?

In what he says of the essence of religion being the strong and earnest direction of the emotions and desires towards an object of that kind, is he not being drawn by that passion of his for seizing above all else the ethical aspects of things human or divine, into leaving out those vital elements of religion which are not and never can be reducible to ethical expression? In the *Autobiography* (p. 46) he declares the principal worth of all religions whatever to be constituted by their possession of "an ideal conception of a Perfect Being, to which men habitually refer as the guide of their conscience." Undoubtedly this is the principal worth of religion, from the point of view of the moralist, that it should guide conscience, that it should direct emotions and desires towards highly excellent ends, that it should tend to subordinate egoism to altruism. Religion, like everything else, may be moral or immoral. But morality is not of the essence of religion; is not its vital or constitutive element; does not give us the secret of its deep attachments in the human heart. Religion is not in any way the outcome of the moral part of us; it is at its root wholly unconnected with principles of conduct; it has its rise in a sphere of feeling as absolutely independent of all our moral relations, as a poem like Shelley's *Skylark* is independent of them, or a piece of ineffable heart-searching melody by Beethoven or Handel. Why is it that in reading the religious compositions of the eighteenth century (always excepting certain pages of Rousseau) we all feel that the breath of religious sentiment has never passed over them? In all these books the morality of religion seems to quench that spirituality which is its true essence. The characteristic deliverances of the religious emotions are not to be described in terms of ethics. Take the *Imitatio,* and read that in the light of a guide to conscience, or a direction to an object of the highest excellence, or an exaltation of altruism over egoism. Is not to do this to lose the whole soul of those divine musings, that ethereal meditation, those soft-glowing ecstasies, that passion of contemplation by the inmost eye? To put the matter shortly, what are we to say is the note of Holiness as something beyond and apart from Virtue?

Before leaving the second essay, I should like to make some observations on a rather remarkable parenthesis which it contains. After expanding the proposition that there never can be any conflict between truth and utility, Mr. Mill proceeds to assert a very important qualification of this proposition.

> It is not enough [he says] to aver, in general terms, that there never can be any conflict between truth and utility; that if religion be false, nothing but good can be the consequence of rejecting it. For, though the knowledge of every positive truth is an useful acquisition, this doctrine cannot without reservation be applied to negative truth. When the only truth ascertainable is that nothing can be known, we do not, by this knowledge, gain any new fact by which to guide ourselves; we are, at best, only disabused of our trust in some former guide-mark, which, though itself fallacious, may have pointed in the same direction with the best indications we have, and if it happens to be more conspicuous and legible, may have kept us right when they might have been overlooked. [P. 73.]

The distinction between positive and negative truths, although a real and important one, is surely here pressed too hard. If it be true that nothing can be known in a given direction in which men have been accustomed both to search for knowledge and to persuade themselves that they have found it, then to ascertain that *is* a new fact by which to guide ourselves. To become "disabused of our trust in some former guide-mark" is the first condition of curiosity and energy in seeking guide-marks which shall be more worthy of trust. Or, to borrow Mr. Mill's own phrases, "a frank recognition that certain subjects are inaccessible to our faculties" —and this is a negative truth, if ever there was one—is the first step towards the positive process of "strengthening and enlarging those other sources of virtue and happiness which stand in no need of the support or sanction of supernatural beliefs and inducements." It is true that the positive propositions of supernatural religions do now and then point in the same direction with the best indications we have. But then it is alleged by unbelievers that such religions on the whole have the effect of enervating the reasoning faculties, of engendering vicious habits of spiritual self-indulgence, of encouraging intellectual and moral sophistication. If this be so, then the mere negation of them will do less harm than good.

This is made the more clear by two considerations. First, the beneficial moral tendencies which are associated with certain theological propositions, lie in the nature of things. They possess an independent fitness. This fitness and conformity to circumstance may be trusted to keep such tendencies alive after the theological association has ceased to be defensible. The assertion of mere negative truths leaves the way all the more open for these natural fitnesses to disclose themselves, and for the substitution of the strong defence of reality instead of the weak defence of superstition. And let us add, if this argument be not admitted, that if there may have been at first some support for useful truths in their association with theological beliefs, there is this set-off; namely, that in proportion as the theological beliefs become untenable, there is a risk of the useful truths being involved in the same ruin. The connection between the two was therefore from the first of equivocal utility, if we only take a sufficiently ample survey to comprehend the bearings of the connection from beginning to end. The second consideration is this. Though the guide-mark may have pointed in the right direction—towards charity, humility, brotherly love, and so forth —and in so far may have been useful, yet the motives which prompted men in accepting its authority, may be so debilitating, retarding, distorting, as to more than counterbalance the advantage of occasional and partial rightness of direction. In that case, even mere negation is the removal of something which happens to have the advantage of confirming rational conclusions in one or two directions, while it has the fundamental disadvantage of weakening rational habits of thinking.

This seems to be the answer to another sentence of Mr. Mill's in the same passage. He pronounces it "perfectly conceivable that religion may be morally useful without being intellectually sustainable." This is a truly remarkable sentence considering its authorship. For one thing, it is ambiguous. Does it mean that religion may be morally useful to the man who knows it to be intellectually indefensible? Or only to people who are not yet alive to its want of intellectual foundation? Does it mean that a creed may be morally beneficial to us, after we have discerned that it is untrue? Or that, in spite of its being untrue, it may be morally beneficial to other persons who have not found out how little true it is?

If the meaning be the latter, the proposition is expressed in a misleading way, because then the religion *is* intellectually sustainable in the minds of those to whom it is morally useful. The sentence ought in such a case to run, that religion may be morally useful to some persons, even without being intellectually sustainable to other persons. The tendency of such a proposition is undoubtedly towards maxims of reserve, conformity, and compromise. Because if there are still societies and portions of society in such a condition as to receive moral advantage from an untrue religion, a serious man would certainly think twice before by conduct or speech doing anything to weaken its utility. A phrase in the next part of the sentence, however, perhaps makes it probable that Mr. Mill did not mean this, but that a religion might be morally useful to a man after he had ceased to believe it true. There is even in that sense something misleading in such a way of stating an undeniable fact. For instance, it might be said that Christianity remains morally useful to men, after they have ceased to believe in its supernatural pretensions. But if we consider what we mean by such a statement, it is this; that we may still find usefulness in certain of the Christian moralities which are intellectually sustainable, even after repudiating certain other parts of the scheme which are not intellectually sustainable. In other words, some of the moral truths that have been associated with a religion remain useful, after the intellectual base has been changed. But then they only remain useful because, and in so far as, they are true. This surely is very different in significance and intention from the bald and crude proposition that a religion may be morally useful after it has ceased to be intellectually sustainable. Whatever may be the force of these criticisms, it must at any rate be counted extremely unfortunate that Mr. Mill should have enunciated in this indeterminate and unqualified form a proposition so important, so complex, so dependent for whatever truth it may contain upon a number of indispensable qualifications. As it stands the passage is fatally well fitted—though assuredly without any such design in the mind of the author—to justify all those conformities, compliances, economies, and accommodations, that men are naturally so ready to practise, partly because they are unwilling to face the untold discomforts of dissent, partly from a more creditable reluctance to do anything to shake the foundations of a fabric in which good men and women still find spiritual shelter.

The general conclusions of the second essay, then, are that the religion of duty is capable of fulfilling the functions of religion better than any form whatever of supernaturalism. The third essay, strange to say, is on its most important side a qualified rehabilitation of supernatural hypotheses.

The essay on Theism has both a negative and a positive aspect. It overthrows some of the most commonly defended arguments in favour of a benevolent and omnipotent Creator of the universe, of the immortality of the soul, and of a miraculously accredited revelation. On this side of the treatise we have nothing to say. Its positive or reconstructive side is much more important. The reconstruction, it is true, results in a very modest and unsubstantial fabric. The principles, however, on which the foundations of this very unpretending edifice of belief are laid, are capable of supporting much more elaborate structures. Shortly put, the central or fundamental conclusions are these.

To deny that there is any evidence on either side in the question of the existence of a Deity, is a form of atheism not less inconsistent with a rational attitude in a thinking mind, than the dogmatic denial of his existence. There is evidence, amounting to one of the lower degrees of probability, that the present order of the universe has been devised by an Intelligent Mind. Such evidence is found in the adaptations to be observed in Nature; in the nice and intricate combinations of vegetable and animal life, showing a connection through causation between the origin of the arrangements of nature and the ends they fulfil.

The same evidences in nature lead us to suppose that the author of the Kosmos worked under limitations. He is not omnipotent, but is obliged to adapt himself to conditions independent of his will, and to reach his ends by such devices and arrangements as these conditions permit.

The appearances in nature which make it in a low degree probable that there is a Creator of limited power, furnish a certain amount of justification for the inference that benevolence is one of his attributes. There are many signs that pleasure is agreeable to him, and few or none that pain is so.

As we do not know the limits either of the power or the goodness of the Creator, whose existence is in a low degree probable, there is room to hope that he may be both powerful enough and good enough to grant us the gift of immortality, or life after bodily dissolution, provided that gift should seem to him to be likely to do us any good.

Finally, "Considering that the order of nature affords some evidence of the reality of a Creator, and of his bearing goodwill to his creatures, though not of its being the sole prompter of his conduct towards them: considering, again, that all the evidence of his existence is evidence also that he is not all-powerful, and considering that in our ignorance of the limits of his power we cannot positively decide that he was able to provide for us by the original plan of Creation all the good which it entered into his intentions to bestow upon us, or even to bestow any part of it at any earlier period than that at which we actually received it—considering these things, when we consider further that a gift, extremely precious, came to us which though facilitated was not apparently necessitated by what had gone before, but was due, as far as appearances go, to the peculiar mental and moral endowments of one man, and that man openly proclaimed that it did not come from himself but from God through him,—then we are entitled to say that there is nothing so inherently impossible or absolutely incredible in this supposition, as to preclude any one from hoping that it may perhaps be true."

In making some observations on this remarkable scheme of probabilities and potentialities, I shall begin with the position assigned by Mr. Mill to Christianity. The reader will bear in mind that the objections which I feel to this position, lie only as against an avowedly positive and scientific thinker such as Mr. Mill was, and neither have, nor are meant to have, any force against the transcendentalist or the mystic.

Firstly, we have to consider the following position: that "to the conception of the rational sceptic it remains a possibility that Christ actually was what he supposed himself to be . . . a man charged with a special, express, and unique commission from God to lead mankind to truth and virtue" (p. 255). Now whether this is a possibility in the abstract, we are not here called upon to discuss. The question which interests us is whether the acceptance of such a possibility is reconcilable with that positive or scientific conception of the movement of human society and the development of human nature which Mr. Mill himself was the first to propagate and partially popularise in this country. Was the commission with which God charged Christ, *special, express, and unique,* in any sense which would not apply equally well to all other conspicuous moral reformers, from Socrates and Confucius downwards? If it was not, surely Mr. Mill, for the first time in the work of his whole life, is doing nothing less than trifling with words. And if it was, if on a given occasion God specially and expressly conferred upon a certain personage gifts which would not and could not have devolved upon him in the undisturbed course of ordinary cause and effect, then what becomes of sociology and the science of history? For no theist can believe in the possibility of a science of social development, or in there being scientific laws of ethnological growth, if he believes also that a most critical and important step in that development was due to special, express, and unique intervention on the part of the Supreme Being. This very obvious line of objection, however, would seem to be accepted by Mr. Mill himself, for twenty pages further back we find the following passage:—

"Let it be remembered also that the goodness of God affords no presumption in favour of a deviation from his general system of government, unless the good purpose could not have been attained without deviation. If God intended that mankind should receive Christianity or any other gift, it would have agreed better with all that we know of his government to have made provision in the scheme of creation for its arising at the appointed time by *natural development; which, let it be added, all the knowledge we now possess concerning the history of the human mind, tends to the conclusion that it actually did.*" (p. 236).

But then, if this be so, what kind of meaning are we to attach to the emphatic words of the passage we are discussing—"special, express, and unique"? If they hint that Christ was charged with a mission in a sense in which Socrates or Confucius,—yes, or any other opener of the human mind, intellectual as well as moral, an Aristotle, or a Descartes, or a Newton,—was not charged with a mission, then there was a deviation from the general system of the government of the world. If, on the contrary, there was no deviation, then to speak of the transaction as even potentially special, express, and unique is illusory. And considering the use which is sure to be made of such an account of the matter, we will add, it is not only illusory but directly and practically injurious. We are not now contending with the theologians, but with a positive thinker, if ever there was one. If a person has once grasped the conception that the phenomena of human nature are as much reducible to general laws as the phenomena of the heavenly bodies—and the writer of the sixth book of the *System of Logic* would hardly have conceded the name of "rational" sceptic to any one falling short of this amount of scientific belief —I am unable to conceive how such a person can admit the possibility of Christ's mission being special or express, any more readily than the possibility of the sun having stood still at the command of Joshua in the valley of Ajalon. If "all the knowledge we now possess concerning the history of the human mind tends to the conclusion that Christianity arose at the appointed time by natural development"—(in what sense, by the way, can the time have been *appointed?*)—then is it not worse than futile to dwell on the possibility of its having arisen otherwise than by natural development, specially, expressly, and uniquely?

Let us turn to another passage in which there is the same singular uncertainty of note. After enumerating certain considerations about the reality of a Creator, the limitation of his powers, and so forth, Mr. Mill says:—"When we consider further that a gift [namely the moralities enunciated by Christ], extremely precious, came to us which though facilitated was not apparently necessitated by what had gone before, but was due, as far as appearances go, to the peculiar mental and moral endowments of one man, and that man openly proclaimed that it did not come from himself but from God through him, then we are entitled to say that there is nothing so inherently impossible or absolutely incredible in this supposition as to preclude any one from hoping that it may perhaps be true." (p. 240). We may note, in passing, how perplexing it is that Mr. Mill should have thought it worth while to refer to Christ's own ascription of his discourse to God, when in the next sentence he reminds us that "in pre-scientific times men always supposed that any unusual faculties which came to them, they knew not how, were an inspiration from God," and declines to attach "any evidentiary value even to the testimony of Christ on such a subject." Whether strictly evidentiary or not, he clearly wished value of some kind or other to be attached to Christ's claim to be divinely inspired, or else he would not have enumerated it among the grounds of rational hope that the gift of revelation may perhaps be true. Though Hope may exist upon less substantial nutriment in the way of evidence than Belief, yet Mr. Mill did not intend it in this case to live upon air. And Christ's own account of the origin of his gift is unmistakably designed both here and also at p. 255, already quoted, to count for something in the mind of any one who is anxious to hope after the authenticity of Christ's credentials. And this, though we are told at the same time that in pre-scientific ages men always did what Christ did, in attributing to God any unusual faculties of their own.

Apart from this, however, we are perplexed as to the purport of the proposition in the above extract, that what the writer justly calls the extremely precious gift of Christ's moral sayings and the impressiveness of his character, *"though facilitated, was not apparently necessitated by what had gone before,* but was due to the peculiar mental and moral endowments of one man." But we have been already told (p. 236) that all the knowledge we now possess concerning the history of the human mind tends to the conclusion that the gift of Christianity arose "by natural development." Then, if so, what are we to understand by the proposition that it was facilitated but not apparently necessitated by antecedent conditions? What other idea of natural development can a scientific thinker have, than one which connects a consequent by way of necessity with its antecedents? And what other idea of a phenomenon being necessitated can a scientific thinker have, than that it arose by natural development? In short was the appearance of Christ in the world, and was his type of character, free from necessary connection with what had gone before, in any sense in which we might not say with equal truth that the appearance and the character of Socrates, or the appearance and character of Descartes, were free from such necessary connection? Was it so, or not? If it was, what becomes of natural development? If it was not, what is the significance of the distinction between necessity and faculty? The effect and purport, not only of this distinction, but of the whole passage in which it occurs (p. 240), are to encourage the believer to hope that the account of Christianity as in some degree due to a supernatural interposition of some kind is a true account. I am not now denying the propriety of this encouragement, nor stating any opinion as to the grounds for it: I am only insisting how profoundly irreconcilable it is with the scientific principles which Mr. Mill inculcated, and with passages in the very volume before us.

And let us make one or two remarks with reference to those "peculiar mental and moral endowments" on which Mr. Mill lays so much stress. No fair-minded man, most certainly not the present writer, can feel any inclination to disparage these in themselves, provided they are not made the basis of conclusions that are too wide for them to bear.

> Whatever else may be taken away from us by rational criticism [Mr. Mill says] Christ is still left; a unique figure, not more unlike all his precursors than all his followers, even those who had the direct benefit of his personal teaching. It is of no use to say that Christ as exhibited in the Gospels is not historical, and that we know not how much of what is admirable has been superadded by the tradition of his followers. The tradition of followers suffices to insert any number of marvels, and may have inserted all the miracles which he is reputed to have wrought. But who among his disciples or among their proselytes was capable of inventing the sayings ascribed to Jesus or of imagining the life and character revealed in the Gospels? . . . About the life and sayings of Jesus there is a stamp of personal originality combined with profundity of insight, which, if we abandon the idle expectation of finding scientific precision where something very different was aimed at, must place the Prophet of Nazareth, even in the estimation of those who have no belief in his inspiration, in the very first rank of the men of sublime genius of whom our species can boast. When this pre-eminent genius is combined with the qualities of probably the greatest moral reformer, and martyr to that mission, who ever existed upon earth, religion cannot be said to have made a bad choice in pitching on this man as the ideal representative and guide of humanity; nor, even now, would it be easy, even for an unbeliever, to find a better translation of the rule of virtue from the abstract into the concrete, than to endeavour so to live that Christ would approve our life. [P. 264.]

From all this few persons will feel inclined seriously to dissent, if only we can be sure that we precisely seize the sense in which

Mr. Mill means it to be taken. Few persons can be seriously disposed to deny the claims of the Prophet of Nazareth to a place in the very first rank of sublime benefactors of mankind. But it will seem a matter of regret to those who are accustomed to the precision of Mr. Mill's other writings, that he did not here too suggest the proper limitations. They are in this case all the more needful, because common opinion and belief is already drawn by a variety of most powerful forces to exaggerate the beauty and worth of the character of the central figure in the Christian scheme. Mr. Mill cannot be held responsible for the interpretation which may be unjustly foisted upon his written words. At the same time it would have been well, and what is more, it would only have been consistent with his usual practice, if he had guarded himself against misunderstandings which he could hardly fail to foresee. It is an invidious thing even to seem to disparage a lovely and noble character, but Mr. Mill's excessive panegyric is so sure to be abused, that in common honesty a critic is bound to hint at some warnings against such an abuse. In the first place, the attempts to separate the noble moralities which may be selected from the Gospels from all the men who had gone before Christ or who gathered round him is thoroughly unhistoric. There is not one of the ethical maxims mentioned by Mr. Mill (p. 98) as the imperishable gifts of Christ, which is not in substance to be found before his time. Readers receive so many shocks to their faith in these days that the impression of any one of them seldom lasts more than a few weeks. Perhaps therefore they have had ample time to forget a shock they received seven years ago. A learned scholar then showed them that the sublimest dicta of the Gospels found exact parallels in the Talmud, and warned them that to assume that the Talmud borrowed from the New Testament would be like assuming that Sanskrit sprang from Latin, or that French was developed from the Norman words found in English. And the wider our knowledge extends, the fainter become the claims made for the Gospel moralities as original, new, or exceptionally profound in insight. The whole mental atmosphere was charged with these moralities. The spirituality of the Judaism of the age in which Christ appeared was fully as high among the better sort, as Christ ever succeeded in making it. Can we forget, it has been justly asked, the summary of religion given by Micah, to do justly, and to love mercy, and to walk humbly with God? "The Jewish synagogues have probably varied in religious attainments as much as Christian churches; but there is no ostensible reason to think that they are indebted to Jesus for any of their spirituality; while ostensibly Jesus must have learnt from them. Rather, they and we and all the world learn from one another and from Time, a richer and richer experience accumulating, while many hearts seek their common Father" (F. W. Newman).

Apart from the positive historic evidence against the exalted and absolute isolation in which Mr. Mill insists upon placing the Prophet of Nazareth, is it not contrary to our whole experience that there should be any such prodigious distance in the capacity for noble feeling between a moral teacher drawing souls after him, and the best of those who are so drawn; between a great master in moral things and the best of his followers? Those whose hearts were touched by his teaching, so that they gave up all and followed him, must already have had within them the stir of the same aspiration to which he had the gift of imparting such pathetic and attaching expression. The Corinthian vine-dresser, who after reading the *Gorgias* was so mastered by admiration that he forsook his fields and his vines and fared to Athens and besought Plato to be his teacher, must already have had alive within him the love of virtue for its own sake, before Plato's words thus quickened the germ.

Secondly, the moralities are admitted to be imperfect. We may have the satisfaction of quoting Mr. Mill's own words about the sayings of Christ, that "they contain and were only meant to contain part of the truth; *many essential elements of the highest morality* are not provided for nor attempted to be provided for" (*Liberty*). "Other ethics," he says, "than any which can be evolved from exclusively Christian sources, must exist side by side with Christian ethics to produce the moral regeneration of mankind" (Ibid.). "Even the Christ of the Gospels," he says in the second of the essays before us (p. 111), "holds out the direct promise of reward from heaven as a primary inducement to the noble and beautiful beneficence towards our fellow-creatures which he so impressively inculcates. This is a radical inferiority of the best supernatural religions, compared with the Religion of Humanity." I will not say that passages like these are logically irreconcilable with the proposition that it would not be easy to find "a better translation of the rule of virtue from the abstract into the concrete, than to endeavour so to live that Christ would approve our life" (p. 255). But at least such passages make an enormous deduction from the significance of that proposition. And so also do they make an enormous deduction from the value of the possibility of a special, express, and unique mission to lead mankind to truth and virtue—truth and virtue, mark, with "many essential elements of the highest morality not provided for nor attempted to be provided for."

Thirdly, this unconditioned exaltation of the Christ of the Gospels as "the pattern of perfection for humanity," as "the ideal representative and guide," and so forth, can only be possible to such a moralist as Mr. Mill was, or as any enlightened person of our day must be, by means of a process of selection and arbitrary rejection. We may, no doubt, and many of us do, construct an ideal figure out of the sayings, the life, and the character of the great figure of the Gospel. Mr. Mill's panegyric should remind us that we do this only on condition of shutting our eyes to about one half of the portraits as drawn in the Gospels. I mean that not merely are some essential elements of the highest morality omitted, but that there are positive injunctions and positive traits recorded which must detract in the highest degree from the justice of an unqualified eulogium. Mr. Mill allows in one place (p. 98) that the noble moralities of Christ are "mixed with some poetical exaggerations and some maxims of which it is difficult to ascertain the precise object." This is far too moderate an account of the matter. There are sayings morally objectionable and superstitious in the highest degree, and we have no more right arbitrarily to shift the discredit of these on to the shoulders of the disciples or narrators, than we have to deny to them all possibility of credit for what is admirable. This, however, is a side of the argument which it would perhaps do more harm than good to press. Even an excessive admiration for a benign and nobly pitiful character is so attractive and so wholesome that one can have little satisfaction in searching for defective traits. That Mr. Mill should have committed himself to a position which calls for this deprecatory withdrawal from the critic, is one of the puzzles and perplexities of the book. It is astonishing that he should not have seen that his conception of the character of the Prophet of Nazareth was moulded in obedience to his own subjective requirement in the way of ethical beauty, and could only be made to correspond with the objective picture in the Gospel record by means of an arbitrary suppression of some of the most remarkable sayings and striking traits. It is a process in fashion. Human experience has widened; many narrow superstitions have dropped off; the notion of right and duty has been impregnated with new ingredients; the ideal has changed. Then we proceed to the anachronism of fastening the new ideal on our favourite figures of antique days, without regard either to obvious historic conditions or to the plain and unmistakable letter of the antique record. "One of the hardest burdens," as Mr. Mill says, "laid upon the other good influences of human nature, has been that of improving religion itself" (p. 75). Let us carefully abstain then from falsifying the history of the development of human nature by imputing, either to the religion of the past, or to their founders, perfections of which it is historically impossible that either one or the other should have been possessed. Let us not assume that Christ was so infinitely "over the heads of his reporters," to use Mr. Arnold's phrase, and then proceed to construct an arbitrary anthology of sayings, which we choose to accept as Christ's on the strength of this assumption. It were surely more consonant with intelligence of method to content ourselves with tracing in Christ, as in the two or three other great teachers of the world who are not beneath him in psychagogic efficacy, such words and traits as touch our spiritual sense and fit in with the later and more mature perceptions of the modern time. And why should we not do this without fretting against discords in act or speech, which were only to be expected from the conditions; and still more without straining our own intelligence and coercing the record into yielding us a picture of transcendent and impossible faultlessness?

Let us now proceed to examine the idea of an Intelligent Mind, working under conditions only partially modifiable, and animated by a certain measure of benevolence. Our first remark is upon the arbitrary character of the idea of limiting the Creator's power. It is in this case an interpretation of the facts of the universe invented for the purpose of saving the Creator's moral goodness. "Nor, then, can God," says Plato, "since he is good, be the author of all things, as people commonly say, but only of a few of the things that occur to men; and for many things he is not responsible; for far fewer are the goods of human life than its evils, and it is the good only that we are to set down to him; for the evil we must seek any cause rather than God."[1] Now if it is indispensable that we should think of the deity as clothed with attributes which are essential elements of human morality, this theory of him as partially responsible would in so far meet the difficulty. And in the next place, if it is indispensable that we should praise and worship the deity, clearly we must impute to him those moral qualities which we praise and admire in the best types of our own species. Mr. Mill has rendered no greater service to morals than by his denunciation, first, in a memorable declamatory passage in the volume on Hamilton, and now in many energetic passages in the volume before us, of the practice of offering homage and flattery to a person whom in the same liturgy we treat as having the most iniquitous of imaginable characters. If the deity is not good in the same sense as men are said to be good, then it is a depraving mockery to make morality consist in doing his will, and to chant litanies expressive of our deep sense how good he is. But it is conceivable that the world may have been created by a Being who is not good, not pitiful, not benevolent, not just; a Being no more entitled to our homage or worship, than Francesco Cenci was entitled to the filial piety of his unhappy children. Why not? Morality concerns the conduct and relations of human beings, and of them only. We cannot know, nor indeed does it seem easy to believe, that the principles which cover the facts of social relationship, must therefore be adequate to guide or explain the motions of a Demiurgus holding the universal ordering in the hollow of his hand. To insist on rejecting any theory of creation which forbids us to predicate anything of the Creator in terms of morality, seems as unphilosophical as to insist on rejecting the evolutional theory of the origin of the human species on the ground that it robs man of his nobility and dignity. If anyone feels bound to praise and

---

1. *Republic,* bk. ii., p. 379: Οὐδ' ἄρα ὁ θεός, κ. τ. λ.

worship the Creator, he is bound to invest the object of his worship with praiseworthy attributes. But a philosopher is not bound to do anything except to explain the facts. Our first objection then to Mr. Mill's permissive explanation of the facts by a limitation of creative power is that it springs from a sentiment which is out of place in an inquiry that pretends to be scientific.

Paley admitted the possibility of the same kind of explanation on a different ground. "Contrivance," he said, "by its very definition and nature, is the refuge of imperfection. Why resort to contrivance where power is omnipotent?" He answered this by saying that it is only by the display of contrivance that the existence, the agency, the wisdom of the Deity could be testified to his rational creatures. So "God has been pleased to prescribe limits to his own power, and to work his ends within those limits."[2] The difference between Mr. Mill's idea and Paley's (both Paley and Mr. Mill are content to rank it as a more or less plausible hypothesis) is that the latter hypothetically conceives God as voluntarily fixing bounds to his own power for the sake of proving his own existence to men, while the former hypothetically conceives him as struggling with intractable matter and its stubborn conditions. Mr. Mill's idea is simply that of the *Timæus,* of which Mr. Grote's account will suffice. "The Demiurgus of Plato is not conceived as a Creator, but as a Constructor or Artist. . . . He represents provident intelligence or art, and beneficent purpose, contending with a force superior and irresistible, so as to improve it so far as it will allow itself to be improved. . . . The genesis of

2. Paley's *Natural Theology,* ch. iii. The passage concludes thus:—"As we have said, therefore, God prescribes limits to his power, that he may let in the exercise, and thereby exhibit demonstrations of his wisdom. For then, *i.e.* such laws and limitations being laid down, it is as though one Being should have fixed certain rules; and, if we may so speak, provided certain materials; and, afterwards, have committed to another Being, out of these materials, and in subordination to these rules, the task of drawing forth a creation; a supposition which evidently leaves room, and induces indeed a necessity, for contrivance. Nay, there may be many such agents, and many ranks of these. We do not advance this as a doctrine either of philosophy or of religion; but we say that the subject may safely be represented under this view; because the Deity, acting himself by general laws, will have the same consequences upon our reasoning, as if he had prescribed these laws to another. It has been said that the problem of creation was, 'attraction and matter being given, to make a world out of them;' and, as above explained, this statement perhaps does not convey a false idea."

the Kosmos thus results from a combination of intelligent force with the original primordial Necessity, which was persuaded, and consented to have its irregular agency regularised up to a certain point, but no further. Beyond this limit the systematizing arrangements of the Demiurgus could not be carried; but all that is good or beautiful in the Kosmos was owing to them."[3]

In short, each of these hypotheses is as arbitrary as the rest, and we are hardly to be blamed for having expected that the last word of the great positive thinker of our day would have been a warning to people to remember how arbitrary all such hypotheses must be, and a clear-voiced counsel to abandon them. And the surprise with which Mr. Mill's countenance to such a hypothesis affects us, is all the greater because in an earlier passage he speaks of the evidence for it as "shadowy and unsubstantial." He is doubtful even whether it can be called evidence at all (p. 117).

Next, when we are told that such evidence as there is points to the arrangement of the present order of the universe by an Intelligent Mind, what are we to understand by an Intelligent Mind? Surely this is to define the supernatural in terms of the natural, the Unknowable in terms of the Known. It is a sublimation of anthropomorphism, but it is essentially anthropomorphic. Mind is no individual and integral entity. It is an abstract term conveniently invented to describe a set of complex psychological energies. It comprehends reason, volition, appetite, affection, and as many subdivisions as the ingenuity of psychologists may form. They do not call them material phenomena, but they are phenomena which we only find united in a material synthesis. No scientific psychologist can realise the occurrence of a mental operation without a corresponding change in nervous structure. In the case of the individual man, what scientific person seriously thinks that his mind (*i.e.* a set of complex energies) is something with an independent objective existence, external to his body? Mind is a general conception, an abstract idea, like motion or heat, and any one who ascribes to it the position of an independent entity, existing apart from the phenomenal conditions in which only we know it, has no right to laugh at Plato's doctrine of archetypal Ideas. To talk of a Mind without a personality attached to it, as the framer

3. Grote's *Plato,* iii. pp. 248–49.

of the Kosmos, is every bit as unmeaning as it was in Pythagoras to fix on Number for the ruling power of the universe. And the moment you attempt to attach elements of personality to this mere name and empty abstraction, there is no reason why man should not forthwith proceed to make God after his own image. If you attach personality to this Intelligent Mind, it can only be a finer version of the rude anthropomorphism of the fetishist. If you do not, then the notion of a bare Mind or a bare Will busying itself over the Kosmos is to me as utterly without meaning, as the old theory of the universe being generated by Contradictories. It was scarcely worth while to forsake the jingle of the Anthanasian Creed, if we are still to find ourselves invited to give a nominally intelligent adherence to another form of the Uncreate and Incomprehensible, the reasonable soul without human flesh subsisting.

My second objection, then, to Mr. Mill's probability of creation by an Intelligent Mind is that it implies the transformation of an abstract name for certain attributes of animals into a superhuman causative agency. And I will venture to lend authoritative support to this objection by a quotation from Mr. Mill himself. "It would, no doubt," he says in the work upon Hamilton, "be absurd to assume that our words exhaust the possibilities of Being. There may be innumerable modes of it which are inaccessible to our faculties, and which consequently we are unable to name. But we ought not to speak of these modes of Being by any of the names we possess. These are all inapplicable, because they all stand for known modes of Being. We might invent new names for such unknown modes, but the new names would have no more meaning than the x, y, z of Algebra. The only name we can give them which really expresses an attribute is the word Unknowable."[4] It is impossible to contend that an impersonal Mind brooding over inorganic and rigidly conditioned Matter is a known mode of Being, and we have therefore no right to predicate anything of such a force—if it be a force—except Unknowableness.

Mr. Mill, however, finds some evidence for another attribute besides Intelligence in this supernatural Mind—namely a partial

4. *Examination of Sir W. Hamilton's Philosophy,* p. 14, 3rd edit.

measure of Benevolence. If this be so, most of the tremendous indictment against Nature, which has been already quoted from the first essay, must assuredly be considered as cancelled and abandoned. "It does appear," Mr. Mill now says, "that granting the existence of design, there is a preponderance of evidence that the Creator desired the pleasure of his creatures."

> This is indicated by the fact that pleasure of one description or another is afforded by almost everything, the mere play of the faculties, physical and mental, being a never-ending source of pleasure, and even painful things giving pleasure by the satisfaction of curiosity and the agreeable sense of acquiring knowledge; and also that pleasure, when experienced, seems to result from the normal working of the machinery, while pain usually arises from some external interference with it, and resembles in each particular case the result of an accident. Even in cases when pain results, like pleasure, from the machinery itself, the appearances do not indicate that contrivance was brought into play purposely to produce pain: what is indicated is rather a clumsiness in the contrivance employed for some other purpose. The author of the machinery is no doubt accountable for having made it susceptible of pain; but this may have been a necessary condition of its susceptibility to pleasure; a supposition which avails nothing on the theory of an Omnipotent Creator, but is an extremely probably one in the case of a contriver working under the limitation of inexorable laws and indestructible properties of matter. The susceptibility being conceded as a thing which did enter into design, the pain itself usually seems like a thing undesigned; a casual result of the collision of the organism with some outward force to which it was not intended to be exposed, and which, in many cases, provision is even made to hinder it from being exposed to. There is, therefore, much appearance that pleasure is agreeable to the Creator, while there is very little if any appearance that pain is so: and there is a certain amount of justification for inferring on grounds of Natural Theology alone, that benevolence is one of the attributes of the Creator. [P. 191.]

What then becomes of the strength of the proposition that "even when Nature does not intend to kill, she inflicts the same tortures in apparent wantonness?" If anything shows contrivance, it would seem to be the arrangements for reproducing. Why should we allow that "there is very little if any appearance that

pain is agreeable to the Creator," who is supposed to have designed this contrivance, if the following lines be true:—"In the
clumsy provision which she [*i.e.* Nature] has made for that perpetual renewal of animal life, rendered necessary by the prompt
termination she puts to it in every individual instance, no human
being ever comes into the world but another human being is
literally stretched on the rack for hours or days, not unfrequently
issuing in death" (p. 30)? Nothing can be more arbitrary than
this attribution of all the pains to Nature, and all the pleasures
to the Demiurgus. How can we apply to the process of birth
such propositions as that the pain arises from external interference with the normal working of the machinery, and resembles
an accident; that the pain seems like a thing undesigned; that it
is a casual result of the collision of the organism with some outward force to which it was not intended to be exposed? And the
same difficulties arise in connection with some other functions
and liabilities of the body, to which I will not more specially
refer. Both in these and all other cases the partition of the phenomena of animal and vegetable life between Nature and an
Intelligent Mind, between a tyrannic Zeus and a beneficent Prometheus, and the attribution of all the good to one, and all the
ill to the other, is tainted with arbitrariness and anthropomorphism from beginning to end. It is irreconcilable with that idea
of Nature as a vast unity, a Whole of continuous processes, which
the discoveries of science are every day pressing more irresistibly
upon the minds of men as the true conception of the universe of
which we are pygmy constituents.

One or two remarks may be made here upon Mr. Mill's modified acceptance of the argument from Design. "I think it must be
allowed," he says, "that in the present state of our knowledge, the
adaptations in Nature afford a large balance of probability in
favour of creation by intelligence." To begin with, one cannot
help feeling that Mr. Mill's reasoning on this critical point in the
discussion loses greatly in interest, from the circumstance that it
does not grapple with the most important scientific hypothesis of
our time—a hypothesis which, if it can ever be completely verified, will make short work with the evidence from which Mr.
Mill's balance of probability is procured. Mr. Mill, with his
invariable candour, admits that the Darwinian theory, the prin-

ciple of the Survival of the Fittest, while "in no way whatever inconsistent with Creation," still would undoubtedly "greatly attenuate the evidence for it" (p. 174). It would be ungracious to make too much of the omission to deal at length with this great dominant hypothesis. It must, however, be said that a treatise whose main positive proposition is that Nature furnishes appearances of design and contrivance by an Intelligent Mind or Will, and yet fails to reconcile that proposition with the principle of modification by natural selection, has not encountered the central problem. In face of the Darwinian hypothesis, with the immense mass of evidence already accumulated in its favour, the inference from contrivance exists, to say the best of it, in a state of suspended animation.

There is another discovery of modern science, which, taken together with the corollaries belonging to it, reduces the evidence from certain special nice and intricate combinations in organic nature to a still weaker quality. I mean the principle of the Persistence of Force and the Transformation and Equivalence of Forces. The explanation of the distribution of matter to which this law points, if it does not finally exclude the idea of a designer or contriver, sedulously inventing adaptations, at least makes a terrible deduction from the small balance of probability which was all that Mr. Mill left us, after making the other deductions which he found necessary. Mr. Mill justly admits that "signs of contrivance are most conspicuous in the structure and processes of vegetable and animal life," while "similar though less conspicuous marks of creation are recognised in inorganic Nature" (p. 188). Now the evidence is daily growing more irresistible to the minds of the most competent observers, that the law of the transforming process in the phenomena of inorganic no less than of organic nature has been one and the same. The quantity of force in the universe is a constant quantity; its metamorphosis takes place over the whole field of concrete phenomena in obedience to uniform laws. The Kosmos is one and integral. Its component parts may be grouped into various divisions for our convenience, astronomic, biologic, organic, inorganic, animal, vegetable; but they are all alike manifestations of one fundamental and all-pervading process. "A Power of which the nature remains for ever inconceivable, and to which no limits in Time or Space can be imagined, works in us certain effects. These effects have certain likenesses of kind, the most general of which we class together under the names of Matter, Motion, and Force; and between these effects there are likenesses of connection, the most constant of which we class as laws of the highest certainty. Analysis reduces these several kinds of effect to one kind of effect; and these several kinds of uniformity to one kind of uniformity. And the highest achievement of Science is the interpretation of all orders of phenomena as differently conditioned manifestations of this one kind of effect, under differently conditioned modes of this one kind of uniformity."[5] Whatever value we may choose to set upon any special way of working out the theory of cosmic evolution, we can hardly be blind either to the evidence there is for its general truth, or to the force with which that evidence makes against the notion of special contrivance and provident adaptation. The scientific principles which lead to the doctrine of Evolution, are not logically inconsistent with Theism. But they are inconsistent with the inference of a creative deity from any of the supposed phenomena of design.

Lastly, upon this part of the subject, I would urge that Mr. Mill has not said anything, in dealing with the argument from design, to weaken the following strong and non-familiar objection to all forms of that argument; namely, that it implies a transfer to regions beyond experience, of an idea which springs from experience and is limited by it. We derive from practical experience the notion that contrivance must come from a contriving intelligence—that is to say, from one or more human beings exercising their faculties with a view to procuring a given end. Let us put aside the objection to inferring a *nisus formativus* from a *nexus formativus*.* Let us grant the proposition in which Mr. Mill widens and fortifies the older statement of the Design argument: let us grant that considerations properly inductive establish that there is some connection through causation between the origin of the arrangements of nature and the ends they fulfil. This does not entitle us to proceed to attribute this causative association to an Intelligent Mind or Will. We know from experience that in the case of the products of human ingenuity the

5. Spencer's *First Principles*, p. 557.
* "formative effort . . . formative connection"—ed.

result may be traced to a provident intention in a man. But how can we infer from this that non-human adaptations are to be traced to a provident intention in ———. In what? We cannot complete the sentence. Whatever word we may choose must be a word directly or indirectly of human experience, and to use it would be to transport the ideas of natural agency into a region where the agency is supernatural.

To turn for a moment to Mr. Mill's treatment of the question of the Immortality of the Soul. His conclusion on this subject is that there is no reason, if we admit the ordering of the world to be the work of an Intelligent Mind, who sometimes appears to desire the happiness of human creatures, why the same Intelligence should not intend human consciousness to be prolonged after the dissolution of the body. Of course to one who denies the alleged evidence for Creation—or the alleged inferences of the benevolence of the Demiurgus—this chain of reasoning, only potential and contingent as it is, breaks asunder. Mr. Mill, however, deals also with the question from the point of view of those indications of immortality which are independent of any theory respecting the Creator and his intentions. His conclusion on this side of the matter is that there is really a total absence of evidence either way; and that the absence of evidence for the affirmative does not, as in so many cases it does, create a strong presumption in favour of the negative (p. 203). There is no evidence in science against the immortality of the soul but that negative evidence which consists in the absence of evidence in its favour (201). Now how far is this really so? Mr. Mill states the case of those who resist the common doctrine thus:—"The evidence is well-nigh complete that all thought and feeling has some action of the bodily organism for its immediate antecedent or accompaniment; that the specific variations, and especially the different degree of complication of the nervous and cerebral organization, correspond to differences in the development of the mental faculties; and though we have no evidence, except negative, that the mental consciousness ceases for ever when the functions of the brain are at an end, we do know that diseases of the brain disturb the mental functions, and that decay or weakness of the brain enfeebles them. We have therefore sufficient evidence that cerebral action is, if not the cause, at least, in our present state of existence, a condition *sine quâ non* of mental operations; and that assuming the mind to be a distinct substance, its separation from the body would not be, as some have vainly flattered themselves, a liberation from trammels and restoration to freedom, but would simply put a stop to its functions and remand it to unconsciousness, unless and until some other set of conditions supervenes, capable of recalling it into activity, but of the existence of which experience does not give us the smallest indication" (p. 198). "The relation of thought to a material brain," however, he warns us, "is no metaphysical necessity, but simply a constant coexistence within the limits of observation."

Without presuming to discuss so far-reaching a problem at the end of an article, I may suggest for consideration whether Mr. Mill's account of the matter is adequate. It has all the marks common to every approach to this question from the Idealistic side. Is that group of attributes which we call the mind or soul a consequence of bodily organization? Biology, not psychology, is the field in which we should seek for an answer. The effect of such evidence as we have on this side is understated by Mr. Mill. We know more than that cerebral action is an indispensable condition of mental operations. This would only show a constant coexistence of mental energies with affections of the bodily organism. We have to add to that the result of the Method of Concomitancy of Variation. Administer a narcotic; the stream of thinking and feeling is suspended. Take alcohol: the mental faculties are stimulated. Take it in excess: their power of coordination gradually disappears. Certain drugs fill the mind of the person addicted to them with special and absorbing images. Facts of this sort might be multiplied without end out of the daily experience of all of us. The canon of the Method of Concomitant Variations is this (Mr. Mill's *Logic,* bk. III., ch. viii. § 6) :—
"Whatever phenomenon varies in any manner whenever another phenomenon varies in some particular manner, is either a cause or an effect of that phenomenon, or is connected with it through some fact of causation." And the writer explains as to the last clause, that it is inserted for the following reason. Two phenomena might accompany one another in their variation, without the one necessarily being the cause of the other; they might both

be different effects of some common cause. How are we to tell which is the proper solution of a given case of concomitancy of variation? The only way to solve the doubt, he tells us, is to endeavour to ascertain whether we can produce the one set of variations by means of the other.

This is exactly what I do when I administer a narcotic or a stimulant. A special variation is effected in the bodily organism of the patient, followed by a corresponding variation of mental energy.

If Mr. Mill's canon above quoted be sound, and if we follow out this method fully, we shall surely see reason for thinking that the bodily organism is truly the cause, and not merely "a condition *sine quâ non*" of mental operations. The facts of mental pathology are tantamount to a series of experiments performed by Nature herself. Cerebral inflammation produces mental delirium; makes the soul delirious, if you choose to express it so. Cerebral malformation makes the soul idiotic. Comparative anatomy in the same manner serves the purpose of experiment by "varying the circumstances," as Bacon bade us do. The soul, or in plainer English, the intellectual faculties of the whole set of animal species, is quantitatively and qualitatively related to the size and structure of the cerebral hemispheres and their contents.

Mr. Mill says that science does not prove experimentally that any mode of organization has the power of producing feeling or thought, and that to make this proof good "it would be necessary that we should be able to produce an organization, and try whether it would feel" (p. 198). I am aware that it may be denied that in the case of narcotics, stimulants and the rest, we are artificially producing the antecedents of mental variations; such cases may be described as "merely setting in motion the exact process by which nature produces them." Even however if the above argument from concomitancy of variations should be deemed insufficient experimental proof to be worth taking into account, I fail to see why the method of Observation should be left out of sight. Observation, if aided by correct deduction, is not confined to the mere ascertaining of sequences and co-existences. It is able to establish causation. This being so, and considering the tenor of the propositions which observation and deduction are gradually building up with an ever increasing force and significance, I submit that Mr. Mill's remarks on the evidence as to the relations between soul and body involve a distinct understatement.

The line of argument followed in pp. 200–203, is extremely important from the Idealist side. It demands a far more careful discussion than can be attempted here. It is substantially identical with the passage in Berkeley on the Natural Immortality of the Soul (*Of the Principles of Human Knowledge,* § 141). There is even nothing in Mr. Mill's way of handling this question inconsistent with a passage quoted by Professor Fraser from one of Berkeley's letters:—"Now it seems very easy to conceive the soul to exist in a separate state, and to exercise herself on new ideas, without the intervention of those tangible things which we call bodies. It is even very possible to conceive how the soul may have ideas of colour without an eye, or of sound without an ear." We do not see how sterile or irrelevant all this is, until we approach the phenomena from the biological side. To do this is not to find proof that such propositions as Mr. Mill lays down on p. 200, and p. 203, are false. But it is to perceive that they would apply equally well to all human knowledge; that they would equally well serve to nullify our conclusions upon the properties of all other kinds of matter, as they are here used to nullify our conclusions from the phenomena of cerebral matter. The line of ontological argument taken by Mr. Mill here no more damages propositions reducing mental operations to functions of a physical organism, than it damages propositions connecting heat and light and growth with the sun. This is at once seen to be the case by any one who first approaches the study of Man in the same attitude in which he would approach the study of any other organized object. Mr. Mill's warning (pp. 200–203) would be just as much in place, and just as efficient, in vindicating the Real Presence.

One more remark. Whatever force the section on Immortality may possess, that force would be exactly as great, if in every place where Immortality is used, we choose to substitute Metempsychosis. When controversialists are disposed to use Mr. Mill's essay as a weapon against those who doubt the immortality of the soul, they will do well to remember that it is exactly as strong a weapon against those who doubt the Transmigration of the soul.

One of the most important subjects of discussion raised in the third of the Essays, I must leave for some future occasion which may present itself: I mean the question, "whether the indulgence of hope in a region of imagination merely, in which there is no prospect that any probable grounds of expectation will ever be obtained, is irrational, and ought to be discouraged as a departure from the rational principle of regulating our feelings as well as opinions strictly by evidence."

Part III

Mr. Pater's Essays

There is no more hopeful sign for that general stir of intellectual energy which is now slowly making itself visible in this country, than the rise among us of a learned, vigorous, and original school of criticism. The amount of contemporary English contribution to the research and thought of Europe seems still to be unequal to our national reputation a hundred and fifty years ago, and the most popular of our two elder living poets is too narrowly provincial, too blind to the new forces, too content with moral prettinesses, as the other of them is too singular in form and too metaphysical in direction, to be in the central current of European ideas in the way in which an English poet, in many respects decidedly the inferior of either of them, and a Scottish romance-writer, were confessed to be sixty years ago. It is not too much to say, however, that if the whole sum of English contribution is still small in proportion to our older fame, as well as to our material and political authority, yet there is now no important department of intellectual activity in which we cannot boast at least one workman of the first order, and in which such a workman may not count upon finding a competent and appreciative public, though possibly less considerable in point of numbers than is completely satisfactory. In truth, we are perhaps beginning to realise in literature what men have long realised in

Studies in the History of the Renaissance. By Walter H. Pater, Fellow of Brasenose College, Oxford. London: Macmillan & Co. [This essay was first published in *Fortnightly Review,* n.s., 76 (April 1873):469–77—ed.]

science, that one of the first conditions of success is to care more for the quality of a public than for its size; perhaps even to work in that half-stoical spirit which counts every individual listener, admirer, sympathiser, as one more than was expected, and all the help derived from sympathizing and competent praise as of the nature of happy windfall, rather than as a goal attained. We are perceiving that content with his public, whatever it may be, is an essential element in one who would bring all his faculties in uncrippled freedom to his work. There is a growing seriousness and sense of responsibility and respect at once for elevation and thoroughness, which is both excellent in its effect on the productions of the given workman, and eminently stimulating and encouraging to all who follow his labours. Such men as Mr. Darwin in one field, and Mr. Freeman in another, exert a general influence upon the method and the standard of good workmanship, which is a gain quite independent of their success in the region of special acquisition. The fatuous association of genius with disorder and haste is giving way to the more rational association of sound and powerful work with minute, searching, disciplined industry; and the poverty and triviality of much of the printed criticism of the day are a very unimportant circumstance to one who is acquainted with the active and cultivated spirit of a younger generation, as yet unknown beyond limited circles, and still wavering in intellectual direction, but from which there is good reason for expecting a literature that may unite, as English tradition makes it not unjustifiable to suppose, German excellence of research and power of historic vision with French excellence of presentation and skill in grouping.

Criticism of the highest kind is the natural forerunner of such a movement as we are all hoping for; indeed, criticism of the highest kind is the earliest form of the movement itself. The speculative distractions of the epoch are noisy and multitudinous, and the first effort of the serious spirit must be to disengage itself from the futile hubbub which is sedulously maintained by the bodies of rival partisans in philosophy and philosophical theology. This effort after detachment naturally takes the form of criticism of the past, the only way in which a man can take part in the discussion and propagation of ideas, while yet standing in some sort aloof from the agitation of the present. But no serious spirit can content itself with discussion that has no aim and is only discharged into the air, nor with the criticism that is no more than an industriously compiled catalogue of notions and opinions. An actively stirred generation craves a doctrine. What we see in our time is that men are beginning to go through the following process: to come by a doctrine by one means or another; to assume it as proven to themselves, and to be indifferent as to its direct demonstration to others; then to use it indirectly and obliquely as an instrument for examining the life, character, and work of others. Criticism thus conceived is apt, if unchecked, to degenerate into a trick of forced and artificial illustration. At present this danger is not very close to us. The criticism of the three or four younger writers to whom these remarks refer is genuine, and wholly disinterested. They use their doctrines as an instrument, and their subject as an illustration, but they do the fullest justice to the subject on independent grounds, and make that their first and not their secondary aim. Thus they help to create a literary atmosphere which is not choked with the acrid fumes of battle, they spread a disposition for positive thought, and they distribute knowledge. And thus, too, what is in superficial appearance merely an appreciation of the production of others, is in fact tantamount to constructive production of a really original kind.

Mr. Pater's studies in the history of the Renaissance and the essay on Winckelmann which he has appropriately enough attached to them, constitute the most remarkable example of this younger movement towards a fresh and inner criticism, and they are in themselves a singular and interesting addition to literature. The subjects are of the very kind in which we need instruction and guidance, and there is a moral in the very choice of them. From the point of view of form and literary composition they are striking in the highest degree. They introduce to English readers a new and distinguished master in the great and difficult art of writing prose. Their style is marked by a flavour at once full and exquisite, by a quality that mixes richness with delicacy, and a firm coherency with infinite subtlety. The peril that besets a second-rate writer who handles a style of this kind lies in the direction of effeminate and flaccid mannerism, and the peril is especially great when he is dealing with æsthetic subjects; they tempt to an expansion of feeling, for the expression of which no prose can ever become a proper medium. Mr. Pater escapes the danger, first by virtue of his artistic sense which reveals to him the limits of prose and gives him spontaneous respect for them, keeping him well away from all bastard dithyramb, and secondly by virtue of a strain of clear, vigorous, and ordered thought, which underlies and compacts his analysis of sensuous impressions. Hence his essays, while abounding in passages of an exquisite and finished loveliness that recall the completeness of perfected verse, are saved by a marked gravity and reserve from any taint of the sin of random poetical expatiation and lyric effusion. Mr. Pater's style is far too singular in its excellence not to contain the germs of possible excess in some later day. All excellent style does so; if it is of a large and noble eloquence, like Burke's or Bossuet's, it holds the seeds of turgidity; if it is racy and generously imaginative, it may easily degenerate into vulgarity or weedy rankness or the grotesque; if it is of a severe and chastened elevation, it is apt to fall over, and substitute ætherialised phrase for real and robust ideas. And so subtlety and love of minor tones may lead a writer who is not in constant and rigorous discipline, into affectation and a certain mawkishness. Meantime we trust to Mr. Pater's intellectual firmness, to his literary conscience and scrupulosity, and above all to his reserve. This fine reserve, besides the negative merit of suppressing misplaced effusion, has a positive effect of its own, an effect of subtle and penetrating suggestiveness that but for the sobriety and balance of the general colour would leave one with half weird, unsatisfied, unreal impressions. Thus at the close of the beautiful piece on Joachim du Bellay, after giving us the song which is the writer's title to commemoration, Mr. Pater justly says that nearly all the pleasure of it "is in the surprise at the happy and dexterous way in which a thing slight in itself is handled," and then concludes generally: "One seems to hear the measured falling of the fans with a child's pleasure on coming across the incident for the first time in one of those great barns of Du Bellay's own country, La Beauce, the granary of France. A sudden light transfigures a trivial thing, a weather-vane, a wind-mill, a winnowing flail, the dirt in the barn-door; a moment,—and the thing has vanished, because it was pure effect; but it leaves a relish behind it, a long-

ing that the accident may happen again." This brief sentence is
the happiest summary of criticism, leaving the reader with the
key, and leaving him, too, with a desire to use it and explore what
further may be locked up in verse or picture. This is the manner
of Mr. Pater's criticism throughout. The same passage illustrates
another of its qualities. It is concrete and positive, not metaphysical; a record or suggestion of impressions, not an analysis
of their ultimate composition, nor an abstract search for the law
of their effects. "The more you come to understand what imaginative colouring really is, that *all colour is no mere delightful
quality of outward things, but a spirit upon them by which they
become expressive to the spirit,* the better you will like this peculiar quality of colour" (p. 48). How full at once of suggestion,
and of explanation, yet without that parade of speculative and
technical apparatus, which has made most art criticism, especially
among ourselves, so little nourishing, so little real or life-like.
"What is important," as Mr. Pater says in words that define his
own method and position, "is not that the critic should possess
a correct abstract definition of beauty, but a certain kind of
temperament, the power of being deeply moved by the presence
of beautiful objects. He will remember that beauty exists in
many forms. And often," he continues, "it will require great
nicety to disengage this virtue from the commoner elements with
which it may be found in combination." It is probably this keen
susceptibility to minute suggestions that underlies the writer's
care for the lesser stars in the great firmament, his love for bits
of work other than the gigantic or sublime, the attraction to him
of hints of beauty and faintly marked traces of exquisite peculiarity, rather than the noon-day splendour of master works. We
can suppose that the simplicity of some Gregorian chant would
please him better than a great Beethoven symphony, and that the
church at Gernerode or St. Cunibert's at Cologne would give him
more heartfelt delight than the glories of the great Cölner Dom
itself. After all anybody may be stirred by the sublime or the
superb. We can well afford to welcome to literature one of the
less common spirits, gifted with a sense for the dimmer beauties,
and to whom the more distant tones are audible and harmonious.
Such gifts are extraordinarily welcome to our own literature,
which rich as it is in magnificent as in sweet and homely produc-

tions, is anything but rich in work marked by subtlety of æsthetic vision. If Mr. Pater continues to remember that it is exactly in the region of a man's gifts where he most needs caution and self-discipline, lest the fatal law of excess turns his strength into his weakness, we may expect from him delight and instruction of the rarest kind.

In one or two places there is perhaps to be noticed a tinge of obscurity, or at least of doubtfulness of meaning, the result of a refining of thought into excess of tenuity. It is so difficult a thing rigorously to put aside as taken for granted all common-place impression and obvious phrase, and only to seize what is the inner virtue of the matter, without going beyond the sight and grasp of plainer men. We have one man of genius who is as great a master of subtle insight into character, as Mr. Pater is of analysis of beautiful impressions; Mr. Meredith, like Mr. Pater, is not always easy to follow, and for the same reason. After all the plain men are at least as much in fault as those who touch them with perplexity. This fault, however, in Mr. Pater's case, if it is really there, and not merely a fancy of my own, is only to be found in the essay on Winckelmann, which is the earliest of the composi-tions in the volume; and so we may suppose that it is a fault of which the writer has already cured himself. We may, perhaps, also venture to notice the occasional appearance of a very minor de-fect, which is far too common in all contemporary writing and conversation, but which jars more than usually in so considerable a stylist as Mr. Pater; I mean the use of German and French phrases, like *intimité, Allgemeinheit, Heiterkeit,* and the rest. It seems just now to be peculiarly the duty of a writer who re-spects his own language, and has the honourable aspiration of maintaining its purity, strength, and comprehensiveness, care-fully to resist every temptation to introduce a single foreign word into his prose upon any pretext whatever. Even quotations from foreign writers ought, as I presume to think, to be given in English, and not in French, German, Greek, Italian, excepting of course quotations in verse, and of these the good prose writer is naturally most sparing in any language.

Concreteness, prevented from running to unprofitable ampli-tude of description alike by the reserve of the writer's style, and by the subtlety of the only impressions which he thinks worth recording, is connected with a prime characteristic of Mr. Pater's work, its constant association of art with the actual moods and purposes of men in life. He redeems beautiful production in all its kinds from the arid bondage of their technicalities, and unfolds its significance in relation to human culture and the perplexities of human destiny. This is to make art veritably fruitful, and criticism too. His criticism is endowed with strength and substance by the abundance of intellectual ideas which have come to him from the union of careful cultivation with an original individuality, and these intellectual ideas are grouped in an unsystematic way round a distinct theory of life and its purport, which thus in the manner we pointed out at first gives colour and meaning to all that Mr. Pater has to say about the special objects of his study. This theory is worth attention. The exponent of it sees only the fluid elements in life, only its brevity and the inevitable abyss that lies at the end of our path. "We have an interval and then our place knows us no more. Some spend their interval in listlessness, some in high passions, the wisest in art and song. For our one chance is in expanding that interval, in getting as many pulsations as possible into the given time. High passions give one this quickened sense of life, ecstasy and sorrow of love, political or religious enthusiasm, or 'the enthusiasm of humanity.' Only, be sure that it does yield you this fruit of a quickened multiplied consciousness. Of this wisdom, the poetic passion, the desire of beauty, the love of art for art's sake has most; for art comes to you professing frankly to give nothing but the highest quality to your moments as they pass and simply for those moments' sake" (p. 212). Of course this neither is, nor is meant to be, a complete scheme for wise living and wise dying. The Hedonist, and this is what Mr. Pater must be called by those who like to affix labels, holds just the same maxims with reference to the bulk of human conduct, the homespun substance of our days, as are held by other people in their senses. He knows perfectly well that the commonplace virtues of honesty, industry, punctuality, and the like, are the conditions of material prosperity, and moral integrity. Here he stands on the same ground as the rest of the world. He takes all that for granted, with or without regret that these limitations should be imposed by inexorable circumstance upon the capacity of human nature for fine delight in the passing moments. He has no design of interfering with the minor or major morals of the world, but only of dealing with what we may perhaps call the accentuating portion of life. In the majority of their daily actions a Catholic, a Protestant, a Positivist, are indistinguishable from one another; just as they are indistinguishable in the clothes they wear. It is the accentuating parts of conduct and belief that reveal their differences, and this is obviously of the most extreme importance,—less in its effect upon commonplace external morality which can take care of itself on independent grounds, than in its influence over the spiritual drift of the believer's life. It is what remains for a man seriously to do or feel, over and above earning his living and respecting the laws. What is to give significance and worth to his life, after complying with the conditions essential to its maintenance and outward order? A great many people in all times, perhaps the most, give a practical answer to the question by ignoring it, and living unaccented lives of dulness or frivolity. A great many others find an answer in devotion to divine mysteries, which round the purpose of their lives and light the weariness of mechanical days. The writer of the essays before us answers it as we have seen, and there is now a numerous sect among cultivated people who accept his answer and act upon it. So far as we know, there never was seen before in this country so distinct an attempt to bring the æsthetical element closely and vividly round daily life. It is an exaggerated side. Dutch farmhouses are systematically swept by brokers, that the vulgarity of ormolu may be replaced by delft, and nankin, and magic bits of oriental blue and white. There is an orthodoxy in wall-papers, and you may commit the unpardonable sin in discordant window-curtains. Members of the sect are as solicitous about the right in tables and the correct in legs of chairs, as members of another sect are careful about the cut of chasuble or dalmatica. Bric-a-brac rises to the level of religions, and the whirligig of time is bringing us back to fetishism and the worship of little domestic gods, not seldom bleak and uncouth.

In all this, notwithstanding its exaggeration, there is something to be glad of. It is the excess of a reaction, in itself very wholesome, against the vulgar luxury of commonplace decoration, and implies a certain appreciation of the permanent principles of beautiful ornament. But there is something deeper than this underneath, at least in the minds of the vigorous leaders of the movement, and in such men as Mr. Pater, just as there was something deeper than the puerilities of the fussier and sillier sort of ritualists in the mind of Mr. Ward or Dr. Newman. Indeed, this more recent pagan movement is one more wave of the great current of reactionary force which the Oxford movement first released. It is infinitely less powerful, among other reasons because it only appeals to persons with some culture, but it is equally a protest against the mechanical and graceless formalism of the modern era, equally an attempt to find a substitute for a narrow popular creed in a return upon the older manifestations of the human spirit, and equally a craving for the infusion of something harmonious and beautiful about the bare lines of daily living. Since the first powerful attempt to revive a gracious spirituality in the country by a renovation of sacramentalism, science has come. The Newmanite generation in Oxford was followed by a generation who were formed on Mr. Mill's Logic and Grote's Greece. The æsthetic spirits were no longer able to find rest in a system associated with theology. Then Mr. Ruskin came, and the Præ-Raphaelite painters, and Mr. Swinburne, and Mr. Morris, and now lastly a critic like Mr. Pater, all with faces averted from theology, most of them indeed blessed with a simple and happy unconsciousness of the very existence of the conventional gods. Many of them are as indifferent to the conventional aims and phrases of politics and philanthropy as they are to things called heavenly. Mr. Ruskin indeed, as we all know, has plunged chivalrously into the difficult career of the social reconstructor, but hardly with a success that any man can call considerable. And Mr. Swinburne, like that most powerful of all French poets whom he calls master, has always shown a generous ardour in the greater human causes. But here is Mr. Pater courageously saying that the love of art for art's sake has most of the true wisdom that makes life full. The fact that such a saying is possible in the mouth of an able and shrewd-witted man of wide culture and knowledge, and that a serious writer should thus raise æsthetic interest to the throne lately filled by religion, only shows how void the old theologies have become.

And if such a doctrine fails of their inspiring earnestness and gravity, at the same time it escapes their cramping narrowness. It is pregnant with intellectual play and expansion, and it is this intellectual play and expansion that we require, before the social changes craved by so many can fully ripen. It is assuredly good for us to possess such a school. There is no reason to be afraid of their taking too firm a hold, or occupying too much ground, to the detriment of energetic social action in the country. We have suffered more from the excessive absorption of national interest in theological strife and the futilities of political faction, than we are at all likely to suffer from the devotion of a few men of special impulses to the subjects where those impulses will tell with most effect. The prodigious block of our philistinism needs to have wedges driven in at many points, and even then they will be all too few. Sincere and disinterested work by competent hands upon exactly such subjects as Mr. Pater has chosen, real yet detached from the clamour of to-day, is one of the first among the many fertilising agents that the time demands. To excite people's interests in numerous fields, to persuade them of the worth of other activity than material and political activity, is to make life more various, and to give the many different aptitudes of men an ampler chance of finding themselves.

Politics and the acquisition of wealth do not constitute the only peril to the growth of culture in England. The specialism of physical science threatens dangers of a new kind. On this side too we need protection for other than scientific manifestations of intellectual activity and fruitfulness. Only on condition of this spacious and manifold energizing in diverse directions, can we hope in our time for that directly effective social action which some of us think calculated to give a higher quality to the moments as they pass than art and song, just because it is not "simply for those moments' sake." For after all, the Heraclitean word which Mr. Pater has expounded with such singular attractiveness both of phrase and sentiment only represents one aspect of the great world. If all is very fluid, yet in another way how stable it all is. Our globe is whirling through space like a speck of dust borne on a mighty wind, yet to us it is solid and fixed. And so with our lives and all that compasses them. Seen in reference to the long æons, they are as sparks that glow for an indivisible moment of time, and then sink into darkness, but for ourselves the months are threads which we may work into a stout and durable web.

Harriet Martineau

In 1850 Charlotte Brontë paid a visit to Harriet Martineau at Ambleside, and she wrote to her friends various emphatic accounts of her hostess. "Without adopting her theories," Miss Brontë said, "I yet find a worth and greatness in herself, and a consistency, benevolence, perseverance in her practice, such as wins the sincerest esteem and affection. She is not a person to be judged by her writings alone, but rather by her own deeds and life, than which nothing can be more exemplary or noble."

The division which Miss Brontë thus makes between opinions and character, and again between literary production and character, is at the root of any just criticism of the two volumes of autobiography which have just been given to the public. Of the third volume, *The Memorials,* by Mrs. Chapman, it is impossible to say anything serious. Mrs. Chapman fought an admirable fight in the dark times of American history for the abolition of slavery, but unhappily she is without literary gifts; and this third volume is one more illustration of the folly of intrusting composition of biography to persons who have only the wholly irrelevant claim of intimate friendship, or kinship, or sympathy in public causes. The qualification for a biographer is not in the least that he is a virtuous person, or a second cousin, or a dear friend, or a trusty colleague; but that he knows how to write a book, has tact, style, taste, considerateness, senses of proportion, and a good eye for

This essay was first published in *Macmillan's Magazine,* 36 (May 1877): 47–60, and was reprinted in *Critical Miscellanies,* vol. 3 (London, 1886)—ed.

the beginnings and ends of things. The third volume, then, tells us little about the person to whom they relate. The two volumes of autobiography tell all that we can seek to know, and the reader who judges them in an equitable spirit will be ready to allow that, when all is said that can be said of her hardness, arbitrariness, and insularity, Harriet Martineau is still a singular and worthy figure among the conspicuous personages of a generation that has now almost vanished. Some will wonder how it was that her literary performances acquired so little of permanent value. Others will be pained by the distinct repudiation of all theology, avowed by her with a simple and courageous directness that can scarcely be counted other than honourable to her. But everybody will admit, as Charlotte Brontë did, that though her books are not of the first nor of the second rank, and though her anti-theological opinions are to many repugnant, yet behind books and opinions was a remarkable personality, a sure eye for social realities, a moral courage that never flinched; a strong judgment, within its limits; a vigorous self-reliance both in opinion and act, which yet did not prevent a habit of the most neutral self-judgment; the commonplace virtues of industry and energy devoted to aims too elevated, and too large and generous, to be commonplace; a splendid sincerity, a magnificent love of truth. And that all these fine qualities, which would mostly be described as manly, should exist not in a man but a woman, and in a woman who discharged admirably such feminine duties as fell to her, fills up the measure of our interest in such a character.

Harriet Martineau was born at Norwich in 1802, and she died, as we all remember, in the course of last summer (1876). Few people have lived so long as three-quarters of a century, and undergone so little substantial change of character, amid some very important changes of opinion. Her family was Unitarian, and family life was in her case marked by some of that stiffness, that severity, that chilly rigour, with which Unitarians are sometimes taxed by religionists of a more ecstatic doctrine. Her childhood was very unhappy; the household seems to have been unamiable, and she was treated with none of that tenderness and sympathy, for which firm and defiant natures are apt to yearn as strongly as others that get the credit of greater sensibility.

With that singular impulse to suicide which is frequent among children, though rarer with girls than boys, she went one day into the kitchen for the carving knife, that she might cut her throat; luckily the servants were at dinner, and the child retreated. Deafness, which proved incurable, began to afflict her before she was sixteen. A severe, harsh, and mournful kind of religiosity seized her, and this "abominable spiritual rigidity," as she calls it, confirmed all the gloomy predispositions of her mind. She learned a good deal, mastering Latin, French, and Italian in good time; and reading much in her own tongue, including constant attention to the Bible, with all sorts of commentaries and explanations, such as those of us who were brought up in a certain spiritual atmosphere, have only too good reasons never to forget. This expansion of intellectual interest, however, did not make her less silent, less low in her spirits, less full of vague and anxious presentiment. The reader is glad when these ungracious years of youth are at an end, and the demands of active life stirred Harriet Martineau's energies into vigorous work.

In 1822 her father died, and seven years later, his widow and his daughters lost at a single blow nearly all that they had in the world. Before this event, which really proved to be a blessing in the disguise of a catastrophe, Harriet Martineau had written a number of slight pieces. They had been printed, and received a certain amount of recognition. They were of a religious cast, as was natural in one with whom religious literature, and religious life and observance, had hitherto taken in the whole sphere of her continual experience. *Traditions of Palestine* and *Devotional Exercises* are titles that tell their own tale, and we may be sure that their authoress was still at the antipodean point of the positive philosophy in which she ended her speculative journey. She still clung undoubtingly to what she had been brought up to believe, when she won three prizes for essays intended to present Unitarianism to the notice of Jews, of Catholics, and of Mahometans. Her success in these and similar efforts, turned her mind more decidedly towards literature as a profession.

Miss Martineau is at some pains to assure us on several occasions that it was the need of utterance now and always that drove her to write, and that money, although welcome when it came, was never her motive. This perhaps a little savours of affectation.

Nobody would dream of suspecting Miss Martineau of writing anything that she did not believe to be true or useful, merely for the sake of money. But there is plenty of evidence that the prospect of payment stirred her to true and useful work, as it does many other authors by profession, and as it does the followers of all professions whatever. She puts the case fairly enough in another place:—"Every author is in a manner an adventurer; and no one was ever more decidedly so than myself; but the difference between one kind of adventurer and another is, I believe, simply this—that the one has something to say which presses for utterance, and is uttered at length without a view to future fortunes; while the other has a sort of general inclination towards literature, without any specific need of utterance, and a very definite desire for the honours and rewards of the literary career." Even in the latter case, however, honest journeyman's work enough is done in literature by men and women who seek nothing higher than a reputable source of income. Miss Martineau did, no doubt, seek objects far higher and more generous than income, but she lived on the income which literature brought to her; and there seems a certain failure of her usually admirable common sense in making any ado about so simple a matter. When doctors and counsel refuse their guineas, and the parson declines a stipend, it will be quite soon enough for the author to be especially anxious to show that he has a right to regard money much as the rest of the human race regard it.

Miss Martineau underwent the harsh ordeal which awaits most literary aspirants. She had a scheme in her head for a long series of short tales to illustrate some of the propositions of political economy. She trudged about London day after day, through mud and fog, with weary limbs and anxious heart, as many an author has done before and since. The times were bad; cholera was abroad; people were full of apprehension and concern about the Reform Bill; and the publishers looked coldly on a doubtful venture. Miss Martineau talks none of the conventional nonsense about the cruelty and stupidity of publishers. What she says is this:—"I have always been anxious to extend to young or struggling authors the sort of aid which would have been so precious to me in that winter of 1829–30, and I know that, in above twenty years, I have never succeeded but once." One of the most dis-

tinguished editors in London, who had charge of a periodical for
many years, told us what comes to the same thing, namely, that in
no single case during all these years did a volunteer contributor of
real quality, or with any promise of eminence, present himself or
herself. So many hundreds think themselves called, so few are
chosen. In Miss Martineau's case, however, the trade made a
mistake. When at length she found some one to go halves with
her in the enterprise, on terms extremely disadvantageous to herself, the first of her tales was published (1832), and instantly had
a prodigious success. The sale ran up to more than ten thousand
of each monthly volume. In that singular autobiographical sketch
of herself which Miss Martineau prepared for the *Daily News,*
to be printed as her obituary notice, she pronounced a judgment
upon this work which more disinterested, though not more im-
partial, critics will confirm. Her own unalterable view, she says,
of what the work could and could not effect, "prevented her
from expecting too much from it, either in regard to its social
operations or its influence on her own fame. The original idea of
exhibiting the great natural laws of society by a series of pictures
of selected social action was a fortunate one; and her tales initiated
a multitude of minds into the conception of what political economy is, and how it concerns everybody living in society. Beyond
this there is no merit of a high order in the work. It popularised
in a fresh form some doctrines and many truths long before
made public by others." James Mill, one of the acutest economists
of the day, and one of the most vigorous and original characters
of that or any other day, had foretold failure; but when the time
came he very handsomely admitted that his prophecy had been
rash. In after years, when Miss Martineau had acquired from
Comte a conception of the growth and movement of societies as a
whole, with their economic conditions controlled and constantly
modified by a multitude of other conditions of various kinds, she
rated the science of her earlier days very low. Even in those days,
however, she says, "I believe I should not have been greatly surprised or displeased to have perceived, even then that the pretended science is no science at all, strictly speaking; and that so
many of its parts must undergo essential change, that it may be a
question whether future generations will owe much more to it
than the benefit (inestimable, to be sure) of establishing the

grand truth that social affairs proceed according to general laws, no less than natural phenomena of every kind."

Harriet Martineau was not of the class of writers, most of them terribly unprofitable, who merely say literary things about social organisation, its institutions, and their improvement. Her feeling about society was less literary than scientific: it was not sentimental, but the business-like quality of a good administrator. She was moved less by pity or by any sense of the pathos and the hardness of the world, than by a sensible and energetic interest in good government and in the rational and convenient ordering of things. Her tales to illustrate the truths of political economy are what might be expected from a writer of this character. They are far from wanting—many of them—in the genuine interest of good story-telling. They are rapid, definite, and without a trace of either slovenliness or fatigue. We are amazed as we think of the speed and prompt regularity with which they were produced; and the fertile ingenuity with which the pill of political economy is wrapped up in the confectionery of a tale, may stand as a marvel of true cleverness and inventive dexterity. Of course, of imagination or invention in a high sense there is not a trace. Such a quality was not in the gifts of the writer, nor could it in any case have worked within such limitations as those set by the matter and the object of the series.

Literary success was followed in the usual order by social temptation. Miss Martineau removed from Norwich to London, and she had good reasons for making the change. Her work dealt with matters of a political kind, and she could only secure a real knowledge of what was best worth saying by intercourse with those who had a better point of view for a survey of the social state of England than could be found in a provincial town like Norwich. So far as evening parties went, Miss Martineau soon perceived how little "essential difference there is between the extreme case of a cathedral city and that of literary London, or any other place, where dissipation takes the turn of book-talk instead of dancing or masquerading." She went out to dinner every night except Sundays, and saw all the most interesting people of the London of five-and-forty years ago. While she was free from presumptuousness in her judgments, she was just as free from a foolish willingness to take the reputations of the hour on trust. Her attitude was friendly and sensible, but it was at the same time critical and independent; and that is what every frank, upright, and sterling character naturally becomes in face of an unfamiliar society. Harriet Martineau was too keen-sighted, too aware of the folly and incompetent pretension of half the world, too consciously self-respecting and proud, to take society and its ways with any diffidence or ingenuous simplicity. On the importance of the small *littérateur* who unreasonably thinks himself a great one, on the airs and graces of the gushing blue-stockings who were in vogue in that day, on the detestable vulgarity of literary lionising, she had no mercy. She recounts with caustic relish the story about a certain pedantical lady, of whom Tierney had said that there was not another head in England that could encounter hers on the subject of Cause and Effect. The story was that when in a country house one fine day she took her seat in a window, saying, in a business-like manner (to David Ricardo), "Come, now, let us have a little discussion about Space." We remember a story about a certain Mademoiselle de Launay, afterwards well known to the Paris of the eighteenth century, being introduced at Versailles by a silly great lady who had an infatuation for her. "This," the great lady kept saying, "is the young person whom I have told you about, who is so wonderfully intelligent, who knows so much. Come, Mademoiselle, pray talk. Now, Madame, you will see how she talks. Well, first of all, now, talk a little about religion; then you can tell us about something else."

We cannot wonder that Miss Martineau did not go a second time to the house where Space might be the unprovoked theme of a casual chat. Pretension in every shape she hated most heartily. Her judgments in most cases were thoroughly just—at this period of her life at any rate—and sometimes even unexpectedly kindly, and the reason is that she looked at society through the medium of a strong and penetrating kind of common sense, which is more often the gift of clever women than of clever men. If she is masculine, she is, like Mrs. Colonel Poyntz, in one of Bulwer's novels, "masculine in a womanly way." There is a real spirit of ethical divination in some of her criticism of character. Take the distinguished man whose name we have just written. "There was Bulwer on a sofa," she says, "sparkling and languishing among a set of female votaries—he and they dizened out, perfumed, and presenting the nearest picture to a seraglio to be seen on British ground—only the indifference or hauteur of the lord of the harem being absent." Yet this disagreeable sight does not prevent her from feeling a cordial interest in him, amidst any amount of vexation and pity for his weakness. "He seems to be a woman of genius inclosed by misadventure in a man's form. He has insight, experience, sympathy, letters, power and grace of expression, and an irrepressible impulse to utterance, and industry which should have produced works of the noblest quality; and these have been intercepted by mischiefs which may be called misfortune rather than fault. His friendly temper, his generous heart, his excellent conversation (at his best), and his simple manners (when he forgot himself), have many a time 'left me mourning' that such a being should allow himself to sport with perdition." Those who knew most about Bulwer, and who were most repelled by his terrible faults, will feel in this page of Miss Martineau's the breath of social equity in which charity is not allowed to blur judgment, nor moral disapproval to narrow, starve, and discolour vision into lost possibilities of character. And we may note in passing how even here, in the mere story of the men and women whom she met in London drawing-rooms, Harriet Martineau does not lose herself in gossip about individuals looked at merely in their individual relations. It is not merely the "blighting of promise nor the forfeiture of a career" that she deplores in the case of a Bulwer or a Brougham; it is "the intercepting of national blessings." If this view of natural gifts as a source of blessing to society, and not merely of power or fame to their privileged possessor, were more common than it is, the impression which such a thought is calculated to make would be the highest available protection against those blighted promises and forfeited careers of which Brougham and Bulwer were only two out of a too vast host of examples.

It is the very fulness with which she is possessed by this large way of conceiving a life in its manifold relations to the service of the world, that is the secret of Harriet Martineau's firm, clear, calm, and almost neutral way of judging both her own work and character and those of others. By calm we do not mean that she was incapable of strong and direct censure. Many of her judgments, both here and in her *Biographic Sketches,* are stern; and some—like that on Macaulay, for instance—may even pass for harsh. But they are never the product of mere anger or heatedness, and it is a great blunder to suppose that reasoned severity is incompatible with perfect composure, or that calm is another name for amiable vapidity.

> Thöricht ist's
> In allen Stücken billig sein; es heisst
> Sein eigen Selbst zerstören.

Her condemnation of the Whigs, for example, is as stringent and outspoken as condemnation can be; yet it is a deliberate and reasoned judgment, not a mere bitterness or prejudice. The Whigs were at that moment, between 1832 and 1834, at the height of their authority, political, literary, and social. After a generation of misgovernment they had been borne to power on the tide of national enthusiasm for parliamentary reform, and for all those improvements in our national life to which parliamentary reform was no more than the first step. The harshness and darkness of the past generation were the measure of the hopes of the new time. These hopes, which were at least as strong in Harriet Martineau as in anybody then living, the Whigs were soon felt to have cheated. She cannot forgive them. Speaking of John and Edward Romilly, "they had virtuous projects," she says, "and had every hope of achieving service worthy of their father's fame; but their aspirations were speedily tamed down—as all high aspirations *are* lowered by Whig influences." A certain peer is described as "agreeable enough in society to those who are not very particular in regard to sincerity; and was, as Chancellor of the Exchequer or anything else, as good a representative as could be found of the flippancy, conceit, and official helplessness and ignorance of the Whig administration." Charles Knight started a new periodical for the people under the patronage of the official Whigs. "But the poverty and perverseness of their ideas, and the insolence of their feelings, were precisely what might be expected by all who really knew that remarkably vulgar class of men. They purposed to lecture the working classes, who were by far the wiser party of the two, in a jejune, coaxing, dull, religious-tract sort of tone, and criticised and deprecated everything like vigour, and a manly and genial tone of address in the new publication, while trying to push in as contributors effete and exhausted writers and friends of their own, who knew about as much of the working classes of England as of those of Turkey." This energetic description, which belongs to the year 1848, gives us an interesting measure of the distance that has been traversed during the last thirty years. The workmen have acquired direct political power; they have organised themselves into effective groups for industrial purposes; they have produced leaders of ability and sound judgment; and the Whig who seeks their support must stoop or rise to talk a Radicalism that would have amply satisfied even Harriet Martineau herself.

The source of this improvement in the society to which she bade farewell, over that into which she had been born, is set down by Miss Martineau to the most remarkable literary genius with whom, during her residence in London, she was brought into contact. "What Wordsworth did for poetry," she says, "in bringing us out of a conventional idea and method to a true and simple one, Carlyle has done for morality. He may be himself the most curious opposition to himself,—he may be the greatest mannerist of his age while denouncing conventionalism,—the greatest talker while eulogising silence,—the most woeful complainer while glorifying fortitude,—the most uncertain and stormy in mood, while holding forth serenity as the greatest good within the reach of man; but he has nevertheless infused into the mind of the English nation a sincerity, earnestness, healthfulness, and courage which can be appreciated only by those who are old enough to tell what was our morbid state when Byron was the representative of our temper, the Clapham church of our religion, and the rotten-borough system of our political morality." We have no quarrel with this account of the greatest man of letters of our generation. But Carlyle has only been one influence among others. It is a far cry indeed from *Sartor Resartus* to the *Tracts for the Times,* yet they were both of them protests against the same thing, both of them attempted answers to the same problem, and the *Tracts* perhaps did more than *Sartor* to quicken spiritual life, to shatter "the Clapham church," and to substitute a mystic faith and not unlovely hope for the frigid, hard, and mechanical lines of official orthodoxy on the one hand, and the egotism and sentimental despair of Byronism on the other. There is a third school, too, and Harriet Martineau herself was no insignificant member of it, to which both the temper and the political morality of our time have owed a deep debt; the school of those utilitarian political thinkers who gave light rather than heat, and yet by the intellectual force with which they insisted on the right direction of social reform, also stirred the very impulse which made men desire social reform. The most illustrious of this body was undoubtedly John Mill, because to accurate political science he added a fervid and vibrating social sympathy, and a power of quickening it in the best minds of a scientific turn. It is odd, by the way, that Miss Martineau, while so lavish in deserved panegyric on Carlyle, should be so grudging and disparaging in the case of Mill, with whom her intellectual affinities must have been closer than with any other of her contemporaries. The translator of Comte's *Positive Philosophy* had better reasons than most people for thinking well of the services of the author of the *System of Logic:* it was certainly the latter book which did more than any other to prepare the minds of the English philosophic public for the former.

It is creditable to Miss Martineau's breadth of sympathy that she should have left on record the tribute of her admiration for Carlyle, for nobody has written so harshly as Carlyle on the subject which interested Harriet Martineau more passionately than any other events of her time. In 1834 she had finished her series of illustrations of political economy; her domestic life was fretted by the unreasonable exigences of her mother; London society had perhaps begun to weary her, and she felt the need of a change of scene. The United States, with the old European institutions placed amid new conditions, were then as now a natural object of interest to everybody with a keen feeling for social improvement. So to the Western Republic Miss Martineau turned her face. She had not been long in the States before she began to feel that the Abolitionists, at that moment a despised and persecuted handful of men and women, were the truly moral and regenerating party in the country. Harriet Martineau no sooner felt this conviction driving out her former prejudice against them as fanatical and impracticable, than she at once bore public testimony, at serious risk of every kind to herself, in favour of the extreme Anti-

Slavery agitators. And for thirty years she never slackened her sympathy nor her energetic action on English public opinion, in this most vital matter of her time. She was guided not merely by humanitarian disgust at the cruel and brutal abominations of slavery,—though we know no reason why this alone should not be a sufficient ground for turning Abolitionist,—but also on the more purely political ground of the cowardice, silence, corruption, and hypocrisy that were engendered in the Free States by purchased connivance at the peculiar institution of the Slave States. Nobody has yet traced out the full effect upon the national character of the Americans of all those years of conscious complicity in slavery, after the moral iniquity of slavery had become clear to the inner conscience of the very men who ignobly sanctioned the mobbing of Abolitionists.

In the summer of 1836 Miss Martineau returned to England, having added this great question to the stock of her foremost objects of interest and concern. Such additions, whether literary or social, are the best kind of refreshment that travel supplies. She published two books on America: one of them abstract and quasi-scientific, *Society in America;* the other, *A Retrospect of Western Travel,* of a lighter and more purely descriptive quality. Their success with the public was moderate, and in after years she condemned them in very plain language, the first of them especially as "full of affectations and preachments." Their only service, and it was not inconsiderable, was the information which they circulated as to the condition of slavery and of the country under it. We do not suppose that they are worth reading at the present day, except from a historical point of view. But they are really good specimens of a kind of literature which is not abundant, and yet which is of the utmost value—we mean the record of the sociological observation of a country by a competent traveller, who stays long enough in the country, has access to the right persons of all kinds, and will take pains enough to mature his judgments. It was a happy idea of O'Connell's to suggest that she should go over to Ireland, and write such an account of that country as she had written of the United States. And we wish at this very hour that some one as competent as Miss Martineau would do what O'Connell wished her to do. A similar request came to her from Milan: why should she not visit Lombardy, and then tell Europe the true tale of Austrian rule?

But after her American journey Miss Martineau felt a very easily intelligible desire to change the literary field. For many years she had been writing almost entirely about fact: and the constraint of the effort to be always correct, and to bear without solicitude the questioning of her correctness, had become burdensome. She felt the danger of losing nerve and becoming morbidly fearful of criticism on the one hand, and of growing narrow and mechanical about accuracy on the other. "I longed inexpressibly," she says, "for the liberty of fiction, while occasionally doubting whether I had the power to use that freedom as I could have done ten years before." The product of this new mental phase was *Deerbrook,* which was published in the spring of 1839. *Deerbrook* is a story of an English country village, its petty feuds, its gentilities, its chances and changes of fortune. The influence of Jane Austen's stories is seen in every chapter; but Harriet Martineau had none of the easy flow, the pleasant humour, the light-handed irony of her model, any more than she had the energetic and sustained imaginative power of Charlotte or Emily Brontë. There is playfulness enough in *Deerbrook,* but it is too deliberate to remind us of the crooning involuntary playfulness of *Pride and Prejudice* or *Sense and Sensibility. Deerbrook* is not in the least a story with a moral; it is truly and purely a piece of art; yet we are conscious of the serious spirit of the social reformer as haunting the background, and only surrendering the scene for reasons of its own. On the other hand, there is in *Deerbrook* a gravity of moral reflection that Jane Austen, whether wisely or unwisely, seldom or never attempts. In this respect *Deerbrook* is the distant forerunner of some of George Eliot's most characteristic work. Distant, because George Eliot's moralising is constantly suffused by the broad light of a highly poetic imagination, and this was in no degree among Miss Martineau's gifts. Still there is something above the flat touch of the common didactic in such a page as that in which (chapter xix.) she describes the case of "the unamiable —the only order of evil ones who suffer hell without seeing and knowing that it is hell: nay, they are under a heavier curse than even this, they inflict torments second only to their own, with an unconsciousness worthy of spirits of light." However, when all is said, we may agree that this is one of the books that give a rational person pleasure once, but which we hardly look forward to reading again.

Shortly after the publication of her first novel, Miss Martineau was seized by a serious internal malady, from which recovery seemed hopeless. According to her usual practice of taking her life deliberately in her hands, and settling its conditions for herself instead of letting things drift as they might, she insisted on declining the hospitable shelter pressed upon her by a near relative, on the excellent ground that it is wrong for an invalid to impose restraints upon a healthy household. She proceeded to establish herself in lodgings at Tynemouth, on the coast of Northumberland. Here she lay on a couch for nearly five years, seeing as few persons as might be, and working at such literary matters as came into her head with steadfast industry and fortitude. The ordeal was hard, but the little book that came of it, *Life in a Sickroom,* remains to show the moods in which the ordeal was borne.

At length Miss Martineau was induced to try mesmerism as a possible cure for her disease, and what is certain is, that after trying mesmeric treatment, the invalid whom the doctors had declared incurable shortly recovered as perfect health as she had ever known. A virulent controversy arose upon the case, for by some curious law, physicians are apt to import into professional disputes a heat and bitterness at least as marked as that of their old enemies, the theologians. It is said that Miss Martineau had begun to improve before she was mesmerised, and what was still more to the point, that she had been taking heavy doses of iodine. "It is beyond all question or dispute," as Voltaire said, "that magic words and ceremonies are quite capable of most effectually destroying a whole flock of sheep, if the words be accompanied by a sufficient quantity of arsenic."

Mesmerism was indirectly the means of bringing Miss Martineau into an intimate acquaintance with a gentleman who soon began to exert a decisive influence upon the most important of her opinions. Mr. Atkinson is still alive, and we need not say much about him. He seems to have been a grave and sincere person, using his mind with courageous independence upon the great speculative problems which were not in 1844, as they are in 1877, the common topics of everyday discourse among educated people. This is not the place for an examination of the philosophy in which Miss Martineau was finally landed by Mr. Atkinson's influence. That philosophy was given to the world in 1851 in a volume called *Letters on the Laws of Man's Nature and Development.* The greater part of it was written by Mr. Atkinson in reply to short letters, in which Miss Martineau stated objections and propounded questions. The book points in the direction of that explanation of the facts of the universe which is now so familiar under the name of Evolution. But it points in this way only as the once famous *Vestiges of Creation* pointed towards the scientific hypotheses of Darwin and Wallace; or as Buckle's crude and superficial notions about the history of civilisation pointed towards a true and complete conception of sociology. That is to say, the Atkinson Letters state some of the difficulties in the way of the explanations of life and motion hitherto received as satisfactory; they insist upon approaching the facts exclusively by the positive, Baconian, or inductive method; and then they hurry to an explanation of their own, which may be as plausible as that which they intend it to replace, but which they leave equally without ordered proof and strict verification.

The only point to which we are called upon to refer is that this way of thinking about man and the rest of nature led to repudiation by Miss Martineau of the whole structure of dogmatic theology. For one thing, she ceased to hold the conception of a God with any human attributes whatever; also of any principle or practice of Design; "of an administration of life according to human wishes, or of the affairs of the world by the principles of human morals." All these became to her as mere visions; beliefs necessary in their day, but not philosophically nor permanently true. Miss Martineau was not an Atheist in the philosophic sense; she never denied a First Cause, but only that this Cause is within the sphere of human attributes, or can be defined in their terms.

Then, for another thing, she ceased to believe in the probability of there being a continuance of conscious individual life after the dissolution of the body. With this, of course, fell all expectation of a state of personal rewards and punishments. "The real and justifiable and honourable subject of interest," she said, "to human beings, living and dying, is the welfare of their fellows surrounding them or surviving them." About that she cared supremely, and about nothing else did she bring herself to care at all.

It is painful to many people even to hear of a person holding such beliefs as these. Yet it would plainly be the worst kind of spiritual valetudinarianism to insist on the omission from even the shortest account of this remarkable woman, of what became the very basis and foundation of her life for those thirty years of it, which she herself always counted the happiest part of the whole.

Although it was Mr. Atkinson who finally provided her with a positive substitute for her older beliefs, yet a journey which Miss Martineau made in the East shortly after her restoration to health (1846) had done much to build up in her mind a historic conception of the origin and order of the great faiths of mankind —the Christian, the Hebrew, the Mahometan, the old Egyptian. We need not say more on this subject. The work in which she published the experiences of the journey which was always so memorable to her deserves a word. There are few more delightful books of travel than *Eastern Life, Past and Present.* The descriptions are admirably graphic, and they have the attraction of making their effect by a few direct strokes, without any of the wordy elaboration of our modern picturesque. The writer shows a true feeling for nature, and she shows a vigorous sense, which is not merely pretty sentiment, like Chateaubriand's, for the vast historic associations of those old lands and dim cradles of the race. All is sterling and real; we are aware that the elevated reflection and the meditative stroke are not due to mere composition, but did actually pass through her mind as the suggestive wonders passed before her eyes. And hence there is no jar as we find a little homily on the advantage of being able to iron your own linen on a Nile boat, followed by a lofty page on the mighty pair of solemn figures that gaze as from eternity on time amid the sand at Thebes. The whole, one may say again, is sterling and real, both the elevation and the homeliness. The student of the history of opinion may find some interest in comparing Miss Martineau's work with the famous book, *Ruins; or, Meditations on the Revolutions of Empires,* in which Volney, between fifty and sixty years before, had drawn equally dissolvent conclusions with her own, from the same panorama of the dead ages. Perhaps Miss Martineau's history is not much better than Volney's, but her brisk sense is preferable to Volney's high *à priori* declamation and artificial rhetoric.

Before starting for the East, Miss Martineau had settled a new plan of life for herself, and built a little house where she thought she could best carry her plan out. To this little house she returned, and it became her cherished home for the long remainder of her days. London, during the years of her first success, had not been without its usual attractions to the new-comer, but she had always been alive to the essential incompleteness, the dispersion, the want of steadfast self-collection, in a life much passed in London society. And we may believe that the five austere and lonely years at Tynemouth, with their evening outlook over the busy waters of the harbour-bar into the stern far off sea, may have slowly bred in her an unwillingness to plunge again into the bustling triviality, the gossip, the distracting lightness of the world of splendid fire-flies. To have discerned the Pale Horse so near and for so long a space awakens new moods, and strangely alters the old perspectives of our life. Yet it would imply a misunderstanding of Harriet Martineau's character to suppose that she turned her back upon London, and built her pretty hermitage at Ambleside, in anything like the temper of Jean Jacques Rousseau. She was far too positive a spirit for that, and far too full of vivid and concentrated interest in men and their doings. It would be unjust to think of Harriet Martineau as having no ear for the inner voices, yet her whole nature was objective; it turned to practice and not to reverie. She had her imaginative visions, as we know, and as all truly superior minds have them, even though their main superiority happens to be in the practical order. But her visions were limited as a landscape set in a rigid frame; they had not the wings that soar and poise in the vague unbounded empyrean. And she was much too sensible to think that these moods were strong, or constant, or absorbing enough in her case to furnish material and companionship for a life from day to day and year to year. Nor again was it for the sake of undisturbed acquisition of knowledge, nor cultivation of her finer faculties that she sought a hermitage. She was not moved by thought of the famous maxim which Goethe puts into the mouth of Leonore—

Es bildet ein Talent sich in der Stille,
Sich ein Charakter in dem Strom der Welt.

Though an intense egotist, in the good and respectable sense of insisting on her own way of doing things, of settling for herself what it was that she was living for, and of treading the path with a firm and self-reliant step, yet Harriet Martineau was as little of an egotist as ever lived, in the poor and stifling sense of thinking of the perfecting of her own culture as in the least degree worthy of ranking among Ends-in themselves. She settled in the Lake district because she thought that there she would be most favourably placed for satisfying the various conditions which she had fixed as necessary to her scheme of life. "My own idea of an innocent and happy life," she says, "was a house of my own among poor improvable neighbours, with young servants whom I might train and attach to myself, with pure air, a garden, leisure, solitude at command, and freedom to work in peace and quietness."

"It is the wisest step in her life," Wordsworth said, when he heard that she had bought a piece of land and built a pretty house upon it; and then he added the strangely unpoetic reason—"because the value of the property will be doubled in ten years." Her poetic neighbour gave her a characteristic piece of advice in the same prudential vein. He warned her that she would find visitors a great expense. "When you have a visitor," he said, "you must do as we did; you must say, 'If you like to have a cup of tea with us, you are very welcome; but if you want any meat, you must pay for your board.' " Miss Martineau declined to carry thrift to this ungracious extremity. She constantly had guests in her house, and, if they were all like Charlotte Brontë, they enjoyed their visits in spite of the arbitrary ways of their energetic hostess.

Her manner of life during these years is pleasant to contemplate; cheerful, active, thoroughly wholesome. "My habit," she says, "was to rise at six and to take a walk, returning to my solitary breakfast at half-past seven. My household orders were given for the day, and all affairs settled out of doors and in by a quarter or half-past eight, when I went to work, which I continued without interruption, except from the post, till three o'clock or later, when alone. While my friend was with me we dined at two, and that was of course the limit of my day's work." De Tocqueville, if we remember, never saw his guests until after he had finished his morning's work, of which he had done six hours by eleven o'clock. Schopenhauer was still more sensitive to the jar of external interruption on that finely-tuned instrument, the brain, after a night's repose, for it was as much as his housekeeper's place was worth to allow either herself or any one else to appear to the philosopher before mid-day. After the early dinner at the Ambleside cottage came little bits of neighbourly business, exercise, and so forth. "It is with singular alacrity that in winter evenings I light the lamp and unroll my wool-work, and meditate or dream till the arrival of the newspaper tells me that the tea has stood long enough. After tea, if there was news from the seat of war, I called in my maids, who brought down the great atlas and studied the chances of the campaign with me. Then there was an hour or two for Montaigne, or Bacon, or Shakespeare, or Tennyson, or some dear old biography."

The only productions of this time worth mentioning are the *History of the Thirty Years' Peace* (1849) and the condensed version of Comte's *Positive Philosophy* (1853), both of them meritorious and useful pieces of work, and both of them undertaken, as nearly all Miss Martineau's work was, not from merely literary motives, but because she thought that they would be meritorious and useful, and because nothing more useful came into her head or under her hand at the moment. The condensation of Comte is easy and rapid, and it is said by those who have looked very closely into it, to be hardly free from some too hasty renderings. It must, however, on the whole be pronounced a singularly intelligent and able performance. The pace at which Comte was able to compose is a standing marvel to all who have pondered the great and difficult art of composition. It must be admitted that the author of the English version of him was in this respect no unworthy match for her original. Miss Martineau tells us that she despatched the last three volumes, which number over 1,800 pages, in some five months. She thought the rendering of thirty pages of Comte a fair morning's work. If we consider the abstract and difficult nature of the matter, this must be pronounced something of a feat. We have not space to describe her method, but any reader who happens to be interested in the mechanism of literary productions, will find the passage in vol. ii. p. 391. The *History of the Thirty Years' Peace* is no less astonishing an example of rapid industry. From the first opening of the books to study for the history, to the depositing of the MS. of the first volume at press, was exactly six months. The second volume took six months to do, with an interval of some weeks of holiday and other work!

We think all this worth mentioning, because it is an illustration of what is a highly important maxim; namely, that it is a great mistake to expend more time and labour on a piece of composition than is enough to make it serve the purpose in hand. The immeasurable moment and far-reachingness of the very highest kinds of literature are apt to make men who play at being students forget that there are many other kinds of literature, which are not in the least immeasurably far-reaching, but which, for all that, are extremely useful in their own day and generation. Those highly fastidious and indolent people, who sometimes live at Oxford and Cambridge, with whom indeed for the most part their high fastidiousness is only a fine name for impotence and lack of will, forget that the less immortal kinds of literature are the only kinds within their own reach. Literature is no doubt a fine art—the finest of the arts—but it is also a practical art, and it is deplorable to think how much stout, instructive work might and ought to be done by people who, in dreaming of ideals in prose or verse beyond their attainment, end, like the poor Casaubon of fiction, in a little pamphlet on a particle, or else in mediocre poetry, or else in nothing. By insisting on rearing nothing short of a great monument more durable than brass, they are cutting themselves off from building the useful little mud-hut, or some of the other modest performances, by which only they are capable of serving their age. It is only one volume in a million that is not meant to perish, and to perish soon, as flowers, sunbeams, and all the other brightnesses of the earth are meant to perish. There are some forms of composition in which perfection is not only good but indispensable. But the most are designed for the purpose of a day, and if they have the degree of elaboration, accuracy, grasp, and faithfulness that suffice for the given purpose, then we may say that it is enough. There is literature proper, for which only two or three men and women in a generation have the true gift. This cannot be too good. But besides this there is a mass of honest and needful work to be done with the pen, to which literary form is only accidental, and in which consummate literary finish or depth is a sheer work of supererogation. If Miss Martineau had given twice as many years as she gave months to the condensation of Comte, the book would not have been a whit more useful in any possible respect—indeed, over-elaboration might easily have made it much less so—and the world would have lost many other excellent, if not dazzling or stupendous services.

"Her original power," she wrote of herself in that manly and outspoken obituary notice to which we have already referred, "was nothing more than was due to earnestness and intellectual clearness within a certain range. With small imaginative and suggestive powers, and therefore nothing approaching to genius, she could see clearly what she did see, and give a clear expression to what she had to say. In short, she could popularise, while she could neither discover nor invent. . . . She could obtain and keep a firm grasp of her own views, and moreover she could make them understood. The function of her life was to do this, and in as far as it was done diligently and honestly, her life was of use." All this is precisely true, and her life was of great use; and that makes what she says not only true, but an example worth much weighing by many of those who meddle with literature.

Miss Martinetu was never tired of trying to be useful in directing and improving opinion. She did not disdain the poor neighbours at her gates. She got them to establish a Building Society, she set them an example of thrifty and profitable management by her little farm of two acres, and she gave them interesting and cheerful courses of lectures in the winter evenings. All this time her eye was vigilant for the great affairs of the world. In 1852 she began to write leading articles for the *Daily News,* and in this department her industry and her aptitude were such that at times she wrote as many as six leading articles in a week. When she died, it was computed that she had written sixteen hundred. They are now all dead enough, as they were meant to die, but they made an impression that is still alive in its consequences upon some of the most important social, political, and economical matters of five and twenty important years. In what was by far the greatest of all the issues of those years, the Civil War in the United States, Harriet Martineau's influence was of the most inestimable value in keeping public opinion right against the strong tide of ignorant Southern sympathies in this country. If she may seem to some to have been less right in her views of the Crimean War, we must admit that the issues were very complex, and that complete assurance on that struggle is not easy even at this distance of time.

To this period belong the Biographic Sketches which she contributed to a London newspaper. They have since been collected in a single volume, now in its fourth edition. They are masterpieces in the style of the vignette. Their conciseness, their clearness in fact, their definiteness in judgment, and above all the rightly-graduated impression of the writer's own personality in the background, make them perfect in their kind. There is no fretting away of the portrait in over-multiplicity of lines and strokes. Here more than anywhere else, Miss Martineau shows the true quality of the writer, the true mark of literature, the sense of proportion, the modulated sentence, the compact and suggestive phrase. There is a happy precision, a pithy brevity, a condensed argumentativeness. And this literary skill is made more telling by the writer's own evident interest and sincerity about the real lives and characters of the various conspicuous people with whom she deals. It may be said that she has no subtle insight into the complexities of human nature, and that her philosophy of character is rather too little analytical, too downright, too content with averages of motive, and too external. This is so in a general way, but it does not spoil the charm of these sketches, because the personages concerned, though all of them conspicuous, were for the most part commonplace in motive, though more than commonplace in strength of faculty. Subtle analysis is wholly unreasonable in the case of Miss Martineau herself, and she would probably have been unable to use that difficult instrument in criticising characters less downright and objective than her own.

The moment of the Crimean War marked an alarming event in her own life. The doctors warned her that she had a heart disease which would end her days suddenly and soon. Miss Martineau at once set her affairs in order, and sat down to write her Autobiography. She had the manuscript put into type, and the sheets finally printed off, just as we now possess them. But the hour was not yet. The doctors had exaggerated the peril, and the strong woman lived for twenty years after she had been given up. She used up the stuff of her life to the very end, and left no dreary remnant nor morbid waste of days. She was like herself to the last—English, practical, positive. Yet she had thoughts and visions which were more than this. We like to think of this faithful woman and veteran worker in good causes, in the stroll which she always took on her terrace before retiring to rest for the night:—

On my terrace there were two worlds extended bright before me, even when the midnight darkness hid from my bodily eyes all but the outlines of the solemn mountains that surround our valley on three sides, and the clear opening to the lake on the south. In the one of those worlds I saw now the magnificent coast of Massachusetts in autumn, or the flowery swamps of Louisiana, or the forests of Georgia in spring, or the Illinois prairie in summer; or the blue Nile, or the brown Sinai, or the gorgeous Petra, or the view of Damascus from the Salahiey; or the Grand Canal under a Venetian sunset, or the Black Forest in twilight, or Malta in the glare of noon, or the broad desert stretching away under the stars, or the Red Sea tossing its superb shells on shore in the pale dawn. That is one world, all comprehended within my terrace wall, and coming up into the light at my call. The other and finer scenery is of that world, only beginning to be explored, of Science. . . . It is truly an exquisite pleasure to dream, after the toil of study, on the sublime abstractions of mathematics; the transcendent scenery unrolled by astronomy; the mysterious, invisible forces dimly hinted to us by physics; the new conception of the constitution of matter originated by chemistry; and then, the inestimable glimpses opened to us, in regard to the nature and destiny of man, by the researches into vegetable and animal organisation, which are at length perceived to be the right path of inquiry into the highest subjects of thought. . . . Wondrous beyond the comprehension of any one mind is the mass of glorious facts and the series of mighty conceptions laid open; but the shadow of the surrounding darkness rests upon it all. The unknown always engrosses the greater part of the field of vision, and the awe of infinity sanctifies both the study and the dream.

It would be a pity if difference of opinion upon subjects of profound difficulty, remoteness, and manifold perplexity, were to prevent any one from recognising in such words and such moods as these what was, in spite of some infirmities, a character of many large thoughts and much generous purpose. And with this feeling we may part from her.

Memorials
of a
Man of Letters

What are the qualities of a good contributor? What makes a good Review? Is the best literature produced by the writer who does nothing else but write, or by the man who tempers literature by affairs? What are the different recommendations of the rival systems of anonymity and signature? What kind of change, if any, has passed over periodical literature since those two great periodicals, the *Edinburgh* and the *Quarterly,* held sway? These and a number of other questions in the same matter—some of them obviously not to be opened with propriety in these pages—must naturally be often present to the mind of any one who is concerned in the control of a Review, and a volume has just been printed which sets such musings once more astir. Mr. Macvey Napier was the editor of the *Edinburgh Review* from 1829—when Jeffrey, after a reign of seven and twenty years, resigned it into his hands—until his death in 1847. A portion of the correspondence addressed to Mr. Napier during this period has been recently printed for private circulation by his son. By his courteous permission I am allowed to refer to a volume that is full of personal interest both to the man of letters and to that more singular being, the Editor, the impresario of men of letters, the *entrepreneur* of the spiritual power.

To manage an opera house is usually supposed to tax human powers more urgently than any position save that of a general in

This essay was first published in *Fortnightly Review,* n.s., 136 (April 1878): 596–610, and was reprinted in *Studies in Literature* (London, 1891)—ed.

the very heat and stress of battle. The orchestra, the chorus, the subscribers, the first tenor, a pair of rival prima donnas, the newspapers, the box-agents in Bond Street, the army of hangers-on in the flies—all combine to demand such gifts of tact, resolution, patience, foresight, tenacity, flexibility, as are only expected from the great ruler or the great soldier. The editor of a periodical of public consideration—and the *Edinburgh Review* in the hands of Mr. Napier was the avowed organ of the ruling Whig powers— is sorely tested in the same way. The rival house may bribe his stars. His popular epigrammatist is sometimes as full of humours as a spoiled soprano. The favourite pyrotechnist is systematically late and procrastinatory, or is piqued because his punctuation or his paragraphs have been meddled with. The contributor whose article would be in excellent time if it did not appear before the close of the century, or never appeared at all, pesters you with warnings that a month's delay is a deadly blow to progress, and stays the great procession of the ages. The contributor who would profitably fill a sheet, insists on sending a treatise. Sir George Cornewall Lewis, who had charge of the *Edinburgh* for a short space, truly described prolixity as the *bête noir* of an editor. "Every contributor," he said, "has some special reason for wishing to write at length on his own subject."

"Ah, que de choses dans un menuet," cried Marcel, the great dancing-master, and ah, what things in the type and *idea* of an article, cries an editor with the enthusiasm of his calling; such proportion, measure, comprehension, variety of topics, pithiness of treatment, all within a space appointed with Procrustean rigour. This is what the soul of the volunteer contributor is dull to. Of the minor vexations who can tell?

> Semper ego auditor tantum? Nunquamne reponam
> Vexatus toties rauci Theseide Codri?*

There is one single tribulation dire enough to poison life—even if there were no other—and this is disorderly manuscript. Empson, Mr. Napier's well-known contributor, was one of the worst offenders; he would never take the trouble to mark his paragraphs. I have the misfortune to have a manuscript before me at this

* "Must I be listening always, and not pay them back? How they bore me. / Authors like Cordus the crude, with that epic he calls the Theseid!"—ed.

moment that would fill thirty of these pages, and yet from beginning to end there is no indication that it is not to be read at a single breath. The paragraph ought to be, and in all good writers it is, as real and as sensible a division as the sentence. It is an organic member in prose composition with a beginning, a middle, and an end, just as a stanza is an organic and definite member in the composition of an ode. "I fear my manuscript is rather disorderly," says another, "but I will correct carefully in print." Just so. Because he is too heedless to do his work in a workmanlike way, he first, inflicts fatigue and vexation on the editor whom he expects to read his paper; second, he inflicts considerable and quite needless expense on the publisher; and thirdly, he inflicts a great deal of tedious and thankless labour on the printers, who are for the most part far more meritorious persons than fifth-rate authors. It is true that Burke returned such disordered proofs that the printer usually found it least troublesome to set the whole afresh, and Miss Martineau tells a story of a Scotch compositor who fled from Edinburgh to avoid a great living author's manuscript, and to his horror was presently confronted with a piece of copy which made him cry, "Lord have mercy! Have *you* got that man to print for!" But most editors will cheerfully forgive such transgressions to all contributors who will guarantee that they write as well as Burke or Carlyle. Alas, it is usually the case that those who have least excuse are the worst offenders. The slovenliest manuscripts come from persons to whom the difference between an hour and a minute is of the very smallest importance. This, however is a digression, only to be excused partly by the natural desire to say a word against one's persecutors, and partly by a hope that some persons of sensitive conscience may be led to ponder whether there may not be after all some moral obligations even towards editors and printers.

Mr. Napier had one famous contributor, who stands out alone in the history of editors. Lord Brougham's traditional connection with the Review,—he had begun to write either in its first or third number, and had written in it ever since—his encyclopædic ignorance, his power, his great fame in the country, and the prestige which his connection reflected on the Review, all made him a personage with whom it would have been most imprudent to quarrel. Yet the position in which Mr. Napier was placed after

Brougham's breach with the Whigs, was one of the most difficult
in which the conductor of a great organ could possibly be placed.
The Review was the representative, the champion, and the mouth-
piece of the Whig party, and of the Whigs who were in office.
Before William IV. dismissed the Whigs in 1834 as arbitrarily
as his father had dismissed the Whigs in 1784, Brougham had
covered himself with disrepute among his party by a thousand
pranks, and after the dismissal he disgusted them by asking the
new Chancellor to make him Chief Baron of the Exchequer.
When Lord Melbourne returned to power in the following year,
this and other escapades were remembered against him. "If left
out," said Lord Melbourne, "he would indeed be dangerous; but
if taken in, he would simply be destructive." So Brougham was
left out, Pepys was made Chancellor, and the Premier compared
himself to a man who has broken with a termagant mistress and
married the best of cooks. Mr. Napier was not so happy. The
termagant was left on his hands. He had to keep terms with a
contributor who hated with a deadly hatred the very government
that the Review existed to support. No editor ever had such a
contributor as Brougham in the long history of editorial torment
since the world began. He scolds, he storms, he hectors, he lectures; he is for ever threatening desertion and prophesying ruin;
he exhausts the vocabulary of opprobrium against his correspondent's best friends; they are silly slaves, base traitors, a vile clique
"whose treatment of me has been the very *ne plus ultra* of in-
gratitude, baseless, and treachery." He got the Review and its
editor into a scrape which shook the world at the time (1834), by
betraying Cabinet secrets to spite Lord Durham. His cries against
his adversaries are as violent as the threats of Ajax in his tent,
and as loud as the bellowings of Philoctetes at the mouth of his
cave. Here is one instance out of a hundred:—

> That is a trifle, and I only mention it to beg of you to pluck
> up a little courage, and not be alarmed every time any of the little
> knot of threateners annoy you. *They want to break off all kind
> of connection between me and the Edinburgh Review.* I have
> long seen it. Their fury against the article in the last number
> knows no bounds, and they will never cease till they worry you
> out of your connection with me, and get the whole control of the
> Review into their own hands, by forcing you to resign it your-

self. *A party and a personal* engine is all they want to make it. What possible right can any of these silly slaves have to object to my opinion being—what it truly is—against the Holland House theory of Lord Chatham's madness? I *know* that Lord Grenville treated it with contempt. I know others now living who did so too, and I know that so stout a Whig as Sir P. Francis was clearly of that opinion, and he knew Lord Chatham personally. I had every ground to believe that Horace Walpole, a vile, malignant, and unnatural wretch, though a very clever writer of Letters, was nine-tenths of the Holland House authority for the tale. I knew that a baser man in character, or a meaner in capacity than the first Lord Holland existed not, even in those days of job and mediocrity. Why, then, was I bound to take a false view because Lord Holland's family have inherited his hatred of a great rival?

Another instance is as follows:—

I solicit your best attention to the fate which seems hastening upon the *Edinburgh Review*. The having always been free from the least control of booksellers is one of the principal distinctions, and long was peculiarly so—perhaps it still has it *nearly* to itself. But if it shall become a *Treasury* journal, I hardly see any great advantage in one kind of independence without the rest. Nay, I doubt if its *literary* freedom, any more than its political, will long survive. Books will be treated according as the Treasury, or their understrappers, regard the authors. . . . But, it is after all possible that the Review should be suffered to sink into such a state of subserviency that it dares not insert any discussion upon a general question of politics because it might give umbrage to the Government of the day? I pass over the undeniable fact that it is *underlings* only whom you are scared by, and that the Ministers themselves have no such inordinate pretension as to dream of interfering. I say nothing of those underlings generally, except this, that I well know the race, and a more despicable, above all, in point of judgment, exists not. Never mind their threats, they *can* do no harm. Even if any of them are contributors, be assured they never will withdraw because you choose to keep your course free and independent.

Mr. Napier, who seems to have been one of the most considerate and high-minded of men, was moved to energetic remonstrance on this occasion. Lord Brougham explained his strong language away, but he was incapable of really controlling himself, and the strain was never lessened until 1843, when the correspondence ceases, and we learn that there had been a quarrel between him and his too long-suffering correspondent. Yet John Allen,—that able scholar and conspicuous figure in the annals of Holland House—wrote of Brougham to Mr. Napier:—"He is not a malignant or bad-hearted man, but he is an unscrupulous one, and where his passions are concerned or his vanity irritated, there is no excess of which he is not capable." Of Brougham's strong and manly sense, when passion or vanity did not cloud it, and even of a sort of careful justice, these letters give more than one instance. The *Quarterly Review,* for instance, had an article on Romilly's Memoirs, which to Romilly's friends seemed to do him less than justice. Brougham took a more sensible view.

Surely we have no right whatever to expect that they whom Romilly had all his life so stoutly opposed, and who were treated by him with great harshness, should treat him as his friends would do, and at the very moment when a most injudicious act of his family was bringing out all his secret thoughts against them. Only place yourself in the same position, and suppose that Canning's private journals had been published,—the journals he may have kept while the bitterest enemy of the Whigs, and in every page of which there must have been some passage offensive to the feelings of the living and of the friends of the dead. Would any mercy have been shown to Canning's character and memory by any of the Whig party, either in society or in Reviews? Would the line have been drawn of only attacking Canning's executors, who published the papers, and leaving Canning himself untouched? Clearly and certainly not, and yet I am putting a very much weaker case, for we had joined Canning, and all political enmity was at an end: whereas the Tories and Romilly never had for an hour laid aside their mutual hostility.

And if he was capable of equity, Brougham was also capable of hearty admiration, even of an old friend who had on later occasions gone into a line which he intensely disliked. It is a relief in the pages of blusterous anger and raging censure to come upon what he says of Jeffrey.

I can truly say that there never in all my life crossed my mind one single unkind feeling respecting him, or indeed any feeling but that of the warmest affection and the most unmingled admiration of his character, believing and knowing him to be as excellent and amiable as he is great in the ordinary, and, as I think, the far less important sense of the world.

Of the value of Brougham's contributions we cannot now judge. They will not, in spite of their energy and force, bear re-reading to-day, and perhaps the same may be said of three-fourths of Jeffrey's once famous essays. Brougham's self-confidence is heroic. He thought he could make a speech for Bolingbroke, but by-and-bye he had sense enough to see that, in order to attempt this, he ought to read Bolingbroke for a year, and then practise for another year. In 1838 he thought nothing of undertaking, amid all the demands of active life, such a bagatelle as a History of the French Revolution. "I have some little knack of narrative," he says, "the most difficult by far of all styles, and never yet attained in perfection but by Hume and Livy; and I bring as much oratory and science to the task as most of my predecessors." But what sort of science? And what has oratory to do with it? And how could he deceive himself into thinking that he could retire to write a history? Nobody that ever lived would have more speedily found out the truth of Voltaire's saying, "Le repos est un bonne chose, mais l'ennui est son frère." The truth is that one learns, after a certain observation of the world, to divide one's amazement pretty equally between the literary voluptuary or over-fastidious collegian, on the one hand, who is so impressed by the size of his subject that he never does more than collect material and make notes, and the presumptuous politician, on the other hand, who thinks that he can write a history or settle the issues of philosophy and theology in odd half hours. The one is so enfeebled in will and literary energy after his *viginti annorum lucubrationes;** the other is so accustomed to be content with the hurry, the unfinishedness, the rough-and-ready methods of practical affairs, and they both in different ways measure the worth and seriousness of literature so wrongly in relation to the rest of human interests.

The relations between Lord Brougham and Mr. Napier naturally suggest a good many reflections on the vexed question of the comparative advantages of the old and the new theory of

* "nightly study of twenty years"—ed.

a periodical. The new theory is that a periodical should not be an organ but an open pulpit, and that each writer should sign his name. Without disrespect to ably conducted and eminent contemporaries of long standing, it may be said that the tide of opinion and favour is setting in this direction. Yet, on the whole, experience perhaps leads to a doubt whether the gains of the system of signature are so very considerable as some of us once expected. An editor on the new system is no doubt relieved of a certain measure of responsibility. Lord Cockburn's panegyric on the first great editor may show what was expected from a man in such a position as Jeffrey's. "He had to discover, and to train, authors; to discern what truth and the public mind required; to suggest subjects; to reject, and, more offensive still, to improve, contributions; to keep down absurdities; to infuse spirit; to excite the timid; to repress violence; to soothe jealousies; to quell mutinies; to watch times; and all this in the morning of the reviewing day, before experience had taught editors conciliatory firmness, and contributors reasonable submission. He directed and controlled the elements he presided over with a master's judgment. There was not one of his associates who could have even held these elements together for a single year. . . . Inferior to these excellences, but still important, was his dexterity in revising the writings of others. Without altering the general tone or character of the composition, he had great skill in leaving out defective ideas or words, and in so aiding the original by lively or graceful touches, that reasonable authors were surprised and charmed on seeing how much better they looked than they thought they would." (Cockburn's *Life of Jeffrey*)

From such toils and dangers as these, the editor of a Review with signed articles is in the main happily free. He has usually suggestions to make, for his experience has probably given him points of view as to the effectiveness of this or that feature of an article for its own purpose, which would not occur to a writer. The writer is absorbed in his subject, and has been less accustomed to think of the public. But this exercise of a claim to a general acquiescence in the judgment and experience of a man who has the best reasons for trying to judge rightly, is a very different thing from the duty of drilling contributors and dressing contributions as Jeffrey dressed and drilled. As Southey said, when groaning under the mutilations inflicted by Gifford on his contributions to the *Quarterly,* "there must be a power expurgatory in the hands of the editor; and the misfortune is that editors frequently think it incumbent on them to use that power merely because they have it" (Southey's *Life*). This is probably true on the anonymous system, where the editor is answerable for every word, and for the literary form no less than for the substantial soundness or interest of an article. In a man of weakish literary vanity—Jeffrey was evidently full of it—there may well be a constant itch to set his betters right in trifles, as Gifford thought he could mend Southey's adjectives. To a vain editor, or a too masterful editor, the temptation under the anonymous system is no doubt strong. M. Buloz, it is true, the renowned editor of the *Revue des deux Mondes,* is said to have insisted on, and to have freely practised, the fullest editorial prerogative over articles that were openly signed by the most eminent names in France. But M. Buloz had no competitor, and those who did not choose to submit to his Sultanic despotism, were shut out from the only pulpit whence they were sure of addressing the congregation that they wanted. In England contributors are better off; and no editor of a signed periodical would feel either bound or permitted to take such trouble about mere wording of sentences as Gifford and Jeffrey were in the habit of taking.

There is, however, another side to this, from an editor's point of view. With responsibility—not merely for commas and niceties and literary kickshaws, but in its old sense—disappears also a portion of the interest of editorial labour. One would suppose it must be more interesting to command a man-of-war than a trading vessel; it would be more interesting to lead a regiment than to keep a tilting-yard. But the times are not ripe for such enterprises. Of literary ability of a good and serviceable kind there is a hundred or five hundred times more in the country than there was when Jeffrey, Smith, Brougham, and Horner devised their Review in a ninth storey in Edinburgh seventy-six years ago. It is the cohesion of a political creed that is gone, and the strength and fervour of a political school. The principles that inspired that group of strong men have been worked out. After their reforms had been achieved, the next great school was economic, and though it produced a fine orator, its work was at no time literary.

The Manchester school with all their shortcomings had at least the signal distinction of attaching their views on special political questions to a general and presiding conception of the modern phase of civilisation, as industrial and pacific. The next party of advance, when it is formed, will certainly borrow from Cobden and Bright their hatred of war and their hatred of the silly policy of imperialism. After the sagacity and enlightenment of this school, came the school of persiflage. A knot of vigorous and brilliant men towards 1856 rallied round the late editor of the *Saturday Review*,—and a strange chief he was for such a group, —but their flag was that of the Red Rover. They gave Philistinism many a shrewd blow, but perhaps at the same time helped to some degree—with other far deeper and stronger forces—to produce that sceptical and centrifugal state of mind, which now tends to nullify organized liberalism and paralyse the spirit of improvement. The Benthamites, led first by James Mill, and afterwards in a secondary degree by Mr. John Mill, had pushed a number of political improvements in the radical and democratic direction during the time when the *Edinburgh* so powerfully represented more orthodox liberalism. They were the last important group of men who started together from a set of common principles, accepted a common programme of practical applications, and set to work in earnest and with due order and distribution of parts to advocate the common cause.

At present there is no similar agreement either among the younger men in parliament, or among a sufficiently numerous group of writers outside of parliament. The Edinburgh Reviewers were most of them students of the university of that city. The Westminster Reviewers had all sat at the feet of Bentham. Each group had thus a common doctrine and a positive doctrine. In practical politics it does not much matter by what different roads men have travelled to a given position. But in an organ intended to lead public opinion towards certain changes, or to hold it steadfast against wayward gusts of passion, its strength would be increased a hundredfold if all the writers in it were inspired by that thorough unity of conviction which comes from sincerely accepting a common set of principles to start from, and reaching practical conclusions by the same route. We are probably not very far from a time when such a group might form itself, and its

work would for some years lie in the formation of a general body
of opinion, rather than in practical realisation of this or that
measure. The success of the French Republic, the peaceful order
of the United States, perhaps some trouble within our own
borders, will lead men with open minds to such a conception of
a high and stable type of national life as will unite a sufficient
number of them in a common project for pressing with systematic iteration for a complete set of organic changes. A country
with such a land-system, such an electoral system, such a monarchy, as ours, has a trying time before it. Those will be doing
good service who shall unite to prepare opinion for the inevitable
changes. At the present moment the only motto that can be
inscribed on the flag of a liberal Review is the general device of
Progress, each writer interpreting it in his own sense, and within
such limits as he may set for himself. For such a state of things
signature is the natural condition, and an editor, even of a signed
Review, would, I suppose, not decline to accept the account of
his function which we find Jeffrey giving to Mr. Napier:—
"There are three legitimate considerations by which you should
be guided in your conduct as editor generally, and particularly
as to the admission or rejection of important articles of a political
sort. 1. The effect of your decision on the other contributors upon
whom you mainly rely; 2, its effect on the sale and circulation,
and on the just authority of the work with the great body of its
readers; and, 3, your own deliberate opinion as to the safety or
danger of the doctrines maintained in the article under consideration, and its tendency either to promote or retard the practical
adoption of those liberal principles to which, and *their practical
advancement,* you must always consider the journal as devoted."

As for discovering and training authors, the editor under the
new system has inducements that lie entirely the other way;
namely, to find as many authors as possible whom the public has
already discovered and accepted for itself. Young unknown
writers certainly have not gained anything by the new system.
Neither perhaps can they be said to have lost, for though of two
articles of equal merit an editor would naturally choose the one
which should carry the additional recommendation of a name of
recognised authority, yet any marked superiority in literary brilliance or effective argument or originality of view would be only

too eagerly welcomed in any Review in England. So much public interest is now taken in periodical literature, and the honourable competition in securing variety, weight, and attractiveness is so active, that there is no risk of a literary candle remaining long under a bushel. Miss Martineau says:—"I have always been anxious to extend to young or struggling authors the sort of aid which would have been so precious to me in that winter of 1829–30, and I know that, in above twenty years, I have never succeeded but once." One of the most distinguished editors in London, who had charge of a periodical for many years, told the present writer what comes to the same thing, namely, that in no single case during all these years did a volunteer contributor of real quality, or with any promise of eminence, present himself or herself. So many hundreds think themselves called, so few are chosen. It used to be argued that the writer under the anonymous system was hidden behind a screen and robbed of his well-earned distinction. In truth, however, it is impossible for a writer of real distinction to remain anonymous. If a writer in a periodical interests the public, they are sure to find out who he is. The writer on Goethe in the last number of the *Quarterly Review* is as well known as the writer on Equality in the last number of the *Fortnightly Review*.

Again, there is unfathomable folly in a periodical affecting an eternal consistency, and giving itself the airs of continuous individuality, and being careful not to talk sense on a given question to-day because its founders talked nonsense upon it fifty years ago. This is quite true. There is a monstrous charlatanry about the old editorial We, but perhaps there are some tolerably obvious openings for charlatanry of a different kind under our own system. The man who writes in his own name may sometimes be tempted to say what he knows he is expected from his position or character to say, rather than what he would have said if his personality were not concerned. As far as honesty goes, signature perhaps offers as many inducements to one kind of insincerity, as anonymity offers to another kind. And on the public it might perhaps be contended that there is an effect of a rather similar sort. They are in some cases tempted away from serious discussion of the matter, into frivolous curiosity and gossip about the man. All this criticism of the principle of which the *Fortnightly Review* was the earliest English adherent, will not be taken as the result in the present writer of Chamfort's *maladie des désabusés;* that would be both extremely ungrateful and without excuse or reason. It is merely a fragment of disinterested contribution to the study of a remarkable change that is passing over a not unimportant department of literature. One gain alone counterbalances all the drawbacks, and that is a gain that could hardly have been foreseen or expected; I mean the freedom with which the great controversies of religion and theology have been discussed in the new Reviews. The removal of the mask has led to an outburst of plain speaking on these subjects, which to Mr. Napier's generation would have seemed simply incredible. The frank avowal of unpopular beliefs or non-beliefs has raised the whole level of the discussion, and perhaps has been even more advantageous to the orthodox in teaching them more humility, than to the heterodox in teaching them more courage and honesty.

Let us return to Mr. Napier's volume. We have said that it is impossible for a great writer to be anonymous. No reader will need to be told who among Mr. Napier's correspondents is the writer of the following:—

> I have been thinking sometimes, likewise, of a paper on Napoleon, a man whom, though handled to the extreme of triteness, it will be long years before we understand. Hitherto in the English tongue, there is next to nothing that betokens insight into him, or even sincere belief of such, on the part of the writer. I should like to study the man with what heartiness I could, and form to myself some intelligible picture of him, both as a biographical and as a historical figure, in both of which senses he is our chief contemporary wonder, and in some sort the epitome of his age. This, however, was a task of far more difficulty than Byron, and perhaps not so promising at present.

And if there is any difficulty in recognising the same hand in the next proposal, it arises only from the circumstance that it is this writer above all others who has made Benthamism a term of reproach on the lips of men less wise than himself:—

> A far finer essay were a faithful, loving, and yet critical, and in part condemnatory, delineation of Jeremy Bentham, and his

place and working in this section of the world's history. Bentham will not be put down by logic, and should not be put down, for we need him greatly as a backwoodsman: neither can reconciliation be effected till the one party understands and is just to the other. Bentham is a denyer; he denies with a loud and universally convincing voice; his fault is that he can *affirm* nothing, except that money is pleasant in the purse, and food in the stomach, and that by this simplest of all beliefs he can reorganize society. He can shatter it in pieces—no thanks to him, for its old fastenings are quite rotten—but he cannot reorganize it; this is work for quite others than he. Such an essay on Bentham, however, were a great task for any one; for me a very great one, and perhaps rather out of my road.

Perhaps Mr. Carlyle would agree that Mr. Mill's famous pair of essays on Bentham and Coleridge have served the purpose which he had in his mind, though we may well regret the loss of such a picture of Bentham's philosophic personality as he would surely have given us. It is touching to think of him whom we all know as the most honoured name among living veterans of letters, passing through the vexed ordeal of the young recruit, and battling for his own against the waywardness of critics and the blindness of publishers. In 1831 he writes to Mr. Napier: "All manner of perplexities have occurred in the publishing of my poor book, which perplexities I could only cut asunder, not unloose; so the MS. like an unhappy ghost still lingers on the wrong side of Styx; the Charon of ———— Street durst not risk it in his *sutilis cymba,** so it leaped ashore again." And three months later, "I have given up the notion of hawking my little Manuscript Book about any further; for a long time it has lain quiet in its drawer, waiting for a better day." And yet this little book was nothing less than the History of the French Revolution.

It might be a lesson to small men to see the reasonableness, sense, and patience of these greater men. Macaulay's letters show him to have been a pattern of good sense and considerateness. Mr. Carlyle seems indeed to have found Jeffrey's editorial vigour more than could be endured.

> My respected friend your predecessor had some difficulty with me in adjusting the respective prerogatives of Author and Editor,

* "tied-together skiff"—ed.

for though not, as I hope, insensible to fair reason, I used sometimes to rebel against what I reckoned mere authority, and this
partly perhaps as a matter of literary conscience; being wont to
write nothing without studying it if possible to the bottom, and
writing always with an almost painful feeling of scrupulosity,
that light editorial hacking and hewing to right and left was in
general nowise to my mind.

But we feel that the fault may have lain with Jeffrey; the qualifications that Lord Cockburn admired so much, were not likely to
be to the taste of a man of Mr. Carlyle's grit. That did not prevent
the most original of Mr. Napier's contributors from being one
of the most just and reasonable.

> I have, barely within my time, finished that paper ["Character-
> istics"], to which you are now heartily welcome, if you have room
> for it. The doctrines here set forth have mostly long been familiar
> convictions with me; yet it is perhaps only within the last twelve-
> month that the public utterance of some of them could have
> seemed a duty. I have striven to express myself with what guard-
> edness was possible; and, as there will now be no time for
> correcting proofs, I must leave it wholly in your editorial hands.
> Nay, should it on due consideration appear to you in your place
> (for I see that matter dimly, and nothing is clear but in my own
> mind and the general condition of the world), unadvisable to
> print the paper at all, then pray understand, my dear Sir, now
> and always, that I am no unreasonable man; but if dogmatic
> enough (as Jeffrey used to call it) in my own beliefs, also truly
> desirous to be just towards those of others. I shall, in all sincerity,
> beg of you to do, without fear of offence (for in *no* point of view
> will there be any), what you yourself see good. A mighty work
> lies before the writers of this time.

It is always interesting, to the man of letters at any rate if not
to his neighbours, to find what was first thought by men of
admitted competence of the beginnings of writers who are now
seen to have made a mark on the world. "When the reputation
of authors is made," said Ste. Beuve, "it is easy to speak of them
convenablement: we have only to guide ourselves by the common
opinion. But at their débuts, at the moment when they are trying
their first flight and are in part ignorant of themselves, then to
judge them with tact, with precision, not to exaggerate their

scope, to predict their flight, or divine their limits, to put the reasonable objections in the midst of all due respect—this is the quality of the critic who is born to be a critic." We have been speaking of Mr. Carlyle. This is what Jeffrey thought of him in 1832.

> I fear Carlyle will not do, that is, if you do not take the liberties and the pains with him that I did, by striking out freely, and writing in occasionally. The misfortune is, that he is very obstinate, and unluckily in a place like this, he finds people enough to abet and applaud him, to intercept the operation of the otherwise infallible remedy of general avoidance and neglect. It is a gerat pity, for he is a man of genius and industry, and with the capacity of being an elegant and impressive writer.

The notion of Jeffrey occasionally writing elegantly and impressively into Carlyle's proof-sheets is rather striking. Some of Jeffrey's other criticisms sound very curiously in our ear in these days. It is startling to find Mill's *Logic* described (1843) as "a great unreadable book, and its elaborate demonstration of axioms and truism." A couple of years later Jeffrey admits, in speaking of Mr. Mill's paper on the Claims of Labour—"Though I have long thought very highly of his powers as a reasoner, I scarcely gave him credit for such large and sound views of *realities* and practical results as are displayed in this article." Sir James Stephen—the distinguished sire of two distinguished contributors, who may remind more than one editor of our generation of the Horatian saying, that

> Fortes creantur fortibus et bonis,
> . . . neque imbellem feroces
> Progenerant aquilæ columbam.*

—this excellent writer took a more just measure of the book which Jeffrey thought unreadable.

> My more immediate object in writing is to remind you of John Mill's book [System of Logic], of which I have lately been reading a considerable part, and I have done so with the conviction that it is one of the most remarkable productions of the nine-

---

* "Brave, noble men father brave, noble children. [In bulls and horses likewise the male's stamp shows./ Clearly;] we never find fear bred from fierceness, eagles hatching doves"—ed.

teenth century. Exceedingly debatable indeed, but most worthy
of debate, are many of his favourite tenets, especially those of
the last two or three chapters. No man is fit to encounter him
who is not thoroughly conversant with the moral sciences which
he handles; and remembering what you told me of your own
studies under Dugald Stewart, I cannot but recommend the affair
to your own personal attention. You will find very few men fit
to be trusted with it. You ought to be aware that, although with
great circumspection, not to say timidity, Mill is an opponent of
Religion in the abstract, not of any particular form of it. That is,
he evidently maintains that superhuman influences on the mind
of man are but a dream, whence the inevitable conclusion that all
acts of devotion and prayer are but a superstition. That such is
his real meaning, however darkly conveyed, is indisputable. You
are well aware that it is in direct conflict with my own deepest
and most cherished convictions. Yet to condemn him for holding, and for calmly publishing such views, is but to add to the
difficulties of fair and full discussion, and to render truth (or
supposed truth), less certain and valuable than if it had invited,
and encountered, and triumphed over every assault of every
honest antagonist. I, therefore, wish Mill to be treated respect-
fully and handsomely.

Few of Mr. Napier's correspondents seem to have been more
considerate. At one period (1844) a long time had passed without any contribution from Sir James Stephen's pen appearing in
the Review. Mr. Senior wrote a hint on the subject to the editor,
and Napier seems to have communicated with Sir James Stephen,
who replied in a model strain.

> Have you any offer of a paper or papers from my friend John
> Austin? If you have, and if you are not aware what manner of
> man he is, it may not be amiss that you should be apprized that
> in these parts he enjoys, and deservedly, a very high and yet a
> peculiar reputation. I have a great attachment to him. He is, in the
> best sense of the word, a philosopher, an earnest and humble
> lover of wisdom. I know not anywhere a larger minded man, and
> yet, eloquent as he is in speech, there is, in his written style, an
> involution and a lack of vivacity which renders his writings a
> sealed book to almost everyone. Whether he will be able to
> assume an easier and a lighter manner, I do not know. If not,
> I rather fear for him when he stands at your bar. All I ask is,
> that you would convey your judgment in measured and (as far as

you can honestly) in courteous terms; for he is, for so considerable a man, strangely sensitive. You must have an odd story to
tell of your intercourse with the knights of the Order of the Quill.

And the letter closed with what an editor values more even than
decently Christian treatment, namely the suggestion of a fine
subject. This became the admirable essay on the Clapham Sect.

Mr. Trevelyan has published the letter to Mr. Napier in which
Macaulay speaks pretty plainly what he thought about Brougham
and the extent of his services to the Review. Brougham in turn
hated Macaulay, whom he calls the third or greatest bore in
society that he has ever known. He is furious—and here Brougham was certainly not wrong—over the "most profligate political
morality" of Macaulay's essay on Clive.

> In my eyes, his defence of Clive, and the audacious ground of
> it, merit execration. It is a most serious, and, to me, a painful
> subject. No—no—all the sentences a man can turn, even if he
> made them in pure taste, and not in Macaulay's snip-snap taste of
> the lower empire,—all won't avail against a rotten morality. The
> first and the most sacred duty of a public man, and, above all, an
> author, is to keep by honest and true doctrine—never to relax—
> never to countenance vice—ever to hold fast by virtue. What?
> Are we gravely to be told, at this time of day, that a set-off may be
> allowed for public, and, therefore, atrocious crimes, though he
> admits that a common felon pleads it in vain? Gracious God,
> where is this to end! What horrors will it not excuse! Tiberius's
> great capacity, his first-rate wit, that which made him the charm
> of society, will next, I suppose, be set up to give a splendour to
> the inhabitants of Capreæ. Why, Clive's address, and his skill,
> and his courage are not at all more certain, nor are they qualities
> of a different cast. Every great ruffian, who has filled the world
> with blood and tears, will be sure of an acquittal, because of his
> talents and his success. After I had, and chiefly in the *Edinburgh
> Review,* been trying to restore a better, a purer, a higher standard
> of morals, and to wean men from the silly love of military glory,
> for which they are the first to pay, I find the *Edinburgh Review*
> preaching, not merely the old and common heresies, but ten
> thousand times worse, adopting a vile principle never yet avowed
> in terms, though too often and too much taken for a guide, un-
> known to those who followed it, in forming their judgments of
> great and successful criminals.

Of the essay on Warren Hastings he thought better, "bating some vulgarity and Macaulay's usual want of all power of reasoning." Lord Cockburn wrote to Mr. Napier (1844) a word or two on Macaulay. "Delighting as I do," says Lord Cockburn, "in his thoughts, views, and knowledge, I feel too often compelled to curse and roar at his words and the structure of his composition. As a corrupter of style, he is more dangerous to the young than Gibbon. His seductive powers greater, his defects worse." All good critics now accept this as true. Jeffrey, by the way, speaking of the same essay, thinks that Macaulay rates Chatham too high. "I have always had an impression," he says "(though perhaps an ignorant and unjust one), that there was more good luck than wisdom in his foreign policy, and very little to admire, except his general purity, in any part of his domestic administration."

It is interesting to find a record, in the energetic speech of contemporary hatred, of the way in which orthodox science regarded a once famous book of heterodox philosophy. Here is Professor Sedgwick on the Vestiges of Creation:—

> I now know the Vestiges well, and I detest the book for its shallowness, for the intense vulgarity of its philosophy, for its gross, unblushing materialism, for its silly credulity in catering out of every fool's dish, for its utter ignorance of what is meant by induction, for its gross (and I dare to say, filthy) views of physiology,—most ignorant and most false,—and for its shameful shuffling of the facts of geology so as to make them play a rogue's game. I believe some woman is the author; partly from the fair dress and agreeable exterior of the Vestiges: and partly from the ignorance the book displays of all sound physical logic. A *man* who knew so much of the surface of Physics must, at least on some one point or other, have taken a deeper plunge; but *all* parts of the book are shallow. . . . From the bottom of my soul, I loathe and detest the Vestiges. 'Tis a rank pill of asafœtida and arsenic, covered with gold leaf. I do, therefore, trust that your contributor has stamped with an iron heel upon the head of the filthy abortion, and put an end to its crawlings. There is not one subject the author handles bearing on life, of which he does not take a degrading view.

Mr. Napier seems to have asked him to write on the book, and

Sedgwick's article, the first he ever wrote for a review, eventually appeared (1845),—without, it is to be hoped, too much of the raging contempt of the above and other letters. "I do feel contempt, and, I hope, I shall express it. Rats hatched by the incubations of a goose—dogs playing dominos—monkeys breeding men and women—all distinctions between natural and moral done away—the Bible proved all a lie, and mental philosophy one mass of folly, all of it to be pounded down and done over again in the cooking-vessels of Gall and Spurzheim!" This was the beginning of a long campaign, which is just now drawing near its close. Let us at least be glad that orthodoxy, whether scientific or religious, has mended its temper. One among other causes of the improvement, as we have already said, is probably to be found in the greater self-restraint which comes from the fact of the writer appearing in his own proper person.

Valedictory

The present number of the Review marks the close of a task which was confided to me no less than fifteen years ago—*grande mortalis ævi spatium,* a long span of one's mortal days. Fifteen years are enough to bring a man from youth to middle age, to test the working value of convictions, to measure the advance of principles and beliefs, and, alas, to cut off many early associates and to extinguish many lights. It is hardly possible that a Review should have been conducted for so considerable a time without the commission of some mistakes; articles admitted which might as well have been left out, opinions expressed which have a crudish look in the mellow light of years, phrases dropped in the heat or hurry of the moment which one would fain obliterate. Many a regret must rise in men's minds on any occasion that compels them to look back over a long reach of years. The disparity between aim and performance, the unfulfilled promise, the wrong turnings taken at critical points—as an accident of the hour draws us to take stock of a complete period of our lives, all these things rise up in private and internal judgment against anybody who is not either too stupid or too fatuously complacent to recognise facts when he sees them. But the mood passes. Ephemera must not take themselves too seriously. Time, happily, is merciful, and men's memories are benignly short.

More painful is the recollection of those earlier contributors of

This essay was first published in *Fortnightly Review,* n.s., 190 (October 1882): 511–21, and was reprinted in *Studies in Literature* (London, 1891)—ed.

ours who have vanished from the world. Periodical literature is like the manna in the wilderness; it quickly loses its freshness, and to turn over thirty volumes of old Reviews can hardly be exhilarating at the best: least of all so, when it recalls friends and coadjutors who can give their help no more. George Henry Lewes, the founder of the Review, and always cordially interested in its fortunes, has not survived to see the end of the reign of his successor. His vivacious intelligence had probably done as much as he was competent to do for his generation, but there were other important contributors, now gone, of whom this could not be said. In the region of political theory, the loss of J. E. Cairnes was truly lamentable and untimely. He had, as Mill said of him, "that rare qualification among writers on political and social subjects— a genuine scientific intellect." Not a month passes in which one does not feel how great an advantage it would have been to be able to go down to Blackheath, and discuss the perplexities of the time in that genial and manly companionship, where facts were weighed with so much care, where conclusions were measured with such breadth and comprehension, and where even the great stolid idols of the Cave and the Market Place were never too rudely buffeted. Of a very different order of mind from Cairnes, but not less to be permanently regretted by all of us who knew him, was Mr. Bagehot, whose books on the English Constitution, on Physics and Politics, and the fragment on the Postulates of Political Economy, were all published in these pages. He wrote, in fact, the first article in the first number. Though himself extremely cool and sceptical about political improvement of every sort, he took abundant interest in more ardent friends. Perhaps it was that they amused him; in return his good-natured ironies put them wholesomely on their mettle. As has been well said of him he had a unique power of animation without combat; it was all stimulus and yet no contest; his talk was full of youth, yet had all the wisdom of mature judgment (R. H. *Hutton*). Those who were least willing to assent to Bagehot's practical maxims in judging current affairs, yet were well aware how much they profited by his Socratic objections, and knew, too, what real acquaintance with men and business, what honest sympathy, and what serious judgment and interest lay under his playful and racy humour.

More untimely, in one sense, than any other was the death of

Professor Clifford, whose articles in this Review attracted so
much attention, and I fear that I may add, gave for a season so
much offence six or seven years ago. Cairnes was scarcely fifty
when he died, and Bagehot was fifty-one, but Clifford was only
four-and-thirty. Yet in this brief space he had not merely won a
reputation as a mathematician of the first order, but had made a
real mark on his time, both by the substance of his speculations in
science, religion, and ethics, and by the curious audacity with
which he proclaimed at the pitch of his voice on the housetops
religious opinions that had hitherto been kept among the family
secrets of the *domus Socratica.* It is melancholy to think that
exciting work, done under pressure of time of his own imposing,
should have been the chief cause of his premature decline. How
intense that pressure was the reader may measure by the fact that
a paper of his on *The Unseen Universe,* which filled eighteen
pages of the Review, was composed at a single sitting that lasted
from a quarter to ten in the evening till nine o'clock the following morning. As one revolves these and other names of eminent
men who actively helped to make the Review what it has been,
it would be impossible to omit the most eminent of them all.
Time has done something to impair the philosophical reputation
and the political celebrity of J. S. Mill; but it cannot alter the
affectionate memory in which some of us must always hold his
wisdom and goodness, his rare union of moral ardour with a
calm and settled mind. He took the warmest interest in this Review from the moment when I took it up, partly from the friendship with which he honoured me, but much more because he
wished to encourage what was then—though it is now happily no
longer—the only attempt to conduct a periodical on the principles of free discussion and personal responsibility. While recalling these and others who are no more, it was naturally impossible for me to forget the constant and valuable help that has
been so freely given to me, often at much sacrifice of their own
convenience, by those friends and contributors who are still with
us. No conductor ever laid down his *bâton* with a more cordial
and sincere sense of gratitude to those who took their several parts
in his performance.

One chief experiment which the Review was established to try
was that of signed articles. When Mr. Lewes wrote his Farewell

Causerie, as I am doing now, he said: "That we have been enabled to bring together men so various in opinion and so distinguished in power has been mainly owing to the principle
adopted of allowing each writer perfect freedom; which could
only have been allowed under the condition of personal responsibility. The question of signing articles had long been debated;
it has now been tested. The arguments in favour of it were mainly
of a moral order; the arguments against it, while admitting the
morality, mainly asserted its inexpediency. The question of expediency has, I venture to say, been materially enlightened by the
success of the Review." The success of other periodicals, conducted still more rigorously on the principle that every article
ought to bear its writer's signature, leaves no further doubt on the
subject; so that it is now almost impossible to realise that only
fifteen or sixteen years ago scarcely anybody of the class called
practical could believe that the sacred principle of the Anonymous
was doomed. One of the shrewdest publishers in Edinburgh, and
also himself the editor of a famous magazine (the colour of
whose Toryism, by the way, is almost of itself enough to explain
why a sensible country like Scotland is so intensely Liberal), once
said to me while Mr. Lewes was still editor of this Review, that
he had always thought highly of our friend's judgment "until he
had taken up the senseless notion of a magazine with signed
articles and open to both sides of every question." Nobody will
call the notion senseless any longer. The question is rather how
long the exclusively anonymous periodicals will resist the in-
novation.

Personally I have attached less stern importance to signature as
an unvarying rule than did my predecessor; though even he was
compelled by obvious considerations of convenience to make
his chronique of current affairs anonymous. Our practice has been
signature as the standing order, occasionally suspended in favour
of anonymity when there seemed to be sufficient reason. On the
whole it may be said that the change from anonymous to signed
articles has followed the course of most changes. It has not led to
one-half either of the evils or of the advantages that its advocates
and its opponents foretold. That it has produced some charlatanry, can hardly be denied. Readers are tempted to postpone

serious and persistent interest in subjects, to a semi-personal curiosity about the casual and unconnected deliverances of the literary or social "star" of the hour. That this conception has been worked out with signal ability in more cases than one; that it has made periodical literature full of actuality; that it has tickled and delighted the palate—is all most true. The obvious danger is lest we should be tempted to think more of the man who speaks than of the precise value of what he says.

One indirect effect that is not unworthy of notice in the new system is its tendency to narrow the openings for the writer by profession. If an article is to be signed, the editor will naturally seek the name of an expert of special weight and competence on the matter in hand. A reviewer on the staff of a famous journal once received for his week's task, *General Hamley on the Art of War,* a three-volume novel, a work on dainty dishes, and a translation of Pindar. This was perhaps taxing versatility and omniscience overmuch, and it may be taken for granted that the writer made no serious contribution to tactics, cookery, or scholarship. But being a man of a certain intelligence, passably honest, and reasonably painstaking, probably he produced reviews sufficiently useful and just to answer their purpose. On the new system we should have an article on General Hamley's work by Sir Garnet Wolseley, and one on the cookery-book from M. Trompette. It is not certain that this is all pure gain. There is something to be said for the writer by profession, who without being an expert, will take trouble to work up his subject, to learn what is said and thought about it, to penetrate to the real points, to get the same mastery over it as an advocate or a judge does over a patent case or a suit about rubrics and vestments. He is at least as likely as the expert to tell the reader all that he wants to know, and at least as likely to be free from bias and injurious prepossession.

Nor does experience, so far as it has yet gone, quite bear out Mr. Lewes's train of argument that the "first condition of all writing is sincerity, and that one means of securing sincerity is to insist on personal responsibility," and that this personal responsibility can only be secured by signing articles. The old talk of "literary bravoes," "men in masks," "anonymous assassins," and so forth, is out of date. Longer experience has only confirmed the present writer's opinion, expressed here from the very beginning: "Everybody who knows the composition of any respectable journal in London, knows very well that the articles which those of our own way of thinking dislike most intensely, are written by men whom to call bravoes in any sense whatever would be simply monstrous. Let us say, as loudly as we choose, if we see good reason, that they are half informed about some of the things which they so authoritatively discuss; that they are under strong class feeling; that they have not mastered the doctrines which they are opposing; that they have not sufficiently meditated their subject; that they have not given themselves time to do justice even to their scanty knowledge. Journalists are open to charges of this kind; but to think of them as a shameless body, thirsting for the blood of better men than themselves, or ready to act as an editor's instrument for money, involves a thoroughly unjust misconception."

As to the comparative effects of the two systems on literary quality, no prudent observer with adequate experience will lay down an unalterable rule. Habit no doubt counts for a great deal, but apart from habit there are differences of temperament and peculiar sensibilities. Some men write best when they sign what they write; they find impersonality a mystification and an incumbrance; anonymity makes them stiff, pompous, and over-magisterial. With others, however, the effect is just the reverse. If they sign, they become self-conscious, stilted, and even pretentious; it is only when they are anonymous that they recover simplicity and ease. It is as if an actor who is the soul of what is natural under the disguises of his part, should become extremely artificial if he were compelled to come upon the stage in his own proper clothes and speaking only in his ordinary voice.

The newspaper press has not yet followed the example of the new Reviews, but we are probably not far from the time when here, too, the practice of signature will make its way. There was an unwise cry at one time for making the disuse of anonymity compulsory by law. But we shall no more see this than we shall see legal penalties imposed for publishing a book without an index, though that also has been suggested. The same end will be reached by other ways. Within the last few years a truly surprising shock has been given to the idea of a newspaper, "as a sort of impersonal thing, coming from nobody knows where, the readers never thinking of the writer, nor caring whether he thinks what he writes, so long as *they* think what he writes." Of course it is still true, and will most likely always remain true, that, like the Athenian Sophist, great newspapers will teach the conventional prejudices of those who pay for it. A writer will long be able to say that, like the Sophist, the newspaper reflects the morality, the intelligence, the tone of sentiment, of its public, and if the latter is vicious, so is the former. But there is infinitely less of this than there used to be. The press is more and more taking the tone of a man speaking to a man. The childish imposture of the editorial We is already thoroughly exploded. The names of all important journalists are now coming to be as publicly known as the names of important members of parliament. There is even something over and above this. More than one editor—the editors of the *Spectator* and of the *St. James's Gazette* are conspicuous instances, in very different ways—have boldly aspired to create and educate a public of their own, and they have succeeded. The press is growing to be much more personal, in the sense that its most important directors are taking to themselves the right of pursuing an individual line of their own, with far less respect than of old to the supposed exigencies of party or the *communiqués* of political leaders. The editor of a Review of great eminence said to the present writer (who, for his own part, took a slightly more modest view) that he regarded himself as equal in importance to twenty-five members of parliament. It is not altogether easy to weigh and measure with this degree of precision. But what is certain is that there are journalists on both sides in politics to whom the public looks for original suggestion, and from whom leading politicians seek not merely such mechanical support as they expect from their adherents in the House of Commons, nor merely the uses of the vane to show which way the wind blows, but ideas, guidance, and counsel, as from persons of co-equal authority with themselves. England is still a long way from the point at which French journalism has arrived in this matter. We cannot count an effective host of Girardins, Lemoinnes, Abouts, or even Cassagnacs and Rocheforts, each recognised as the exponent of his own opinions, and each read because the opinions written are known to be his own. But there is a distinctly nearer approach to this as the general state of English journalism than there was twenty years ago.

Of course nobody of sense supposes that any journalist, however independent and however possessed by the spirit of his personal responsibility, tries to form his opinions out of his own head, without reference to the view of the men practically engaged in public affairs, the temper of Parliament and the feeling of constituencies, and so forth. All these are part of the elements that go to the formation of his own judgment, and he will certainly not neglect to find out as much about them as he possibly can. Nor, again, does the increase of the personal sentiment about our public prints lessen the general working fidelity of their conductors to a party. It is their duty, no doubt, to discuss the merits of measures as they arise. In this respect any one can see how radically they differ from the Member of Parliament, whose business is not only to discuss but to act. The Member of Parliament must look at the effect of his vote in more lights than one. Besides the merits of the given measure, it is his duty to think of the wishes of those who chose him to represent them; and if, moreover, the effect of voting against a measure of which he disapproves would be to overthrow a whole Ministry of which he strongly approves, then, unless some very vital principle indeed were involved, to give such a vote would be to prefer a small object to a great one, and would meet a very queasy monkish sort of conscience. The journalist is not in the same position. He is an observer and a critic, and can afford, and is bound, to speak the truth. But even in his case, the disagreement, as Burke said, "will be only enough to indulge freedom, without violating concord or disturbing arrangement." There is a certain "partiality which becomes a well-chosen friendship." "Men thinking freely will, in particular instances, think differently. But still as the greater part of the measures which arise in the course of public business are related to, or dependent on, some great leading general principles in government, a man must be peculiarly unfortunate in the choice of his political company if he does not agree with them at least nine times in ten." The doctrine that was good enough for Burke in this matter may be counted good enough for most of us. Some of the current talk about political independence is mere hypocrisy and *blague;* some of it is mere vanity. For the new priest of Literature is quite as liable to the defects of spiritual pride and ambition as the old priest of the Church, and it is quite as well for him that he should be on his guard against these scarlet and high-crested sins.

The success of Reviews, of which our own was the first English type, marks a very considerable revolution in the intellectual habits of the time. They have brought abstract discussion from the library down to the parlour, and from the serious student down to the first man in the street. We have passed through a perfect cyclone of religious polemics. The popularity of such Reviews means that really large audiences, *le gros public,* are eagerly interested in the radical discussion of propositions which twenty years ago were only publicly maintained, and then in their crudest, least true, and most repulsive form, in obscure debating societies and little secularist clubs. Everybody, male or female, who reads anything serious at all, now reads a dozen essays a year to show, with infinite varieties of approach and of demonstration, that we can never know whether there be a Supreme Being or not, whether the soul survives the body, or whether the soul is more and other than a mere function of the body. No article that has appeared in any periodical for a generation back excited so profound a sensation as Mr. Huxley's memorable paper "On the Physical Basis of Life," published in this Review in February, 1869. It created just the same kind of stir that, in a political epoch, was made by such a pamphlet as the *Conduct of the Allies* or the *Reflections on the French Revolution.* This excitement was a sign that controversies which had hitherto been confined to books and treatises were now to be admitted to popular periodicals, and that the common man of the world would now listen and have an opinion of his own on the bases of belief, just as he listens and judges in politics, or art, or letters. The clergy no longer have the pulpit to themselves, for the new Reviews became more powerful pulpits, in which heretics were at least as welcome as orthodox. Speculation has become entirely democratised. This is a tremendous change to have come about in little more than a dozen years. How far it goes, let us not be too sure. It is no new discovery that what looks like complete tolerance may be in reality only complete indifference. Intellectual fairness is often only another name for indolence and inconclusiveness of mind, just as love of truth is sometimes a fine phrase for temper. To be piquant counts for much, and the interest of seeing on the drawing-room tables of devout Catholics and high-flying Anglicans article after article, sending divinities, creeds, and Churches all headlong into limbo, was indeed piquant. Much of all this elegant dabbling in infidelity has been a caprice of fashion. The Agnostic has had his day with the fine ladies, like the black footboy of other times, or the spirit-rapper and table-turner of our own. When one perceived that such people actually thought that the Churches had been raised on their feet again by the puerile apologetics of Mr. Mallock, then it was easy to know that they had never really fallen. What we have been watching, after all, was perhaps a tournament, not a battle.

It would not be very easy for us now, and perhaps it would not be particularly becoming at any time, to analyze the position that has been assigned to this Review in common esteem. Those who have watched it from without, can judge better than those who have worked within. Though it has been open, so far as editorial good will was concerned, to opinions from many sides, the Review has unquestionably gathered round it some of the associations of sect. What that sect is, people have found it difficult to describe with anything like precision. For a long time it was the fashion to label the Review as Comtist, and it would be singularly ungrateful to deny that it has had no more effective contributors than some of the best-known disciples of Comte. By-and-by it was felt that this was too narrow. It was nearer the truth to call it the organ of Positivists in the wider sense of that designation. But even this would not cover many directly political articles that have appeared in our pages, and made a mark in their time. The memorable programme of Free Labour, Free Land, Free Schools, Free Church had nothing at all Positivist about it. Nor could that programme and many besides from the same pen and others be compressed under the nickname of Academic Liberalism. There was too strong a flavour of action for the academic and the philosophic. This passion for a label, after all, is an infirmity. Yet people justly perceived that there seemed to be a certain undefinable concurrence among writers coming from different schools and handling very different subjects. Perhaps the instinct was right which fancied that it discerned some common drift, a certain pervading atmosphere. People scented a subtle connection between speculations on the Physical Basis of Life and the Unseen Universe, and articles on Trades Unions and National Education; and Professor Tyndall's eloquence in impugning the authority of miracles was supposed to work in the same direction as Mr. Frederic Harrison's eloquence in demolishing Prince Bismarck and vindicating the Commune as the newest proof of the political genius of France.

So far as the Review has been more specially identified with one set of opinions than another, it has been due to the fact that a certain dissent from received theologies has been found in company with new ideas of social and political reform. This suspicious combination at one time aroused considerable anger. The notion of anything like an intervention of the literary and scientific class in political affairs touched a certain jealousy which is always to be looked for in the positive and practical man. They think as Napoleon did of men of letters and savans:—"Ce sont des coquettes avec lesquelles il faut entretenir un commerce de galanterie, et dont il ne faut jamais songer à faire ni sa femme ni son ministre." Men will listen to your views about the Unknowable with a composure that instantly disappears if your argument comes too near to the Rates and Taxes. It is amusing, as we read the newspapers to-day, to think that Mr. Harrison's powerful defence of Trades Unions fifteen years ago caused the Review to be regarded as an incendiary publication. Some papers that appeared here on National Education were thought to indicate a deliberate plot for suppressing the Holy Scriptures in the land. Extravagant misjudgment of this kind has passed away. But it was far from being a mistake to suppose that the line taken here by many writers did mean that there was a new Radicalism in the air, which went a good deal deeper than fidgeting about an estimate or the amount of the Queen's contribution to her own taxes. Time has verified what was serious in those early apprehensions. Principles and aims are coming into prominence in the social activity of to-day which would hardly have found a hearing twenty years ago, and it would be sufficient justification for the past of our Review if some writers in it have been instrumental in the process of showing how such principles and aims meet the requirements of the new time. Reformers must always be open to the taunt that they find nothing in the world good enough for them. "You write," said a popular novelist to one of this un-thanked tribe, "as if you believed that everything is bad." "Nay," said the other, "but I do believe that everything might be better." Such a belief naturally breeds a spirit which the easy-goers of the world resent as a spirit of ceaseless complaint and scolding. Hence our Liberalism here has often been taxed with being un-genial, discontented, and even querulous. But such Liberals will wrap themselves in their own virtue, remembering the cheering apophthegm that "those who are dissatisfied are the sole bene-factors of the world."

This will not be found, I think, too lofty, or too thrasonical an estimate of what has been attempted. A certain number of people have been persuaded to share opinions that fifteen years ago were more unpopular than they are now. A certain resistance has been offered to the stubborn influence of prejudice and use and wont. The original scheme of the Review, even if there had been no other obstacle, prevented it from being the organ of a systematic and constructive policy. There is not, in fact, a body of systematic political thought at work in our own day. The Liberals of the Benthamite school, as was said here not many months ago,[1] surveyed society and institutions as a whole; they connected their advocacy of political and legal changes with carefully formed theories of human nature; they considered the great art of Gov-ernment in connection with the character of man, his proper education, his potential capacities. Yet, as we then said, it cannot be pretended that we are less in need of systematic politics than our fathers were sixty years since, or that general principles are now more generally settled even among members of the same party than they were then. The perplexities of to-day are as embarrassing as any in our history, and they may prove even more dangerous. The renovation of Parliamentary government; the transformation of the conditions of the ownership and occu-

1. *Fortnightly Review,* April, 1882.

pation of land; the relations between the Government at home and our adventurers abroad in contact with inferior races; the limitations on free contract and the rights of majorities to restrict the private acts of universities; these are only some of the questions that time and circumstances are pressing upon us. These are in the political and legislative sphere alone. In Education, in Economics for realisation in Literature, the problems are as many. Yet ideas are hardly ripe. We shall need to see great schools before we can make sure of powerful parties. Meanwhile, whatever gives freedom and variety to thought, and earnestness to men's interest in the world, must contribute to a good end. The Review has been an attempt to do something in this direction. I may well hope that the energy and intelligence of my successor will enable it to do more.

The Life
of
George Eliot

The illustrious woman who is the subject of these volumes makes
a remark to her publisher which is at least as relevant now as it
was then. Can nothing be done, she asks, by dispassionate criticism towards the reform of our national habits in the matter of
literary biography? "Is it anything short of odious that as soon
as a man is dead his desk should be raked, and every insignificant
memorandum which he never meant for the public be printed for
the gossiping amusement of people too idle to reread his books?"
Autobiography, she says, at least saves a man or a woman that the
world is curious about, from the publication of a string of mistakes called Memoirs. Even to autobiography, however, she con-
fesses her deep repugnance unless it can be written so as to involve
neither self-glorification nor impeachment of others—a condition, by the way, with which hardly any, save Mill's, can be said
to comply. "I like," she proceeds, "that *He being dead yet speak-
eth* should have quite another meaning than that" (iii. 226, 297,
307). She shows the same fastidious apprehension still more
clearly in another way. "I have destroyed almost all my friends'
letters to me," she says, "because they were only intended for my
eyes, and could only fall into the hands of persons who knew little
of the writers, if I allowed them to remain till after my death. In
proportion as I love every form of piety—which is venerating

George Eliot's Life. By J. W. Cross. Three volumes. Blackwood and Sons. 1885.
[This essay was first published in *Macmillan's Magazine,* 51 (February 1885):
241–56, and was reprinted in *Critical Miscellanies,* vol. 3 (London, 1886)—ed.]

love—I hate hard curiosity; and, unhappily, my experience has impressed me with the sense that hard curiosity is the more common temper of mind" (ii. 286). There is probably little difference among us in respect of such experience as that.

Much biography, perhaps we might say most, is hardly above the level of that "personal talk," to which Wordsworth sagely preferred long barren silence, the flapping of the flame of his cottage fire, and the undersong of the kettle on the hob. It would not, then, have much surprised us if George Eliot had insisted that her works should remain the only commemoration of her life. There be some who think that those who have enriched the world with great thoughts and fine creations, might best be content to rest unmarked "where heaves the turf in many a mouldering heap," leaving as little work to the literary executor, except of the purely crematory sort, as did Aristotle, Plato, Shakespeare, and some others whose names the world will not willingly let die. But this is a stoic's doctrine; the objector may easily retort that if it had been sternly acted on, we should have known very little about Dr. Johnson, and nothing about Socrates.

This is but an ungracious prelude to some remarks upon a book, which must be pronounced a striking success. There will be very little dispute as to the fact that the editor of these memorials of George Eliot has done his work with excellent taste, judgment, and sense. He found no autobiography nor fragment of one, but he has skilfullly shaped a kind of autobiography by a plan which, so far as we know, he is justified in calling new, and which leaves her life to write itself in extracts from her letters and journals. With the least possible obtrusion from the biographer, the original pieces are formed into a connected whole "that combines a narrative of day-to-day life with the play of light and shade which only letters written in serious moods can give." The idea is a good one, and Mr. Cross deserves great credit for it. We may hope that its success will encourage imitators. Certainly there are drawbacks. We miss the animation of mixed narrative. There is, too, a touch of monotony in listening for so long to the voice of a single speaker addressing others who are silent behind a screen. But Mr. Cross could not we think, have devised a better way of dealing with his material: it is simple, modest, and effective.

George Eliot, after all, led the life of a studious recluse, with none of the bustle, variety, motion, and large communication with the outer world, that justified Lockhart and Moore in making a long story of the lives of Scott and Byron. Even here, among men of letters, who were also men of action and of great sociability, are not all biographies too long? Let any sensible reader turn to the shelf where his Lives repose; we shall be surprised if he does not find that nearly every one of them, taking the present century alone, and including such splendid and attractive subjects as Goethe, Hume, Romilly, Mackintosh, Horner, Chalmers, Arnold, Southey, Cowper, would not have been all the better for judicious curtailment. Lockhart, who wrote the longest, wrote also the shortest, the Life of Burns; and the shortest is the best, in spite of defects which would only have been worse if the book had been bigger. It is to be feared that, conscientious and honourable as his self-denial has been, even Mr. Cross has not wholly resisted the natural and besetting error of the biographer. Most people will think that the hundred pages of the Italian tour (vol. ii), and some other not very remarkable impressions of travel, might as well or better have been left out.

As a mere letter-writer, George Eliot will not rank among the famous masters of what is usually considered especially a woman's art. She was too busy in serious work to have leisure for that most delightful way of wasting time. Besides that, she had by nature none of that fluency, rapidity, abandonment, pleasant volubility, which make letters amusing, captivating, or piquant. What Mr. Cross says of her as the mistress of a *salon,* is true of her for the most part as a correspondent:—"Playing around many disconnected subjects, in talk, neither interested nor amused her much. She took things too seriously, and seldom found the effort of entertaining compensated by the gain" (iii. 335). There is the outpouring of ardent feeling for her friends, sobering down, as life goes on, into a crooning kindliness, affectionate and honest, but often tinged with considerable self-consciousness. It was said of some one that his epigrams did honour to his heart; in the reverse direction we occasionally feel that George Eliot's effusive playfulness does honour to her head. It lacks simplicity and *verve.* Even in an invitation to dinner, the words imply a grave sense of responsibility on both sides, and sense of responsibility is fatal to the charm of familiar correspondence.

As was inevitable in one whose mind was so habitually turned to the deeper elements of life, she lets fall the pearls of wise speech even in short notes. Here are one or two:—

> My own experience and development deepen every day my conviction that our moral progress may be measured by the degree in which we sympathise with individual suffering and individual joy.

> If there is one attitude more odious to me than any other of the many attitudes of "knowingness," it is that air of lofty superiority to the vulgar. She will soon find out that I am a very commonplace woman.

> It so often happens that others are measuring us by our past self while we are looking back on that self with a mixture of disgust and sorrow.

The following is one of the best examples, one of the few examples, of her best manner:—

> I have been made rather unhappy by my husband's impulsive proposal about Christmas. We are dull old persons, and your two sweet young ones ought to find each Christmas a new bright bead to string on their memory, whereas to spend the time with us would be to string on a dark shrivelled berry. They ought to have a group of young creatures to be joyful with. Our own children always spend their Christmas with Gertrude's family; and we have usually taken our sober merrymaking with friends out of town. Illness among these will break our custom this year; and thus *mein Mann,* feeling that our Christmas was free, considered how very much he liked being with you, omitting the other side of the question—namely, our total lack of means to make a suitably joyous meeting, a real festival, for Phil and Margaret. I was conscious of this lack in the very moment of the proposal, and the consciousness has been pressing on me more and more painfully ever since. Even my husband's affectionate hopefulness cannot withstand my melancholy demonstration. So pray consider the kill-joy proposition as entirely retracted, and give us something of yourselves only on simple black-letter days, when

the Herald Angels have not been raising expectations early in the morning.

This is very pleasant, but such pieces are rare, and the infirmity of human nature has sometimes made us sigh over these pages at the recollection of the cordial cheeriness of Scott's letters, the high spirits of Macaulay, the graceful levity of Voltaire, the rattling dare-devilry of Byron. Epistolary stilts among men of letters went out of fashion with Pope, who, as was said, thought that unless every period finished with a conceit, the letter was not worth the postage. Poor spirits cannot be the explanation of the stiffness in George Eliot's case, for no letters in the English language are so full of playfulness and charm as those of Cowper, and he was habitually sunk in gulfs deeper and blacker than George Eliot's own. It was sometimes observed of her, that in her conversation, *elle s'écoutait quand elle parlait*—she seemed to be listening to her own voice while she spoke. It must be allowed that we are not always free from an impression of self-listening, even in the most caressing of the letters before us.

This is not much better, however, than trifling. I dare say that if a lively Frenchman could have watched the inspired Pythia on the sublime tripod, he would have cried, *Elle s'écoute quand elle parle*. When everything of that kind has been said, we have the profound satisfaction, which is not quite a matter of course in the history of literature, of finding after all that the woman and the writer were one. The life does not belie the books, nor private conduct stultify public profession. We close the third volume of the biography, as we have so often closed the third volume of her novels, feeling to the very core that in spite of a style that the French call *alambiqué,* in spite of tiresome double and treble distillations of phraseology, in spite of fatiguing moralities, gravities, and ponderosities, we have still been in communion with a high and commanding intellect, and a great nature. We are vexed by pedantries that recall the *précieuses* of the Hôtel Rambouillet, but we know that she had the soul of the most heroic women in history. We crave more of the Olympian serenity that makes action natural and repose refreshing, but we cannot miss the edification of a life marked by indefatigable labour after generous purpose, by an unsparing struggle for duty, and by steadfast and devout fellowship with lofty thoughts.

Those who know Mr. Myers's essay on George Eliot will not have forgotten its most imposing passage:—

> I remember how at Cambridge, I walked with her once in the Fellows' Garden of Trinity, on an evening of rainy May; and she, stirred somewhat beyond her wont, and taking as her text the three words which have been used so often as the inspiring trumpet-calls of men,—the words *God, Immortality, Duty,*—pronounced, with terrible earnestness, how inconceivable was the *first,* how unbelievable the *second,* and how peremptory and absolute the *third.* Never, perhaps, had stearner accents affirmed the sovereignty of impersonal and unrecompensing law. I listened, and night fell; her grave, majestic countenance turned toward me like a Sibyl's in the gloom; it was as though she withdrew from my grasp, one by one, the two scrolls of promise, and left me the third scroll only, awful with inevitable fates.

To many, the relation, which was the most important event in George Eliot's life, will seem one of those irretrievable errors which reduce all talk of duty to a mockery. It is inevitable that this should be so, and those who disregard a social law have little right to complain. Men and women whom in every other respect it would be monstrous to call bad, have taken this particular law into their own hands before now, and committed themselves to conduct of which "magnanimity owes no account to prudence." But if they had sense and knew what they were about, they have braced themselves to endure the disapproval of a majority fortunately more prudential than themselves. The world is busy, and its instruments are clumsy. It cannot know all the facts; it has neither time nor material for unravelling all the complexities of motive, or for distinguishing mere libertinage from grave and deliberate moral misjudgment; it is protecting itself as much as it is condemning the offenders. On all this, then, we need have neither sophistry nor cant. But those who seek something deeper than a verdict for the honest working purpose of leaving cards and inviting to dinner, may feel, as has been observed by a contemporary writer, that men and women are more fairly judged, if judge them we must, by the way in which they bear the burden of an error, than by the decision that laid the burden on their lives. Some idea of this kind was in her own mind when she wrote to her most intimate friend in 1857, "If I live five years longer,

the positive result of my existence on the side of truth and goodness will outweigh the small negative good that would have consisted in my not doing anything to shock others" (i. 461). This
urgent desire to balance the moral account may have had something to do with that laborious sense of responsibility which
weighed so heavily on her soul, and had so equivocal an effect
upon her art. Whatever else is to be said of this particular union,
nobody can deny that the picture on which it left a mark was an
exhibition of extraordinary self-denial, energy, and persistency
in the cultivation and the use of great gifts and powers for what
their possessor believed to be the highest objects for society and
mankind.

A more perfect companionship, one on a higher intellectual
level, or of more sustained mental activity, is nowhere recorded.
Lewes's mercurial temperament contributed as much as the
powerful mind of his consort to prevent their seclusion from degenerating into an owlish stagnation. To the very last (1878) he
retained his extraordinary buoyancy. "Nothing but death could
quench that bright flame. Even on his worst days he had always a
good story to tell; and I remember on one occasion in the drawing-
room at Witley, between two bouts of pain, he sang through
with great *brio,* though without much voice, the greater portion
of the tenor part in the *Barber of Seville,* George Eliot playing
his accompaniment, and both of them thoroughly enjoying the
fun" (iii. 334). All this gaiety, his inexhaustible vivacity, the
facility of his transitions from brilliant levity to a keen seriousness, the readiness of his mental response, and the wide range of
intellectual accomplishments that were much more than superficial, made him a source of incessant and varied stimulation. Even
those, and there were some, who thought that his gaiety bordered
on flippancy, that his genial self-content often came near to
shockingly bad taste, and that his reminiscences of poor Mr.
Fitzball and the green-room and all the rest of the Bohemia in
which he had once dwelt, too racy for his company, still found it
hard to resist the alert intelligence with which he rose to every
good topic, and the extraordinary heartiness and spontaneity with
which the wholesome spring of human laughter was touched in
him.

Lewes had plenty of egotism, not to give it a more unamiable

name, but it never mastered his intellectual sincerity. George
Eliot describes him as one of the few human beings she has
known who will, in the heat of an argument, see, and straightway confess, that he is in the wrong, instead of trying to shift his
ground or use any other device of vanity. "The intense happiness
of our union," she wrote to a friend, "is derived in a high degree
from the perfect freedom with which we each follow and declare our own impressions. In this respect I know *no* man so great
as he—that difference of opinion rouses no egotistic irritation in
him, and that he is ready to admit that another argument is the
stronger, the moment his intellect recognises it" (ii. 279). This
will sound very easy to the dispassionate reader, because it is so
obviously just and proper, but if the dispassionate reader ever
tries, he may find the virtue not so easy as it looks. Finally, and
above all, we can never forget in Lewes's case how much true
elevation and stability of character was implied in the unceasing
reverence, gratitude, and devotion with which for five-and-twenty
years he treated her to whom he owed all his happiness, and who
most truly, in his own words (ii. 76), had made his life a new
birth.

The reader will be mistaken if he should infer from such
passages as abound in her letters that George Eliot had any particular weakness for domestic or any other kind of idolatry.
George Sand, in *Lucrezia Floriani,* where she drew so unkind a
picture of Chopin, has described her own life and character as
marked by "a great facility for illusions, a blind benevolence of
judgment, a tenderness of heart that was inexhaustible; consequently great precipitancy, many mistakes, much weakness, fits
of heroic devotion to unworthy objects, enormous force applied to
an end that was wretched in truth and fact, but sublime in her
thought." George Eliot had none of this facility. Nor was general
benignity in her at all of the poor kind that is incompatible with
a great deal of particular censure. Universal benevolence never
lulled an active critical faculty, nor did she conceive true humility as at all consisting in hiding from an impostor that you have
found him out. Like Cardinal Newman, for whose beautiful passage at the end of the *Apologia* she expresses such richly deserved
admiration (ii. 387), she unites to the gift of unction and
brotherly love, a capacity for giving an extremely shrewd nip to

a brother whom she does not love. Her passion for Thomas-a-Kempis did not prevent her, and there was no reason why it should, from dealing very faithfully with a friend, for instance (ii. 271); from describing Mr. Buckle as a conceited, ignorant man; or castigating Brougham and other people in slashing reviews; or otherwise from showing that great expansiveness of the affections went with a remarkably strong, hard, masculine, positive, judging head.

The benefits that George Eliot gained from her exclusive companionship with a man of lively talents were not without some compensating drawbacks. The keen stimulation and incessant strain, unrelieved by variety of daily intercourse, and never diversified by participation in the external activities of the world, tended to bring about a loaded, over-conscious, over-anxious state of mind, which was not only not wholesome in itself, but was inconsistent with the full freshness and strength of artistic work. The presence of the real world in his life has, in all but one or two cases, been one element of the novelist's highest success in the world of imaginative creation. George Eliot has no greater favourite than Scott, and when a series of little books upon English men of letters was planned, she said that she thought that writer among us the happiest to whom it should fall to deal with Scott. But Scott lived full in the life of his fellowmen. Even of Wordsworth, her other favourite, though he was not a creative artist, we may say that he daily saturated himself in those natural elements and effects, which were the material, the suggestion, and the sustaining inspiration of his consoling and fortifying poetry. George Eliot did not live in the midst of her material, but aloof from it and outside of it. Heaven forbid that this should seem to be said by way of censure. Both her health and other considerations made all approach to busy sociability in any of its shapes both unwelcome and impossible. But in considering the relation of her manner of life to her work, her creations, her meditations, one cannot but see that when compared with some writers of her own sex and age, she is constantly bookish, artificial and mannered. She is this because she fed her art too exclusively, first on the memories of her youth, and next from books, pictures, statues, instead of from the living model, as seen in its actual motion. It is direct calls and personal claims from without that make fiction alive. Jane Austen bore her part in the little world of the parlour that she described. The writer of *Sylvia's Lovers,* whose work George Eliot appreciated with unaffected generosity (i. 305), was the mother of children, and was surrounded by the wholesome actualities of the family. The authors of *Jane Eyre* and *Wuthering Heights* passed their days in one long succession of wild, stormy, squalid, anxious, and miserable scenes—almost as romantic, as poetic, and as tragic, to use George Eliot's words, as their own stories. George Sand eagerly shared, even to the pitch of passionate tumult and disorder, in the emotions, the aspirations, the ardour, the great conflicts and controversies of her time. In every one of these, their daily closeness to the real life of the world has given a vitality to their work which we hardly expect that even the next generation will find in more than one or two of the romances of George Eliot. It may even come to pass that their position will be to hers as that of Fielding is to Richardson in our own day.

In a letter to Mr. Harrison, which is printed here (ii. 441), George Eliot describes her own method, as "the severe effort of trying to make certain ideas thoroughly incarnate, as if they had revealed themselves to me first in the flesh and not in the spirit." The passage recalls a discussion one day at the Priory in 1877. She was speaking of the different methods of the poetic or creative art, and said that she began with moods, thoughts, passions, and then invented the story for their sake, and fitted it to them; Shakespeare, on the other hand, picked up a story that struck him, and then proceeded to work in the moods, thoughts, passions, as they came to him in the course of meditation on the story. We hardly need the result to convince us that Shakespeare chose the better part.

The influence of her reserved fashion of daily life was heightened by the literary exclusiveness which of set purpose she imposed upon herself. "The less an author hears about himself," she says, in one place, "the better." "It is my rule, very strictly observed, not to read the criticisms on my writings. For years I have found this abstinence necessary to preserve me from that discouragement as an artist, which ill-judged praise, no less than ill-judged blame, tends to produce in us." George Eliot pushed this repugnance to criticism beyond the personal reaction of it upon the artist, and more than disparaged its utility, even in the most competent and highly trained hands. She finds that the diseased spot in the literary culture of our time is touched with the finest point by the saying of La Bruyère, that "the pleasure of criticism robs us of the pleasure of being keenly moved by very fine things" (iii. 327). "It seems to me," she writes (ii. 412), "much better to read a man's own writings, than to read what others say about him, especially when the man is first-rate and the others third-rate. As Goethe said long ago about Spinoza, 'I always preferred to learn from the man himself what *he* thought, rather than to hear from some one else what he ought to have thought.' " As if the scholar will not always be glad to do both, to study his author and not to refuse the help of the rightly prepared commentator; as if even Goethe himself would not have been all the better acquainted with Spinoza, if he could have read Mr. Pollock's book upon him. But on this question Mr. Arnold has fought a brilliant battle, and to him George Eliot's heresies may well be left.

On the personal point whether an author should ever hear of himself, George Eliot oddly enough contradicts herself in a casual remark upon Bulwer. "I have a great respect," she says, "for the energetic industry which has made the most of his powers. He has been writing diligently for more than thirty years, constantly improving his position, and profiting by the lessons of public opinion and of other writers" (ii. 322). But if it is true that the less an author hears about himself the better, how are these salutary "lessons of public opinion" to penetrate to him? "Rubens," she says, writing from Munich, in 1858 (ii. 28), "gives me more pleasure than any other painter whether right or wrong. More than any one else he makes me feel that painting is a great art, and that he was a great artist. His are such real breathing men and women, moved by passions, not mincing, and grimacing, and posing in mere imitation of passion." But Rubens did not concentrate his intellect on his own ponderings, nor shut out the wholesome chastenings of praise and blame, lest they should discourage his inspiration. Beethoven, another of the chief objects of George Eliot's veneration, bore all the rough stress of an active and troublesome calling, though of the musician, if any, we may say, that his is the art of self-absorption.

Hence, delightful and inspiring as it is to read this story of diligent and discriminating cultivation, of accurate truth and real erudition and beauty, not vaguely but methodically interpreted, one has some of the sensations of the moral and intellectual hot-house. Mental hygiene is apt to lead to mental valetudinarianism. "The ignorant journalist" may be left to the torment which George Eliot wished that she could inflict on one of those literary slovens whose manuscripts bring even the most philosophic editor to the point of exasperation: "I should like to stick red-hot skewers through the writer, whose style is as sprawling as his handwriting." By all means. But much that even the most sympathetic reader finds repellent in George Eliot's later works might perhaps never have been, if Mr. Lewes had not practiced with more than Russian rigour a censorship of the press and the post office which kept every disagreeable whisper scrupulously from her ear. To stop every draft with sandbags, screens, and curtains, and to limit one's exercise to a drive in a well-warmed brougham with the windows drawn up, may save a few annoying colds in the head, but the end of the process will be the manufacture of an invalid.

Whatever view we may take of the precise connection between what she read, or abstained from reading, and what she wrote, no studious man or woman can look without admiration and envy on the breadth, variety, seriousness, and energy, with which she set herself her tasks and executed them. She says in one of her letters, "there is something more piteous almost than soapless poverty in the application of feminine incapacity to literature" (ii. 16). Nobody has ever taken the responsibilities of literature more ardently in earnest. She was accustomed to read aloud to Mr. Lewes three hours a day, and her private reading, except when she was engaged in the actual stress of composition, must have filled as many more. His extraordinary alacrity and her brooding intensity of mind, prevented these hours from being that leisurely process in slippers and easy chair which passes with many for the practice of literary cultivation. Much of her reading was for the direct purposes of her own work. The young lady who begins to write historic novels out of her own head will find something much to her advantage if she will refer to the lists of books read by George Eliot during the latter half of 1861, when she was meditating *Romola* (ii. 325). Apart from immediate needs and uses, no student of our time has known better the solace, the delight, the guidance that abide in great writings. Nobody who did not share the scholar's enthusiasm could have described the blind scholar in his library in the adorable fifth chapter of *Romola;* and we feel that she must have copied out with keen gusto of her own those words of Petrarch which she puts into old Bardo's mouth—"Libri medullitus delectant, colloquuntur, consulunt, et viva quadam nobis atque arguta familiaritate junguntur."*

As for books that are not books, as Milton bade us do with "neat repasts with wine," she wisely spared to interpose them oft. Her standards of knowledge were those of the erudite and the savant, and even in the region of beauty she was never content with any but definite impressions. In one place in these volumes, by the way, she makes a remark curiously inconsistent with the usual scientific attitude of her mind. She has been reading Darwin's *Origin of Species,* on which she makes the truly astonishing criticism that it is "sadly wanting in illustrative facts," and that "it is not impressive from want of luminous and orderly presentation" (ii. 43–48). Then she says that "the development theory, and all other explanation of processes by which things came to be produce a feeble impression compared with the mystery that lies under processes." This position it does not now concern us to discuss, but at least it is in singular descrepancy with her strong habitual preference for accurate and quantitative knowledge, over vague and misty moods in the region of the unknowable and the unreachable.

George Eliot's means of access to books were very full. She knew French, German, Italian, and Spanish accurately. Greek and Latin, Mr. Cross tells us, she could read with thorough delight to herself; though after the appalling specimen of Mill's juvenile Latinity that Mr. Bain has disinterred, the fastidious collegian may be sceptical of the scholarship of prodigies. Hebrew was her favourite study to the end of her days. People commonly supposed that she had been inoculated with an artificial taste for science by her companion. We now learn that she took a

* "Books thoroughly delight, converse, counsel, and are united with us by a kind of living and lively friendship"—ed.

decided interest in natural science long before she made Mr. Lewes's acquaintance, and many of the roundabout pedantries that displeased people in her latest writings, and were set down to his account, appeared in her composition before she had ever exchanged a word with him.

All who knew her well enough were aware that she had what Mr. Cross describes as "limitless persistency in application." This is an old account of genius, but nobody illustrates more effectively the infinite capacity of taking pains. In reading, in looking at pictures, in playing difficult music, in talking, she was equally importunate in the search, and equally insistent on mastery. Her faculty of sustained concentration was part of her immense intellectual power. "Continuous thought did not fatigue her. She could keep her mind on the stretch hour after hour; the body might give way, but the brain remained unwearied" (iii. 422). It is only a trifling illustration of the infection of her indefatigable quality of taking pains, that Lewes should have formed the important habit of re-writing every page of his work, even of short articles for Reviews, before letting it go to the press. The journal shows what sore pain and travail composition was to her. She wrote the last volume of *Adam Bede* in six weeks; she "could not help writing it fast, because it was written under the stress of emotion." But what a prodigious contrast between her pace, and Walter Scott's twelve volumes a year! Like many other people of powerful brains, she united strong and clear general retentiveness, with a weak and untrustworthy verbal memory. "She never could trust herself to write a quotation without verifying it." "What courage and patience," she says of some one else, "are wanted for every life that aims to produce anything," and her own existence was one long and painful sermon on that text.

Over few lives have the clouds of mental dejection hung in such heavy unmoving banks. Nearly every chapter is strewn with melancholy words. "I cannot help thinking more of your illness than of the pleasure in prospect—according to my foolish nature, which is always prone to live in past pain." The same sentiment is the mournful refrain that runs through all. Her first resounding triumph, the success of *Adam Bede,* instead of buoyancy and exultation, only adds a fresh sense of the weight upon her future life. "The self-questioning whether my nature will be able to meet the heavy demands upon it, both of personal duty and intellectual production—presses upon me almost continually in a way that prevents me even from tasting the quiet joy I might have in the *work done*. I feel no regret that the fame, as such, brings no pleasure; buit it *is* a grief to me that I do not constantly feel strong in thankfulness that my past life has vindicated its uses."

Romola seems to have been composed in constant gloom. "I remember my wife telling me, at Witley," says Mr. Cross, "how cruelly she had suffered at Dorking from working under a leaden weight at this time. The writing of *Romola* ploughed into her more than any of her other books. She told me she could put her finger on it as marking a well-defined transition in her life. In her own words, 'I began it a young woman—I finished it an old woman.' " She calls upon herself to make "greater efforts against indolence and the despondency that comes from too egoistic a dread of failure." "This is the last entry I mean to make in my old book in which I wrote for the first time at Geneva in 1849. What moments of despair I passed through after that—despair that life would ever be made precious to me by the consciousness that I lived to some good purpose! It was that sort of despair that sucked away the sap of half the hours which might have been filled by energetic youthful activity; and the same demon tries to get hold of me again whenever an old work is dismissed, and a new one is being meditated" (ii. 307). One day the entry is: "Horrible scepticism about all things paralysing my mind. Shall I ever be good for anything again? Ever do anything again?" On another, she describes herself to a trusted friend as "a mind morbidly desponding, and a consciousness tending more and more to consist in memories of error and imperfection rather than in a strengthening sense of achievement." We have to turn to such books as Bunyan's *Grace Abounding* to find any parallel to such wretchedness.

Times were not wanting when the sun strove to shine through the gloom, when the resistance to melancholy was not wholly a failure, and when, as she says, she felt that Dante was right in condemning to the Stygian marsh those who had been sad under the blessed sunlight. "Sad were we in the sweet air that is gladdened by the sun, bearing sluggish smoke in our hearts; now lie we sadly here in the black ooze." But still for the most part sad she remained in the sweet air, and the look of pain that haunted her eyes and brow even in her most genial and animated moments, only told too truly the story of her inner life.

That from this central gloom a shadow should spread to her work was unavoidable. It would be rash to compare George Eliot with Tacitus, with Dante, with Pascal. A novelist—for as a poet, after trying hard to think otherwise, most of us find her magnificent but unreadable—as a novelist bound by the conditions of her art to deal in a thousand trivialities of human character and situation, she has none of their severity of form. But she alone of moderns has their note of sharp-cut melancholy, of sombre rumination, of brief disdain. Living in a time when humanity has been raised, whether formally or informally, into a religion, she draws a painted curtain of pity before the tragic scene. Still the attentive ear catches from time to time the accents of an unrelenting voice, that proves her kindred with those three mighty spirits and stern monitors of men. In George Eliot, a reader with a conscience may be reminded of the saying that when a man opens Tacitus he puts himself in the confessional. She was no vague dreamer over the folly and the weakness of men, and the cruelty and blindness of destiny. Hers is not the dejection of the poet who "could lie down like a tired child, And weep away this life of care," as Shelley at Naples; nor is it the despairing misery that moved Cowper in the awful verses of the *Castaway*. It was not such self-pity as wrung from Burns the cry to life, "Thou art a galling load, Along, a rough, a weary road, To wretches such as I;" nor such general sense of the woes of the race as made Keats think of the world as a place where men sit and hear each other groan, "Where but to think is to be full of sorrow, And leaden-eyed despairs." She was as far removed from the plangent reverie of Rousseau as from the savage truculence of Swift. Intellectual training had given her the spirit of order and proportion, of definiteness and measure, and this marks her alike from the great sentimentalists and the sweeping satirists. "Pity and fairness," as she beautifully says (iii. 317), "are two little words which, carried out, would embrace the utmost delicacies of the moral life." But hers is not seldom the severe fairness of the judge, and the pity that may go with putting on the black cap after a conviction for high treason. In the midst of many an easy flowing page, the reader is surprised by some bitter aside, some judgment of intense and concentrated irony with the flash of a blade in it, some biting sentence where lurks the stern disdain and the anger of Tacitus, and Dante, and Pascal. Souls like these are not born for happiness.

This is not the occasion for an elaborate discussion of George Eliot's place in the mental history of her time, but her biography shows that she travelled along the road that was trodden by not a few in her day. She started from that fervid evangelicalism which had made the base of many a powerful character in this century, from Cardinal Newman downwards. Then with curious rapidity she threw it all off, and embraced with equal zeal the rather harsh and crude negations which were then associated with the *Westminster Review*. The second stage did not last much longer than the first. "Religious and moral sympathy with the historical life of man," she said (ii. 363), "is the larger half of culture;" and this sympathy, which was the fruit of her culture, had by the time she was thirty become the new seed of a positive faith and a semi-conservative creed. Here is a passage from a letter of 1862 (she had translated Strauss, we may remind ourselves, in 1845, and Feuerbach in 1854) :—

> Pray don't ask me ever again not to rob a man of his religious belief, as if you thought my mind tended to such robbery. I have too profound a conviction of the efficacy that lies in all sincere faith, and the spiritual blight that comes with no-faith, to have any negative propagandism in me. In fact, I have very little sympathy with Freethinkers as a class, and have lost all interest in mere antagonism to religious doctrines. I care only to know, if possible, the lasting meaning that lies in all religious doctrine from the beginning till now. [ii. 243.]

Eleven years later the same tendency had deepened and gone further:—

> All the great religions of the world, historically considered, are rightly the objects of deep reverence and sympathy—they are the record of spiritual struggles, which are the types of our own. This is to me preeminently true of Hebrewism and Christianity,

on which my own youth was nourished. And in this sense I have no antagonism towards any religious belief, but a strong outflow of sympathy. Every community met to worship the highest Good (which is understood to be expressed by God) carries me along in its main current; and if there were not reasons against my following such an inclination, I should go to church or chapel, constantly, for the sake of the delightful emotions of fellowship which come over me in religious assemblies—the very nature of such assemblies being the recognition of a binding belief or spiritual law, which is to lift us into willing obedience, and save us from the slavery of unregulated passion or impulse. And with regard to other people, it seems to me that those who have no definite conviction which constitutes a protesting faith, may often more beneficially cherish the good within them and be better members of society by a conformity based on the recognised good in the public belief, than by a nonconformity which has nothing but negatives to utter. *Not*, of course, if the conformity would be accompanied by a consciousness of hypocrisy. That is a question for the individual conscience to settle. But there is enough to be said on the different points of view from which conformity may be regarded, to hinder a ready judgment against those who continue to conform after ceasing to believe in the ordinary sense. But with the utmost largeness of allowance for the difficulty of deciding in special cases, it must remain true that the highest lot is to have definite beliefs about which you feel that 'necessity is laid upon you' to declare them, as something better which you are bound to try and give to those who have the worse. [iii. 215–17.]

These volumes contain many passages in the same sense—as, of course, her books contain them too. She was a constant reader of the Bible, and the *Imitatio* was never far from her hand. "She particularly enjoyed reading aloud some of the finest chapters of Isaiah, Jeremiah, and St. Paul's Epistles. The Bible and our elder English poets best suited the organ-like tones of her voice, which required for their full effect a certain solemnity and majesty of rhythm." She once expressed to a younger friend, who shared her opinions, her sense of the loss which they had in being unable to practise the old ordinances of family prayer. "I hope," she says, "we are well out of that phase in which the most philosophic view of the past was held to be a smiling survey of human folly, and when the wisest man was supposed to be one who could sympathise with no age but the age to come" (ii. 308).

For this wise reaction she was no doubt partially indebted, as so many others have been, to the teaching of Comte. Unquestionably the fundamental ideas had come into her mind at a much earlier period, when, for example, she was reading Mr. R. W. Mackay's *Progress of the Intellect* (1850, i. 253). But it was Comte who enabled her to systematise these ideas, and to give them that "definiteness," which, as these pages show in a hundred places, was the quality that she sought before all others alike in men and their thoughts. She always remained at a respectful distance from complete adherence to Comte's scheme, but she was never tired of protesting that he was a really great thinker, that his famous survey of the Middle Ages in the fifth volume of the *Positive Philosophy* was full of luminous ideas, and that she had thankfully learned much from it. Wordsworth, again, was dear to her in no small degree on the strength of such passages as that from the *Prelude,* which is the motto of one of the last chapters of her last novel:—

> The human nature with which I felt
> That I belonged and reverenced with love,
> Was not a persistent presence, but a spirit
> Diffused through time and space, with aid derived
> Of evidence from monuments, erect,
> Prostrate, or leaning towards their common rest
> In earth, *the widely scattered wreck sublime*
> *Of vanished nations.*

Or this again, also from the *Prelude,* (see iii. 389):—

> There is
> One great society alone on earth:
> The noble Living and the noble Dead.

Underneath this growth and diversity of opinion we see George Eliot's oneness of character, just, for that matter, as we see it in Mill's long and grave march from the uncompromising denials instilled into him by his father, then through Wordsworthian mysticism and Coleridgean conservatism, down to the pale belief and dim starlight faith of his posthumous volume. George Eliot was more austere, more unflinching, and of ruder intellectual constancy than Mill. She never withdrew from the position that she had taken up, of denying and rejecting; she stood to that to the end: what she did was to advance to the far higher perception that denial and rejection are not the aspects best worth attending to or dwelling upon. She had little patience with those who fear that the doctrine of protoplasm must dry up the springs of human effort. Any one who trembles at that catastrophe may profit by a powerful remonstrance of hers in the pages before us (iii. 245–50, also 228).

> The consideration of molecular physics is not the direct ground of human love and moral action, any more than it is the direct means of composing a noble picture or of enjoying great music. One might as well hope to dissect one's own body and be merry in doing it, as take molecular physics (in which you must banish from your field of view what is specifically human) to be your dominant guide, your determiner of motives, in what is solely human. That every study has its bearing on every other is true; but pain and relief, love and sorrow, have their peculiar history which make an experience and knowledge over and above the swing of atoms.
>
> With regard to the pains and limitations of one's personal lot, I suppose there is not a single man, or woman, who has not more or less need of that stoical resignation which is often a hidden heroism, or who, in considering his or her past history, is not aware that it has been cruelly affected by the ignorant or selfish action of some fellow-being in a more or less close relation of life. And to my mind, there can be no stronger motive, than this perception, to an energetic effort that the lives nearest to us shall not suffer in a like manner from *us*.
>
> As to duration and the way in which it affects your view of the human history, what is really the difference to your imagination between infinitude and billions when you have to consider the value of human experience? Will you say that since your life has a term of threescore years and ten, it was really a matter of indifference whether you were a cripple with a wretched skin disease, or an active creature with a mind at large for the enjoyment of knowledge, and with a nature which has attracted others to you?

For herself, she remained in the position described in one of her letters in 1860 (ii. 283):—"I have faith in the working out of higher possibilities than the Catholic or any other Church has presented; and those who have strength to wait and endure are bound to accept no formula which their whole souls—their intellect, as well as their emotions—do not embrace with entire reverence. The highest calling and election is *to do without opium,* and live through all our pain with conscious, clear-eyed endurance." She would never accept the common optimism. As she says here:—"Life, though a good to men on the whole, is a doubtful good to many, and to some not a good at all. To my thought it is a source of constant mental distortion to make the denial of this a part of religion—to go on pretending things are better than they are."

Of the afflicting dealings with the world of spirits, which in those days were comparatively limited to the untutored minds of America, but which since have come to exert so singular a fascination for some of the most brilliant of George Eliot's younger friends (see iii. 204), she thought as any sensible Philistine among us persists in thinking to this day:—

> If it were another spirit aping Charlotte Brontë—if here and there at rare spots and among people of a certain temperament, or even at many spots and among people of all temperaments, tricksy spirits are liable to rise as a sort of earth-bubbles and set furniture in movement, and tell things which we either know already or should be as well without knowing—I must frankly confess that I have but a feeble interest in these doings, feeling my life very short for the supreme and awful revelations of a more orderly and intelligible kind which I shall die with an imperfect knowledge of. If there were miserable spirits whom we could help—then I think we should pause and have patience with their trivial-mindedness; but otherwise I don't feel bound to study them more than I am bound to study the special follies of a peculiar phase of human society. Others, who feel differently, and are attracted towards this study, are making an experiment for us as to whether anything better than bewilderment can come of it. At present it seems to me that to rest any fundamental part of religion on such a basis is a melancholy misguidance of men's minds from the true sources of high and pure emotion. [iii. 161.]

The period of George Eliot's productions was from 1856, the date of her first stories, down to 1876, when she wrote, not under brightest star, her last novel of *Daniel Deronda.* During this

time the great literary influences of the epoch immediately pre-
ceding had not indeed fallen silent, but the most fruitful seed
had been sown. Carlyle's *Sartor* (1833–34), and his *Miscellaneous Essays* (collected, 1839), were in all hands; but he had
fallen into the terrible slough of his Prussian history (1858–65),
and the last word of his evangel had gone forth to all whom it
concerned. *In Memoriam,* whose noble music and deep-browed
thought awoke such new and wide response in men's hearts, was
published in 1850. The second volume of *Modern Painters,* of
which I have heard George Eliot say, as of *In Memoriam* too,
that she owed much and very much to it, belongs to an earlier
date still (1846), and when it appeared, though George Eliot was
born in the same year as its author, she was still translating Strauss
at Coventry. Mr. Browning, for whose genius she had such admiration, and who was always so good a friend, did indeed produce during this period some work which the adepts find as full
of power and beauty as any that ever came from his pen. But Mr.
Browning's genius has moved rather apart from the general
currents of his time, creating character and working out motives
from within, undisturbed by transient shadows from the passing
questions and answers of the day.

The romantic movement was then upon its fall. The great
Oxford movement, which besides its purely ecclesiastical effects,
had linked English religion once more to human history, and
which was itself one of the unexpected outcomes of the romantic
movement, had spent its original force, and no longer interested
the stronger minds among the rising generation. The hour had
sounded for the scientific movement. In 1859 was published the
Origin of Species, undoubtedly the most far-reaching agency of
the time, supported as it was by a volume of new knowledge
which came pouring in from many sides. The same period saw
the important speculations of Mr. Spencer, whose influence on
George Eliot had from their first acquaintance been of a very
decisive kind. Two years after the *Origin of Species* came Maine's
Ancient Law, and that was followed by the accumulations of Mr.
Tylor and others, exhibiting order and fixed correlation among
great sets of facts which had hitherto lain in that cheerful chaos
of general knowledge which has been called general ignorance.
The excitement was immense. Evolution, development, heredity,

adaptation, variety, survival, natural selection, were so many patent pass-keys that were to open every chamber.

George Eliot's novels, as they were the imaginative application of this great influx of new ideas, so they fitted in with the moods which those ideas had called up. "My function," she said (iii. 330), "is that of the æsthetic, not the doctrinal teacher—the rousing of the nobler emotions which make mankind desire the social right, not the prescribing of special measures, concerning which the artistic mind, however strongly moved by social sympathy, is often not the best judge." Her influence in this direction over serious and impressionable minds was great indeed. The spirit of her art exactly harmonised with the new thoughts that were shaking the world of her contemporaries. Other artists had drawn their pictures with a strong ethical background, but she gave a finer colour and a more spacious air to her ethics, by showing the individual passions and emotions of her characters, their adventures and their fortunes, as evolving themselves from long series of antecedent causes, and bound up with many widely operating forces and distant events. Here, too, we find ourselves in the full stream of evolution, heredity, survival, and fixed inexorable law.

This scientific quality of her work may be considered to have stood in the way of her own aim. That the nobler emotions roused by her writings tend to "make mankind desire the social right," is not to be doubted; that we are not sure that she imparts peculiar energy to the desire. What she kindles is not a very strenuous, aggressive, and operative desire. The sense of the iron limitations that are set to improvement in present and future by inexorable forces of the past, is stronger in her than any intrepid resolution to press on to whatever improvement may chance to be within reach if we only make the attempt. In energy, in inspiration, in the kindling of living faith in social effort, George Sand, not to speak of Mazzini, takes a far higher place.

It was certainly not the business of an artist to form judgments in the sphere of practical politics, but George Eliot was far too humane a nature not to be deeply moved by momentous events as they passed. Yet her observations, at any rate after 1848, seldom show that energy of sympathy of which we have been speaking, and these observations illustrate our point. We can hardly think that anything was ever said about the great civil war in America, so curiously far-fetched as the following reflection:—"My best consolation is that an example on so tremendous a scale of the need for the education of mankind through the affections and sentiments, as a basis for true development, will have a strong influence on all thinkers, and be a check to the arid narrow antagonism which in some quarters is held to be the only form of liberal thought" (ii. 335).

In 1848, as we have said, she felt the hopes of the hour in all their fulness. To a friend she writes (i. 179):—

> You and Carlyle (have you seen his article in last week's *Examiner?*) are the only two people who feel just as I would have them—who can glory in what is actually great and beautiful without putting forth any cold reservations and incredulities to save their credit for wisdom. I am all the more delighted with your enthusiasm because I didn't expect it. I feared that you lacked revolutionary ardour. But no—you are just as *sans-culottish* and rash as I would have you. You are not one of those sages whose reason keeps so tight a rein on their emotions that they are too constantly occupied in calculating consequences to rejoice in any great manifestation of the forces that underlie our everyday existence.
>
> I thought we had fallen on such evil days that we were to see no really great movement—that ours was what St. Simon calls a purely critical epoch, not at all an organic one; but I begin to be glad of my date. I would consent, however, to have a year clipt off my life for the sake of witnessing such a scene as that of the men of the barricades bowing to the image of Christ, "who first taught fraternity to men." One trembles to look into every fresh newspaper lest there should be something to mar the picture; but hitherto even the scoffing newspaper critics have been compelled into a tone of genuine respect for the French people and the Provisional Government. Lamartine can act a poem if he cannot write one of the very first order. I hope that beautiful face given to him in the pictorial newspaper is really his: it is worthy of an aureole. I have little patience with people who can find time to pity Louis Philippe and his moustachioed sons. Certainly our decayed monarchs should be pensioned off: we should have a hospital for them, or a sort of zoological garden, where these worn-out humbugs may be preserved. It is but justice that we should keep them, since we have spoiled them for any

honest trade. Let them sit on soft cushions, and have their dinner regularly, but, for heaven's sake, preserve me from sentimentalising over a pampered old man when the earth has its millions of unfed souls and bodies. Surely he is not so Ahab-like as to wish that the revolution had been deferred till his son's days: and I think the shades of the Stuarts would have some reason to complain if the Bourbons, who are so little better than they, had been allowed to reign much longer.

The hopes of '48 were not very accurately fulfilled, and in George Eliot they never came to life again. Yet in social things we may be sure that undying hope is the secret of vision.

There is a passage of Coleridge's *Friend* which seems to represent the outcome of George Eliot's teaching on most, and not the worst, of her readers:—"The tangle of delusions," says Coleridge, "which stifled and distorted the growing tree of our well-being has been torn away; the parasite weeds that fed on its very roots have been plucked up with a salutary violence. To us there remain only quiet duties, the constant care, the gradual improvement, the cautious and unhazardous labours of the industrious though contented gardener—to prune, to strengthen, to engraft, and one by one to remove from its leaves and fresh shoots the slug and the caterpillar." Coleridge goes further than George Eliot, when he adds the exhortation—"Far be it from us to under-value with light and senseless detraction the conscientious hardihood of our predecessors, or even to condemn in them that vehemence to which the blessings it won for us leave us now neither temptation nor pretext."

George Eliot disliked vehemence more and more as her work advanced. The word "crudity," so frequently on her lips, stood for all that was objectionable and distasteful. The conservatism of an artistic moral nature was shocked by the seeming peril to which priceless moral elements of human character were exposed by the energumens of progress. Their impatient hopes for the present appeared to her rather unscientific; their disregard of the past, very irreverent and impious. Mill had the same feeling when he disgusted his father by standing up for Wordsworth, on the ground that Wordsworth was helping to keep alive in human nature elements which utilitarians and innovators would need when their present and particular work was done. Mill, being free from the exaltations that make the artist, kept a truer balance. His famous pair of essays on Bentham and Coleridge were published (for the first time, so far as our generation was concerned) in the same year as *Adam Bede,* and I can vividly remember how the "Coleridge" first awoke in many of us, who were then youths at Oxford, that sense of truth having many mansions, and that desire and power of sympathy with the past, with the positive bases of the social fabric, and with the value of Permanence in States, which form the reputable side of all conservatisms. This sentiment and conviction never took richer or more mature form than in the best work of George Eliot, and her stories lighted up with a fervid glow the truths that minds of another type had just brought to the surface. It was this that made her a great moral force at that epoch, especially for all who were capable by intellectual training of standing at her point of view. We even, as I have said, tried hard to love her poetry, but the effort has ended less in love than in a very distant homage to the majestic in intention and the sonorous in execution. In fiction, too, as the years go by, we begin to crave more fancy, illusion, enchantment, than the quality of her genius allowed. But the loftiness of her character is abiding, and it passes nobly through the ordeal of an honest biography. "For the lessons," says the fine critic already quoted, "most imperatively needed by the mass of men, the lessons of deliberate kindness, of careful truth, of unwavering endeavour,—for these plain themes one could not ask a more convincing teacher than she whom we are commemorating now. Everything in her aspect and presence was in keeping with the bent of her soul. The deeply-lined face, the too marked and massive features, were united with an air of delicate refinement, which in one way was the more impressive because it seemed to proceed so entirely from within. Nay, the inward beauty would sometimes quite transform the external harshness; there would be moments when the thin hands that entwined themselves in their eagerness, the earnest figure that bowed forward to speak and hear, the deep gaze moving from one face to another with a grave appeal,—all these seemed the transparent symbols that showed the presence of a wise, benignant soul." As a wise, benignant soul George Eliot will still remain for all right-judging men and women.

On Pattison's Memoirs

To reckon the subject of this volume among leading minds who have stamped a deep influence on our generation, is not possible even to the friendliest partiality. That was not his position, and nobody could be less likely than he would himself have been to claim it. Pattison started no new problem. His name is associated with no fertile speculation, and with no work of the first degree of importance. Nor was he any more intended for a practical leader than for an intellectual discoverer. He did not belong to the class of authoritative men who are born to give decisions from the chair. Measured by any standard commensurate to his remarkable faculties, Pattison's life would be generally regarded as pale, negative, and ineffectual. Nevertheless, it is undeniable that he had a certain singular quality about him that made his society more interesting, more piquant, and more sapid than that of many men of a far wider importance and more commanding achievement.

Critics have spoken of his learning, but the description is only relatively accurate. Of him, in this respect, we may say, what he said of Erasmus. "Erasmus, though justly styled by Muretus, *eruditus sane vir ac multæ lectionis,** was not a learned man in the

Memoirs. By Mark Pattison, late Rector of Lincoln College, Oxford. London, 1885. [This essay was first published in *Macmillan's Magazine*, 51 (April 1885):446–61, and was reprinted in *Critical Miscellanies*, vol. 3 (London, 1886)—ed.]

* "a very erudite and well-read man"—ed.

special sense of the word—not an *érudit*. He was the man of letters. He did not make a study apart of antiquity for its own sake, but used it as an instrument of culture." The result of culture in Pattison's actual life was not by any means ideal. For instance, he was head of a college for nearly a quarter of a century, and except as a decorative figurehead with a high literary reputation, he did little more to advance the working interests of his college during these five-and-twenty years, than if he had been one of the venerable academic abuses of the worst days before reform. But his temperament, his reading, his recoil from Catholicism, combined with the strong reflective powers bestowed upon him by nature to produce a personality that was unlike other people, and infinitely more curious and salient than many who had a firmer grasp of the art of right living. In an age of effusion to be reserved, and in days of universal professions of sympathy to show a saturnine front, was to be an original. There was nobody in whose company one felt so much of the ineffable comfort of being quite safe against an attack of platitude. There was nobody on whom one might so surely count in the course of an hour's talk for some stroke of irony or pungent suggestion, or, at the worst, some significant, admonitory, and almost luminous manifestation of the great *ars tacendi*. In spite of his copious and ordered knowledge, Pattison could hardly be said to have an affluent mind. He did not impart intellectual direction like Mill, nor morally impress himself like George Eliot. Even in pithy humour he was inferior to Bagehot, who was certainly one of the most remarkable of the secondary figures of our generation. But he made everyone aware of contact with the reality of a living intelligence. It was evident that he had no designs upon you. He was not thinking of shaking a conviction, nor even of surprising admiration.

Everlasting neutrality, no doubt, may soon become a tiresome affectation. But we can afford to spare a few moments from our solid day to the Sage, if we are so lucky as to hit upon one; always provided that he be not of those whom La Bruyère has described as being made into sages by a certain natural mediocrity of mind. Whatever else may be said of Pattison, at least he was never mediocre, never vapid, trite, or common. Nor was he one of those false pretenders to the judicial mind, who "mistake for sober sense And wise reserve, the plea of indolence." On the contrary, his industry and spirit of laborious acquisition were his best credentials. He was invested to our young imaginations with the attraction of the literary explorer, who had "voyaged through strange seas of thought alone," had traversed broad continents of knowledge, had ransacked all the wisdom of printed books, and had by native courage and resource saved himself from the engulfing waters of the great Movement.

The Memoirs of such a man may not be one of the monuments of literature. His little volume is not one of those romantic histories of the soul, from the Confessions of Augustine to the Confessions of Jean Jacques, by which men and women have been beguiled, enlightened, or inspired in their pilgrimage. It is not one of those idealised and highly embellished versions of an actual existence, with which such superb artists as George Sand, Quinet, and Renan have delighted people of good literary taste. What the Rector has done is to deliver a tolerably plain and unvarnished tale of the advance of a peculiar type of mind along a path of its own, in days of intellectual storm and stress. It stirs no depths, it gives no powerful stimulus to the desire after either knowledge or virtue—in a word, it does not belong to the literature of edification. But it is an instructive account of a curious character, and contains valuable hints for more than one important chapter in the mental history of the century.

Mark Pattison, born in 1813, passed his youthful days at the rectory of Hauxwell, a village in Wensleydale, on the edge of the great uplands that stretch northwards towards Richmond and Barnard Castle, and form an outwork of the Pennine range and the backbone of northern England. The scene has been described in that biography of his Sister Dora, which he here so unceremoniously despatches as a romance.

> Hauxwell is a tiny village lying on the southern slope of a hill, from whence an extensive view of the moors and Wensleydale is obtained. It contains between two and three hundred inhabitants. The rectory is a pretty little dwelling, some half-mile from the church, which is a fine old building much shut in by trees. The whole village, even on a bright summer day, gives the traveller an impression of intense quiet, if not of dullness; but in winter, when the snow lies thickly for weeks together in the narrow lane, the only thoroughfare of the place; when the distant

moors also look cold in their garment of white, and the large expanse of sky is covered with leaden-coloured clouds; when the very streams with which the country abounds are frozen into silence—then indeed may Hauxwell be called a lonely village.

Pattison's father had been educated, badly enough, at Brasenose, but though his own literary instincts were of the slightest, he had social ambition enough to destine his son from the first to go to Oxford and become the fellow of a college. But nothing systematic was done towards making the desired consummation a certainty or even a probability. The youth read enormously, but he did not remember a tenth of what he read, nor did he even take in the sense of half of it as he went along. "Books as books," he says, "were my delight, irrespective of their contents. I was already marked out for the life of a student, yet little that was in the books I read seemed to find its way into my mind." He found time for much besides reading. He delighted in riding, in shooting rooks in the Hall rookery, and in fishing for trout with clumsy tackle and worm. Passion for country sports was followed by passion for natural history in the ordinary shape of the boy's fancy for collecting insects and observing birds. He fell in with White's *Natural History of Selborne,* read it over and over again, and knew it by heart.

> The love of birds, moths, butterflies, led on to the love of landscape; and altogether, in the course of the next six or seven years, grew and merged in a conscious and declared poetical sentiment, and a devoted reading of the poets. I don't suppose the temperament was more inclined to æsthetic emotions in me than in other youths; but I was highly nervous and delicate, and having never been at school had not had sentiment and delicacy crushed out of me; also, living on the borderland of oak woods, with green lanes before me, and an expanse of wild heather extending into Northumberland behind, I was favourably placed for imbibing a knowledge by contrast of the physical features of England. My eye was formed to take in at a glance, and to receive delight from contemplating, as a whole, a hill and valley formation. Geology did not come in till ten years later to complete the cycle of thought, and to give that intellectual foundation which is required to make the testimony of the eye, roaming over an undulating surface, fruitful and satisfying. When I came in after years to read *The Prelude* I recognised, as if it were my own

history which was being told, the steps by which the love of the country-boy for his hills and moors grew into poetical suscepti-bility for all imaginative presentations of beauty in every direc-tion. [Pp. 34, 35.]

Perhaps it may be added that this was a preparation for some-thing more than merely poetical susceptibility. By substituting for the definite intellectual impressions of a systematic education, vague sensibilities as the foundation of character, this growth of sentiment, delicacy, and feeling for imaginative presentations of beauty, laid him peculiarly open to the religious influences that were awaiting him in days to come at Oxford.

In 1832 Pattison went up as a freshman at Oriel. His career as an undergraduate was externally distinguished by nothing un-common, and promised nothing remarkable. He describes him-self as shy, awkward, boorish, and mentally shapeless and inert. In 1833, however, he felt what he describes as the first stirrings of intellectual life within him. "Hitherto I have had no mind, prop-erly so-called, merely a boy's intelligence, receptive of anything I read or heard. I now awoke to the new idea of finding the reason of things; I began to suspect that I might have much to unlearn, as well as to learn, and that I must clear my mind of much current opinion which had lodged there. The principle of rationalism was born in me, and once born it was sure to grow, and to be-come the master idea of the whole process of self-education on which I was from this time forward embarked." In other words, if he could have interpreted and classified his own intellectual type, he would have known that it was the Reflective. Reflection is a faculty that ripens slowly; the prelude of its maturity is often a dull and apparently numb-witted youth. Though Pattison con-ceived his ideal at the age of twenty, he was five-and-forty before he finally and deliberately embraced it and shaped his life in conformity to it. The principle of rationalism, instead of grow-ing, seemed for twelve whole years to go under, and to be com-pletely mastered by the antagonistic principles of authority, tradi-tion, and transcendental faith.

The secret is to be found in what is the key to Pattison's whole existence, and of what he was more conscious at first than he seems to have been in later days. He was affected from first to last by a profound weakness of will and character. Few men of

eminence have ever lived so destitute of nerve as Pattison was—
of nerve for the ordinary demands of life, and of nerve for those
large enterprises in literature for which by talent and attainment
he was so admirably qualified. The stamp of moral *défaillance*
was set upon his brow from the beginning. It was something
deeper in its roots than the temporary self-consciousness of the
adolescent, that afflicted him in his early days at Oxford. The shy
and stiff undergraduate is a familiar type enough, and Pattison
is not the only youth of twenty of whom such an account as his
own is true:—

> This inability to apprehend the reason of my social ill-success
> had a discouraging consequence upon the growth of my character.
> I was so convinced that the fault was in me, and not in the others,
> that I lost anything like firm footing, and succumbed to or imi-
> tated any type, or set, with which I was brought in contact, es-
> teeming it better than my own, of which I was too ashamed to
> stand by it and assert it. Any rough, rude, self-confident fellow,
> who spoke out what he thought and felt, cowed me, and I yielded
> to him, and even assented to him, not with that yielding which
> gives way for peace' sake, secretly thinking itself right, but with a
> surrender of the convictions to his mode of thinking, as being
> better than my own, more like men, more like the world. [P. 48.]

This fatal trait remained unalterable to the very end, but as
time went on, things grew worse. Nobody knows what deliberate
impotence means who has not chanced to sit upon a committee
with Pattison. Whatever the business in hand might be, you
might be sure that he started with the firm conviction that you
could not possibly arrive at the journey's end. It seemed as if the
one great principle of his life was that the Sons of Zeruiah must
be too hard for us, and that nobody but a simpleton or a fanatic
would expect anything else. "With a manner," he says of himself,
"which I believe suggested conceit, I had really a very low estimate of myself as compared with others. I could echo what
Bishop Stanley says of himself in his journal: 'My greatest obstacle to success in life has been a want of confidence in myself,
under a doubt whether I really was possessed of talents on a par
with those around me.'" Very late in life, talking to Mr. Morison, he said in his pensive way, "Yes, let us take our worst opinion of ourselves in our most depressed mood. Extract the cube

root of that, and you will be getting near the common opinion of your merits."

He describes another side of the same overspreading infirmity when he is explaining why it was always impossible for him ever to be anything but a Liberal. "The restlessness of critical faculty," he says, "has done me good service when turned upon myself. *I have never enjoyed any self-satisfaction in anything I have ever done,* for I have inevitably made a mental comparison with how it might have been better done. The motto of one of my diaries, 'Quicquid his operis fiat pœnitet'* may be said to be the motto of my life" (p. 254). A man who enters the battle on the back of a charger that has been hamstrung in this way, is predestined to defeat. A frequent access of dejection, self-abasement, distrust, often goes with a character that is energetic, persevering, effective, and reasonably happy. To men of strenuous temper it is no paradox to say that a fit of depression is often a form of repose. It was D'Alembert, one of the busiest of the workers of a busy century, who said this, or something to this effect—that low spirits are only a particular name for the mood in which we see our aims and acts for what they really are. Pattison's case was very different. With him, except for a very few short years, despair was a system and an unreasoned pessimism the most rooted assurance of his being. He tells a thoroughly characteristic story of himself in his days as an undergraduate. He was on the coach between Birmingham and Sheffield. Two men shared the front seat with him, and conversed during the whole of the journey about the things which he was yearning to know and to learn. "I tried once or twice to put in my oar, but it was a failure: I was too far below their level of knowledge; I relapsed into enchanted listening. I thought to myself, 'There exists there such a world, but I am shut out of it, not by the accidents of college, but by my own unfitness to enter.' " (p. 148). Mankind suffers much from brassy incompetency and over-complacency, but Pattison is only one of many examples how much more it may lose in a man who has ability, but no fight and no mastery in him. As we have all been told, in this world a man must be either anvil or hammer, and it always seems as if Pattison deliberately chose to be anvil—not merely in

* "Whatever work this one may do he is displeased with"—ed.

the shape of a renunciation of the delusive pomps and vanities of life, but in the truly questionable sense of doubting both whether he could do anything, and whether he even owed anything to the world in which he found himself.

The earliest launch was a disappointment. He had set his heart upon a first class, but he had not gone to work in the right way. Instead of concentrating his attention on the task in hand, he could only in later days look back with amazement "at the fatuity of his arrangements and the snail-like progress with which he seemed to be satisfied." He was content if, on his final review of Thucydides, he got through twenty or thirty chapters a day, and he re-read Sophocles "at the lazy rate of a hundred and fifty lines a day, instead of going over the difficult places only, which might have been done in a week." There must, he says, "have been idleness to boot, but it is difficult to draw the line between idleness and dawdling over work. I dawdled from a mixture of mental infirmity, bad habit, and the necessity of thoroughness if I was to understand, and not merely remember." The dangerous delights of literary dispersion and dissipation attracted him. Among his books of recreation was Johnson's *Lives of the Poets.* "This I took in slowly, page by page, as if by an instinct; but here was a congenial subject, to which, when free, I would return, and where I would set up my habitation."

It was probably a reminiscence of these vacations at Hauxwell that inspired the beautiful passage in his *Milton,* where he contrasts the frosty *Ode to the Nativity* with the *Allegro and Penseroso.* "The two idylls," he says, "breathe the free air of spring and summer and of the fields round Horton. They are thoroughly naturalistic; the choicest expression of our language has yet found of the fresh charm of country life, not as that life is lived by the peasant, but as it is felt by a young and lettered student, issuing at early dawn or at sunset from his chamber and his books. All such sights and sounds and smells are here blended in that ineffable combination which, once or twice perhaps in our lives has saluted our young senses before their perceptions were blunted by alcohol, by lust, or ambition, or diluted by the social distractions of great cities." (Pattison's *Milton,* 24).

For the examination school no preparation could have been worse. It was no wonder that so uncalculating an adjustment of means and ends resulted in a second class (1836). The class was not merely a misfortune in itself, but threatened to be a bar to the fulfilment of his lifelong dream of a fellowship. He tried his fortunes at University, where he was beaten by Faber; and at Oriel, his own college, where he was beaten by the present Dean of St. Paul's. "There was such a moral beauty about Church," it was said by a man not peculiarly sensitive about moral beauty, "that they could not help liking him." Though Pattison had failed, Newman sent him word that there were some who thought that he had done the best. He made two more unsuccessful attempts, in one of them the triumphant competitor being Stanley, the famous Dean of a later day. At last, in November, 1838, he was elected to a Yorkshire fellowship at Lincoln College. "No moment in all my life," he says, "has ever been so sweet as that Friday morning, when Radford's servant came in to announce my election, and to claim his five shillings for doing so." Yet if the curtain of fate could have been raised, his election to the Lincoln fellowship might have disclosed itself as the central misfortune of his life.

"All this while," he says, "I was rushing into the whirlpool of Tractarianism; was very much noticed by Newman—in fact fanaticism was laying its deadly grip around me." He had come up from Yorkshire with what he calls his "home Puritan religion almost narrowed to two points—fear of God's wrath and faith in the doctrine of the Atonement." He found Newman and his allies actively dissolving this hard creed by means of historical, philosophical, and religious elements which they summed up in the idea of the Church. This idea of the Church, as Pattison truly says, and as men so far removed from sympathy with dogma as J. S. Mill always admitted, "was a widening of the horizon." In another place (*Mind*), the Rector shows the stages of speculation in Oxford during the present century. From 1800 or 1810 to 1830, the break-up of the old lethargy took the form of a vague intellectualism; free movement, but blind groping out of the mists of insular prejudice in which reaction against the French Revolution had wrapped us. Then came the second period from 1830 to 1845. Tractarianism was primarily a religious movement; it was a revival of the Church spirit which had been dormant since the expiry of Jacobitism at the accession of George III. But it rested on a conception, however imperfect, of universal history;

and it even sought a basis for belief in a philosophic exposition of the principle of authority.

Pattison, like most of the superior minds then at Oxford, was not only attracted, but thoroughly overmastered by this great tide of thought. He worked at the Lives of the Saints, paid a visit to the cloisters at Littlemore, and was one of Newman's closest disciples, though he thinks it possible that Newman even then, with that curious instinct which so often marks the religious soul, had a scent of his latent rationalism. A female cousin, who eventually went over to Rome, counted for something among the influences that drove him into "frantic Puseyism." When the great secession came in 1845, Pattison somehow held back and was saved for a further development. Though he appeared to all intents and purposes as much of a Catholic at heart as Newman or any of them, it was probably his constitutional incapacity for heroic and decisive courses that made him, according to the Oxford legend, miss the omnibus. The first notion of the Church had expanded itself beyond the limits of the Anglican Communion, and been transformed into the wider idea of the Catholic Church. This in time underwent a further expansion.

> Now the idea of the Catholic Church is only a mode of conceiving the dealings of divine Providence with the whole race of mankind. Reflection on the history and condition of humanity, taken as a whole, gradually convinced me that this theory of the relation of all living beings to the Supreme Being was too narrow and inadequate. It makes an equal Providence, the Father of all, care only for a mere handful of species, leaving the rest (such is the theory) to the chances of eternal misery. If God interferes at all to procure the happiness of mankind, it must be on a far more comprehensive scale than by providing for them a Church of which far the majority of them will never hear. It was on this line of thought, the details of which I need not pursue, that I passed out of the Catholic phase, but slowly, and in many years, to that highest development when all religions appear in their historical light as efforts of the human spirit to come to an understanding with that Unseen Power whose pressure it feels, but whose motives are a riddle. Thus Catholicism dropped off me as another husk which I had outgrown. [Pp. 327–28.]

So a marked epoch came to its close, and this was one of the many forms in which the great Anglican impulse expended itself. While Newman and others sank their own individuality in religious devotion to authority and tradition, Pusey turned what had been discussion into controversy, and from a theologian became a powerful ecclesiastical manager. Others dropped their religious interests, and cultivated cynicism and letters. The railway mania, the political outbursts of 1848, utilitarian liberalism, all in turn swept over the Oxford field, and obliterated the old sanctuaries. Pattison went his own way alone. The time came when he looked back upon religion with some of the angry contempt with which George Eliot makes Bardo, the blind old humanist of the fifteenth century, speak of his son, who had left learning and liberal pursuits, "that he might lash himself and howl at midnight with besotted friars—that he might go wandering on pilgrimages befitting men who knew no past older than the missal and the crucifix."

It is a critical moment in life when middle age awakens a man from the illusions that have been crowning the earlier years with inward glory. Some are contemptuously willing to let the vision and the dream pass into easy oblivion, while they hasten to make up for lost time in close pursuit of the main chance. Others can forgive anything sooner than their own exploded ideal, and the ghost of their dead enthusiasm haunts them with an embittering presence. Pattison drops a good many expressions about his Anglo-Catholic days, that betray something like vindictiveness— which is certainly not philosophical, whatever else it was. But his intellectual faculties were too strong to let him feed on the poison of a reactionary antipathy to a deserted faith. Puseyism, as he says, dropped away from him for lack of nutrition of the religious brain,—which perhaps at the best was more like an artificial limb than a natural organ in a man of Pattison's constitution. For some five years he was inspired by a new and more genuine enthusiasm —for forming and influencing the minds of the young. He found that he was the possessor of what for lack of a better name he calls a magnetic power in dealing with the students, and his moral ascendency enabled him to make Lincoln the best managed college in Oxford.

From 1848 to 1851 he describes his absorption in the work of the college as complete. It excluded all other thoughts. In November that incident occurred which he calls the catastrophe of his life. The headship of the college fell vacant, and for several weeks he was led to believe that this valuable prize was within his grasp. At first the invincible diffidence of his nature made it hard for him to realise that exaltation so splendid was possible. But the prospect once opened, fastened with a fatally violent hold upon his imagination. The fellows of Lincoln College, who were the electors, were at that time a terribly degraded body. The majority of them were no more capable of caring for literature, knowledge, education, books, or learning than Squire Western or Commodore Trunnion. One of them, says Pattison, had been reduced by thirty years of the Lincoln common-room to a torpor almost childish. Another was "a wretched *crétin* of the name of Gibbs, who was always glad to come and booze at the college port a week or two when his vote was wanted in support of college abuses." The description of a third, who still survives, is veiled by editorial charity behind significant asterisks. That Pattison should be popular with such a gang was impossible. Such an Alceste was a standing nuisance and reproach to the rustic Acastes and Clitandres of the Lincoln bursary. They might have tolerated his intellect and overlooked his industry, if his intellect and his industry had not spoiled his sociability. But irony and the *ars tacendi* are not favourite ingredients in the boon companion. Pattison never stayed in the common-room later than eight in the evening, and a man was no better than a skeleton at a feast who left good fellows for the sake of going over an essay with a pupil, instead of taking a hand at whist or helping them through another bottle.

We need not follow the details of the story. Pattison has told them over again with a minuteness and a sourness that show how the shabby business rankled in his soul to the very last. It was no battle of giants, like the immortal Thirty Years' War between Bentley and the Fellows of Trinity. The election at Lincoln College, which was a scandal in the university for many a long day after, was simply a tissue of paltry machinations, in which weakness, cunning, spite, and a fair spice of downright lying showed that a learned society, even of clergymen, may seethe and boil with the passions of the very refuse of humanity. Intricate and unclean intrigues ended, by a curious turn of the wheel, in the election of a grotesque divine, whom Pattison, with an energy of phrase that recalls the amenities of ecclesiastical controversy in the sixteenth century, roundly designates in so many words as a satyr, a ruffian, and a wild beast. The poor man was certainly illiterate and boorish to a degree that was a standing marvel to all ingenuous youths who came up to Lincoln College between 1850 and 1860. His manners, bearing, and accomplishments were more fitted for the porter of a workhouse than for the head of a college. But he served the turn by keeping out Pattison's rival, and whatever discredit he brought upon the society must be shared by those who, with Pattison at their head, brought him in against a better man. All this unsavoury story might as well have been left where it was.

The reaction was incredibly severe. There has been nothing equal to it since the days of the Psalmist were consumed like smoke, and his heart was withered like grass. "My mental forces," says Pattison, "were paralysed by the shock; a blank, dumb despair filled me; a chronic heartache took possession of me, perceptible even through sleep. As consciousness gradually returned in the morning, it was only to bring with it a livelier sense of the cruelty of the situation into which I had been brought." He lay in bed until ten o'clock every morning, to prolong the semi-oblivion of sleep. Work was impossible. If he read, it was without any object beyond semi-forgetfulness. He was too much benumbed and stupefied to calculate the future. He went through the forms of lecturing, but the life and spirit were gone. Teaching became as odious to him as it had once been delightful. His Satan, as he calls the most active of the enemies who had thus ruined his paradise, planned new operations against him, by trying, on the grounds of some neglected formality, to oust him from his fellowship. "Here," cries Pattison, "was a new abyss opened beneath my feet! My bare livelihood, for I had nothing except my fellowship to live upon, was threatened; it seemed not unlikely that I should be turned into the streets to starve. Visitatorial law, what it might contain! It loomed before me like an Indian jungle, out of which might issue venomous reptiles, man-eating tigers, for my destruction."

This is not the language of half-humorous exaggeration, but a literal account of a mind as much overthrown from its true balance, as is disclosed in the most morbid page of Rousseau's

Confessions. For months and months after, the burden of "dull, insensible wretchedness," "bitter heartache," weighed upon him with unabated oppression. More than a year after the catastrophe the sombre entries still figure in his diary:—"Very weary and wretched both yesterday and to-day: all the savour of life is departed:"—"Very wretched all yesterday and to-day: dull, gloomy, blank; sleep itself is turned to sorrow." Nearly two whole years after, the same clouds still blacken the sky. "I have nothing to which I look forward with any satisfaction: no prospects; my life seems to have come to an end, my strength gone, my energies paralysed, and all my hopes dispersed."

It is true that frustrated ambition was not the only key to this frightfully abject abasement. We may readily believe him when he says that the personal disappointment was a minor ingredient in the total of mental suffering that he was now undergoing. His whole heart and pride had in the last few years been invested in the success of the college; it was the thing on which he had set all his affections; in a fortnight the foundation of his work was broken up; and the wretched and deteriorated condition of the undergraduates became as poison in his daily cup. That may all be true enough. Still, whatever elements of a generous public spirit sharply baffled may have entered into this extraordinary moral breakdown, it must be pronounced a painfully unmanly and unedifying exhibition. It says a great deal for the Rector's honesty and sincerity in these pages, that he should not have shrunk from giving so faithful and prominent an account of a weakness and a self-abandonment which he knew well enough that the world will only excuse in two circumstances. The world forgives almost anything to a man in the crisis of a sore spiritual wrestle for faith and vision and an Everlasting Yea; and almost anything to one prostrated by the shock of an irreparable personal bereavement. But that anybody with character of common healthiness should founder and make shipwreck of his life because two or three unclean creatures had played him a trick after their kind, is as incredible as that a three-decker should go down in a street puddle.

It will not do to say that lack of fortitude is a mark of the man of letters. To measure Pattison's astounding collapse, we have a right to recall Johnson, Scott, Carlyle, and a host of smaller men, whom no vexations, chagrins, and perversities of fate could daunt from fighting the battle out. Pattison was thirty-eight when he missed the headship of his college. Diderot was about the same age when the torments against which he had struggled for the best part of twenty arduous years in his gigantic task seemed to reach the very climax of distraction. "My dear master," he wrote to Voltaire, in words which it is a refreshment under the circumstances to recall and to transcribe, "my dear master, I am over forty. I am tired out with tricks and shufflings. I cry from morning till night for rest, rest; and scarcely a day passes when I am not tempted to go and live in obscurity and die in peace in the depths of my old country. Be useful to men! Is it certain that one does more than amuse them, and that there is much difference between the philosopher and the flute player? They listen to one and the other with pleasure or with disdain, and they remain just what they were. But there is more spleen than sense in all this, I know—and back I go to the Encyclopædia." And back he went— that is the great point—with courage unabated and indomitable, labouring with sword in one hand and trowel in the other, until he had set the last stone on his enormous fabric.

Several years went by before Pattison's mind recovered spring and equilibrium, and the unstrung nerves were restored to energy. Fishing, the open air, solitude, scenery, slowly repaired the moral ravages of the college election. The fly rod "was precisely the resource of which my wounded nature stood in need." About the middle of April, after long and anxious preparation of rods and tackle, with a box of hooks and a store of tobacco, he used to set out for the north. He fished the streams of Uredale and Swaledale; thence he pushed on to the Eden and the waters of the Border, to Perthshire, to Loch Maree, Gairloch, Skye, and the far north. When September came, he set off for rambles in Germany. He travelled on foot, delighting in the discovery of nooks and corners that were not mentioned in the guidebooks. Then he would return to his rooms in college, and live among his books. To the undergraduates of that day he was a solemn and mysterious figure. He spoke to no one, saluted no one, and kept his eyes steadily fixed on infinite space. He dined at the high table, but uttered no word. He never played the part of host, nor did he ever seem to be a guest. He read the service in chapel when his turn came; his voice had a creaking and impassive tone, and his pace was too deliberate to please young men with a morning appetite. As he says here, he was a complete stranger in the college. We looked upon him with the awe proper to one who was supposed to combine boundless erudition with an impenetrable misanthropy. In reading the fourth book of the Ethics, we regarded the description of the High-souled Man, with his slow movements, his deep tones, his deliberate speech, his irony, his contempt for human things, and all the rest of the paraphernalia of that most singular personage, as the model of the inscrutable sage in the rooms under the clock. Pattison was understood to be the Megalopsuchos in the flesh. It would have been better for him if he could have realised the truth of the healthy maxim that nobody is ever either so happy or so unhappy as he thinks. He would have been wiser if he could have seen the force in the monition of Goethe:—

> Willst du dir ein hübsch Leben zimmern,
> Must ums Vergangne dich nicht bekümmern,
> Und wäre dir auch was verloren,
> Musst immer thun wie neu geboren;
> Was jeder Tag will, sollst du fragen,
> Was jeder Tag will, wird er sagen;
> Musst dich an eignem Thun ergetzen,
> Was andre thun, das wirst du schätzen;
> Besonders keinen Menschen hassen,
> Und das Uebrige Gott überlassen."
> [*Zahme Xenien, iv.*]

> *Wouldst fashion for thyself a seemly life?—*
> *Then fret not over what is past and gone;*
> *And spite of all thou mayst have lost behind*
> *Yet act as if thy life were just begun:*
> *What each day wills, enough for thee to know,*
> *What each day wills, the day itself will tell;*
> *Do thine own task, and be therewith content,*
> *What others do, that shalt thou fairly judge;*
> *Be sure that thou no brother mortal hate.*
> *And all besides leave to the master Power.*

At length "the years of defeat and despair," as he calls them, came to an end, though "the mental and moral deterioration" that belonged to them left heavy traces to the very close of his life. He took a lively interest in the discussions that were stirred by the famous University Commission, and contributed ideas to the subject of academic reform on more sides than one. But such matters he found desultory and unsatisfying; he was in a state of famine; his mind was suffering, not growing; he was becoming brooding, melancholy, taciturn, and finally pessimist (pp. 306–7). Pattison was five-and-forty before he reached the conception of what became his final ideal, as it had been in a slightly different shape his first and earliest. He had always been a voracious reader. When "the flood of the Tractarian infatuation" broke over him, he naturally concentrated his studies on the Fathers and on Church History. That phase, in his own term, took eight years out of his life. Then for five years more he was absorbed in teaching and forming the young mind. The catastrophe came, and for five or six years after that he still remained far below "the pure and unselfish conception of the life of the true student, which dawned upon him afterwards, and which Goethe, it seems, already possessed at thirty." Up to this time—the year 1857, or a little later—his aims, and thoughts had been, in his own violent phrase, polluted and disfigured by literary ambition. He had felt the desire to be before the world as a writer, and had hitherto shared "the vulgar fallacy that a literary life meant a life devoted to the making of books." "It cost me years more of extrication of thought before I rose to *the conception that the highest life is the art to live,* and that both men, women, and books are equally essential ingredients of such a life" (p. 310).

We may notice in passing, what any one will see for himself, that in contrasting his new conception so triumphantly with the vulgar fallacy from which he had shaken himself free, the Rector went very near to begging the question. When Carlyle, in the strength of his reaction against morbid introspective Byronism; cried aloud to all men in their several vocations, *"Produce, produce; be it but the infinitesimallest product, produce,"* he meant to include production as an element inside the art of living, and an indispensable part and parcel of it. The making of books may or may not belong to the art of living. It depends upon the faculty and gift of the individual. It would have been more philosophical if, instead of ranking the life of study for its own sake above the life of composition and the preparation for composition, Pattison had been content with saying that some men have the impulse towards literary production, while in others the impulse is strongest for acquisition, and that he found out one day that nature had placed him in the latter and rarer class. It is no case of ethical or intellectual superiority, as he fondly supposed, but only diversity of gift.

We must turn to the volume on Casaubon for a fuller interpretation of the oracle. "The scholar," says the author, "is greater than his books. The result of his labours is not so many thousand pages in folio, but himself. . . . Learning is a peculiar compound of memory, imagination, scientific habit, accurate observation, all concentrated, through a prolonged period, on the analysis of the remains of literature. The result of this sustained mental endeavour is not a book, but a man. It cannot be embodied in print, it consists in the living word. True learning does not consist in the possession of a stock of facts—the merit of a dictionary—but in the discerning spirit, a power of appreciation, *judicium* as it was called in the sixteenth century—which is the result of the possession of a stock of facts."

The great object, then, is to bring the mind into such a condition of training and cultivation that it shall be a perfect mirror of past times, and of the present, so far as the incompleteness of the present will permit, "in true outline and proportion." Mommsen, Grote, Droysen, fall short of the ideal, because they drugged ancient history with modern politics. The Jesuit learning of the sixteenth century was sham learning, because it was tainted with the interested motives of Church patriotism. To search antiquity with polemical objects in view, is destructive of "that equilibrium of the reason, the imagination, and the taste, that even temper of philosophical calm, that singleness of purpose," which were all required for Pattison's ideal scholar. The active man has his uses, he sometimes, but never very cheerfully, admits. Those who at the opening of the seventeenth century, fought in literature, in the council-chamber, in the field, against the Church revival of their day, may be counted among worthies and benefactors. "But for all this, it remains true, that in the intellectual sphere grasp and mastery are incompatible with the exigencies of a struggle."

The reader will hardly retain gravity of feature before the self-indulgent, self-deceiving sophistication of a canon, which actually excludes from grasp and mastery in the intellectual sphere, Dante, Milton, and Burke. Pattison repeats in his closing pages his lamentable refrain that the author of *Paradise Lost* should have forsaken poetry for more than twenty years "for a noisy pamphlet brawl, and the unworthy drudgery of Secretary to the Council Board" (p. 332). He had said the same thing in twenty places in his book on Milton. He transcribes unmoved the great poet's account of his own state of mind, after the physicians had warned him that if he persisted in using his remaining eye for his pamphlet, he would lose that too. "The choice lay before me," says Milton, "between dereliction of a supreme duty and loss of eyesight: in such a case I could not listen to the physician, not if Æsculapius himself had spoken from his sanctuary. I could not but obey that inward monitor, I knew not what, that spake to me from heaven. I considered with myself that many had purchased less good with worse ill, as they who give their lives to reap only glory, and I therefore concluded to employ the little remaining eyesight I was to enjoy in doing this, the greatest service to the common weal it was in my power to render." And so he wrote the *Second Defence,* and yet lived long enough, and preserved sublimity of imagination enough, to write the *Paradise Lost* as well. Mr. Goldwin Smith goes nearer the mark than the Rector when he insists that "the tension and elevation which Milton's nature had undergone in the mighty struggle, together with the heroic dedication of his faculties to the most serious objects, must have had not a little to do both with the final choice of his subject and with the tone of his poem. 'The great Puritan epic' could hardly have been written by any one but a militant Puritan" (*Lectures and Essays*). In the last page of his *Memoirs,* Pattison taxes the poet with being carried away by the aims of "a party whose aims he idealised." As if the highest fruitfulness of intellect were ever reached without this generous faculty of idealisation, which Pattison, here and always, viewed with such icy coldness. Napoleon used to say that what was most fatal to a general was a knack of combining objects into pictures. A good officer, he said, never makes pictures; he sees objects, as through a field-glass, exactly as they are. In the art of war let us take

Napoleon's word for this; but in "the art to live," a man who dreads to idealise aims or to make pictures, who can think of nothing finer than being what Aristotle calls αὐθέκαστος,* or taking everything literally for what it is, will sooner or later find his faculties benumbed and his work narrowed to something for which nobody but himself will care, and for which he will not himself always care with any sincerity or depth of interest.

Let us take another illustration of the false exclusiveness of the definition, in which Pattison erected a peculiar constitutional idiosyncrasy into a complete and final law for the life literary. He used to contend that in many respects the most admirable literary figure of the eighteenth century was the poet Gray. Gray, he would say, never thought that devotion to letters meant the making of books. He gave himself up for the most part to ceaseless observation and acquisition. By travelling, reading, noting, with a patient industry that would not allow itself to be diverted or perturbed, he sought and gained the discerning spirit and the power of appreciation which make not a book but a man. He annotated the volumes that he read with judgment; he kept botanical calendars and thermometrical registers; he had a lively curiosity all round; and, in Gray's own words, he deemed it a sufficient object of his studies to know, wherever he was, what lay within reach that was worth seeing—whether building, ruin, park, garden, prospect, picture, or monument—to whom it had ever belonged, and what had been the characteristic and taste of different ages. "Turn author," said Gray, "and straightway you expose yourself to pit, boxes, and gallery: any coxcomb in the world may come in and hiss if he pleases; ay, and what is almost as bad, clap too, and you cannot hinder him."

Nobody will be inclined to quarrel with Gray's way of passing his life, and the poet who has produced so exquisite a masterpiece as the Elegy had a fair right to spend the rest of his days as he pleased. But the temptations to confound a finnicking dilettantism with the "art to live" are so strong, that it is worth while to correct the Rector's admiration for Gray by looking on another picture—one of Gray's most famous contemporaries, who in variety of interest and breadth of acquired knowledge

* "one who calls things by their right names"—ed.

was certainly not inferior to him, but enormously his superior. Lessing died when he was fifty-two (1729–81); his life was two years shorter than Gray's (1716–71), and nearly twenty years shorter than Pattison's (1813–84). The Rector would have been the last man to deny that the author of *Laoköon* and the *Wolfenbüttel Fragments* abounded in the discerning spirit and the power of appreciation. Yet Lessing was one of the most incessantly productive minds of his age. In art, in religion, in literature, in the drama, in the whole field of criticism, he launched ideas of sovereign importance, both for his own and following times, and in *Nathan the Wise* the truest and best mind of the eighteenth century found its gravest and noblest voice. Well might George Eliot at the Berlin theatre feel her heart swelling and the tears coming into her eyes, as she "listened to the noble words of dear Lessing, whose great spirit lives immortally in this crowning work of his" (*Life*). Yet so far were "grasp and mastery" from being incompatible with the exigencies of a struggle, that the varied, supple, and splendid powers of Lessing were exercised from first to last in an atmosphere of controversy. Instead of delicately nursing the theoretic life in the luxury of the academic cloister, he was forced to work like a slave upon the most uncongenial tasks for a very modest share of daily bread. "I only wished to have things like other men," he said in a phrase of pathetic simplicity, at the end of his few short months of wedded happiness; "I have had but sorry success." Harassed by small persecutions, beset by paltry debts, passing months in loneliness and in indigence, he was yet so possessed, not indeed by the winged dæmon of poetic creation, but by the irrepressible impulse and energy of production, that the power of his intellect triumphed over every obstacle, and made him one of the greatest forces in the wide history of European literature. Our whole heart goes out to a man who thus, in spite alike of his own impetuous stumbles and the blind buffets of unrelenting fate, yet persevered to the last in laborious, honest, spontaneous, and almost artless fidelity to the use of his talent, and after each repulse only came on the more eagerly to "live and act and serve the future hours." It was Lessing and not Rousseau whom Carlyle ought to have taken for his type of the Hero as Man of Letters.

The present writer will not be suspected of the presumption of hinting or implying that Pattison himself was a *dilettante,* or any-think like one. There never was a more impertinent blunder than when people professed to identify the shrewdest and most widely competent critic of his day with the Mr. Casaubon of the novel, and his absurd Key to all Mythologies. The Rector's standard of equipment was the highest of our time. "A critic's education," he said, "is not complete till he has in his mind a conception of the successive phases of thought and feeling from the beginning of letters. Though he need not read every book, he must have surveyed literature in its totality. Partial knowledge of literature is no knowledge" (*Fortnightly Review,* Nov., 1877, p. 670). For a man to know his way about in the world of printed books, to find the key to knowledge, to learn the map of literature, "requires a long apprenticeship. This is a point few men can hope to reach much before the age of forty" (*Milton*).

There was no dilettantism here. And one must say much more than that. Many of those in whom the love of knowledge is live-liest, omit from their curiosity that part of knowledge which is, to say the least of it, as interesting as all the rest—insight, namely, into the motives, character, conduct, doctrines, fortunes of the individual man. It was not so with Pattison. He was essentially a bookman, but of that high type—the only type that is worthy of a spark of our admiration—which explores through books the voyages of the human reason, the shifting impulses of the human heart, the chequered fortunes of great human conceptions. Pattison knew that he is very poorly equipped for the art of criticism who has not trained himself in the observant analysis of character, and has not realised that the writer who seeks to give richness, body, and flavour to his work must not linger exclusively among texts or abstract ideas or general movements or literary effects, but must tell us something about the moral and intellectual configuration of those with whom he deals. I had transcribed, for an example, his account of Erasmus, but the article is growing long, and the reader may find it for himself in the *Encyclopædia Britannica.*

Though nobody was ever much less of a man of the world in one sense, yet Pattison's mind was always in the world. In company he often looked as if he were thinking of the futility of dinner-party dialectics, where all goes too fast for truth, where people miss one another's points and their own, where nobody convinces or is convinced, and where there is much surface excite-ment with little real stimulation. That so shrewd a man should have seen so obvious a fact as all this was certain. But he knew that the world is the real thing, that the proper study of mankind is man, and that if books must be counted more instructive and nourishing than affairs, as he thought them to be, it is still only because they are the most complete record of what is permanent, elevated, and eternal in the mind and act of man. Study with him did not mean the compilation of careful abstracts of books, nor did it even mean the historic filiation of thoughts and beliefs. It was the building up before the mind's eye of definite concep-tions as to what manner of men had been bred by the diversified agencies of human history, and how given thoughts had shaped the progress of the race. This is what, among other things, led him to spend so much time on the circle of Pope, and Addison and Swift.

We have let fall a phrase about the progress of the race, but it hardly had a place in Pattison's own vocabulary. "While the advances," he said, "made by objective science and its industrial applications are palpable and undeniable everywhere around us, it is a matter of doubt and dispute if our social and moral advance towards happiness and virtue has been great or any." The selfish-ness of mankind might seem to be a constant quantity, neither much abated nor much increased since history began. Italy and France are in most material points not more civilised than they were in the second century of our era. The reign of law and justice has no doubt extended into the reign of hyperborean ice and over Sarmatian plains: but then Spain has relapsed into a double barbarism by engrafting Catholic superstition upon Iberian ferocity. If we look Eastward, we see a horde of bar-barians in occupation of the garden of the Old World, not as settlers, but as destroyers (*Age of Reason,* in *Fortnightly Review,* March, 1877, 357–61).

The same prepossessions led him to think that all the true things had been said, and one could do no better than hunt them up again for new uses. Our business was, like Old Mortality, to clear out and cut afresh inscriptions that had been made illegible by time and storm. At least this delivered him from the senseless vanity of originality and personal appropriation. We feel sure that if he found that a thought which he had believed to be new had been expressed in literature before, he would have been pleased and not mortified. No reflection of his own could give him half as much satisfaction as an apt citation from some one else. He once complained of the writer of the article on Comte in the *Encyclopædia* for speaking with too much deference as to Comte's personality. "That overweening Franch vanity and egotism not only overshadows great gifts, but impoverishes the character which nourished such a sentiment. It is not one of the weaknesses which we overlook in great men, and which are to go for nothing." Of overweening egotism, Pattison himself at any rate had none. This was partly due to his theory of history, and partly, too, no doubt, to his inborn discouragement of spirit. He always professed to be greatly relieved when an editor assured him that his work was of the quality that might have been expected from him. "Having lived to be sixty-three," he wrote on one of these occasions, "without finding out why the public embrace or reject what is written for their benefit, I presume I shall now never make the discovery." And this was perfectly sincere.

The first draft of his *Life of Milton* was found to exceed the utmost limits of what was possible by some thirty or forty pages. Without a single movement of importunity or complaint he cut off the excess, though it amounted to a considerable fraction of what he had done. "In any case," he said, "it is all on Milton; there is no digression on public affairs, and much which might have gone in with advantage to the completeness of the story, has been entirely passed over, *e.g.,* history of his posthumous fame, Bentley's emendations, *et cetera.*" It almost seemed as if he had a private satisfaction in a literary mishap of this kind: it was an unexpected corroboration of his standing conclusion that this is the most stupid and perverse of all possible worlds.

"My one scheme," he wrote to a friend in 1877, "that of a history of the eighteenth century, having been forestalled by Leslie Stephen, and the collections of years having been rendered useless, I am entirely out of gear, and cannot settle to anything." His correspondent urged the Rector to consider and re-consider. It would be one of the most deplorable misfortunes in literature if he were thus to waste the mature fruit of the study of a lifetime.

It was as unreasonable as if Raphael or Titian had refused to paint a Madonna, simply because other people had painted Madonnas before them. Some subjects, no doubt, were treated once for all; if Southey had written his history of the Peninsular war after Napier, he would have done a silly thing, and his book would have been damned unread. But what reason was there why we should not have half a dozen books on English thought in the eighteenth century? Would not Grote have inflicted a heavy loss upon us, if he had been frightened out of his plan by Thirlwall? And so forth, and so forth. But all such importunities were of no avail. "I have pondered over your letter," Pattison replied, "but without being able to arrive at any resolution of any kind." Of course one knew that in effect temperament had already cast the resolution for him in letters of iron before our eyes.

We are not aware whether any considerable work has been left behind. His first great scheme, as he tells us here (p. 319), was a history of learning from the Renaissance. Then he contracted his views to a history of the French school of Philology, beginning with Budæus and the Delphin classics. Finally, his ambition was narrowed to fragments. The book on *Isaac Casaubon,* published ten years ago, is a definite and valuable literary product. But the great work would have been the vindication of Scaliger, for which he had been getting materials together for thirty years. Many portions, he says, were already written out in their definitive form, and twelve months would have completed it. Alas, a man should not go on trusting until his seventieth year that there is still plenty of daylight. He contributed five biographies to the new edition of the *Encyclopædia Britannica.* The articles, on Bentley, Erasmus, Grotius, More, and Macaulay are from his pen. They are all terse, luminous, and finished, and the only complaint that one can make against them is that our instructor parts company from us too soon. It is a stroke of literary humour after Pattison's own heart that Bentley, the mightiest of English scholars, should fill no more space in the Encyclopædic pantheon than Alford, who was hardly even the mightiest of English deans. But the fault was more probably with the rector's parsimony of words than with the editor. In 1877 he delivered a lecture, afterwards reprinted in one of the reviews, on Books and Critics. It is not without the usual piquancy and the usual cynicism, but he

344

had nothing particular to say, except to tell his audience that a small house is no excuse for absence of books, inasmuch as a set of shelves, thirteen feet by ten, and six inches deep, will accommodate nearly a thousand octavos; and to hint that a man making a thousand a year, who spends less than a pound a week on books, ought to be ashamed of himself. There are some other fugitive pieces scattered in the periodicals of the day. In 1871 and 1872 he published editions on the *Essay on Man* and *The Satires and Epistles* of Pope. Ten years before that he had been at last elected to the headship of his college, but the old enthusiasm for influencing young minds was dead. We have spoken of the Rector's timidity and impotence in practical things. Yet it is fair to remember the persevering courage with which he pleaded one unpopular cause. As Mr. Morison said not long ago in these pages, his writings on university organisation, the most important of which appeared in 1868, are a noble monument of patient zeal in the cause for which he cared most. "Pattison never lost heart, never ceased holding up his ideal of what a university should be, viz., a metropolis of learning in which would be collected and grouped into their various faculties the best scholars and *savants* the country could produce, all working with generous emulation to increase the merit and renown of their chairs. If England ever does obtain such a university, it will be in no small measure to Pattison that she will owe it."

Yet when the record is completed, it falls short of what might have been expected from one with so many natural endowments, such unrivalled opportunities, such undoubted sincerity of interest. Pattison had none of what so much delighted Carlyle in Ram-Dass, the Hindoo man-god. When asked what he meant to do for the sins of men, Ram-Dass at once made answer that he had fire enough in his belly to burn up all the sins of the world. Of this abdominal flame Pattison had not a spark. Nor had he that awful sense which no humanism could extinguish in Milton, of service as "ever in the great Taskmaster's eye." Nor had he, finally, that civil and secular enthusiasm which made men like Bentham and Mill into great workers and benefactors of their kind. Pattison was of the mind of Fra Paolo in a letter to Casaubon. "As long as there are men there will be fanaticism. The wisest man has warned us not to expect the world ever to improve so much that the better part of mankind will be the majority. No wise man ever undertakes to correct the disorders of the public estate. He who cannot endure the madness of the public, but goeth about to think he can cure it, is himself no less mad than the rest. So sing to yourself and the muses." The muses never yet inspired with their highest tunes, whether in prose or verse, men of this degree of unfaith.

Matthew Arnold

The first canon in the art of unsophisticated letter-writing is that, just as a speech is intended for hearers rather than for readers, so a letter is meant for the eye of a friend, and not for the world. Even the lurking thought in anticipation of an audience destroys true epistolary charm. This is one reason why stories told in that form, or portions of stories so told, in spite of some famous old-fashioned examples to the contrary, have fallen out of vogue, give but inferior pleasure, and are even found thoroughly tiresome. The very essence of good letter-writing is, in truth, the deliberate exclusion of outsiders, and the full surrender of the writer to the spirit of egotism; amiable, free, light-handed, unpretending, harmless, but still egotism. A French Jesuit once wrote a Latin piece called *Ratio conscribendæ epistolæ,* which the present writer has never read, but which, I hope, contains the indisputable maxim that a good letter, like good talk, must always be an improvisation. The best letters are always improvisations, directly or indirectly, about yourself and your correspondent, and the personal things which you and your correspondent happen to be interested in and to care about. The public breaks the spell.

The great battle between ancients and moderns, which once kindled such wrath among the celestial minds of the day, has

Letters of Matthew Arnold (1848–88). Collected and arranged by George W. E. Russell. 2 vols. Macmillan & Co., 1895. [This essay was first published in *The Nineteenth Century,* 38 (December 1895): 1041–55—ed.]

long been over, and the moderns are understood to have given themselves the literary palm. Yet few will deny that the highest performance in epistolary art is to be sought in the letters of Cicero. Mommsen may tell us as loudly as he will that Cicero had no insight, opinion, nor purpose as a statesman; that he was a thorough dabbler and a short-sighted egotist; that he was by nature a journalist in the worst sense of the term; that his letters may be interesting and clever, so long as they reflect the town and villa life of the world of quality, but when he is thrown on his own resources, as in exile or in Cilicia, they are as stale and empty as ever was the soul of a feuilletoniste banished from the boulevards. All this may or may not be true; but, true or untrue, it does not affect the delight which long generations of educated men have found in these intimate effusions of that expansive, lively, and impressionable nature, in contact with great personages and stirring times, and the master of the most copious and varied style that ever was known since men first learned to write.

Next to Cicero the critics place Madame de Sévigné. Adding to native genius good literary training and the habit of cultivated society, this great woman wrote letters of such rare quality, distinction, and enduring charm, that fourteen volumes of them were the first foundation of that massive and imposing structure, *Les Grands Ecrivains de la France.* No other modern letters that I know of, have risen to the dignity of an established classic of the first rank.

No English writer of letters, as most competent judges are agreed, is comparable to Cowper. His letters fill half a score volumes of Southey's edition, and there is surely no such delightful reading of that kind in our language. This is because they are the genuine outpouring of the writer's own feelings; of all his simplicity, purity, gaiety, despondency, affectionateness, just as mood follows mood, and as this trivial daily incident or that or the other interests or moves a refined, sensitive, gentle, and pure nature. Somebody told him that one of his correspondents found his letters clever, entertaining, and so forth. It stayed his pen. "This foolish vanity," wrote Cowper, in explaining his silence to his friend, "would have spoiled me quite, and would have made me as disgusting a letter-writer as Pope, who seems to have thought that, unless a sentence was well turned, and every period pointed with some conceit, it was not worth the carriage. Accordingly he is to me, except in very few instances, the most disagreeable writer of epistles that ever I met with. I was willing, therefore, to wait till the impression your commendation had made upon the foolish part of me was worn off, that I might scribble away as usual, and write my uppermost thoughts, and those only." (iv. 15).

The famous letters of Horace Walpole, interesting, invaluable as they are for the manners, politics, and general gossip of his age, have no more epistolary charm than a leading article; so self-conscious are they, so affected, artificial, and full of smirking animation. That he had underneath his frivolity and his forced and incessant efforts at satire a firm understanding, or that he may have deserved Carlyle's praise as about the clearest-sighted man of his time, does not affect the proposition that his letters are essentially not letters, but annals composed with a view to ultimate publication, like the letters of Grimm in French, or of Howell in English. The correspondence of Gray with Mason, and with Walpole himself, is for the most part marked by the same evil qualities; it is nearly all written as with printer and publisher before them, and the whole literary and fine world looking over their shoulders. Scott's letters are like all else that came from that brave, manly, whole-hearted genius; they are sincere, unaffected, friendly, cheerful, and humane. "You know I don't care a curse about what I write!" This was the temper to make a good letter-writer. Charles Lamb, of course, has a high rank among the letter-writers of mark and genius, with his inexhaustible vein of whim and drollery, with his many strokes of pathos and tender humour, with the flashes of serious and admirable criticism in the midst of all his quips and jestings. Byron's are undoubtedly the best letters after Cowper, and some may possibly choose to put Byron first; their happy carelessness, their wit, their flash, their boldness, their something dæmonic, all give them a place among the pleasantest and liveliest reading for idle hours to be found in any library, whether English or foreign. In our own day, Mill wrote generous replies to all comers; but they deal with serious subjects, and answer grave riddles propounded to the most patient of oracles. George Eliot's letters have a suspicion of the episcopal charge about them. Emerson to Carlyle is adequate and sufficient, but without much colour or feature. Carlyle to Emerson, and to every other correspondent, has colour and feature enough for a dozen men, and nowhere does the more genial, friendly, and fraternal aspect of him come into pleasanter light. Dickens is observant, graphic, bright, and full of high spirits. The letters and journals of Miss Caroline Fox admit the reader to an enchanting circle of intellectual refinement and spiritual delicacy.

Macaulay's letters and journals are so stamped with the love of literature and the glory of it as the best companionship for a man's life, that, just as Heine said, whenever he read Plutarch, he immediately resolved to take the next mail-post and become a great man, so Macaulay stirs a reader to take a pen on the instant, and immediately write something which the world will never willingly let die.

On the whole, of volumes of letters very recently given to the world, those of Edward Fitzgerald, the translator of Omar Khayyam, seem to have most of the genuine epistolary spirit in them, in association with a true feeling for good books, and the things that good books bring into the mind; with an easy view of human nature; with a kindly eye for the ups and downs of human life, and a clear perception that one of the prime secrets is not to expect more from life than life is capable of giving. One who was an expert connoisseur in good music, who could seriously master strange and hard tongues, could enjoy and judge the weightiest books and the lightest, who was never so happy as in his herring lugger, with a Montaigne on board, or "smoking a pipe every night with a delightful chap who is to be captain," or sailing for hours, days, and weeks on the river Deben, "looking at the crops as they grow green, yellow, russet, and are finally carried away in the red and blue waggons with the sorrel horse"—here was the man who should write, and did write to the friends that he loved, letters that, without his ever meaning or designing it, are not only letters, but agreeable and diverting literature.

What place in this catalogue will ultimately be taken by the two new volumes of the *Letters of Matthew Arnold,* nobody can now decide. Those who looked for a grand literary correspondence, rich in new instruction, fresh inspiration, profound social observation, will be disappointed; and they deserve to be, for Arnold was one of the most occupied men of his time. Those, on the other hand, who had the happiness to count him among faithful and affectionate friends, and to whom his disappearance leaves a truly painful void in familiar haunts and meditative hours—and those others who know his books only, and would wish to know something of his personality—will not be disappointed at all, but will be grateful to the relatives who have consented to give to the world these memorials of a fine genius and a high and most attractive character.

Arnold formally prohibited a biography, and, in view of some excesses perpetrated in that direction within the last few years, we may appreciate his reserve. There are probably not six Englishmen over fifty now living, whose lives need to be written, or should be written; yet, with equal probability, we may guess that nearer sixty than six, *si, ut sapientibus placet, non cum corpore extinguuntur magnæ animæ,* * and, if their shades are suffered to revisit the bookshops, will find themselves the heroes of these elaborate, overdone, disproportioned performances. It was thought, however, that Arnold would not so much object to a collection of letters, and he himself considered George Sand's a good instance of what such a collection should be. Beyond his own family, he was no great correspondent. He was, as I have said, one of the most occupied men of his time; and though busy men are usually, as is well known, the best able to find time to do most, Arnold had no leisure in which to add large promiscuous epistolising in private, to his various duties and performances in public. On principle, moreover, he always thought that the little notes and letters in which many people find such singular pleasure every day of their lives, are a grievous waste of time and a grievous dispersion of spirit. Nor did writing come very easily to him. He had none of the lively and untiring facility of Voltaire, for instance, who was never happy unless he was writing a history, a tragedy, a romance, a satire, a controversial article, graceful and pointed verse, long letters to friends, the pleasantest and most piquant of notes to fine ladies. Of this extraordinary

* "if, as the wise say, great souls are not destroyed with their bodies"—ed.

facility Arnold had none, and he was not of the class of men who would have cared to have it. His letters to his family constitute the bulk of the present volume, and the reader will recognise him in them for what he truly was: as Mr. Russell says, "gentle, generous, enduring, laborious; a devoted husband, a most tender father, an unfailing friend"; and, above all, let us add, a thoroughly good citizen and lover of his country.

Some will think that the editor has given us more letters than were wanted for the purpose which he has so aptly conceived. Most modern books are indeed far too long. The *Agricola* of Tacitus is the imperishable biography in literature, and Agricola does not fill much more than a score of pages of this periodical, just as, according to Mr. Frederic Harrison's computation, all Thucydides does not contain more words than a single copy of the *Times*. Many of us have good ground for some remorse under this head, even the author of a book of mine that happens to be benevolently mentioned in one of these letters. Mr. Russell, however, may reply that, as there was to be no biography, the only way of bringing out the personality of his friend was to print his letters just as they came, and on all sorts of topics, and not to trim them up into anything like an orderly series of discourses. He might say, further, that almost every letter, though the bulk of it may be somewhat trivial or commonplace, yet contains some good thought or phrase. One does not see, however, why the thought or phrase should not stand by itself, though it may be true that the gem looks best in its setting. Perhaps Mr. Russell has erred on the right side, for no age can so little as ours be called *incuriosa suorum ætas:** it may be that two volumes will give twice as much gratification to his public as one; and, after all, the judicious reader always has the remedy in his own hands.

In other respects the editor has done his work with the diligence, judgment, and taste that were to be expected from one endowed with literary conscience and literary faculty, and with a deep and sincere feeling in the business that he was about. He has achieved what he describes as his anxious desire, that "no handiwork of his should impertinently obtrude itself between

* "an age indifferent to its own men"—ed.

the writer and his readers, or obscure the effect of Arnold's unique and fascinating character." One damning sin of omission Mr. Russell has indeed perpetrated: the two volumes have no index, nor even table of contents. In such a book, with its multiplicity of heterogeneous topics touched in no regular order, this is fatal to reference. Unlike some other sins, however, this is not wholly irreparable.

If Mr. Russell found anything in the letters likely to give pain or reasonable offence to living persons—as he probably did not— he has left such things out. Literary or political judgments on contemporaries, as apart from matters personal, he has very properly allowed to stand, much as some of them run counter to the popular verdict of our day. Thackeray is not, to Arnold's thinking, a great writer. The author of the *Angel of the House* is worthy, but mildish. The elevation of Tennyson above Wordsworth is ridiculous. "I do not think Tennyson a great and powerful spirit in any line—as Goethe was in the line of modern thought, Wordsworth in that of contemplation, Byron even in that of passion" (i. 239). Oddly enough, in the same letter (1864) *Enoch Arden* is declared to be very good indeed, "perhaps the best thing Tennyson has done," which is a very hard saying indeed. Of Cicero, "what a pedant is Mommsen, who runs this charming personage down!" (ii. 216). Freeman's school of history "has done much to explore our early history and to throw light on the beginnings of our system of government and of our liberty; but they have not had a single man of genius, with the *étincelle* and the instinctive good sense and moderation which make a guide really attaching and useful. Freeman is an ardent, learned, and honest man; but he is a ferocious pedant, and Stubbs, though not ferocious, is not without his dash of pedantry" (ii. 149).

Politicians fare almost as badly at Arnold's hands as they fare at the hands of one another. Severities are frequently levelled at a statesman whose name Mr. Russell discreetly leaves a blank, but the discerning reader will not be greatly puzzled to fill in the name. Lord Salisbury is a dangerous man, because he only cares for science and for the Church, and fears and dislikes literature; and it is no doubt true that in those days Dr. Pusey and his associates in the University had no fear of science, but in the interests of ecclesiasticism bitterly dreaded literature and philosophy, and very likely their instinct was right. Mr. Disraeli comes better off than anybody else, because he cared for literature, and knew about it, and was interested in those who produced it. The political judgment is appalling: the writer preferred Grant to Lincoln (ii. 349).

Arnold was Liberal, but only in a non-party sense. The Liberal party is always in the wrong, and deserved its great eviction in 1874, "because they had no body of just, clear, well-ordered thought upon politics, and were only superior to the Conservative in not having for their rule of conduct merely the negative instinct against change; now they will have to examine their minds, and find what they really want and mean to try for" (ii. 112). Very true, and by-and-bye, in the fulness of time, the Liberals examined their minds and, taking the advice which Arnold himself so ardently pressed upon his countrymen, they tried to disestablish the Church of England in Wales, and this was followed by a mightier disaster than even in 1874, in spite of twenty-one years of enlightened teaching and preaching from apostles of light. So little way has been made in rousing and impressing "quiet and reasonable opinion in the country" on that matter.

As to Ireland, Arnold had, long before the great evolution of 1886, been exercised by that dire problem. He had written more than one essay of his own upon it, and he had collected and published Burke's writings on Irish affairs. In England and Scotland, he says in one of these letters (ii. 335), government has been conducted in accordance with the wishes of the majority in the respective countries; in Ireland, "government has been conducted in accordance with the wishes of the minority and of the British Philistine." Ireland, he said, has good cause to hate us. Nobody saw the mischief and the active necessity more clearly. The attempt of the Liberal party to meet the necessity in 1886 altogether displeased him. He wrote more than one piece of sharp criticism on that great effort in this *Review,* and he rejoiced in the Ministerial defeat. It gave Lord Salisbury and Lord Hartington, he thinks, an opportunity which, if they missed it now, would never return, of introducing a system of local government of an effective kind for all the three kingdoms, just as Germans, Swiss, and Americans have such a system (ii. 337). Writing to Mrs.

Forster, his sister, two or three months after Mr. Forster's death, he says:—

> I regretted his [Mr. Forster's] expression of general objection to Home Rule, but I know that by this he meant only Home Rule as understood by Parnell. In this country [America], it is supposed that England refuses every kind of Home Rule; and as this is eminently the country of local government, almost everyone goes for Gladstone as the only propounder of a scheme of local government. The moment any politician produces a counter-scheme, free from the great danger of Gladstone's, the separate National Parliament, but giving real powers of local government, opinion here, which is extremely important if for no other reason than that most of Parnell's friends come from America, will undergo a change. The Americans are not really indisposed to England, I believe, but they are not closely informed on Irish matters, and they see no Home Rule proposed but Gladstone's measure. I doubt if Salisbury is disposed, or Hartington laborious enough, to make one; William [Forster] and Goschen together would have been invaluable for this purpose. [ii. 333.]

A stout wall of *non possumus* still blocks the way, and Ireland is still governed, to repeat Arnold's own description, "in accordance with the wishes of the minority and of the British Philistine."

The political and party world was none the worse for the active incursions of a man like Matthew Arnold, and he had the right and the duty of a good citizen to speak his mind about the affairs of the commonwealth. But it is doubtful whether he had much, or even any, influence in that somewhat complicated sphere of things. It fell to me to have to express in the House of Commons, one night shortly after his death, our sense of his services to education, and of the loss of them to the country. It was felt that a proper ceremony had been gone through, but, except for a few of the elect on both sides, the recognition was received with respect, without any particular warmth or comprehension. Direct incursions into questions of party were in fact a departure from the principle of the exhortations so systematically addressed by him, as he says, to his young literary and intellectual friends, not to be rushing into the arena of politics themselves, but "rather to work inwardly upon the predominant force in our politics—

the great middle class—and to cure its spirit."[1] This was the
real task that he had set himself, and his quarrels with the way of
politicians are of no importance. As he says in one of these letters
about another and more renowned of the world's teachers, "What
the English public cannot understand is that a man is a just and
fruitful object of contemplation, much more by virtue of what
spirit he is of, than he is by virtue of what system of doctrine he
elaborates" (i. 179).

Mr. Birrell has put this admirably in the course of what is much
the most acute, just, manly, and felicitous of all the many criticisms of which Arnold has been the subject:

> Liberalism is not a creed, but a frame of mind. Mr. Arnold's
> frame of mind was Liberal. No living man is more deeply per-
> meated with the grand doctrine of Equality than was he. He
> wished to see his countrymen and countrywomen all equal: Jack
> as good as his master, and Jack's master as good as Jack; and
> neither talking clap-trap. He had a hearty un-English dislike of
> anomalies and absurdities. He fully appreciated the French Rev-
> olution, and was consequently a democrat. He was not a democrat
> from irresistible impulse, or from love of mischief, or from
> hatred of priests, or, like the average British workman, from a
> not unnatural desire to get something on account of his share of
> the family inheritance; but all roads lead to Rome, and Mr.
> Arnold was a democrat from a sober and partly sorrowful con-
> viction that no other form of government was possible. He was an
> Educationalist, and Education is the true Leveller. His almost
> passionate cry for better middle-class education arose from his
> annoyance at the exclusion of the large numbers of this great class
> from the best education the country afforded. It was a ticklish job
> telling this great wealthy middle class, which, according to the
> newspapers, had made England what she is and what everybody
> else wished to be—that it was, from an educational point of view,
> beneath contempt.[2]

Arnold says, in a letter to his mother, that in his notions about
the State he was quite his father's son, and his continuator. "I
inherit from him a deep sense of what in the Greek and Roman
world was sound and rational" (i. 226). Yet in the department

---

1. *Nineteenth Century*, May, 1886, p. 645.
2. *Res Judicatæ*, p. 170; 1892.

in which Arnold made a deep mark, he was not quite his father's son. He did not think that his father "thought of the Saxon and Celt mutually needing to be completed by each other; on the contrary, he was so full of the sense of the Celt's vices, want of steadiness, and want of plain truthfulness, vices to him particularly offensive, that he utterly abhorred him and thought him of no good at all. Jane, too, to whom I spoke of this, is clearly of the same opinion, and, indeed, I have not a doubt of it. He thought our rule in Ireland cruel and unjust, no doubt. He was not blind to faults in the Saxon; but can you show me a single line, in all he has written, testifying to his sense of any virtues and graces in the Celt?" (i. 320).

Arnold may have differed from his father about Celt and Saxon, and about a hundred other things, and some of them were important things in the eyes of both of them; but to his father he did no doubt owe that point of fundamental resemblance which made them both take the social view of human life and duty. That Matthew Arnold will live by his verse, and not by his prose, does not affect the fact that the mainspring of his activity was his sense of the use and necessity of England as a great force in the world, and his conviction that she could not exert this force effectively or wisely until her educational system had been vivified, her ideas of conduct and character clarified and widened, and all her standards of enlightenment raised. For this literature was to be the great instrument. But along with literature, organisation.

What is a man of letters? The answer of a French writer may at least serve to show one side of him:—

> The man of letters properly so called is a peculiar being; he does not look at things exactly with his own eyes; he has not merely his own impressions; you could not recover the imagination which was once his; 'tis a tree on which have been grafted Homer, Virgil, Milton, Dante, Petrarch; hence, singular flowers, which are not natural any more than they are artificial. . . . With Homer, he has looked at the plain of Troy, and there lingers in his brain something of the light of the sky of Greece; he has taken something of the pensive beauty of Virgil as he wanders on the Aventine slopes; he sees the world like Milton through the grey mists of England, like Dante through the limpid, burning

sky of Italy. Out of all these colours he makes for himself a new colour that is unique; from all these glasses through which his life passes to reach the real world there is formed a particular tint, which is the imagination of the man of letters.[3]

This natural assimilation of ideal in form and phrase from the great mainsprings of literature, this identification of himself with all that the master-spirits have poured into him from all their sources, is the mark of most, though not of the whole, of Arnold's poetry. What Pattison, who was so much a friend of his and mine, said of the *Allegro* and *Penseroso* is just as true, and even still more true, of more than half of Arnold's poetic work:—"The two idylls breathe the air of spring and summer, and the fields round Horton. They are thoroughly naturalistic: the choicest expression our language has yet found of the charm of country life, not as that life is lived by the peasant, but as it is felt by a young and lettered student, issuing at early dawn or at sunset into the fields from his chamber and his books. All rural sights, and sounds, and smells are here blended in that ineffable combination, which once or twice, perhaps, in our lives has saluted our young senses before their perceptions were blunted by alcohol, by lust, by ambition, or diluted by the social distractions of great cities."

Yet, saturated as he was with literature and the literary spirit, Arnold was never caught by the delusion that literature is an end in itself, apart from life, conduct, character, and all that makes either the base or superstructure of society. Sainte-Beuve was his master, and in the small but sharply outlined vignette of that illustrious writer, which Arnold drew for the *Encyclopedia Britannica,* he quotes some words of Sainte-Beuve that are no bad account of his own temper in these things. Somebody talked of his being tenacious of his literary opinions. "I hold very little," Sainte-Beuve answered, "to literary opinions. Literary opinions occupy very little place in my life and in my thoughts. What does occupy me seriously is life itself, and the object of it." This was exactly Arnold's point of view, and from that point of view he brought the best ideas that literature and wide observation and many standards of comparison could furnish (and an inspector of schools who travelled abroad so much and so systematically as

3. Doudan.

Arnold, has considerable opportunities of large observation of his countrymen, and of the relation of their doings to those of other people) to the furthering of what he conceived to be the full growth of the very roots of national well-being. In that noble and touching passage, where Dante makes Virgil quit the side of his companion for ever, the Master of those who Know tells Dante that now,

> Libero, dritto, e sano è lo tuo arbitrio.

This was the device of all that miscellaneous prose-writing of Arnold's which wearied some, vexed some, and shocked others, ranging over so wide a field, and touching so many things for which men had cared very deeply or cared not at all, to make for wider circles of the community, the springs and the rules of their action and their judgment more free, more true, more sound.

He knew from the first what he was about. In 1863 he wrote: "One cannot change English ideas, so much as, if I live, I hope to change them, without saying imperturbably what one thinks, and making a good many people uncomfortable. The great thing is to speak without a particle of vice, malice, or rancour." In another place he talks of his "sinuous, easy, unpolemical mode of proceeding" as the best mode of getting at and keeping with truth, and the surest means of procuring access for such ideas as his to the British mind. And again: 'It is very animating to think that one at last has a chance of *getting at* the English public. Such a public as it is, and such a work as one wants to do with it! Partly nature, partly time and study, have also by this time taught me thoroughly the precious truth, that everything turns upon one's exercising the power of *persuasion,* of *charm;* that without this all fury, energy, reasoning power, acquirement, are thrown away, and only render their owner more miserable. Even in one's ridicule, one must preserve a sweetness and good humour" (i. 201). This is all very true, and it is the note of the strangely winning style of Newman and Church, and the Oxford of their day. But one is not sure that Arnold did not make too much of persuasion and charm, so that he interposed it between the reader and the thing for the very sake of which the reader was to be got at, until the mannerisms of the preacher attracted more attention than the substance of his excellent sermon. The witty satire of Mr. Frederic Harrison in *Culture, a Dialogue,* which made Arnold laugh till he cried (i. 372), hit his peril in persuasion and charm at an early date. There are causes that demand and deserve fury and energy, and the public is to be got at upon no other terms; say, Anti-slavery, or Reform; and men are properly adjured to strip off coat and waistcoat, charm or no charm. On the other hand, there have been, and there are, great public causes where Arnold's exaltation of persuasion over passion is thoroughly warranted. The profoundest change in our fiscal policy was effected, as everybody knows, far less by the speeches of Mr. Bright, grand as they were, than by the reasoning power, the full knowledge, and the persuasive charm of Cobden; and Cobden had less mannerism than any speaker of his time.

And, by the way, in days when any crude and inexpert politician feels free to lift up his heel against the Manchester School, it is satisfactory to come upon an emphatic tribute to Cobden in these volumes from no less a personage than Lord Beaconsfield:

> After a little talk to the bishop, he turned to me and asked me very politely if this was my first visit to Buckinghamshire, how I like the country, &c.: then he said he thought he had seen me somewhere, and I said Lord Houghton had introduced me to him eight or nine years ago at a literary dinner among a crowd of other people. "Ah, yes, I remember," he said, and then went on: "At that time I had a great respect for the name you bore, but you yourself were little known. Now you are well known. You have made a reputation, but you will go further yet. You have a great future before you, and you deserve it." I bowed profoundly, and said something about his having given up literature. "Yes," he said, "one does not settle these things for oneself, and politics and literature both are very attractive; still, in the one one's work lasts, and in the other it doesn't." He went on to say that he had given up literature because he was not one of those people who can do two things at once, but that he admired most the men, like Cicero, who could. Then we talked of Cicero, Bolingbroke, and Burke. Later in the evening, in the drawing-room, we talked again. I mentioned William Forster's name, telling him my connection with him, and he spoke most highly of him and of his prospects, saying, just as I always say, how his culture and ideas distinguished him from the mob of Radicals. He spoke strongly of the harm he and Stansfield and such men suffered in

letting themselves be "appropriated," as he called it, by Palmerston, with whom they really had not the least agreement. Of Bright's powers as a speaker he spoke very highly, but thought his cultivation defective and his powers of mind not much; for Cobden's powers of mind he professed the highest admiration. "He was born a statesman," he said, "and his reasoning is always like a statesman's and striking" [i. 221].

A judgment like this, backed by Sir Robert Peel and Mr. Gladstone, may be trusted to stand.

The future historian of the time covered by these volumes will mark, as the most far-reaching of all the changes in the English society of the period, the signal enlargement of the education, the position, and the opportunities of women. From the fine ladies in great houses, through the daughters of doctors and lawyers and tradesmen, down to the shop-girl who lives by herself in a flat, it is among women that a revolution in ideals and possibilities is working its way, far exceeding in real significance any mere political changes, and perhaps even the transformation both in speculative religious beliefs and the temper in which they are held. This momentous operation owes its first great direct impulse to Mill's memorable little book on the *Subjection of Women* and others of his writings. Arnold does not, I think, touch upon this remarkable phase of contemporary things; but he gives to a female relative an incidental piece of advice which is worth pressing in days when women in certain circles are beginning to exercise an influence, not quite beyond comparison with the influence of women in France in more than one great epoch in French history.

"If I were you," writes Arnold, "I should now take to some regular reading, if it were only an hour a day. It is the best thing in the world to have something of this sort as a point in the day, and far too few people know and use this secret. You would have your district still, and all your business as usual, but you would have this hour in your day in the midst of it all, and it would soon become of the greatest solace to you. Desultory reading is a mere anodyne; regular reading, well chosen, is restoring and edifying" (ii. 110). No wiser counsel could be devised either for women or for men, and if an hour a day be for some a counsel of unattainable perfection, half an hour well used might suffice to keep the flame of intellectual interest alive and steady.

In this connection, too, there is no harm in quoting a remark of Sainte-Beuve, made to some old friend, and recorded by Arnold, about the French Academy: "All these academies, between you and me, are pieces of childishness. Our least quarter of an hour of solitary reverie, or of serious talk, yours and mine, in our youth, was better employed; as one gets old, one falls into the power of these nothings; only it is well to know that nothings they are."

Arnold says something in the same vein in one of these letters, after a party of celebrities at the country house which he liked best of all. "These occasional appearances in the world I like—no, I do not like them, but they do one good, and one learns something from them; but, as a general rule, I agree with all the men of soul, from Pythagoras to Byron, in thinking that this type of society is the most drying, wasting, depressing, and fatal thing possible" (i. 225).

Arnold, in fact, took Milton's genial view that

> He who of these delights can judge, and spare
> To interpose them oft, is not unwise.

Unfortunately, "the lute well touched" said little to him, and he thought it as strange as Benedick "that sheep's guts should hale souls out of men's bodies." A lack of ear and musical sense certainly betrays itself in his verse. Flowers and plants and a garden were his special delight, and he had, as Mr. Russell says, a frank enjoyment of light and colour, a pretty room, a neat repast like Milton's, a good vintage. In one of those catechisms which are circulated from time to time to satisfy the curiosity of the public about people whose names they see often in the newspapers, he was asked whether he drank wine; then the further question whether he drank it for health or infirmities, and he gave the adequate reply, "I drink it because it is pleasant." A still better pleasure was his kindness and friendship for what are called the lower animals, the humble ministers and comrades of man. His letter to Mrs. Arnold about the death of Lola, the pony (ii. 318), is as beautiful as Cowper's tenderness for his tame hares; while the verses on Geist move the lover of dogs almost as deeply as the immortal lines, where the Father of Poetry makes the old hound Argos prick up his ears at the voice of Odysseus, and vainly try to draw nearer to the long absent master of his youth, and then to close his eyes in dark death.

It is true to say that Arnold talked, wrote, and thought much about himself, but not really much more than most other men and women who take their particular work and purpose in life seriously to heart. He was not the least of an egotist, in the common ugly and odious sense of that terrible word. He was incapable of sacrificing the smallest interest of anybody else to his own; he had not a spark of envy or jealousy; he stood well aloof from all the hustlings and jostlings by which selfish men push on; he bore life's disappointments, and he was disappointed in some reasonable hopes and anticipations, with good nature and fortitude; he cast no burden upon others, and never shrank from bearing his own share of the daily load to the last ounce of it; he took the deepest, sincerest, and most active interest in the well-being of his country and his countrymen. It is not absurd to think of such a man as an egotist, simply because he took a child's pleasure in his own performance, and liked to know that somebody thought well of his poetry, or praised his lecture, or laughed at his wit? As if a certain sheep-faced and insipid modesty, and spurious reserve in speaking of self, does not constantly conceal an egotism of the most intense and poisonous species. Somebody attacked him, and somebody else defended him. "I had rather it was not done," he told his mother, "as these bitter answers increase and perpetuate hatreds, which I detest." "Fiery hatred and malice are what I detest, and would always allay or avoid, if I could." This is the great thing after all, as nobody knows better than some of those who have by fortune of eager and great issues been drawn into too sharp contention.

To refuse vindication on these terms, or almost on any terms, is not the temper of the egotist. "To the last day I live, I shall never get over a sense of gratitude and surprise at finding my productions acceptable when I see so many people all round me so hard put to it to find a market. This comes from a deep sense of the native similarity of people's spirits, and that if one spirit seems richer than another, it is rather that it has been given to him to *find* more things, which it might have been equally given to others to find, than that he has seized or invented them by superior power and merit" (i. 228). There does not seem to be much difference, and it is little more than a question of words, but such language in the intimacy of a letter to his mother illustrates Arnold's real modesty. What does it matter that he would often in honest gaiety of heart cry out, "Did I say that? How good that was!"

It is the grave occasions in mortal life that test the stuff of which a man is made—whether he faces them with serenity or sullenness, with mutiny or resignation. One hardly wishes to draw the curtain aside from the sacred sorrow of the parent over his dead son; the two letters of 1868 (i. 381–84) will reveal to any reader, not only the tenderness of the writer's soul, but his courageous piety, in the noblest sense of a word too often used in narrow and contracted senses:—

> And so this loss comes to me just after my forty-fifth birthday, with so much other "suffering in the flesh"—the departure of youth, cares of many kinds, an almost painful anxiety about public matters—to remind me that *the time past of our life may suffice us!* words which have haunted me for the last year or two; and that we "should no longer live the rest of our time in the flesh to the lusts of men, but to the will of God." However different the interpretation we put on much of the facts and history of Christianity, we may unite in the bond of this call, which is true for all of us, and for me, above all, how full of meaning and warning. [i. 382.]

In the same year the same cruel stroke fell a second time upon him. The editor of these volumes tells us how he was with the bereaved father on the morning after his boy's death, and the author with whom he was consoling himself was Marcus Aurelius—that saint or sage whom he had described as "wise, just, self-governed, tender, thankful, blameless, yet with all this agitated, stretching out his arms for something beyond"—

> Tendentemque manus ripæ ulterioris amore.*

There is a sublime figure, not unworthy of the Dante whom its author so much loved and so well understood, in a letter written to a kinsman by that admirable man, the late Dean of St. Paul's,

---

* "And reaching out his hands with love of the distant shore"—ed.

in many ways by far the most attaching personage produced by the Oxford Movement. "I often have a kind of waking dream," he wrote not long before his death; "up one road, the image of a man decked and adorned as if for a triumph, carried up by rejoicing and exulting friends, who praise his goodness and achievements; and on the other road, turned back to back to it, there is the very man himself, in sordid and squalid apparel, surrounded not by friends, but by ministers of justice, and going on, while his friends are exulting, to his certain and perhaps awful judgment." As we close these volumes, we have the assured feeling that in the case of him of whom we have been reading and thinking the image and the man were one and the same.

Index

Data B